Harry Speight

Through Airedale from Goole to Malham

Harry Speight

Through Airedale from Goole to Malham

ISBN/EAN: 9783337212025

Printed in Europe, USA, Canada, Australia, Japan

Cover: Foto ©Andreas Hilbeck / pixelio.de

More available books at **www.hansebooks.com**

THROUGH
AIREDALE
FROM
GOOLE TO MALHAM,

BY

JOHNNIE GRAY,

AUTHOR OF "PLEASANT WALKS AROUND BRADFORD,"
"A TOURIST'S VIEW OF IRELAND," ETC., ETC.

WITH ILLUSTRATIONS AND MAP.

Leeds: WALKER & LAYCOCK.
Bradford: T. BREAR & CO., LTD.
Skipton: EDMONDSON & CO.   Goole: GARDINER & CO.
1891.

PREFACE.

S a native of the district comprised in the following pages, the author has been long intimate with the greater portion of the country described. Considering the number of books there are relating to our other Yorkshire dales, it has long remained a matter of surprise to him, as no doubt to many others, that Airedale (none the less noteworthy) should not have been similarly distinguished. In order, therefore, to provide a book separately dealing with the whole of the Aire valley, he has traversed the entire area from the fall of the river near Goole, upwards to its source at Malham, noting everything of interest on either bank, besides a large tract of country around the principal places. The value of such a work must be obvious, as all the Yorkshire valleys differ, often very conspicuously, alike in their ethnic and physical aspects, and Airedale, in common with the rest of our dales, has its own special features and characteristics. Abounding in old market-towns, pleasant villages, castles, monasteries, and other famous buildings, in historical events, and in its natural history and landscape scenery, arising from the great diversity of its rock formations, it is certainly in no way inferior to any other of our great Yorkshire dales.

Although Airedale on the whole has been unjustly neglected, yet there are several places in the Dale which have their local and indeed valuable histories. Of the majority of places, however, little or nothing has been written, and especially of the hamlets and the country and scenes of interest around them, it may be said that these have remained practically a *terra incog.* even to a very large proportion of the inhabitants themselves. To such places and objects, especially in the upper Dale, hitherto unnoticed, more attention has been given, and, wherever possible, published history, derived from an infinitude of sources, has been supplemented, and new facts, data, and other interesting particulars introduced.

Necessarily in a work of this class, involving a large amount of enquiry, correspondence, and research, the author is indebted for much extraneous help. To the vicars, churchwardens, secretaries, and various members of many of the public offices and institutions in the Dale, as well as at the British Museum and Record Office, he is indebted for many valuable particulars and for material obtained from ancient documents, Town Books, Parish Registers, &c. From various residents in the Dale he has obtained the loan of manuscript and diverse information of an interesting local character, and especially is he obliged to the representatives of the late indefatigable antiquary, Mr. Jonathan Hindle, of Steeton, whose collection of manuscript memoranda has been of essential service.

Many of the views are from original sketches and photographs supplied by resident artists and others in the Dale, and have been engraved by Mr. G. W. Shepherd, of Bradford. For these the author is especially indebted to Mr. W. H. Lambert, Silsden; Mr. Alex. Keighley, Keighley; Dr. Stuart, Heckmondwike; Mr. Wm. Scruton, Bradford; the Rev. T. C. Henley, M.A., Kirkby-Malham; Messrs. Edmondson and Co., Skipton; and Messrs. Gardiner & Co., Goole.

To the Secretaries of Angling Clubs he is under obligation for information supplied in the Angling chapter of the book. The Botanical section has been somewhat exhaustively dealt with, as the Dale being exceedingly rich in wild plants, both in respect to the number and variety of indigenous species, it was thought that some tolerably complete list would be useful as a standard reference to working botanists especially, and to all, in fact, interested in our native wildings. The lists have been compiled up to date, and revised by Mr. H. T. Soppitt, ex-President of the Bradford Naturalists' Society. The chapter on the Birds of the Dale has been specially written for the work by that well-known authority, Mr. E. P. Butterfield, of Wilsden.

In conclusion, the author desires to express his thanks to those ladies and gentlemen who have manifested a friendly interest in the work by obtaining subscribers to it, and to the subscribers themselves he is especially grateful for their encouraging support.

GEOLOGY.

WITH the exception of the Don, which covers a drainage area of about 600 square miles, the Aire has a larger watershed than any other of the West Yorkshire rivers. In its social and industrial, as well as in its physical aspects, this is a most important fact. It comprises about 480 square miles; the Wharfe coming next, (470 sq. m.), and the Calder fourth (380 sq. m.) among the great streams of the West Riding. As our river has carved its way through all the main geological formations in Yorkshire, a great diversity in its contour lines is apparent, and to this circumstance is owing its eminent natural picturesqueness. Tracts of luxuriant forest still clothe the high-ascending steeps; wide stretches of game-haunted moorlands extend northward and southward above the upper Dale, and to the north-west the great scar limestone and circumjacent rocks give rise to a class of scenery of unrivalled attractiveness. The rich and various earthy matters brought down by the river to the lower Aire lands likewise contribute much to the luxuriant fertility and generally well-wooded character of this portion of the landscape. By far the largest sectional area of the Dale is occupied by the Millstone grits,—about 150 miles, the Coal Measures being next in extent, 120 miles, or about one-fifth of their entire surface-area in the Riding; whilst the Mountain Limestone and Magnesian Limestone cover an area of 100 and 30 square miles respectively. The Silurians, Yoredales, New Red Sandstone, and recent river deposits make up the quota of our chief local rocks.

The **Silurians**, which in point of age rank next to the Cambrian and Laurentian, (the latter the oldest formation known, and exposed in this country only in the Hebrides and in Sutherland), occupy a small area in the neighbourhood of Malham Tarn. They range from the bluish-green fissile slates and porphyries of the lower group to the tough grits, flags, and Bannisdale slates of the upper division. Of enormous thickness (in the vicinity of Sedbergh and Horton, estimated at two miles thick) they extend eastwards by Ingleton, Ribblesdale, and Malham Moor, and disappear just beyond Gordale, where they are thrown down to a great depth by the North Craven Fault. Though the rock is not exposed to view, there is no doubt that Malham Tarn rests on an impervious (Upper) Silurian floor, covered by glacial drift and a loosish sandstone conglomerate. The beach is pebbly; about Capon Hall this deposit of pebbles being over 12 feet thick. Boulders of ice-transported Silurians lie scattered about on the high ground between Clapham and Settle and Kilnsey; the finest examples of which are the well-known *blocs perchè*, at Norber, above Austwick. In the neighbourhood of the upper Aire, the rock may be observed *in situ* at the foot of Gordale Scar, on Black Hill, Catrigg Pasture, Neals Ing, and in the beck at Streets (1240 feet elevation) on Malham Moor. In other places in this district

b

its presence is hidden by the overlying limestone and beds of drift.

Above the Silurians is ranged the **Carboniferous** group of rocks, comprising the various limestones, shales, millstone grits, and coal measures. A vast and incalculable period (not to be reckoned in years) must have elapsed between the formation of the old Silurians and the deposition of the **mountain limestone**. This is evidenced by the irregular, much-worn, and altered character of the older rock, on the jagged upturned edges of which the limestone is often found laid in perfectly horizontal layers. The latter, a marine deposit, must have been formed at a time when the only dry land in our country was the protozoic areas of Wales and Cumberland, then mere rocky islets in the encompassing ocean. Where undivided by shales or sandstones this limestone must have been laid down in a deep and comparatively tranquil water. In Derbyshire are beds of pure limestone, sometimes very compact, crystalline or semi-crystalline, and capable of a high polish, 1200 to 1500 feet thick. As we go north the beds become usually less massive and pure by irregular intercalations of probable estuarine or fresh water origin. South of the Craven Fault the series attains a thickness in some places, as between Clitheroe and Gisburn (where the stone is largely quarried), of more than 3000 feet. North of the Fault the scar limestone, which covers Hard Flask and the Malham plateau, and forms the general base of Fountains Fell, &c., attains its greatest thickness (about 1000 feet) between Kettlewell and Buckden and Great Whernside. The general average, however, is not more than 5-600 feet in the upper Aire division. The limestone takes a direction north-east, dipping under the Yoredales, and lower millstone grits (upper Yoredale grits), which latter rock caps all the higher ground northwards to the county boundary. A striking peculiarity of this area is the rent or fissured character of the tabular surface limestone. This is caused by the mechanical action of the atmosphere and water combining with the resultant carbonic acid, to eat or penetrate along the joints of the rock, which is of a very variable degree of hardness. Sometimes an opening in the rock is sufficiently large to admit a stream, or series of streams along the same crevice, which in process of time enlarges it to the dimensions of a great cave. In fact, from the quantity of water that annually finds its way down into the porous rocky soil, were borings of sufficient depth to be made almost anywhere over this area caverns of greater or less magnitude would be met with. Sometimes the rumbling of underground waters may be heard apparently quite close to the surface. Many of these gloomy and unseen recesses however, doubtless primarily originated with the great system of 'faults' or upheavals which are such a marked and perplexing feature of this district. The main, or great **Craven Fault**, terminated westward by the Penine anticlinal, divides near Clapham, and the dislocation runs eastward in several almost parallel branches. The northern one, which brings up the lower scar limestone against the slates on Malham Moor, a little south of the Tarn, pursues an easterly course as far as Threshfield, in Wharfedale, where it becomes obscure. The slip is about three hundred feet. The south Craven

Fault is again sub-divided, the northern offshoot, or Mid-Craven Fault, following the line of scars from Settle, and between Ryeloaf and Kirkby Fell to Malham. Here the Yoredale and millstone grit series are brought up against the mountain limestone by a drop at Malham, of about 1000 feet, gradually diminishing eastward. Westward, about Ingleton, the throw is estimated at over 3000 feet. The line of fault continues a little to the south of the Cove and Gordale Scar, (which fine mural escarpments are due to this disturbance), and proceeding south of the hamlet of Skirethorns may be traced as far east as Pateley Bridge. Whilst the bold, lofty and picturesque line of scars extending from near Giggleswick to Gordale are owing to this tremendous Fault, it is evident by their position from the axis of disturbance that they have considerably receded, and still are weathering back in the form of terraces by gradual and unceasing denudation. The southern member of this Fault follows the Aire in a south-easterly direction to Skipton. In this neighbourhood we enter upon a system of **anticlinals**, consisting of long ridges of dark coloured and more or less laminated limestone, forming trough-like valleys; the synclinals, or high ground between them, being mostly composed of the more recent Yoredale shales, capped with hard grit. They strike in roughly parallel lines from south-west to north-east. The principal of these extends from Clitheroe through Skipton and Blubberhouses towards Harrogate, disappearing beneath the unconformable Permians; others of lesser extent occupy the Lothersdale and Thornton valleys, forming dry escarpments, separated by the wet, gritstone elevations of Elslack and Carleton Moors. The limestone is much folded, at times is very massive and bossy, at others is thin-bedded, fine-grained, and laminated, and traversed along the faults by veins of lead, calcite, and heavy spar. In Lothersdale there is a rich vein of sulphate of barytes, besides several long-worked veins of calc spar. The limestone of these anticlinals is, as already stated, much contorted, the beds frequently dipping at very sharp angles, and sometimes at the summit-ridges appearing quite vertical. The best local examples of this form of bedding are to be seen at Thornton, Elslack road side, Lothersdale, Skipton Rock, Hambleton Quarry, near Bolton Abbey Station, and at Draughton, where the rock is also quarried, and presents a most remarkable appearance. All the limestones named, including the various shales, abound in fossil organisms, and are especially rich in a variety of *goniatites, crinoids, producta*, &c. Fossil corals also largely abound, forming thick, dense masses in the rock, nowhere, perhaps, better exhibited in Airedale, than near the entrance to Gordale Scar.

In the neighbourhood of Gordale also may be observed several undisturbed mounds of **glacial drift.** These deposits likewise occupy the Dale a considerable distance southwards. They are especially conspicuous in the lower lands and on the level tracts about Gargrave, Bell Busk, and Skipton. Here they form round, grassy isolated hillocks, rising fifty to one hundred or more feet in height, being made up of stiffish clay, or gravel and sand, intermixed with rounded, angular and sub-angular fragments of transported rock (often striated) of varying size and composition. A section of such drift-hills will sometimes reveal a depth of 150 feet of till, enclosing pebbles from an inch or two in diameter to boulders of a ton in weight, before coming upon the stratified rock. Such a boulder, of very unusual dimensions, has quite recently been turned out in excavating at the Leeds and Liverpool Canal Co.'s new reservoir near Winterburn, above Gargrave. It is fully three tons in weight, and is remarkably well smoothed and striated. The morainic mounds referred to were undoubtedly left by the retreating glaciers during the Ice Age; their longer axes indicating the general trend of the frozen mass. Lingering relics of an arctic as well as a maritime flora, prove not only an ice-mass, but that the waves of the sea have at no distant period in geological history beaten against the cliffs of our Airedale uplands. Glacial *debris* has overspread the valley from Malham downwards, occupying either flat denuded beds, filling hollows, or assuming the form of thick, tenacious re-arranged shore-mounds of post-glacial lakes, through which the diminishing waters of the onflowing river have subsequently carved a passage. These raised, re-deposited boulder gravels have been very much denuded, and are composed chiefly of smooth, water-rounded stones, rarely displaying marks of striation. About Marley, Saltaire, and in the town of Bingley, recent excavations shew the gravel to contain pebbles and blocks of various sandstones, grits, and blue limestone from the Skipton anticlinal, with occasional pieces of pale grey crystalline rock derived from the limestone further north. No older rock, such as Silurians or granites, has been found here worth mentioning. These are generally confined to the upper part of the Dale, and to the west side of the Penine anticlinal, as well as to various tracts in the North and East Ridings, where they were deposited by the great North Glacier that swept across Stainmoor into the valleys of the Tees and Swale. Our Yorkshire dales must at this period have been pretty much like the valleys of the High Alps of Switzerland, and Norway at the present day. The Airedale glacier had its origin in the vast snow-field of Malham Moor, and was joined by lesser tributary glaciers, notably from the valleys of the Worth and Silsden. Ice scratches, smoothings, and deposits of till overlaid by esker-gravels, are found in these localities at an elevation of over 1100 feet; perhaps the most perfect assemblage of drift-hills we know of in this neighbourhood, being those locally called the "scars," near Cowlaughton on 'Cornshaw Moor. The Airedale glacier probably extended as far south as Leeds, as well-defined striæ and smoothings are observable on the Rough Rock about 100 feet above the river near Apperley. Deposits of local till (from the general ice-sheet) are also found at a much higher elevation about here. From Bingley northwards to beyond Steeton, there can be no doubt that long after the disappearance of the last ice-flow, this part of the valley was immersed in an immense and gradually shallowing lake, a condition in which it remained, even up to historic times. It is indeed more than probable, that at the time of the Roman invasion the bottom of all the valley from Shipley northwards, was little better than an impassable swamp. Indications of an old river-level are found in several parts of the valley, especially above Keighley, where terraces of gravel and sand occur ten or twelve feet above the recent alluvium.

The next rocks in our series are the **millstone grits,** a fresh-water deposit, occupying longitudinally about thirteen miles of the Dale above Shipley. From the borders of Staffordshire they extend northwards, dipping under the coal measures, and in the West Riding have a total thickness of about 2500 feet. Their south-eastern horizon may be determined locally by a line drawn from Halifax northwards to Denholme, and eastwards by Cottingley to Shipley and Idle; the north boundary covering the high moors of Cononley, Carleton, and by the Skipton anticlinal eastwards to Bolton Abbey. The lowest member of this group, the Kinderscout grit, is remarkably persistent over a wide area, extending northward along the summit of the Penine Chain, entering into our district upon the moors and fells of Cononley, (where galena used to be worked in a fault of this rock), Skipton, Flasby, Embsay, and Cracoe, and westward again occupying the outlying high ground north of Hanlith and the Weets above Malham. The Middle or Third Grits are commonly characterised by a reddish hue, and are of finer grain than the rocks below and above them. They enter Airedale southwards from the Oxenhope and Haworth moors, occupy a part of Keighley, and pursue a northerly direction by Holden Gill, Silsden Moor, (the curious Double Stones being of this grit), and Rumbalds Moor to Ilkley, where they are overlaid by the Rough Rock. This, the topmost bed of the millstone group, occupies a narrow strip (never exceeding five miles in breadth) and immediately underlies the coal measures. It is also contiguous to the flag-rock, and is frequently very false-bedded. It is very coarse, rich in quartz and felspar, and weathers much and blackly. It occurs on Rumbalds Moor, Baildon Hill, &c., and may often be seen denuded in large detached blocks. Shipley Glen and Druids' Altar, Bingley, are notable examples.

Above this uppermost bed of the millstone grits lie the Coal Measures, industrially the most important of all the Airedale strata. These comprise the lower, middle and upper coal series, the latter but scantily and irregularly developed in Yorkshire. The **Lower Coal Measures,** or Ganister Group, include all the various strata intermediate from the Rough Rock to the Silkstone or Blocking Coal, and the thick-bedded, weather-resisting flagrock forms their most striking surface characteristic. This, known as the **Elland Flagstone,** ranges from 600 to 800 feet above the Rough Rock, and in the neighbourhoods of Bradford and Halifax attains an elevation of over 1000 feet above sea level. These flagstones cap all the higher hills in the district, and are very extensively quarried, ranging from the south of Bradford northward to Shipley and Idle, and eastward to beyond Leeds, constituting the summit tracts of Kirkstall Hill, Armley Ridge, Headingley Hill, Woodhouse Ridge, Potternewton, Gledhow, &c. About Bradford the stone attains a thickness of nearly 200 feet, the lower strata forming a valuable building material, and the upper, which is often micaceous and flaggy, providing a good roofing stone. Many exceptionally large and perfect examples of *Lepidodendra* and other fossil remains have been obtained locally from this series. Between the Rough Rock and the Flagstone are the Soft and Hard Bed Coals, with a variable thickness of shale, sandstone and galliard. The shaly roof of the Hard Bed is exceedingly fossiliferous, and, near Idle, yielded perhaps the finest *Megalichthys Hibbertii* ever discovered, and which is now in the Leeds Philosophical Society's Museum. In this neighbourhood the ganister occurs 135 feet above the hard bed coal, and there is also a good stratum of fire clay about 100 feet above the hard bed band clay. The valuable **Galliard** lies usually immediately beneath the coal beds. It is a hard, closely-grained, white and highly silicious sandstone, and possessing great heat-resisting properties, is now largely used in the composition of bricks for lining furnaces. These ganister beds are worked in an outlier on the north side of the Aire at Baildon, and were formerly also pretty extensively worked at Bowling. The beds may be traced along the east side of the Meanwood valley, north of Leeds, where they are cut off near Carr House by the fault which brings up the Rough Rock, and extends eastward by Red Hall to the Permian limestone escarpment. Stratigraphically the order of the series near Leeds is, from the Elland Flag-rock, the Better Bed Coal, the Black Bed Coal, Crow Coal, Oakenshaw Coal, Beeston Coal, and the Barcelona or Silkstone Coal (the base of the Middle Coal Measures), with intermediate shales and partings. The Better Bed Coal is remarkable for its freedom from all impurities, and is used at the Farnley, Bowling, and Low Moor Iron Works, in the manufacture of their well-known specialities. A thin stratum of fossiliferous shale covers the surface of this coal over an extensive area. The remains consist of fishes and labyrinthodonts, and include the following species :

Ctenacanthus hybodoides, *Eg.* Megalichthys Hibbertii, *Ag.*
Lepracanthus Colei, *Eg.* Strepsodus Sauroides, *Hux.*
Pleuracanthus lævissimus, *Ag.* Holoptychius Sauroides, *Ag.*
Pleurodus Rankinii, *Ag.* Cœlacanthus lepturus, *Ag.*
Helodus simplex, *Ag.* Ctenoptychius apicalis, *Ag.*
Orthacanthus cylindricus, *Ag.* Diplodus gibbosus, *Ag.*

Associated with the Black Bed coal, higher up, are the valuable seams or layers of ironstone and fire-clay, which have long been worked in the district. The ironstone varies both in thickness and quality and rarely yields more than 30 per cent of metallic ore. The following is a section of the richest portion of the ore at Bowling :

	Ft.	In.		Ft.	In.
Black shale and ironstone,	4	11½	Black shale,	1	4
Black shale,	1	0	*Ironstone*,	0	4
Ironstone,	0	1½	Black shale,	0	9
Black shale,	0	6	*Ironstone*,	0	1½
Ironstone,	0	1½	Black shale,	1	0
Black shale,	0	9	*Ironstone*,	0	1
Ironstone,	0	2½	Black shale,	0	6

The **Middle Coal Measures** range in our district principally to the south and east of Leeds. Though very variable in character they are much more thickly developed than the lower coal measures, and are lacking in the thick beds of sandstone and lofty escarpments which are a characteristic of the latter. The surface scenery is consequently, if not so bold in outline as the lower series, much more fertile, lying low and warm, and usually picturesquely wooded, where not broken up by pits. The principal coals in the group are the Silkstone, or as it is called near Leeds, Barcelona coal; Middleton Main, Cromwell, or Swilly coal; Parkgate or Brown Metal coal; Flockton; Swallow Wood, Netherton or Haigh Moor; and the Barnsley Nine-Foot or Warren House coal. Of these, perhaps, the Silkstone is the most valuable, being four to five feet thick, of great purity, and providing an excellent house coal. Much of it is sent to London. In the shale above this coal at Middleton has been found a variety of fossil fish remains, including *megalichthys hibbertii*, *cœlacanthus lepturus*, &c. Near Castleford there is a highly fossiliferous seam of coal about a foot thick, over-lying a three-foot bed of good fire-clay. In this locality formerly large quantities of sand used in glass making were obtained from the Red Hills. A sand, however, containing less iron and more silicious is now employed for this purpose, and is obtained chiefly from Lynn, in Norfolk, and from the sands of the French coast near Calais.

A strip of **Magnesian Limestone**, four or five miles wide, abuts upon the coal measures westward, forming a low, undulating, and picturesque escarpment, intersecting the vale of the Aire in a northerly and southerly direction about Knottingley, Pontefract, and Ferry Bridge. In a paper contributed some years ago to the *Proceedings* of the Geological and Polytechnic Society, Mr. Thos. Edwd. Tew, of Pontefract, remarks respecting this limestone : "The rocks of the formation may be divided into five bands or layers; the lower yellowish magnesian rocks resting towards the west on a fringe of the Permian red sandstones. The upper thin-bedded rocks are separated from the lower limetones by a bed of red marl, and over-lapped in some places by layers of marl and grits. This magnesian formation may be called the backbone of Osgoldcross. It runs through the two wapontakes nearly from south to north. It varies in breadth from three to four-and-a-half miles, and it is from eighty to one hundred yards thick. At Brotherton, Knottingley, Cridling Stubbs and Womersley, the limestone is burned and sold for agricultural purposes. It has the property when put upon land, of pulverising strong soils, and to use a farmer's phrase, of fastening or cementing light ones; the Knottingley bed of limestone being held in high estimation by the farmers of the East Riding of Yorkshire and Lincolnshire."

Local outcrops of New Red Sandstone extend east of this limestone escarpment. encompassed by long level tracts of recent warps, clays, and sand, covering, in some places, a thickness of peat, and from Goole westward to Snaith and Drax, overlying an extensive ancient forest-bed, containing remains of a variety of trees, with well-preserved fir-cones, hazel nuts, and quantities of cranberries (*Vac. oxycoccus*). These remarkable deposits are undoubtedly relics of a primæval forest, destroyed, in all probability, during the conquest of Britain by the Romans early in the Christian era. West and south of Goole the peat-bed ranges from six to eighteen or more inches in thickness, overlaid by four or five feet of soil, the whole of which may quite possibly have accumulated since the period of the Roman invasion, now 1800 to 1900 years since. In the Isle of Axholme, Dugdale tells us there were found trees five yards in compass, and sixteen yards long, and some smaller of greater length, with large quantities of acorns near them. Many of the trees, and especially the fir trees, this same old authority observes, had been burnt, sometimes quite through; others chopped, squared, bored through or split, with large wooden wedges and stones in them, and broken axeheads, somewhat like sacrificing axes in shape, and these at depths and under circumstances which exclude all supposition of their having been touched since the destruction of the forest. Below the peat there are alternations of clay, sand, and marl of varying thickness and composition. A town well sunk to a depth of 360 feet, near Goole, exhibits the following section:

		Ft.	In.			Ft.	In.
1	Warpy Sand	4	4	14 Red Marl		1	0
2	Warpy Clay	0	6	15 Hard Sand		61	0
3	Peat	0	6	16 Red Marl		3	0
4	Fine stiff Clay	6	8	17 Hard Coarse Sand-			
5	Red Clay	5	0	stone (with small			
6	Rough Gravel	8	0	pebbles)		3	0
7	Warp Clay	3	0	18 Marl and Red Sand			
8	Red Sand	6	0	(mixed)		84	0
9	Hard Coarse Sand			19 Red Sand		28	0
	(light red)	24	0	20 Stiff Red Marl		2	0
10	Red Marl	10	0	21 Marl and Red Sand-			
11	Hard Sand	11	0	stone		22	0
12	Red Marl	3	0	22 Red Sandy Marl		60	0
13	Hard Sand	26	0				

BOTANY.

THE annexed List of Plants of Airedale has been prepared mainly from the following works: Miall's Sup'ment to Whitaker's "Craven" (Third Edition); Lees "Flora of West Yorkshire"; the "Naturalist," and "Transactions" of the Yorkshire Naturalists' Union; the "Journal of Botany"; Gissing's "Flora of Wakefield"; Roberts' "Lofthouse and its Neighbourhood"; Miall's and Carrington's "Flora of the West Riding"; the Records of the Leeds Naturalists' Club; the Bradford Naturalists' Society; and the Craven Naturalists' Society. The author has also had furnished to him various records by local botanists, in addition to his own individual observations.

The object of the compiler has been to supply a useful, and it is hoped, fairly representative and reliable catalogue of native plants of the Aire valley, a number now estimated at over 700 species. Only those "denizens" and "colonists" are included by reason of a special interest, such as persistent occurrence in certain habitats. Aliens or casuals are, with a few notable exceptions, excluded.

A denizen, (marked thus *), it may be useful to state, is a "species suspected to have been introduced by man, and which maintains its habitat." A colonist (thus †) is "one found only in ground adapted by man for its growth and continuous maintenance."

The classification is according to the Third Edition of Hooker's "Student's Flora," as this handbook is the one most used and recognised by botanists throughout the country. The figures after the localities indicate approximately the month when the plant appears in flower, as 6, June, &c.

Botanical Name.	Common Name.	Where found.
Ranunculaceæ.		
Clematis vitalba*	Traveller's Joy	Near Allerton - Bywater, Ledston, &c.; mainly on Permian limestone, 7
Thalictrum minus, var. montanum	Lesser Meadow Rue	Malham, Gordale, 7
Thalictrum majus, var. flexuosum	Large ,,	Gordale, Monk Fryston, 7
Thalictrum flavum	Common ,,	Goole fields, Pollington, 6
Anemone pulsatilla	Pasque flower	Dry hilly ground near Brotherton, Smeaton (doubtful) 4
,, nemorosa	Wood Anemone	Common in woods, 3

Ranunculaceæ,—continued.

Botanical Name.	Common Name.	Where found.
Ranunculus circinatus	Floating Water Crow-foot	Drains by river Aire, Brotherton, 7
,, fluitans	,,	Cottingley Bridge
,, peltatus	,,	Swift reaches of the Aire above Skipton
,, Lenormandi	Lenormands Water Crow-foot	Malham Moor (1250 ft.), Baildon Common, 5
,, sceleratus	Celery-leaved ,,	Aire side, Methley; Frizinghall, 6
,, auricomus	Goldilocks	Malham, Skipton woods, Shipley Glen, 4
,, hirsutus	Hairy Crow-foot	Hooke road, Goole
,, arvensis †	Corn Crow-foot	Near Eldwick, Meanwood, Marshland (on warp soil)
Caltha palustris	Marsh Marigold	Common, 4
Trollius europæus	Globe-flower	Malham Cove (A.D. 1805), above Holden Gill, 6
Helleborus viridis	Setterwort	Kidhall Lane, near Leeds; Becca Banks, Aberford, (rare), 4
,, fœtidus	Bear's-foot	Malham Cove, Ledston Park, (doubt. native), 4
Actæa spicata	Baneberry or Herb Christopher	Barwick-in-Elmet, Malham Moor and Cove, 6

Berberaceæ.

Berberis vulgaris	Barberry	Between Knottingley and Womersley, 5

Nymphæaceæ.

Nymphæa alba	White Water-lily	Thorne Waste (Goole), 7
Nuphar luteum	Yellow ,,	River Went, Smeaton, 7

Papaveraceæ.

Papaver rhœas †	Scarlet Poppy	Frequent in corn-fields, 8
,, dubium †	,,	Waste ground, Frizinghall
,, argemone †	Prickly head'd ,,	Near Saltaire, Rothwell, Rawcliffe
Meconopsis cambrica*	Welsh Poppy	Nr. Kirkby Malham; river side below Settle, 7
Chelidonium majus	Celandine	Ledsham, 6

Botanical Name.	Common Name.	Where found.
Fumariaceæ.		
Corydalis claviculata .	White Climbing-Fumitory	Bingley Wood, Adel Moor, Brayton Barf, 6
Fumaria officinalis .	Common „	Cultivated fields, generally distributed, 5
Cruciferæ.		
Cheiranthus cheiri .	Wallflower . .	Walls of Skipton Castle, Pontefract Castle
Nasturtium officinale .	Water-cress . .	Generally distributed
„ sylvestre .	Creeping yellow water-cress .	Below Leeds, Airmyn, 6
„ palustre .	Yellow „ .	Meanwood valley, Hawksworth, 6
„ amphibium	Water Radish .	Pond, Carlton Bridge, nr. Snaith, 7
Barbarea vulgaris . .	Winter-cress . .	Common on river banks in Airedale, 5
Arabis hirsuta . . .	Hairy Rock-cress	Malham, Apperley, Kirkstall Abbey up to 1867
Cardamine amara . .	Bitter-cress . .	Aire banks above Leeds, Esholt, 5
„ impatiens .	Impatient „	Malham Cove, 6-7 very rare
Sisymbrium thaliana .	Thale-cress . .	Skipton, Malham. Seven Arches (Cottingley) Hut Green, Kellington, 4
„ officinale.	Hedge Mustard	Common, 7
„ Sophia †.	Flixweed . .	Knottingley, 7
„ Alliaria .	Jack-by-the-Hedge . . .	Common, 5
Brassica sylvestris . .	Wild Turnip . .	Snaith, Bingley
Diplotaxis tenuifolia .	Rocket . . .	Old walls Pontefract Castle and Church
Draba incana . . .	Twisted-podded Whitlow grass	Malham, Gordale
„ muralis . . .	Wall „	About Malham. First record, A.D. 1763
Erophila vulgaris . .	Vernal „	Wall tops, not uncommon
Cochlearia officinalis .	Scurvy grass .	Aire side above Skipton, Malham, Apperley, 5
„ var. alpina	„ .	Gordale
Senebiera coronopus .	Wart-cress . .	Drax, Goole, and Marshland, 7
Lepidium Smithii . .	Pepper-wort . .	Betw. Skipton and Grassington, 7
Thlaspi arvense † . .	Penny-cress . .	Near Drax, 7

Botanical Name.	Common Name.	Where found.
Cruciferæ,—*continued.*		
Thlaspi alpestre, var. occitanum	Alpine Penny-cress . . .	Water side, Airton ; near lead mines, Malham ; Gordale, 5
Hutchinsia petræa . .	Hutchinsia . .	Betw. Malham Cove and Tarn, 3, (very rare)
Resedaceæ.		
Reseda lutea . .	Wild Mignonette	Skipton (Gargrave Road), Ferry Fryston, 6
,, luteola . .	Dyers' Weed .	Garforth, Ferrybridge, 6
Cistaceæ.		
Helianthemum vulgare	Rock-rose . .	Malham Cove, Elbolton, Ledsham, 7
canum	Dwarf Rock-rose	Ledges on front of Malham Cove, (*see* Lees *Flora*), requires confirmation
Violaceæ.		
Viola palustris . . .	Bog Violet . .	Malham Moor, Sharper, above Flasby ; Marley, Esholt, Adel Bog, 5
,, odorata . .	Sweet ,, . .	Broughton, Bingley, Ledston, 4
,, hirta	Hairy ,, . .	Malham Cove, Gordale, 5
,, canina	Dog ,, . .	Camblesforth and Drax, Skipton
,, lactea . . .	,, . .	Rawcliffe 'Rabbit Hills,' 6, (rare)
,, tricolor . . .	Field Pansy . .	Fields at Newlay, Cookridge, Brayton, 5
,, lutea var. amœna	Mountain ,, . .	Malham Cove, Skirethorns nr. Rylstone, and Cracoe
Polygalaceæ.		
Polygala vulgaris . .	Milkwort . .	Hawksworth, Holden Gill, Ferrybridge, 6-7
,, depressa . .	,, . .	Slopes of Rumbalds Moor, Malham Moor, 6

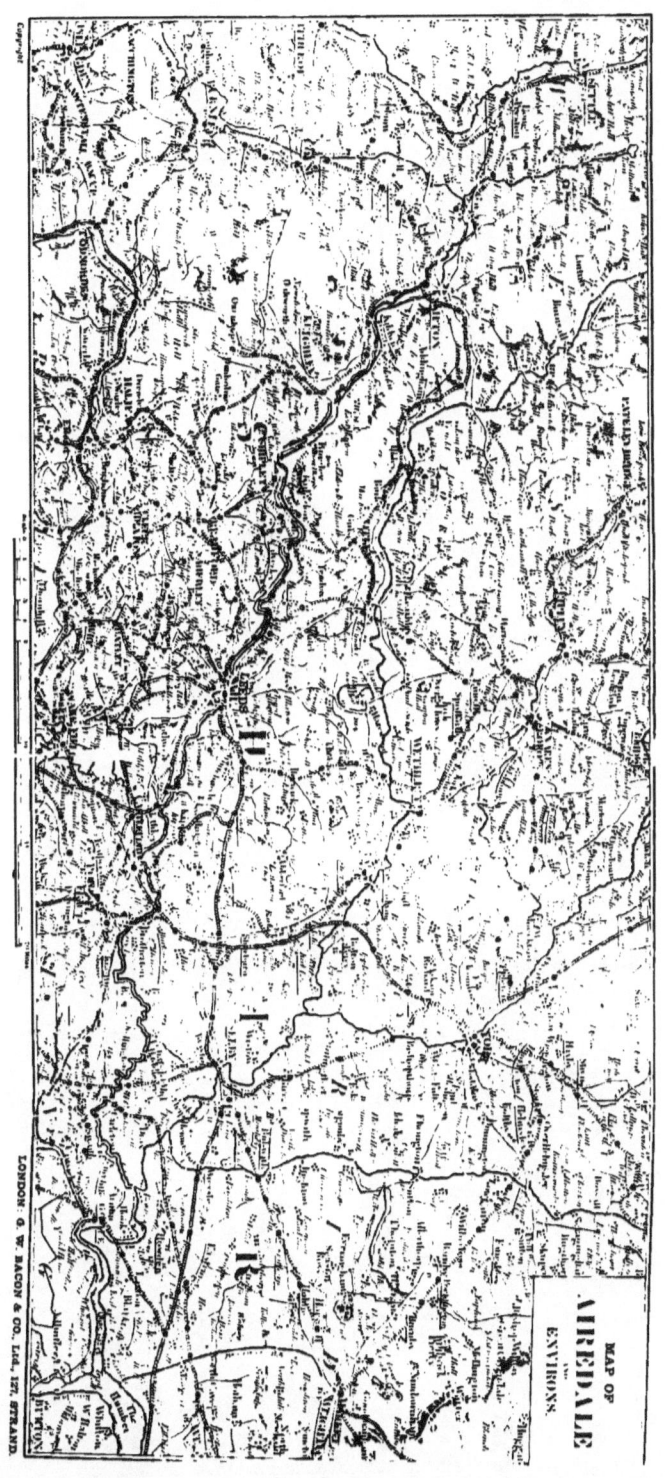

Botanical Name.	Common Name.	Where found.
Caryophyllaceæ.		
Saponaria officinalis *	Soapwort. . .	Near Cowling, River side between Shipley and Esholt, Aire side, Castleford, 8
Silene inflata . . .	Bladder Campion	Airedale generally
„ maritima . . .	Sea-side Catchfly	Limestone scars, Moughton Fell, and above the village of Wharf (Settle)
„ anglica . . .	English „	Clover-field, near Ferry Fryston
„ nutans . . .	Nottingham „	Near foot-road in Bramham Park
„ noctiflora † . .	Night-flowering Catchfly . .	Milford, about Bramham and Wetherby
Lychnis vespertina .	White Campion.	Not uncommon in fields and on dry banks
„ diurna . . .	Red „	Woods, hedges; common
„ flos-cuculi .	Ragged Robin .	Keighley Moor (1200 ft.), Bingley, &c.
Githago segetum † .	Corn-cockle . .	Apperley, Idle
Cerastium semidecandrum	Little Mouse-ear Chickweed .	Malham, 4-5
Cerastium glomeratum	Narrow-leaved Chickweed .	Bingley, Hawksworth, Meanwood, Bardsey, 6
„ triviale . .	Broad-leaved Chickweed .	Fields, road-sides, general
„ arvense . .	Field Chickweed	Hambleton, Smeaton, Kellington, &c., 5
Stellaria aquatica . .	Water Stitchwort	Aire side, near Methley; Snaith
„ nemorum .	Wood „	Bingley woods, Shipley to Apperley
„ glauca . . .	Marsh „	Marshy place by Swillington Bridge, 6
Arenaria trinervia . .	Three-nerved Sandwort . .	Skipton, Bingley, Adel
„ verna . . .	Vernal Sandwort	Frequent about Malham
Sagina ciliata . . .	Pearlwort . .	Malham Tarn shore, Garforth and Selby
„ subulata . . .	„ . .	Malham Tarn shore

Botanical Name.	Common Name.	Where found.
Caryophyllaceæ,—*continued.*		
Sagina nodosa	Knotted Pearl-wort	Malham Tarn shore, Grassington road, Skipton; Hawksworth, Adel Dam
Hypericaceæ.		
Hypericum androsæmum	Tutsan	Shipley Glen, Pontefract (1791). 7
Hypericum perforatum	St. John's Wort.	On sandstone, frequent, 7-8
,, humifusum	Trailing ,,	Esholt, Alwoodley, Brayton Barf
,, hirsutum	Hairy ,,	About Draughton, Esholt, Ledsham
,, montanum	Mountain ,,	Malham Cove, Gordale
Malvaceæ.		
Malva moschata	Musk Mallow	Skipton, nr. Steeton, Gilstead, Apperley, Adel
,, sylvestris	Common ,,	Bingley, Sherburn, Brotherton
,, rotundifolia	Dwarf ,,	About Pontefract
Linaceæ.		
Linum catharticum	Purging-flax	Dry banks; common, 7
Radiola millegrana	All-seed	Blackhill Dam, Adel, 7
Geraniaceæ.		
Geranium sanguineum	Bloody Cranes-bill	Malham Cove, Gordale, 7
,, phœum *	Dusky ,,	Bingley. Rawcliffe, 6
,, sylvaticum	Wood ,,	Airton to Hanlith, Marley
,, pratense	Meadow ,,	Malh'm; Marl'y; by river, Newlay; Ferrybridge, 6
,, pyrenaicum	Mountain ,,	Betw. Bingley & Keighley
,, pusillum	Small-flowered ,,	About Garforth, Ledston
,, columbinum	Dove's-foot ,,	Skipton: Seven Arches, (Cottingley)
,, robertianum	Herb-robert	Hedge-banks and stony places; common
,, lucidum	Shining Cranes-bill	Malham, near Bingley
Erodium cicutarium †	Stork's-bill	Kellington
Oxalis acetosella	Wood Sorrel	Common (up to 2000 ft.)

Botanical Name.	Common Name.	Where found.
Celastraceæ.		
Euonymus europæus	Spindle-tree	Road side, Kirkby Malham; Shipley Glen; Pontefract, &c.
Rhamnaceæ.		
Rhamnus catharticus	Purging Buckthorn	[Kippax Gordale, Malham (1100 ft.),
„ frangula	Alder „	Malham, nr. Adel Bridge and Aqueduct, lime-hills Roundhay
Leguminiferæ.		
Ulex europæus	Furze, Whin, Gorse	Common except on lime-stone, 1-2
„ galli	Autumnal Gorse	Farnhill Moor (800 ft.); Otley Chevin, &c., 8-9
Genista anglica	Needle Furze	Idle, Wilsden. Yeadon Moor, Adel Blackmoor, Rawcliffe, 6
„ tinctoria	Dyers' Greenweed	Saltaire, Esholt, Monk Fryston, Ledsham, 7
Ononis spinosa	Rest-harrow	Skipton, about Pontefract
„ arvensis	„	Bingley; Aire Banks, Methley, &c., 7
Anthyllis vulneraria	Lady's Fingers	Gordale, Pontefract, &c.
Melilotus parviflora †	Melilot	Woodlesford. Methley, &c. Shipley rail.-bank
Trifolium medium	Zig-zag Trefoil	Generally distributed
„ striatum	Knotted „	Brayton Barf
Lotus corniculatus	Bird's-foot	Dry heathy banks, com., 6
„ uliginosus	„	Malham Moor, Marley, Shipley, 7
Astragalus hypoglottis	Purple Milk-vetch	Kippax lime-hills, Jack-daw Crag, Stutton, 6
„ glycyphyllus	Wild Liquorice	Monk Fryston, between Lumby and Ledsham, 6
Ornithopus perpusillus	Common Bird's-foot	Baildon Green, Adel, Hambleton, 5
Hippocrepis comosa	Tufted Horse-shoe Vetch	Malham Gordale, 7
Vicia sylvatica	Wood Vetch	Kirkby Malham, 7
Orobus tuberosus	Wood Pea	Gen. dist., formerly (1865) on Woodhouse Ridge, 4

Botanical Name.	Common Name.	Where found.
Rosaceæ.		
Prunus insititia *	Bullaster	Pontefract, Thorp Arch, 4
,, avium *	Wild Cherry	All down Aire valley from about Gargrave to Castleford, 5
,, cerasus *	Morella	Rawdon woods, 5
,, padus	Bird-cherry	Skipton to Rylstone, Cottingley, 5
Spiræa filipendula	Dropwort	Gargr've, Scarnb'r, W'burn
Rubus chamæmorus	Cloudberry	Near Malham Tarn
,, cæsius	Dewberry	Airton, Gargrave; common on limestone about Micklefield, Aberford, &c.
,, saxatilis	Stone Bramble	Gordale
,, plicatus	Plaited-leaved Bramble	Malham
,, lindleianus		About Hambleton, Horsforth
,, affinis		Skipton Rock, Hawksworth, Adel, &c.
,, leucostachys	Downy-spiked Bramble	Skipton Rock, Bingley, Hawksworth
,, festivus	,,	Allerton (Bradford)
,, Sprengelii	Sprengel's ,,	Cookridge Wood, Meanwood
,, radula	Scraping ,,	Woodhouse Ridge, Baild'n
,, Kœhleri	Koehler's ,,	Allerton (Bradford) ,,
,, corylifolius	Hazel-leaved ,,	Skipton, Roundhay ,,
Dryas octopetala	Mountain Avens	Arncliffe Clouder, (its only West Yorks. stat.), 6-7
Geum urbanum	Common ,,	Common, 6
,, rivale	Water ,,	Malham, Skipton, &c.
,, intermedium	,, ,,	Skipton, betw. Bell Busk and Malham, 6
Potentilla verna	Spring Cinquefoil	About Kippax, and Ledston Park
,, alpestris	Alpine ,,	Rocks above Gordale Scar, Malham Tarn, &c., 7
,, procumbens	Procumbent ,,	Horsfo'th, Hawksw'th, &c.
,, norvegica	,,	Kirkstall, Calder banks near Castleford (not native). 6
Fragaria elatior	Hautboy Strawberry	Near the quarry tramway behind Skipton Castle, 6

xxi.

Botanical Name.	Common Name.	Where found.
Rosaceæ,—*continued.*		
Comarum palustre	Marsh Cinquefoil	Morton, Adel Bog, 7
Agrimonia eupatoria	Common Agrimony	Generally distributed, 7
Poterium sanguisorba	Salad Burnet	On Permian strata, 6
Sanguisorba officinalis	Great „	Abundant in Airedale
Rosa spinosissima	Scotch or Burnet Rose	Gordale, Airton, Ledsham
„ mollis	Red or Apple „	Malham, Skipton, Adel
„ tomentosa	Downy-leav'd „	Malham, Bingley, Camblesforth, 6
„ canina	Dog Rose	Common, 6
„ arvensis	Trailing Dog-rose	Common in lower Airedale
Saxifragaceæ.		
Saxifraga aizoides	Yellow Mt. Saxifrage	Between Malham Tarn and Penyghent, 7-8
„ tridactylites	Rue-leaved „	Malham, Rylstone, Cottingley, 5
„ granulata	White Meadow „	Malham (native), Holden Gill, near Eccleshill. Esholt (adventive), 5
„ hypnoides	Mossy Saxifrage	Malham, Elbolton, &c.
Chrysosplenium alternifolium	Altern-leaved golden „	Malham Moor; Beckfoot. Bingley, 5
Chrysosplenium oppositifolium	Opposite-le'v'd „	Common by streams. 4-5
Parnassia palustris	Grass of Parnassus	Malham, Gordale, Skipton Rock, Adel Bog (1888) 7
Crassulaceæ.		
Sedum telephium	Orpine	Gully above Malham Cove
„ villosum	Hairy Stone-crop	Between Kirkby-Malham and Settle, 7
„ acre	Golden Moss	Frequent on limestone
Droseraceæ.		
Drosera rotundifolia	Round-leaved Sundew	Rumbalds Moor, Shipley Glen, Adel Bog
„ anglica	Great „	Goole Moor, Thorne Waste
„ intermedia	Long-leaved „	„ „

c

Botanical Name.	Common Name.	Where found.
Haloragaceæ.		
Hippuris vulgaris	Mare's-tail	Dikes near Malham Tarn, Mill-dam betw. Micklefield and Sherburn
Myriophyllum verticillatum	Water-milfoil	Old river-bed below Keighley, Milford
,, spicatum	Spiked ,,	Malham Tarn, near Cottingley Bridge
,, alternifolium	Altern-leaved ,,	Dikes at Sherburn
Callitriche verna	Spring Water-starwort	Malham Tarn
,, stagnalis	,,	Common throughout Airedale
Lythrarieæ.		
Lythrum Salicaria	Loosestrife	Near Kildwick, Marley, Milford, 8
Peplis portula	Purslane	Drake Hill, near Morton; Adel lower dam; near Womersley. 7-8
Onagrarieæ.		
Epilobium angustifolium	Rose-bay Willow-herb	Above Gordale, Esholt, 7
,, hirsutum	Gt. Hairy ,,	Generally distributed, 7
,, parviflorum	Small-flow'r'd ,,	,, ,,
,, montanum	Broad smooth-leaved ,,	,, ,,
,, obscurum	Angle-stem'd ,,	,, ,,
,, roseum	Pale sm'th-l'v'd ,,	Waste ground, Frizinghall; Meanwood valley
,, palustre	Narrow-leaved Marsh ,,	Malham Moor, Bingley, &c.
Circæa lutetiana	Enchanter's Nightshade	Malham Cove, frequent in woods
Cucurbitaceæ.		
Bryonia dioica	Red-berried Bryony	Frequent on Permian limestone

Botanical Name.	Common Name.	Where found.
Umbelliferæ.		
Hydrocotyle vulgaris	Marsh Pennywort	Low-lying marshy places, general, 6
Sanicula europæa	Wood Sanicle	Bingley, Shipley Gln. &c., 6
Conium maculatum	Hemlock	Near Gargrave; Castle Hill, Pontefract, 7
Bupleurum rotundifolium †	Hare's-ear	Waste ground, Frizinghall (very rare)
Sium angustifolium	Water-kex	Marsh near Rawdon Crag Wood, between Apperley and Calverley, 7
Ægopodium podagraria	Goutweed	Near Skipton, &c., 7
Pimpinella saxifraga	Common Burnet Saxifrage	Frequent in upper Airedale
„ magna	Greater „	Skipton to Bolton Abbey, Baildon, by Ouse near Selby
Scandix pecten-veneris	Shep'rd's Needle	Infrequent in cultivated fields, 6
Ænanthe fistulosa	Common Water-dropwort	Ferrybridge district, 7
„ crocata	Hemlock „	Skipton, near Wilsden, Hawksworth, near Aire, Castleford
Silaus pratensis	Pepper Saxifrage	Common about Skipton; Rail. bank, Apperley
Angelica sylvestris	Angelica or Holy Ghost	Not infrequent, Shipley Glen, &c.
Daucus carota	Wild Carrot	Not uncom. between Goole and Gargrave, 7
Cornaceæ.		
Cornus sanguinea	Dog-wood or Wild Cornel	Malham, Gisburn, Abundt. on Permian limestone, 6
Caprifoliaceæ.		
Viburnum lantana *	Wayfaring-tree	Skipton Woods, 5
Sambucus ebulus *	Dwarf Elder	Canal side, Calverley
Adoxa moschatellina	Muskweed	Skipton, Rylstone, Hold'n Gill, Seven Ar. (Cott.) 5

Botanical Name.	Common Name.	Where found.
Rubiaceæ.		
Galium mollugo	White Bed-straw	Gisburn, Ry. bank, Esholt
,, boreale	Cross-leaved ,,	West side of Malham Tarn, near Grassington, 7-8
,, tricorne	Corn ,,	Frizinghall sewerage beds (casual)
,, uliginosum	Marsh ,,	Holden Wood, Marley, Heaton, 7
Asperula odorata	Woodruff	Skipton, Holden Gill, Shipley Glen, 6
,, cynanchia	Quinzywort	Quarry near Aberford, 7
Valerianeæ.		
Valeriana dioica	Marsh Valerian	Below Malham Cove, Shipley Glen, 6
,, officinalis	Great ,,	Distrib. generally, 7
Valerianella olitoria	Lamb's Lettuce	Eldwick, Knottingley, not infreq. in cultivated fields
Dipsaceæ.		
Dipsacus sylvestris	Teazel	Eccleshill, (casual), Knottingley
Scabiosa succisa	Devil's-bit Scabious	Generally distributed, 8
,, columbaria	Small Scabious	Malham, Skipton Rock, 7
Compositæ.		
Eupatorium cannabinum	Hemp Agrimony	Nr. Winterburn, Shipley Glen, Tong Park, (Hawksworth), Fryston
Aster tripolium	Aster	By the Ouse to Aire mouth, 8
Erigeron acre	Blue Flea-bane	Garforth ; on Permian limestone chiefly, 7
Solidago virg-aurea	Golden-rod	Skipton, Bingl'y, Nab wo'd. (Saltaire), Hambleton Haugh, 8
Inula conyza	Ploughman's Spikenard	Nr. Castleford and Pontefract, 7
Pulicaria dysenterica	Flea-bane	Bingley, Marley, near Trench Wood, Saltaire ; Seacroft, 7

Compositæ,—*continued.*

Botanical Name.	Common Name.	Where found.
Gnaphalium sylvaticum	Common Everlasting	Fields about Brayton and Selby, 7
,, uliginosum	Marsh Cudweed	Generally distributed
Antennaria dioica	Cat's-foot	Malham, top of Gordale, Ledsham Hall, 7
Filago minima	Small Cudweed	Common abt. Hambleton
,, apiculata	,,	Sandy fields about Hambleton Haugh
Bidens cernua	Bur Marigold	Marsh by the 'Cut,' Selby
,, tripartita	Three-lobed ,,	Nr. Seven Arches (Cottingley), Frizinghall dam
Chrysanthemum segetum †	Corn Marigold	Cornfields, Shipley, near Heaton, &c., 7
,, leucanthemum	Ox-eye or Dog-daisy	Common on rail.banks,&c.
Tanacetum vulgare	Tansy	Gisburn, Aire banks, Marley, Apperley, &c.
Artemisia vulgaris	Mugwort	Infrequent, 7
Doronicum pardalianches *	Leopard's Bane	Plantation nr. Harewood, Ledsham, 7
Senecio sylvaticus	Mountain Groundsel	Malham, old quarry Fagley, Selby
,, erucifolius	Hoary Ragwort	Skipton, near Wilsden, Hawksworth, Castleford
,, saracenicus *	Worm-wort	Near Smithy Mills, Adel; stream side Weetwood Bottoms (long estab.)
Arctium majus	Burdock	Field side nr. Selby (rare)
Carlina vulgaris	Carline-thistle	Frequent betw. Skipton and Malham, &c., 7
Centaurea scabiosa	Great Knapweed	Malham, Gargrave, Skipt'n
,, cyanus †	Blue-bottle or Corn-flower	Hawksworth, Frizinghall, Moortown, 8
Serratula tinctoria	Saw-wort	Malham Tarn bog, Arncliffe Clowder, 7
Carduus nutans	Musk-thistle	Gordale Scar pastures, Garforth, &c., 7
,, crispus	Welted ,,	Gargrave, common about Brotherton, &c., 7

Botanical Name.	Common Name.	Where found.
Compositæ,—*continued.*		
Carduus heterophyllus	Melanch'ly thistle	Malham, Winterburn, 7
Lapsana communis	Nipplewort	Generally distributed, 7
Crepis paludosa	Yellow or Marsh Succory	Malham Tarn shore, Ingrow, Shipley Glen
Hieracium pilosella	Mouse-ear Hawkweed	Generally distributed, 7
,, anglicum	,,	Limestone scars Malham and Gordale
,, iricum	,,	By the stream flowing from Gordale Scar
,, murorum	Wall Hawkweed	Malham Cove and Scars, Skipton
,, cæsium	,,	,, ,, (abundant)
,, pallidum	,,	Malham (very rare), 7
,, Gibsoni	,,	,, and Gordale
,, sylvaticum (vulgatum)	,,	High Close Scar, Malham, Idle
,, gothicum	. . . . . .	Malham, 7
,, tridentatum	. . . . . .	,,
,, crocatum	. . . . . .	,,
,, boreale	Broad-leaved ,,	Keighley, Bingley, Apperley, &c.
Leontodon hirtus	Hawkbit	Skipton, pastures nr. Cottingley and Baildon, Brayton Barf, 8
,, hispidus	,,	Malham downwards, rarer off limestone, 8
Taraxacum officinale var. erythrospermum	Dandelion	Between Gordale Scar top and Malham Tarn, 5
Lactua muralis	Wall Lettuce	Malham, Bingley. Seven Arches (Cottingley)
Sonchus asper	Sow Thistle	Malham Moor, near Keighley, 7
Tragopogon pratensis	Goat's-beard	Gilstead Canal-lock. Saltaire, railway banks, &c. betw. Leeds & Skipton, 6
Campanulaceæ.		
Jasione montana	Mountn. Sheep's-Bit	Quarries nr. Bolton Woods (Bradford), near Oxenhope, about Gateforth and Brayton, 7

Botanical Name.	Common Name.	Where found.
Campanulaceæ,—*continued.*		
Campanula rapunculoides *	Creeping Bell-flower	Betw. Skipt'n & Brought'u
„ latifolia	Broad-leaved „	Frequent in Airedale betw. Skipton & Snaith
„ glomerata	Clustered „	From Selby downwards to mth. of Aire (on warp), 7
Ericaceæ.		
Vaccinium myrtillus	Bilberry	Common; on gritstone moors mainly, 5-6
„ vitis-idæa	Whortleberry	Rumbalds Moor; Black Hills, Wilsden; Moseley Wood, Horsforth, 6-7
„ oxycoccos	Cranberry	Malham; bogs on Rumbalds Moor, 6
Erica cinerea	Fine-leav'd Heath	Otley Chevin, Wilsden, Rumbalds Moor, &c., 8
Calluna vulgaris	Heather or Ling	Common on moors, 8
Plumbagineæ.		
Armeria maritima	Sea-Pink	Betw. Malham and Settle
Primulaceæ.		
Primula vulgaris	Primrose	Com. in some woods, &c., 4
„ officinalis	Cowslip	Common on limestone; Bingley
„ farinosa	Bird's-eye Primrose	Malham, nr. Cracoe, Gisburn, Skipton Rock
Lysimachia vulgaris	Yellow Loose-strife	By Aire near Castleford, Carlton (Snaith)
„ nemorum	Yellow Pimpernel	Skipton Woods, Shipley Glen, Adel Moor, 6
„ nummularia	Moneywort	Nr. Gargrave, Osier-beds, Brotherton
Trientalis europæa	Winter-Green	Rumbalds Moor, above Bingley, *(Yorks. Nat. Un. Exc.,* 1873), 6
Anagallis arvensis	Scarl. Pimpernel	Saltaire and Marley (garden Weed), 6
„ tenella	Bog „	Nr. Cullingworth, nr. Marley old Hall, Adel Bog

Botanical Name.	Common Name.	Where found.
Primulaceæ,—*continued.*		
Hottonia palustris	Water Violet	Marley, nr. Methley, Osier-bed dikes at F'rrybridge
Apocynaceæ.		
Vinca minor *	Periwinkle	Wood between Cottingley Bridge & Seven Arches, Weetwood, 5
Gentianeæ.		
Erythræa centaurium	Centaury	Near Gilstead, pasture above Shipley Glen, frequent on Permian limestone, 7
Gentiana campestris	Field Gentian	Betw. Malham & Arncliffe, nr. Wilsden, fields above Shipley Glen, 9
,, amarella	Autumnal ,,	Top of Gordale Scar, St. Helen's Well, Eshton, pastures nr. Shipley Gln.
,, Pneumonanthe	Marsh ,,	Mort'n Bog, nr. Hamblet'n
Menyanthes trifoliata	Bog-bean	Malham Tarn shore, Rumbalds Moor, ab. Morton, near Wilsden, field near Shipley Glen, 6
Polemoniaceæ.		
Polemonium cæruleum	Jacob's Ladder	Malham (noted by Merrett, A.D. 1666: there yet), 6
Boragineæ.		
Echium vulgare	Viper's-bugloss	Waste ground (casual) Saltaire, Pontefract, &c.
Symphytum officinale*	Comfrey	Field near Nab Wood, (Saltaire), Osier-beds, Ferrybridge, 6
,, tuberosum	Tuberous ,,	Canal-bank, Newlay, 7
Anchusa arvensis	Alkanet	Near old river-bed above Keighley, Frizinghall (casual)
Lithospermum officinale	Gromwell	Garforth and Kippax
,, arvense	Stone-hard	Gilstead, Hawksworth, 6
Myosotis palustris	Water Forget-me-not	Skipt'n, Marley, Baild'n, 6
,, cæspitosa	Tufted ,,	Frequent in sluggish streams throughout Airedale, 6

Botanical Name.	Common Name.	Where found.
Boragineæ,—*continued.*		
Myosotis sylvatica	Wood Forget-me-not	Skipton, Shipley Glen, Esholt Springs, 5-6
,, arvensis	Field ,,	Generally distributed, 6
,, collina	Early ,,	Malham, 4
,, versicolor	Varied ,,	
Cynoglossum officinale	Hound's-tongue	Bingley, &c., 5 Near Skipton, 7
Convolvulaceæ.		
Convolvulus arvensis	Field Bindweed	Commonly distributed
,, sepium	Hedge Convolvulus	Calverl'y, Charlest'n (Shipley), near Roundhay, 7
Solanaceæ.		
Solanum dulcamara	Bitter-sweet or Nightshade	Frequent in Airedale betw. Goole and Airton, 7
Atropa belladonna	Deadly ,,	Wood by Roundhay lime-hills, Sherburn Churchyard, Frizinghall (introduced with sewerage)
Plantaginaceæ.		
Plantago major	Great Plantain	Very common, 6
,, media	Hoary ,,	Most frequent on limest., Hawksworth, warp lands about Goole, 6
,, lanceolata	Ribbed ,,	Generally distributed
,, maritima	Sea-side ,,	Pastures between Bordley and Kilnsey, on Ouse banks about Goole, 7
Littorella lacustris	Shoreweed	Malham Tarn shore, margin of Yeadon dam, Adel dam, 7
Scrophularineæ.		
Verbascum thapsus	Great Mullein	Brotherton and Burton Salmon, waste ground Saltaire (casual)
Linaria cymbalaria *	Ivy-leaved Toad-flax	Skipton Castle walls, and frequent in Airedale down to Castleford
,, elatine		Knottingley, 7

Botanical Name.	Common Name.	Where found.
Scrophularineæ—*continued.*		
Linaria vulgaris	Yellow Toad-flax	Frequent, on sandy soils chiefly, 7
,, minor	,,	Bingley, Frizinghall, Calverley, &c., on rail. ashes
Antirrhinum majus *	Snapdragon	Castle Walls Skipton and Pontefract
Scrophularia nodosa	Figwort	Common by streams, 7
,, Balbisii	Water Betony	Between Gargrave and Airton, Marley, Selby, 7
,, Ehrharti	,,	River-side, Cottingley, 7
Limosella aquatica	Mudwort	By pools, Rawcliffe 'Rabbit Hills' (1877)
Digitalis purpurea	Foxglove	Comm'n, occasionally wht. flowers, rare on limestone, 7
Veronica agrestis	Green Field Speedwell	Throughout Airedale to Malham Moor, 4
,, Buxbaumii †	Buxbaum's ,,	Kippax, 4
,, hederæfolia	Ivy-leaved ,,	Generally distributed, 4
,, arvensis	Field ,,	,, ,, 5
,, serpyllifolia	Thyme-leav'd,,	,, ,, 6
,, Chamædrys	Germander ,,	,, ,, 5
,, montana	Mountain ,,	Malham Cove, Newsholme Dene, Shipley Glen, Hawksw'rth, Moort'wn, 6
,, scutellata	Marsh ,,	Malham Tarn bog, near Bingley woods, Baildon Green, ditch near road, Adel dam, 6
,, Beccabunga	Brooklime :	Generally distributed, 6
,, Anagallis	Water Speedwell	Malham, Marley, 7
Bartsia alpina	Alpine Bartsia	Betw. Gordale Scar top and M'h'm Tarn (Lees *Flora*) 7
,, Odontites	Red Bartsia or Cock's-comb	Generally distributed, 7
Euphrasia officinalis	Eyebright	Common, 6
Rhinanthus Crista-galli	Yellow Rattle	- 6
Pedicularis palustris	Marsh Lousewort	Malham Moor, near Skipton, Marley, &c., 7
,, sylvatica	Wood ,,	Generally distributed, 5
Melampyrum pratense	Meadow Cow-wheat	Shipley Glen, Hawksw'rth, Meanwood Wood

Botanical Name.	Common Name.	Where found.
Scrophularineæ,—*continued.*		
Lathræa squamaria	Toothwort	Malham Cove, Hainworth Wood (Ingrow), near Seven Arches (Cottingley), Shipley Glen, 4
Orobancheæ.		
Orobanche major	Greater Broomrape	Baildon Moor (on gorse), Roundhay lime-hills (1867), 6
Lentibularineæ.		
Pinguicula vulgaris	Butterwort or Bog-violet	Malham Moor, Rumbalds Moor, Marley, 6
Utricularia „	Bladderwort	Dike near Thorne Waste
Labiatæ.		
Mentha piperita	Peppermint	Marley, Hawksworth, Odsal (Bradford), 7
„ sativa	Whorled Hairy-mint	Skipton, Marley, Baildon, 7
„ arvensis	Field-mint	Generally distributed, 8
Lycopus europæus	Gipsy-wort	Canal side betw. Gargrave and Leeds, Frizinghall dam, Blackhill d'm, Adel
Origanum vulgare	Wild Marjoram	Malham, Skipton Rock, (white flowers), 7
Thymus serpyllum	Wild Thyme	Not infrequent, especially on limestone, 7
Calamintha Acinos	Calamint	Malham, Ferrybridge, (*Yorks. Nat. Union, Excursion,* 1873)
Nepeta Cataria	Cat-mint	Kippax, restricted to Permian limestone
„ Glechoma	Ground Ivy	Generally distrib., 5
Scutellaria galericulata	Common Skull-cap	By canal, Skipton; Eldwick, near Calverley, Selby, 7
„ minor	Lesser Skull-cap	By stream south side of Adel Bog, 7
Salvia verbenaca	Clary	About Ferrybridge
Stachys sylvatica	Woundwort	Generally distrib., 7
„ palustris	Marsh „	Not uncommon, 7

Botanical Name.	Common Name.	Where found.
Labiatæ,—*continued.*		
Stachys Betonica	Wood Betony	Common throughout Airedale up to 1250 ft., 7
Galeopsis Tetrahit	Common Hemp-nettle	Common, 7
Lamium purpureum	Red Dead-nettle	Very common, 4
,, amplexicaule	Henbit	Near Skipton, 5
,, album	White Archangel	Very common at low levels, 4
,, Galeobdolon	Archangel	Seven Arches (Saltaire), Esholt, 6
Ballota nigra	Black Horehound	Abundant on Permian limestone, 7
Teucrium Scorodonia	Wild Sage	Not uncommon
Ajuga reptans	Bugle	Not uncommon, 5
Illecebraceæ.		
Scleranthus annuus	Knawell	About quarries, Meanwo'd Wood, com. about Selby
Chenopodiaceæ.		
Chenopodium album	Goose-foot	Common on waste ground
,, Bonus-Henricus *	Good King Henry (VI.)	Malham, Marley, Cottingley, Idle, 6
Atriplex angustifolia	Orache	Common on arable and waste land, 7
Polygonaceæ.		
Polygonum Bistorta	Bistort	Nr. Malham village, Eldwick (750 ft.), Marley, Methley, 6
,, viviparum	Alpine Bistort	Near Malham Tarn, 6
,, amphibium	Water Buckwheat	Canal nr. Steeton, Bingley, Adel dam, Methley, 7
,, ,, v. terrestre	,,	Gargrave, Marley, Apperl'y
,, lapathifolium	Pale-flowered Persicaria	Common on waste ground
,, Persicaria	Spotted Knotgrass	Common, 7
,, Hydropiper	Water-pepper	Generally distrib., lower lands chiefly, 8

Botanical Name.	Common Name.	Where found.
Polygonaceæ,—*continued.*		
Polygonum minus	Small Creeping Persicaria	Gravelly margin of Blackhill dam, Adel, 8
,, aviculare	Knotgrass	Very common, rail. banks, road sides, &c., 5
,, Convolvulus †	Black Bindweed	In cultivated fields, a common garden weed
Rumex obtusifolius	Broad-leaved Dock	Very common, 8
,, crispus	Curled ,,	,,
,, conglomeratus	Pointed ,,	Frequent
,, Acetosella	Sheep's Sorrel	Dry or stony pastures and moors to the highest summits, 6
Thymelæaceæ.		
Daphne Laureola	Spurge Laurel	On Permian limestone mainly, Kippax, 4
Euphorbiaceæ.		
Euphorbia Helioscopia	Sun Spurge	Common, 6
,, Peplus	Garden ,,	,,
,, Lathyris *	Caper ,,	A weed in gardens at Braithwaite (Keighley), and near one of the lodges of Harewood Pk.
Mercurialis perennis	Dog's Mercury	Common up to about 1000 ft.
Urticaceæ.		
Urtica urens	Small Stinging Nettle	Silsden, Bingley, Baildon, 7
Parietaria diffusa	Wall Pellitory	Near Esholt
Humulus Lupulus *	Hop	Nr. Charlestown (Shipl'y)
Ceratophylleæ.		
Ceratophyllum aquaticum	Hornwort	Canal near Methley, Drax, (rare), 7
Orchideæ.		
Neottia Nidus-avis	Birds'-nest Orchis	Formerly at Nab Wood (Saltaire), and Holden Gill (Steeton)
Listera ovata	Tway-blade	Generally distributed, 6

Botanical Name.	Common Name.	Where found.
Orchideæ,—*continued.*		
Listera cordata	Small Tway-blade	Braithwaite Moor near Keighley, 7
Spiranthes autumnalis	Lady's-tresses	Kippax lime-hills, Micklefield, 8
Epipactis latifolia	Broad-leaved Hellebore	Bingley Woods, Heaton Woods, Ledsham
,, ovalis	Purple ,,	Gordale, 7
Orchis mascula	Early Purple Orchis	Woods and pastures, common, 4
,, latifolia	Marsh ,,	Near Oughtershaw, Langstrothdale, 7
,, maculata	Spotted ,,	Common in moist meadows and woods, 6
,, Morio	Green-winged ,,	Pontefract (rare), 6
,, ustulata	Chocolate-tipped Orchis	Barlow, near Drax, and Went Vale (probably gone), 5-6
,, pyramidalis	Pyramidal ,,	Frequent on Permian limestone, very rare off it, 7
Ophrys apifera	Bee ,,	Near Skipton (two localities, 7
,, muscifera	Fly ,,	Malham Cove ? Hetchell's Wood, Scarcroft, 6
Habenaria conopsea	Fragrant ,,	Skipton Rock, Arncliffe Clowders, field near Holden Gill, common on Permian limestone
,, albida	White ,,	Above Gordale (rare), 6-7
,, viridis	Frog ,,	Malham, Bingley, Marley, fields above Ship. Glen, 7
,, bifolia	Butterfly ,,	Malham Moor pastures, 7
,, chlorantha	Gt. ,, ,,	Malham, Marley, Hawksworth, Bramham, mainly on limestone, 7
Irideæ.		
Iris Pseudacorus	Yellow Water-flag	Wet pastures, &c., frequent, 6

Botanical Name.	Common Name.	Where found.
Amaryllideæ.		
Narcissus Pseudo-Narcissus	Daffodil, or Lent Lily	Shelf Wood (Bradford), nr. Coley Hall, Lightcliffe; (noted by Ray in 1724; there yet); 4
Galanthus nivalis . .	Snowdrop . .	Wood betw. Seven Arches and Cottingley Bridge, (naturalized), 3
Discoreæ.		
Tamus communis . .	Black Bryony .	Skipton, Shipley Glen, Esholt, 5
Liliaceæ.		
Polygonatum officinale	Solomon's Seal.	Malham, 6
Convallaria majalis .	Lily of the Valley	Malham, nr. Wilsden, 5
Allium vineale . . .	Crow Garlic . .	Malham, Gateforth to Brayton, 7
,, Scorodoprasum	Sand Leek . .	River bank between Selby and Booth Ferry, 7
,, oleraceum . .	Field Garlic . .	Malham, field by canal between Shipley and Apperley; betw. Stanningley and Armley, 7
,, ursinum . . .	Ramsons . . .	Common in woods, 5
Scilla nutans . . .	Wild Hyacinth or Blue-bell .	Common in woods; white flowers, frequent; pink, very rare, 4
Gagea lutea	Yellow Star-of-Bethlehem .	Wood at Halton East, (Skipton), (650 ft.), 4
Narthecium ossifragum	Bog Asphodel .	Malham, Cullingworth, Bingley, and Baildon moors, 7
Paris quadrifolia . .	Herb Paris . .	Malham, Skipton, Ingrow and Bingley woods, 6
Junceæ.		
Juncus effusus . . .	Soft Rush . .	Wet pastures, &c., com., 7
,, glaucus . . .	Hard Rush . .	,, ,,
,, squarrosus . .	Goose-corn . .	Gen. distrib. on moors

Botanical Name.	Common Name.	Where found.
Junceæ,—*continued.*		
Luzula sylvatica	Great Wood-rush	Bingley, Esholt, Shipley Glen
„ pilosa	Hairy „	Frequent in woods
„ campestris	Field „	Common in pastures
„ muliflora, var. congesta	Many-headed „	Hawksworth, and Baildon Moor, 6
Aroideæ.		
Arum maculatum	Cuckoo-pint	Woods and hedges, com., 5
Alismaceæ.		
Alisma Plantago	Water Plantain	Throughout Airedale to Malham Tarn, 7
Sagittaria sagittifolia	Arrow-head	Skipton, old river-bed above Keighl'y, Bingl'y, canal at Seven Arches (Saltaire), in Aire, Ferrybridge, 7
Butomus umbellatus	Flowering Rush	Near Keighley, Saltaire, canal at Kildwick and Apperley, Selby
Naiadaceæ.		
Potamogeton natans	Broad-leaved Pondweed	Canal at Bingley, Tong Park, Baildon, South Milford
„ densus	Pondweed	Malham, canal at Bingley, Saltaire, 7
„ rufescens	„	Canal nr. Morton (Bingl'y)
„ lucens	Shining „	Malham Tarn
„ perfoliatus	Perfoliate „	Malham Tarn, in Aire between Leeds and Snaith, 8
Cyperaceæ.		
Scripus lacustris	Bulrush	Eshton Tarn, Gargrave (1805), in Aire near Marley, ab. Keighley. &c.
„ setaceus	Bristly Club-rush	Malham Tarn edge, Skipton Rock, Eldwick
„ pauciflorus	Chocol'te-head'd Club-rush	Malham Tarn edge

Botanical Name.	Common Name.	Where found.
Cyperaceæ,—*continued.*		
Eriophorum latifolium	Broad-leaved Cotton-grass.	Near Malham Tarn, Airton, 8
Carex dioica	Diœcious Sedge	Malham Tarn Bog, Adel Bog, &c.
,, divisa	Bracteated Marsh Sedge	Below Malham Cove? marshy dike side, Hooke Road, Goole (very rare)
,, teretiuscula	Lesser Panicled ,,	Malham (very rare), 6
,, paniculata	,, ,,	Tong Park, Hawksworth, Nab Wood, Saltaire. bog near Rawdon Wood
,, muricata	Great Prickly ,,	Near Skipton, infrequent on Permian limestone
,, acuta	Slend'r-spik'd ,,	Canal side near Skipton, 6
,, pallescens	Pale ,,	Gordale Scar, Malham, Shipley Glen, 6
,, capillaris	Capillary ,,	Left-hand rocks of Gordale Scar (its only West Yorks. stat.) Before 1878 unknown south of Teesdale
,, pilulifera	Round-head'd ,,	Rumbalds Moor, Otley Chevin, Shipley Glen, 7
,, lævigata	Broad-leaved ,,	Malham, Shipley Glen, Adel beck
,, vesicaria	Bladder ,,	Malham, Baildon Moor, Adel dam, 7
,, ampullacea	Bottle ,,	Common in old river bed below Keighley
,, paludosa	Marsh ,,	Malham, Airton, nr. Keighley, Adel lower dam
Gramineæ, (Grasses).		
Alopecurus agrestis	Fox-tail Grass	Waste ground, Frizinghall
Phleum pratense	Cat's-tail ,,	Common in meadows
Agrostis canina	Brown Bent-grass	Baildon Moor, Adel Blackhill, Mo'rt'wn to Shadw'll
Aira caryophyllea	Hair-grass	Skipton Rock, nr. Holden Wood, nr. Eldwick and Hawksworth, 6
Avena pratensis	Oat-grass	Malham to Skipton, near Selby, 7

Botanical Name.	Common Name.	Where found.
Gramineæ, (Grasses),—*continued.*		
Avena pubescens	Downy Oat-grass	About Malham, Hainworth (Keighley), frequent on Permian about Brotherton, &c.
Triodia decumbens.	Heath-grass	Common about Shipley Glen, Adel Moor, &c., 7
Sesleria cœrulea	Blue Rock-grass	Malham, Gordale, 6 (confined to mountn. limest.
Phragmitis communis	Reed-grass	Malham Tarn (rare)
Koeleria cristata	Koeler's Crested-grass	Malham, Skipton Rock, Ouse bank, Selby, 7
Molinia cœrulea	Blue Moor-grass	Generally distributed on high moors, heaths, &c.
Catabrosa aquatica	Water Whorl ,,	Sherburn Dikes (very rare in Airedale), 7
Melica nutans	Wood Melic-grass	Near Grassington
Briza media	Trembling-grass	Generally distributed, rare above 900 ft., 6
Poa compressa	Flat-stalked Meadow-grass	Skipton, Baildon Green, Rimmington, Allerton-Bywater, 7
Poa nemoralis	Wood ,,	Malham (rare), Esholt Springs? 6
Festuca sylvatica	Wood Fescue	Wood nr. Airton (rare), 7
,, rubra	Creeping Fescue	Near Heaton, Fagley
Bromus erectus	Upright Brome-grass	Canal-side Saltaire, Apperley, Allerton-Bywater, 6
,, secalinus †	Rye Brome-grass	Baildon
Brachypodium pinnatum	Barren False-Brome-grass	Frequent on Perm. limest.
Brachypodium sylvaticum	Wood ,,	Holden Wood; Bingley, Shipley Glen
Triticum caninum	Couch-grass	Skipton, Shipley Glen
Lolium perenne	Rye-grass	Common up to Airedale summits, 6-7
Hordeum sylvaticum	Wood Barley-grass	Holden Wood (rare) 7
,, pratense	Field ,,	
,, murinum	Wall ,, or Way-bent	Near Pontefract and Knottingley, (rare) 7-8

Botanical Name.	Common Name.	Where found.
Filices, (Ferns).		
(The figures denote the month of fruiting.)		
Trichomanes radicans	Killarney Fern	Observed by Dr. Richardson in Belbank Wood, Bingley, in 1724, and by Bolton in 1758, and again by Bolton and Teesdale in 1782; now long extinct, 8
Pteris aquilina	Bracken	Woods and moors, common up to 1800 ft., 7
Cryptogramme crispa	Parsley Fern	Fountains Fell (nr. summit), nr. Settle (rare), 8
Lomaria Spicant	Common Hard-Fern	Distribution general, rare on limestone, 7
Asplenium Ruta-muraria	Wall Rue	Common on limestone; near Cottingley, near Apperley, 7
,, Trichomanes	Black Maidenhair Spleenwort	Frequent Malham Moor to Skipton; nr. Keighley, walls of Swillington Church. 7
,, viride	Green ,,	Malham and Gordale, 7
Athyrium Filix-fœmina	Lady Fern	Generally distributed, 7
Athyrium Felix-fœm. var. rhæticum	,,	Holden Wood, Harden Woods (Miall), Barden Tower. 7
Athyrium Felix-fœm. var. incisum	,,	In sheltered gills not infrequent
Athyrium Ceterach	Scaly-fern or Rustyback	Nr. Malham Tarn (very rare), 7
Scolopendrium vulgare	Hart's-tongue	Malham Moor, formerly common in Nab Wood, Saltaire, 8
Cystopteris fragilis	Brittle Bladder-Fern	Frequent on limestone; Seven Arches (Cottingley), Heaton Woods, 7

Botanical Name.	Common Name.	Where found.
Filices, (Ferns), *continued.*		
Cystopteris fragilis var. dentata	Brittle Bladder-Fern	Betw. M'lh'm & Settle (rare)
Aspidium Lonchitis	Holly Fern	Moughton Fell (1867), and Scar nr. Feizor, (Settle), in Airedale probably extinct, 7
Aspidium aculeatum	Prickly Shield Fern	Gordale, Malham, Steeton Gill, Newsholme Dene, Hawksworth, 7
„ angulare	Soft „	No Airedale record; near Burley, and Collingham
Nephrodium Filix-mas	Male Fern, or Common Buckler Fern	Generally distributed (to Airedale summits)
„ „ var. abbreviata		Fountains Fell (very rare) 7
Nephrodium cristatum	Crested „	Thorne Waste (very rare) 7
„ rigidum	Rigid „	Malham plateau (rare), 8
„ spinulosum	Spiny „	Shipley Glen; Nab Wood, Saltaire, up to 1886; Hunsworth Wood, (Cleckheaton)
„ dilatatum	Broad Buckler Fern	Common (with varieties) 7
„ Oreopteris	Hay-scented Fern or Mountain Buckler Fern	Fountains Fell, Holden Gill, Marley, Eldwick, Morton Bog, Hambleton, 8
Polypodium vulgare	Common Polypody	Frequent in upper Airedale, Shipley Glen, &c., 8
„ Phegopteris	Beech Fern	Winterburn, Holden Gill, Bingley, Hawksworth, 6
„ Dryopteris	Oak Fern	Steeton Gill, Newsholme Dene, Holden Gill, Nab Wood (Saltaire), Hawksworth, 7
„ Robertianum	Limestone Polypody	Malham and Gordale, (rare), 7

Botanical Name.	Common Name.	Where found.
Filices, (Ferns),—*continued.*		
Osmunda regalis	Royal Fern	Adel Bog, field nr. Birkenshaw (Bradford), (in 1860), Birkin, Camblesforth, all now extinct
Ophioglossum vulgatum	Adder's-tongue	Frequent throughout Airedale to Malham Cove
Botrychium lunaria	Moonwort	High ground behind Malham Tarn, near Bingley woods, Holden Gill, above Shipley Glen, Hooke (Goole), 6
Equisetaceæ.		
Equisetum maximum	Gt. Horse-tail	Skipton, Newsholme Dene, Odsal Wood (Bradford), Rawdon Crag Wood
,, sylvaticum	Wood ,,	Bingley, Allerton (Bradford), Odsal Wood, Camblesforth, &c.
,, limosum	Smooth ,,	Newsholme Dene, Canal nr. Holden Wood, Chellow Dene (Bradford)
,, hyemale	Rough ,,	Newsholme Dene, by Aire between Shipley and Esholt (rare)
Lycopodiaceæ.		
Lycopodium clavatum	Com. Club-moss	Bingley and Keighley Moors (rare)
,, inundatum	,,	"On the east side of Rumble-moor, above Helwick, in the deep heath" (*Merrett*, A.D. 1666)
,, Selago	Fir ,,	Penyghent, Fountains Fell Brayton rail. cutting, in a delving a mile west of Selby (a relic)

Botanical Name.	Common Name.	Where found.
Selaginellaceæ.		
Selaginella selaginoides	Small Fir Club-Moss . . .	Wet ground near Malham Cove and Gordale becks, east side of Malham Tarn, 7
Marsileaceæ.		
Pilularia globulifera	Pill-wort . . .	Rawcliffe (very rare), 7-8

ORNITHOLOGY.

IT has not been the object of this paper to inflate the List by the inclusion of doubtful records, which even if properly authenticated, would be of slight value as affording a basis in estimating the real ornithic wealth of the area under consideration. A bare list of the birds would also have been comparatively worthless without a few notes as to their relative abundance, &c.; and, moreover, no attempt has been made to chronicle in detail the accidental visitants, which are of little significance except as indicating their wanderings. The aim has been rather to give special prominence to those species which have been or are known to breed, or which purposely visit us annually; and my remarks, it should also be stated, apply more especially to the upper Aire valley.

I have followed the classification and nomenclature adopted by Mr. Saunders in his recent "Manual of British Birds,' not that I think it an altogether perfectly natural arrangement, but as respects one aspect at least of the classification it is to be recommended, and in all probability will, with some modifications, be adopted by ornithologists in the future.

Missel Thrush, *Turdus viscivorus*, resident, common.
Song Thrush, *Turdus musicus*, resident, common.
Redwing, *Turdus iliacus*, winter visitant, common.
Fieldfare, *Turdus pilaris*, winter visitant, common.
Blackbird, *Turdus merula*, resident, common. This is the only species in this genus, which winters with us, that was not affected by the severe winter of 1878-9.
Ring Ouzel, *Turdus torquatus*, summer visitant, common on the high moorlands, and occasionally breeds near this village. A few years ago two of my sons brought me a Cuckoo's egg which had been deposited in the nest of this species.
Wheatear, *Saxicola œnanthe*, summer visitant, common.
Whinchat, *Pratincola rubetra*, summer visitant, common. One of this species which bred close by this village possessed the power in a remarkable degree of imitating the notes of other birds, so much so that if I had not actually seen the bird in question I should certainly have taken it to be a Sedge Warbler.
Stonechat, *Pratincola rubicola*. I have never known this species to breed in this district. It is occasionally met with, but chiefly in early spring. It is, however, remarkable that it should not breed, considering what has been written relative to the nature of its favourite haunts.

Redstart, *Ruticilla phœnicurus,* summer migrant, common.
Redbreast, *Erithacus rubecula,* resident, numerous.
Nightingale, *Daulias luscinia.* There have been many reports of this noted songster frequenting this neighbourhood, but I have invariably found them to be of the Sedge Warbler. It is said to occur lower down the valley, near Goole, and one or two other places.
Whitethroat, *Sylvia cinerea,* summer visitant, common.
Lesser Whitethroat, *Sylvia curruca,* summer visitant. I know of but one instance of this species breeding here.
Blackcap, *Sylvia atricapilla,* summer migrant, not common.
Garden Warbler, *Sylvia hortensis,* summer migrant, commoner than the last species, and more generally distributed.
Goldcrest, *Regulus cristatus.* I have never found its nest in this neighbourhood, but it is abundant in winter. When on migration I have seen it in this village.
Chiffchaff, *Phylloscopus rufus,* another species which is not known to breed here.
Willow Wren, *Phylloscopus trochilus,* summer visitant, abundant.
Wood Wren, *Phylloscopus sibilatrix,* summer visitant, common, but somewhat local.
Reed Warbler, *Acrocephalus streperus,* summer visitant, breeds not uncommonly near Keighley and Leeds.
Sedge Warbler, *Acrocephalus phragmitis,* summer visitant, common in suitable localities.
Grasshopper Warbler, *Locustella nævia,* summer visitant, rare.
Hedge Sparrow, *Accentor modularis,* resident, abundant.
Dipper, *Cinclus aquaticus,* resident, fairly common.
Long-tailed Titmouse, *Acredula caudata,* resident, common in winter but rare in summer.
Great Titmouse, *Parus major,* resident, common.
Cole Titmouse, *Parus ater,* resident, common in winter, but breeds in very limited numbers.
Marsh Titmouse, *Parus palustris,* resident, not common either in winter or summer.
Blue Titmouse, *Parus cœruleus,* resident, abundant.
Crested Titmouse, *Parus cristatus,* a casual visitant; one shot in Aug., 1887, near Keighley, and another on Thornton Moor, are the only two records I have for this district.
Wren, *Troglodytes parvulus,* resident, plentiful.
Tree-creeper, *Certhia familiaris,* resident, does not breed in any numbers, more frequent in winter.
Pied Wagtail, *Motacilla lugubris,* resident, plentiful in summer, very seldom seen in winter.
Grey Wagtail, *Motacilla melanope,* resident, not uncommon by our hill-streams.
Yellow Wagtail, *Motacilla raii,* summer migrant, tolerably common.
Tree Pipit, *Anthus trivialis,* summer migrant, numerous.
Meadow Pipit, *Anthus pratensis,* resident, abundant in summer.

Golden Oriole, *Oriolus galbula*, accidental visitant.
Great Grey Shrike, *Lanius excubitor*, casual visitant.
Red-backed Shrike, *Lanius collurio*, summer visitant, breeds rarely.
Waxwing, *Ampelis garrulus*, accidental visitant.
Spotted Fly-catcher, *Musicapa grisola*, summer visitant, common.
Pied Fly-catcher, *Musicapa atricapilla*, summer visitant, breeds but rarely.
Swallow, *Hirundo rustica*, summer visitant, plentiful.
House Martin, *Chelidon urbica*, summer visitant, plentiful.
Sand Martin, *Cotile riparia*, summer visitant, plentiful.
Greenfinch, *Ligurinus chloris*, resident, very common in summer.
Hawfinch, *Coccothraustes vulgaris*, resident, breeds occasionally.
Goldfinch, *Carduelis elegans*, occurs occasionally in winter.
Siskin, *Chrysomitris spinus*, winter visitant, rare.
House Sparrow, *Passer domesticus*, resident, abundant.
Tree Sparrow, *Passer montanus*, local, but breeds in one or two localities.
Chaffinch, *Fringilla cœlebs*, resident, abundant.
Brambling, *Fringilla montifringilla*, winter visitant, common in some winters, in others somewhat scarce.
Linnet, *Acanthis cannabina*, resident, common in summer but scarce in winter.
Mealy Redpoll, *Acanthis linaria*, an irregular winter visitant.
Lesser Redpoll, *Acanthis rufescens*, resident, breeds plentifully.
Twite, *Acanthis flavirostris*, resident, breeds plentifully on the high moorlands, and has occasionally bred close to this village.
Bulfinch, *Pyrrula Europœa*, resident, breeds sparingly.
Crossbill, *Loxia curvirostra*, a scarce and irregular winter visitant.
Corn Bunting, *Emberiza miliaria*, resident, common in summer but exceedingly rare in winter.
Yellow Bunting, *Emberiza citrinella*, resident, very plentiful.
Reed Bunting, *Emberiza schœniclus*, resident, but seldom makes its appearance in this locality, though it breeds commonly in suitable places in the Aire valley.
Snow Bunting, *Plectrophenax nivalis*, an irregular winter visitant.
Starling, *Sturnus vulgaris*, resident, very common, but irregularly so; in this district it rears but one brood in the season.
Jay, *Garrulus glandarius*, resident, but in very limited numbers.
Magpie, *Pica rustica*, resident, common.
Jackdaw, *Corvus monedula*, resident, common.
Carrion Crow, *Corvus corone*, resident, scarce.
Hooded Crow, *Corvus cornix*, winter visitant, scarce.
Rook, *Corvus frugilegus*, resident, abundant.
Skylark, *Alauda arvensis*, resident, abundant in summer.
Swift, *Cypselus apus*, summer visitant, not uncommon.
Nightjar, *Caprimulgus europœus*, summer visitant, not uncommon.
Green Woodpecker, *Gecinus viridis*, breeds occasionally in Bingley woods.

Great Spotted Woodpecker, *Dendrocopus major*, resident, breeds not uncommonly in Bingley wood.
Lesser Spotted Woodpecker, *Dendrocopus minor*, has only once occurred in the district.
Kingfisher, *Alcedo ispida*, resident, not uncommon in the valley, the dipper partially taking its place in this more elevated district.
Roller, *Coracias garrulus*, an accidental visitor.
Hoopoe, *Upupa epops*, an accidental visitant.
Cuckoo, *Cuculus canorus*, summer visitant, deposits its egg chiefly in the nest of the Titlark; plentiful. In the south the nest of the Hedge Sparrow is usually selected in which to deposit its egg. In this locality it seems to have a decided preference to consign its charge to the Titlark and Whinchat.
Barn Owl, *Strix flammea*, not very common in this district.
Long-eared Owl, *Asio otus*, I have never seen it in this locality. Mr. T. Bunker thinks a pair bred near Goole in 1879.
Short-eared Owl, *Asis accipitrinus*, not at all common.
Tawny Owl, *Syrnium aluco*, resident, breeds not uncommonly in Bingley Wood.
Scops Owl, *Scops giu*, one said to have been shot at Skipton, and another at Horsforth.
Eagle Owl, *Bubo ignavus*, one captured on Rumbalds Moor in July, 1876, by two farm servants.
Montague's Harrier, *Circus cineraceus*, although not recorded for Airedale it is interesting to know that a pair has bred just outside its boundary, viz.: on Barden Moor, in 1860.
Rough-legged Buzzard, *Butes lagopus*, several have been taken, but not of late years.
Sparrow Hawk, *Accipiter nisus*, resident, common.
Kite, *Milvus ictinus*, rare.
Honey Buzzard, *Pernis apivorus*, one said to have been obtained at Harewood, in 1848.
Peregrine Falcon, *Falco peregrinus*, a rare visitant.
Hobby, *Falco subbuteo*, two records, one at Bingley and near Leeds.
Merlin, *Falco Æsalon*, resident, breeds not uncommonly.
Kestrel, *Falco tinnunculus*, resident, common.
Osprey, *Pandion haliaetus*, one caught at Harewood.
Heron, *Ardea cinerea*, resident, breeds near Gargrave.
Little Bittern, *Ardetta minuta*, one recorded from Goole.
Mallard, *Anas boscas*, frequently seen.
Shoveller, *Spatula clypeata*, a casual visitant.
Teal, *Querquedula crecca*, not unfrequent about reservoirs.
Pochard, *Fuligula ferina*, is said to be an occasional winter visitant.
Tufted Duck, *Fuligula cristata*, said to have bred at Malham Tarn.
Golden Eye, *Clangula glancion*, an occasional winter visitant.
Common Scoter, *Edemia nigra*, an occasional winter visitant.
Ring Dove, *Columba palumbus*, resident, very common.
Stock Dove, *Columba œnas*, resident, common in Bingley Wood.
Red Grouse, *Lagopus scoticus*, abundant on the moors.
Pheasant, *Phasianus colchicus*, plentiful in the woods.

Common Partridge, *Perdix cinerea,* plentiful in the meadows.
Redlegged Partridge, *Caccabis rufa,* rare.
Quail, *Coturnix communis,* has been occasionally met with, and is said in one instance to have bred and brought off its young.
Landrail, *Crex pratensis,* summer migrant, common in some years, in others comparatively scarce.
Spotted Crake, *Porzana maruetta,* one is said to have flown against a telegraph wire, near Bradford.
Water Rail, *Rallus aquaticus,* a rare visitant.
Moor Hen, *Gallinula chloropus,* resident, common.
Coot, *Fulica atra,* resident, not so common as the last.
Ringed Plover, *Ægialitis hiaticula,* occasionally met with by gunners when on migration.
Golden Plover, *Charadrius pluvialis,* breeds not uncommonly on Rumbalds Moor.
Grey Plover, *Squatarola helvetica,* an occasional winter visitant.
Lapwing, *Vanellus vulgaris.* resident, plentiful.
Woodcock, *Scolopax rusticula,* winter visitant, common. It would appear not to breed in this district.
Great Snipe, *Gallinago major,* rare.
Common Snipe, *Gallinago cœlestis,* resident, common in winter, and breeds sparsely in summer.
Jack Snipe, *Gallinago gallinula,* winter visitant, not very scarce, but more so, I think, of late years.
Dunlin, *Tringa alpina,* breeds commonly at Malham. One of its very few Yorkshire localities.
Common Sandpiper, *Totanus hypoleucus,* a summer visitant. Breeds not uncommonly about our reservoirs, and occasionally beside streams.
Redshank, *Totanus calidris,* resident, breeds plentifully at Malham.
Greenshank, *Totanus canescens,* one specimen shot in 1887 at Manywells.
Common Curlew, *Numenius arquata,* breeds commonly on some parts of the high moorland.
Whimbrel, *Numenius phæopus,* a casual visitant.
Little Auk, *Mergulus alle,* said to have occurred near Leeds. 1878.
Black Throated Diver, *Colymbus acticus,* a casual visitant.
Great Crested Grebe, *Podicipes cristatus,* a casual visitant.
Red Necked Grebe, *Podicipes griseigena.* a casual visitant.
Little Grebe, *Podicipes fluviatilis,* not uncommonly breeds in suitable localities in the Dale.
Storm Petrel, *Procellaria pelagica.* Mr. T. Bunker reports a specimen found dead (probably killed by the telegraph wires) at Howden, in October, 1890.

The following table shews the dates of arrival of our Summer migrants in the **Wilsden district**. The years 1879, 1882, and 1890, have been selected so as to obtain an approximate average.

	1879.	1882.	1890.
Pied Wagtail		Feb. 18th	
Wheatear	April 11th	April 8th	March 30th
Ring Ouzel	,, 11th	,, 10th	,, 30th
Willow Wren	,, 17th	,, 11th	April 18th
Sand Martin	,, 18th	,, 16th	,, 21st
Swallow	,, 22nd	,, 16th	,, 21st
Cuckoo	,, 22nd	May 4th (*see* remarks in type).	,, 20th
Redstart	,, 26th	April 21st	,, 21st
Tree Pipit	,, 26th	,, 21st	,, 7th (one)
Ray's Wagtail	May 2nd (late)	,, 23rd	April 22nd
House Martin	May 2nd	,, 15th (one)	May 2nd
Whinchat	,, 2nd	May 6th	,, 5th
Whitethroat	,, 3rd	April 29th	,, 1st
Swift	,, 15th	May 14th	,, 7th
Wood Wren	,, 16th	,, 6th	
Blackcap	No record	April 23rd	
Garden Warbler	,,	May 7th	
Nightjar	,,	,, 27th	,, 22nd
Landrail	,,		,, 5th
Spotted Flycatcher			,, 20th

In glancing at the above table one cannot fail to observe with what regularity our "feathered friends" arrive, notwithstanding the differences in the temperature of the years placed for comparison.

The spring of 1879 was preceded by a winter which, for extent and severity, was almost arctic; that of 1882, on the contrary, was preceded by a winter which was said to have been one of the mildest on record; whilst the winter of 1889-90 might be said to have been of an intermediate character.

The phenomena of bird-migration is invested with a certain mysteriousness when it is remembered that it is frequently in our coldest seasons,—contrary to what might be expected,—that we have to record exceptionally early arrivals and *vice versa*. For instance, in the year 1879 the cuckoo arrived here on the 22nd April, but there was no record of its arriving in 1882, although a mild spring, until the 4th May. During the present spring (1891), which has been remarkable for its severe and protracted cold, I saw several Ring Ouzels feeding in a ploughed field on the 8th April, although, when seen, it had been snowing fast for three hours, which is an earlier date by two days than their arrival in 1882.

E. P. BUTTERFIELD (Wilsden).

FOLK-LORE.

LET us in this chapter memorize old customs, curious beliefs, and quaint sayings and doings, which once common in our Dale, are now fast dying out. What strange things our forefathers said and did, and what weird romantic stories of fairies, ghosts and goblins, witches and wisemen, were current amongst them, seem almost incredible to us at this day. Though formerly when low-roofed 'creaky' buildings with their sliding panels, long, dark corridors, and narrow windows, were in fashion, 'sensation' and 'mystery' found readier help-meets than they do now. Now the daylight of science and of modern life penetrates all corners, and popular education and the spread of railways are likewise rapidly demolishing the old fictitious boundaries that at one time separated village communities and made each a little world of its own.

But in the age of 'gross darkness,' (a phrase, by the way, piously explained by a last-century country parson to his gullible flock, as 144 times the strength of ordinary darkness!), who had not seen a ghost, or been terribly frightened by some sudden or unusual noise? What it was could not always be exactly defined, but it was sure to be an awful 'something' appearing or happening usually in the night-time, when the alarmed one was alone and in a dreamy mood, (often alack, when in bed) and so startling in its effect that it made his very hair bristle up, his flesh creep, and the perspiration start coldly upon his brow,—and the cause of it all remaining strangely unaccountable and a "mystery even to the present day!" An old folk-lorist tells us, with the knowledge of one who has examined the subject in all its bearings, that our mothers' maids in our childhood "have so frayed us with bullbeggars, spirits, witches, urchins, elves, hags, fairies, satyrs, pans, faunes, sylvans, kit-with-the-candlestick (will-o'-the-wisp), tritons (kelpies), centaurs, dwarfs, giants, imps, calcars, (assy-pods), conjurors, nymphs, changelings, incubus, Robin-Goodfellow (Brownies), the spoorey, the man-in-the-oak, the hellwain, the fire-drake (dead light), the Puckle, Tom Thumb, Hobgoblin, Tom Tumbler, Bouclus, and such other bugbears, that we are afraid of our own shadows." Even so; such fabled monstrosities have had in all ages and at all periods of life, a peculiar fascination to the imagination, which persistently cleaves to the unseen, unsubstantial, and unreal, and in spite of all modern dogmatizing and the strictest scrutiny of science, it is impossible to banish even from the most sceptical belief in the supernatural altogether. Nature, indeed, is made up of "mysteries," which have always taxed and will ever tax human ingenuity to unravel them. Yet, people are certainly much less credulous than they were even a generation ago, and if we go back to the early years of the century, superstition and witchery, and all sorts of odd and out-of-the-way beliefs were, in rural districts especially, all prevalent. An ancestress of the writer's, and a native of Craven, relates a wonderful story of an aunt of hers, who was living not so many miles away from Keighley in the early part of this century, when this event happened, the story of which has been handed down as a perfectly true and authenticated account of the existence of fairies at that time. Indeed, so circumstantially were the facts always narrated, that none of the family dared ever doubt them. This aunt, who lived in a somewhat remote country district, occasionally acted as midwife, and late one very dark night a faint knock summoned her to the door, when she found a surprisingly little grey man on a little grey pony, who plaintively asked her to follow him. Putting on her bonnet and shawl she followed, and by-and-bye was led under some cliffs to a small cave, which they entered, and then they passed into an inner chamber where she found several beautiful fairies in attendance. At first she felt rather afraid, but the pleasant smiles and actions of the sprightly little beings soon put her at her ease. When the child was born, a little bottle and feather were given her with which to anoint the infant's eyes, and wondering what the effect would be, the woman, like a true daughter of Eve, slyly brushed the feather across her own eyes, when she instantly saw the apartment was quite filled with little fairies! It happened, however, that her action was not observed, and the little grey man soon saw her safe home again, rewarding her well for her services. Some weeks afterwards the midwife happened to be in Keighley market, when she observed the little grey man going about taking handfuls of corn, &c., out of the open sacks! She was the more surprised as no one appeared to notice the theft. But she went up to the fairy and asked him how he was and how his wife and baby were. The grey man looked puzzled, but answered they were well, adding "but which eye do you see me with?" She touched the eye, for she thought it best to be truthful, having a wholesome fear of the power of the little people. The little man instantly blew into her eye, and she saw him no more,—the fairy power of sight was lost! The same matronly individual always declared that she knew from her own personal experience that fairies were not imaginary beings, for had she not *seen* their clothes laid on the heather to dry, very much like the clothes worn by ordinary mortals, only remarkaby small and white, proving, too, that the strange little folk had washing days! Perhaps after all, she was one of those fated beings who are said to be gifted with second-sight. It used to be a common belief that children born during the hour after midnight possessed through life the strange power of being able to see the spirits of the departed. The fairies, of course, preferred this uncanny hour of birth; ordinary folk, however, were generally very anxious to avoid such a calamity befalling their little ones.

Witchcraft at one time had a strong hold on the people, and not only in the less accessible wilds of Craven but throughout our Dale we meet with numerous instances of such practices. One of the commonest, and also believed to be one of the most effective, charms against the wiles of witches and wisemen was the nailing of a horse-shoe on the house or stable-door. These may still be seen exhibited about Malham and in out-of-the-way localities, but preserved now more out of a curious veneration for the old custom than for any actual good expected from the practice. Sprigs of mountain-ash, rowan, or "wiggan-tree," were also used for the same purpose, and these might often have been seen suspended in the stalls of ailing cattle, and even hanging above the heads of sick persons while in bed. And an old saying runs,

"If your whipstock's made of row'n,
Your nag you may ride through any town."

No farmer thought of beating an animal with any stick but that made of rowan-wood, and all good house-wives had their churn-staffs made of the same material. Sometimes if a person was going upon an errand of importance, he or she would put ash-tree leaves in the soles of the shoes to ward off the ill-luck that might befall them if they chanced to meet a witch. But these witches and wisemen were often consulted on important family matters, and especially in cases of sickness, when the most remarkable remedies would be prescribed, in which "herbs of power," such as hemlock, nightshade, and other deadly types frequently played a conspicuous part. Sometimes, however, the party concerned would be told after much eccentric manœuvring that the case was hopeless, and the person must be prepared for the worst. Not so long ago the writer had some talk with an octogenarian living not a score miles from Malham, who firmly believes in the occult power of witchery. In his early days he possessed a little stock of six head of cattle, one of which took badly and died. Feeling somewhat alarmed, he forthwith consulted a wiseman, and was told they all would die, *and they did!* Ever since then he has had an unshaken belief in their divinations. Their cases or boxes containing various curious odds and ends with which they plied their mysterious craft, were jealously kept by their owners to themselves, and hidden away in secret places of the house. One such witch-box, containing a number of pins stuck upright, and a nail enclosed in cotton wick, was found in a hole behind an oak beam in the roof of an old house at Bramley, taken down in 1873. Many of the villages in our Dale had their fully-recognised sorcerers, the most noted of them, perhaps, being Mary Bateman, of Leeds, the celebrated "Yorkshire Witch," and, alas! murderess, who was hanged at York on March 20th, 1809, and whose body being publicly exhibited in Leeds, people paid their threepences to the amount of £30 (the money going to the General Infirmary); Hannah Green, of Yeadon, the famous "Lingbob Witch," who died in 1810, having amassed a fortune of £1000 by witchcraft, and Geo. Mason, the wiseman and astrologer, of Calverley, who died in 1807, worth a similar amount. A celebrated wise woman, also named Green, lived at Gargrave during the time of the Commonwealth. The village of Calverley, just mentioned, was moreover the scene of a most remarkable apparition, which frequented a narrow green lane, near the old Hall. This was the ghost of a headless horse bearing a frantic-looking rider (supposed to be the spirit of Sir Walter Calverley, the murderer), who held in his right hand a dagger dripping with blood. The villagers were well aware of the presence of this horrible apparition, but many strangers who were not, and had ventured down this gloomy thoroughfare after dark, had been almost scared to death. But, happily, the ghost, we are told, has not been seen for many years now, nor will it again be "on view" so long as the holly-tree, or "Christ's thorn," with its bright, scarlet berries, typical of His blood, grows on Calverley manor.

Of the many quaint customs and beliefs belonging to our Dale, none are more pleasing or possess a more widespread interest, than those appertaining to births, weddings, and funerals. It is a very old notion or superstition in the north that before a child is baptised it should be well looked after and guarded, lest the fairies make off with it, or do it harm. After baptism there is no such fear. May the little creature cry at its christening, otherwise it is a pretty sure omen that it is too good to live! Observe, also, with which hand the child seizes a spoon to sup, for if it be the left one, ill-luck will mark its future career. To fall upstairs is a pretty sure sign that you intend to be married soon; and if you are going to be married do not delay that most important event until late in the week, for it is a current belief in this part of Yorkshire that,

"Monday for wealth,
Tuesday for health,
Wednesday the best day of all;
Thursday for losses,
Friday for crosses,
And Saturday no luck at all."

The lady ought on no account to attend church during the publication of her banns, and if after she be told she persists in it, then woe betide her hapless children, for they are sure to be born with some sad affliction! The custom of throwing rice and an old shoe after the bridal couple is a common one in the north of England generally. In Craven, up to a comparatively recent date, it was usual for the guests to assemble at the close of the wedding festival in the bedroom of the newly-married couple, and while the latter sat up in bed in full dress, with the exception of their shoes and stockings, the women present standing with their backs to the bed, took in turn the bridegroom's stocking and flung it with the left hand over the right shoulder in the face of the bridegroom. The men then took the bride's stocking and aimed likewise at her face. This by no means easy thing to do naturally caused considerable merriment, and he or she who made the straightest aim was foretold to be married next. The wedding-race was also a common custom formerly, and only a few years ago was revived at Wibsey, near Bradford. The race used to be for a coloured ribbon offered by the bride to the one who reached her future home first after the marriage ceremony. Females took part in these races and sometimes rode on horseback, as it was thought to be very lucky to be the winner of such a wedding-ribbon. In some places the race was to the bride herself, who gave up the ribbon to the winner with a blessing and a kiss. With respect to ceremonies at funerals, it was the custom in Airedale to bury people of distinction by torchlight at a late hour of the evening; and about Skipton, up to 1803, when the practice was officially abolished, interments of this kind took place at midnight on the occasion of a woman dying at the birth of her first child. In this neighbourhood, and in Craven generally, the singularly tender custom prevailed of carrying garlands of flowers before the coffin of a deceased unmarried female. Such garlands or chaplets were afterwards hung up in the church, usually on the screen separating the choir from the nave, and remained there until withered away; an emblem of the frailty of human life, whose beauty, saith the prophet, "shall be as a fading flower." The custom is of very remote origin, being mentioned by Pliny as practised as early as the fourth century before Christ. At many places in Craven, including Kildwick, Carleton, Skipton and Gargrave, the custom lingered until the present century, and in Skipton church the hooks which held these floral tributes were only taken out in 1853, when the church was restored. In some parts of Derbyshire, we may add, it was the custom to hang the garlands over the seats in church previously occupied by the deceased.

Another pleasing relic of high antiquity which survived in our dale until recently was the May-day festivals,

"When all the lusty younkers in a rout,
With merry lasses danced the pole about,
Then friendship to their banquets bid the guests,
And poor men fared the better for their feasts."

This happy rustic carnival was abolished by statute in the time of Charles I. (A.D. 1644), as "a heathenish vanity," and was not revived until very many years afterwards. The only instances of May-poles in Airedale we have met with are at Barwick-in-Elmete, Woodhouse Moor, and Bramley, near Leeds, and at Laycock, near Keighley, but doubtless other of our villages had them once too. At several bordering places, such as Otley, Burnsall, and Coniston in Wharfedale, Ossett-cum-Gawthorpe, and Warley, near Halifax, May-poles still exist. A remarkable and inexplicable custom once widely prevalent in Yorkshire, and other parts of the north, was that of boys and young men on Easter Sunday seizing females and taking off their shoes, which were only redeemed on monetary payment. On the following day the girls would pull off the boys' caps and return them on like conditions. In Lancashire, by the way, it used to be a common practice on Easter Monday for the lasses to 'heave' the lads, that is, they were lifted up from the ground in their arms, and on Tuesday the lads 'heaved' the lasses. The custom, however, became so uproarious that in some parts of the factory districts for the sake of decency and order it had to be threateningly suppressed. Royal Oak Day (May 29th) was observed in our district by the ringing of bells and the decorating of church towers with boughs and sprigs of oak. This was continued at Kildwick and Skipton up to about 1830. In the old Royalist town of Skipton the bells on Gunpowder

e

Plot Day (Nov. 5th) were similarly rung at the expense of the parish and the tower of the church was hung round with large oak-boughs. At night huge bonfires blazed forth, also at the cost of the town. An old local saying (more vigorous than poetical) declares,

"Gunpowder Plot shall never be forgot,
As long as Skipton Castle stands on a rock."

Among the most ancient of our local customs or observances are those connected with springs and wells. The two great elements of fire and water have, of course, been regarded as objects of veneration by mankind in all places and in all ages, and with the worship of these began the very earliest form of sacred ritual. Well worship, indeed, locally continued down almost to our own time. It is, however, impossible to enumerate all these remarkable springs and wells, which were very numerous in our Dale; in fact there is no doubt that at one time almost every spring of note was dedicated to some saint, and the name in lapse of time may have been forgotten, yet these were always remembered as *holy* wells, and in our day still recognized as such. Now, in the Roman Catholic Church, any water may be consecrated to religious purposes, and thus rendered 'holy.' Many springs were furthermore named after some noted local or traditional character, such as Robin Hood, and many again were resorted to for their reputed medicinal virtues, and were known by some distinctive or may-be opprobrious appellation such as Stinking Well, &c. From the *Magna Britannica*, published in 1733, we gather that there were in Leeds several famous springs, viz.: St. Peter's Spring (at the top of what is now Bingley Street), the water of which was intensely cold, but beneficial to such as are troubled with rheumatism, rickets, &c.; Eyebright Well, near the Monk-pits, celebrated as a cure for sore eyes; a spring at the High Dam, 'whose water by the power of galls, will turn into a purple colour;' and the Spaw on Quarry-hill, which surpasses all the rest, 'being a *Panacea*'; and the Ducking-Stool for the cure of scolds, being near it. About Bradford there was a *Holy Well* (latterly called Helliwell), Spink Well, and at Dudley Hill "Our Lady's Well." Leeds had also a Lady's Well, situated in Lady Lane, but this was a common designation given to holy wells, especially to those in the neighbourhood of religious houses. About Skipton there are a number of famous springs, such as St. Helen's Well, near Eshton; Rouland Well, between Rylstone and Hetton; and St. Margaret's Well, at Burnsall. St. Helen's Well doubtless received its name from the celebrated Helena, mother of Constantine the Great, who was a native of York, and in which city there were no fewer than *four* churches dedicated in her honour. Almost within living recollection one might have seen votive offerings, such as pieces of ribbon, &c., tied to the bushes adjoining this and other similar pilgrims' wells. Sometimes an offering of money or piece of metal, such as a crooked pin, was dropped into the water, or into a receptacle provided for the purpose. At the top of Brayton Barf, near Selby, there is a pool of water into which anyone visiting the place must drop a pin, otherwise the omission will be fraught by the person sooner or later contracting the *itch*, at least that was the current belief. Passing now from water to fire worship we have but scant traces left in our Dale, outside the harvest-thanksgivings in our churches, which are an undoubted survival of sun-worship, once celebrated by the *bel* fires on our hills. In some parts of Norway even at the present day such harvest offerings are burnt on stone altars in the open air. Fire was believed to purify from sin and disease, bodies were consequently burnt before interment, and in Craven within the last twenty years or so it was the custom with farmers and others who kept cattle to kindle a so-called 'Need-fire' on the occasion of the outbreak of foot-and-mouth disease or other epidemic. This was done by rubbing two pieces of wood violently together, igniting a large bonfire, and then driving the affected animals among the smoking brands. In some parts of Craven there are still people who have a superstitious dread of fire, and thirty or forty years ago, or even more recently, many old folk might have been met with who regarded it as a positive sin (indeed much the same as telling a lie) to blow or stir up the fire, and on anyone moving to do so they would turn aside in dismay or hide themselves while it was being done.

Other strange superstitions were those connected with birds, animals, flowers, and various objects of local significance, such as certain hills, trees, stones, &c., the stories and traditions of which would occupy too much of our space to tell at length. One of the best known is that appertaining to the far-travelled cuckoo, at the hearing of whose welcome voice for the first time in the Spring, you should not be without money in your pocket, if you desire that good fortune attend your steps throughout the year. The robin, wren, swallow, crow, raven, magpie, &c., have all their traditionary spells. The latter is a witches' bird and of particular ill-omen, and if you are anxious to avoid the evil consequences attendant upon meeting a single magpie, you should make a cross in the air, or respect the bird by taking off your hat. There is a saying,

"I cross one magpie,
And one magpie cross me ;
May the devil take the magpie
And God take me."

and another local one is,

"One for sorrow, two for mirth
Three for a wedding, four for a birth,
Five for heaven, six for hell,
Seven the de'ils ain sell."

The first lamb of the season is a portent of good luck, if on seeing it you turn the money in your pocket ; in some districts the position of the animal when seen is said to augur, if the tail be towards you, plenty of meat to eat during the year, and if the head, then you may expect mostly milk and vegetables for your fare.

With wild herbs and flowers is connected an endless variety of folk-lore. But a few local examples must suffice. Everyone knows the pretty Herb Robert, or Stinking Cranesbill, as it is sometimes called, with its small pink blossoms and deeply-cut leaves, but not everyone may know how it received its name ages ago, from the pious St. Robert, who was Abbot of Fountains in the 12th century, and whose festival is on the 29th of April, this being about the time of the appearance of the flower. The Ragwort, one of our common summer plants, is likewise known as St. James' Wort, from its being generally in full flower about the time of St. James' day, July 25th. And similarly the early-peeping daisy, or "daie's eye" of Chaucer, is called Margaret, that Saint's day being on the 22nd of February; and St. John's Wort, whose Saint-day is June 24th; whilst the "drooping cowslip" is called Herb Peter, from its pendant head of flowers resembling somewhat a bunch of keys, the well-known badge of that apostle. The Lady's-smock Bitter-cress, Milk-maid, or Cuckoo-flower, as it is variously called, is still another of our common favourite wildlings, whose name is said to have originated in mediæval times from its having been dedicated to "Our Lady of Mercy," &c. From the qualities or peculiarities of some of our plants and flowers, have sprung such familiar sayings as "As wick (lively) as a whin;" "As blake (yellow) as a paigle;" "As red as a hep, rose, &c.;" "As clean as a pink;" "As green as gerse (grass);" "As sweet as new mown hay," &c.

In connection with the oak and ash an old weather rhyme tells us that

"If the oak's before the ash,
Then there'll only be a splash,
But if the ash precede the oak,
Then there'll be a jolly soak."

But these vegetable prognostications have no general application; on the thin limestone soils in the upper part of our dale, for instance, where the ash flourishes and the oak is scarce, the former is sure to leaf first if the Spring be mild and showery, which conditions do not so quickly affect the hardier and more deeply rooting oak. In certain places, however, where the soil and conditions are equal, the proverb no doubt will hold good.

Many old weather proverbs have been derived from natural signs and local observation, often much more reliable than the learned forecasts (valuable as these may be) deducted from fine instruments, and transmitted to us often from long distances by telegraph. No amount of scientific inference can ever interfere, for example, with such trusty old observations as "A peck of March dust is worth a king's ransom," and whence the rhyme,

"A March without water,
Dowers the hind's daughter."

Or the belief that a bright, showery April is good. "April weather, rain and sunshine both together," is what the farmers like, and so they say,

"In April, Dove's flood,
Is worth a king's good."

Certain presumably long-observed signs indicate the kind of weather that is to follow a day specially noted in the calendar, such as March 21st, mark which way the wind blows; St. Swithin's day (July 15th), which, like the day of the "Seven Sleepers" (June 27th) in Germany, rules the weather for the ensuing forty days; &c. In Airedale there are a few old weather-signs and sayings, as

"When t' mist's on Hope Hill,
Look out for a swill."

And, similarly,

"When Rawdon Billing puts on his cap,
Calverley mill will get a slap."

Another old saying runs,

"O Skipton in Craven,
'Tis never a haven,
But many a day of foul weather!"

But this is hardly applicable, at anyrate now. Neither, we regret to say, is the famous old rhyme,

"Castleford lasses may weel be fair,
For they wash in the Calder, and rinse in the Aire."

Both streams being, alas! at present as black as filth can make them.

Many odd quips and cranks and stories, lively and sedate, are incident to our Dale, and smartness in repartee has especially always been a characteristic of the humour-loving Dalesman. Instance the following. A couple of cockneys were riding up Airedale when they met a man coming along with a horse. "Here comes a Yorkshire tyke," said one of them, "let us humble him." After a little banter one of the gentlemen said, "Now I can prove you to be either a horse or an ass." "Well," replied the tyke, naively, "I can prove your saddle to be a mule." "How's that," they both then exclaimed, "Because," said the tyke, "it is something between a horse and an ass." Sometimes, however, queer blunders are made. At a public meeting, not a dozen miles from Keighley, a patriotic native, declaiming on the prowess of the English nation suddenly rounded on his audience with the following illustrative remark. "The British Lion," he said, bringing down his fist violently on the desk before him, "whether it is roaming the deserts of India, or at large among the forests of Canada will not draw in its horns or retire into its shell!" And a writer in "Yorkshire Notes and Queries" is responsible for the following. A Methodist preacher at Skipton during the late Irish crisis prayed: "O Lord, at this critical juncture of events, be pleased to grant that Mr. Gladstone and his supporters may hang together;" whereupon a well-known Tory exclaimed, "Amen! Amen!" To remedy matters the minister continued: "O Lord, I mean, may they in accord and concord hang together." "Amen! Amen!" retorted the Tory, "any sort of a cord so long as they hang in it."

Story-telling used to be a favourite pastime of the dales-people in the rural villages on the long winter evenings. In olden times, when books were not so plentiful as they are now, peddlers used to go about the farms and cottages selling cheap illustrated chap-books, and nothing was more entertaining than for some person to read aloud from these small paper tracts a story usually of some horrible crime or tale of thrilling heroism, to a party gathered in the lamp or candle-light round the fireside. In the neighbourhood of the moors little coal was used; the fire being mostly made up of sods of warm, fragrant peat, and brushwood where obtainable. Now the railways bring trucks of coal almost to the tops of the dales, so that even the remotest farm now burns some amount of coal. In the Dale farm-houses on winter nights the time would frequently be occupied in mending such tools as hay-rakes, putting shafts into axes, hammers, hoes, &c., and in making "soles" to put round the cows' necks, instead of chains, to fasten them in their stalls. Also milking-stools would be made, locally called "creckets,"—possibly the name of the game *cricket* owes its origin to these wooden buffets, which were constructed of three staffs or legs. Then again they fashioned those rough, useful baskets called "wiskets"; besoms, either of heather or of birch, and walking-sticks; whilst the lads frequently made knurs from holly-wood, or other articles for their games. There was no fear of covering the hearth with chips, or anything that could be swept up without making dirt, especially if the men were making something the women wanted for use.

In the small farm-houses and cottages there was weaving and winding, and in earlier times spinning,—reminding one very much of that verse in Macaulay's *Lay of Horatius*, "When the girls are weaving baskets," &c. Now, however, things are very different in the rural districts; spinning and weaving are done in 'mills' devoted to the purpose, and agricultural tools, &c., are mostly sent up from large implement works; whilst the poet's 'honest sweat' of the old-time ploughman is being largely superseded by the uses of steam and the ever-increasing number of agricultural contrivances. The following comparative rhymes may aptly sum up farm-life of a century ago, and in the present year of the census. It is to be hoped, however, that the satire contained in the latter verse is somewhat overdrawn.

1791.	1891.
Farmer at the plough,	Farmer gone to see the show,
Wife milking cow;	Daughter at the pi-a-no;
Daughter spinning yarn,	Madam gaily dress'd in satin,
Son threshing in the barn,	All the boys are learning Latin;
All happy to a charm!	With a mortgage on the farm.

But if this, indeed, be the rate of rural 'progress,' where, pray, will 1991 find us?

ANGLING IN AIREDALE.

TO non-anglers, or most people generally, unfamiliar with the actual state of the waters of the Aire and its in-running streams, the title given above will appear like a huge joke. Alas! it is but too true that to a large section,—a good half,—of the river is commonly applied the term "open sewer," in which tons of fish are annually sacrificed; but it is equally true that in the upper reaches of the river we have good fish, large fish, and plenty of fish available to followers of the gentle craft. Indeed, over this length of the water anglers' prospects at present have not been better for many years past, fish being plentiful and above average weight. On the other hand, at the Shipley outlet and on to and below Leeds things have grown worse, and the increasingly deleterious discharges of the Aire into the Ouse, near Goole, are year by year diminishing the products of the local fisheries, and thereby seriously affecting the well-being of a valuable industry. The under given statistics will shew the extent of these losses so far as ascertainable. Above Baildon Bridge (the limit of the Aire fishing eastwards) up to Skipton and northwards to Malham, the results have been good, and last year (1890) were markedly above the average, especially in coarse fishing.

To begin with the head waters of angling in our Dale, **Malham Tarn** yields capital sport,—no better in Yorkshire. It abounds in perch and trout. The latter are of two kinds, the common red and 'silver trout.' The fish are liable to a peculiar malformation of the *operculum* or gill-cover, arising doubtless from long confinement in a limited area, rendered by its position inaccessible to fresh breeding haunts. The fish were in all probability introduced in the thirteenth century by the Fountains Abbey monks, whose vast estates extended thus far west. Formerly trout of 5 lbs. and upwards were commonly caught, but latterly they have much diminished in size, owing, we are told, to the increase of perch. In Lord Ribblesdale's time every trout taken under a pound weight had to be returned. The fishing in the Tarn is now the private property of Walter Morrison, Esq., M.P. From **Malham Cove** down the river, and **Gordale Beck** down to the junction with the Aire, visitors at Malham are granted the liberty to fish. Below this point to **Airton** the river runs through Mrs. Serjeantson's Hanlith Hall estate, and is preserved by C. A. Rickards, Esq., of Bell Busk; and below this again to **Gargrave** it is in the hands of various private owners. The trout fishing throughout this length of the river (some 7 miles) is excellent.

The "Aire Fishing Club" follows with an important length of the river extending from **Gargrave** down to **Kildwick,** a distance of about 8 miles. This old-established Club was originally founded in the year 1838, under the title of the "Craven Anglers' Club," which in course of time was altered to its present name. The Club waters are divided for fishing purposes into two lengths. The upper length, extending from Gargrave to Carleton stone-bridge, (about 5 miles), includes the best trout water of the club. The number of its members is limited to 20. The lower length, from Carleton down to Kildwick, has its members limited to 40. The waters of the upper length are well stocked with trout, and also a considerable number of grayling. In connection with this part of the river the club has built a small fish-breeding establishment, which for some years past has annually turned into the river a goodly number of young trout. The lower length holds mainly coarse fish, chiefly chub, with some pike, and a steadily-decreasing number of perch. The Hon. Sec. of this Club is Mr. T. H. Dewhurst, Whin Field, Skipton.

The "Willow Field Anglers' Club" (Hon. Sec., Mr. A. Crowther, 23, Woodland Street, Bradford) has about 500 yards of the Aire on its north side at Willow Field, adjoining the Skipton Sewage Works, between **Skipton** and **Cononley**. The presence of these works has undoubtedly contributed to the value of the fishing over this short reach of the river; the water being clear and full of feed, and yields abundance of chub, roach, trout (up to 2 lbs.), perch (up to 3 lbs.), gudgeon (big and very plentiful), and a few grayling. Of roach 20 lbs. to 25 lbs. have been taken in a day within the last four years; and last year (1890) a chub scaling 3 lbs. 15 ozs. was caught here. Pike are also occasionally seen; a very fine one weighing over 20 lbs., and measuring 30 inches in length having been captured in 1883 in the old river course between Cononley and Bradley.

The "Bradford Eagle Angling Association" (Hon. Sec., Mr. H. S. Foulds, *Eagle* Inn, Bowling, Bradford) was founded in 1873, and is now about 70 strong. The society has about 1¼ miles of fishing grounds in the Aire at **Kildwick** and **Steeton**. Trout, roach, perch, chub and gudgeon constitute the principal varieties. There used to be a good many cray-fish in and about the river at Steeton, which were first introduced last century by the Garforths into a brook not far from the old family seat at Steeton. Salmon and salmon-smelts from the Ouse used also formerly to ascend the river here to spawn, but they are rarely if ever seen now higher up than about Carleton bridge, near Snaith.

Above **Steeton** bridge there are several fields owned by Mr. Smith, of Kildwick Grange, and Mr. G. S. Taylor, who allow a number of anglers at Silsden the privilege of fishing this reach of the Aire. Sport here is sometimes very good; on August 31st, 1887, one Silsden fisherman having hooked a fine 2½ lbs. trout. There is no properly organised club at Silsden, many of the local fishermen being members of the Keighley club.

The "Bradford Waltonians" (Hon. Sec., Mr. W. H. Hall Ward, 14, Darley Street, Bradford) possess two most excellent fishing waters, viz.: **Chelker** Reservoir (57 acres) and **Silsden** Compensation Reservoir (25 acres), both belonging to the Bradford Corporation.

The fishing rights of the former are vested in the Duke of Devonshire and J. Coulthurst, Esq., of Gargrave House, and of the latter in Lord Hothfield. Both waters abound principally in trout; in Silsden there are a few perch occasionally taken up to 3 lbs. Chelker, after the careful management and attention that has been bestowed upon it, is now one of the finest fishing areas in Yorkshire, and its reputation, both for quality and size of the fish, is not inferior to that so long enjoyed by Malham Tarn above mentioned. The 'feed' consists largely of shell-fish, and the excellent quality of the water seems well suited to the development of the fish. Trout of 1 lb. is a common average, and sometimes a four or five pounder will be hooked. Fly and minnow only are used here. In the Silsden waters trout from ¼ lb. to 2 lbs. are the regular catches, but fish of 3 lbs. to 4 lbs. are taken at odd times. In April, 1886, an expert member of this Club hooked as many as 83 trout in one morning before 12 o'clock! The year following (1887), we may add, was an exceedingly dry one, and during the long summer drought, when the reservoir became nearly empty, and the in-running streams were dried up, the Club computed its loss of trout and perch at fully 20,000. In connection with this reservoir, the "Waltonians" erected some five years ago one of the most perfect hatching-houses in the North of England. As many as 140,000 trout fry have been hatched in a year; and the famous Loch Leven ova have also been largely introduced. The hatching-house is only shewn on application. The waters of the Club are strictly watched, and the Club membership is limited to 25.

The "Stock Bridge and Eastburn Angling Club" (Hon. Sec. Mr. Ellis Town, Keighley) now numbers about 100 members. The club waters extend along the Aire from Stock Bridge (**Keighley**) westwards to Eastburn Beck, a distance of over four miles. They are well stocked with trout, chub, roach, perch, gudgeon, and ruffs. Occasionally a pike is taken. The Club has lately (Spring, 1891) turned into the river 8000 young Loch Leven trout, and there is every prospect of good sport during the coming season. One good principle of this club is that it grants free season-tickets to aged anglers who reside in Keighley, and also those who are not in a position to pay the full subscription fee are admitted at a reduced fare. The Keighley Corporation, we may here state, grant daytickets, at 1s. each, for fishing in the Ponden reservoir, in the upper Worth valley. It is pretty well stocked with trout, though the average weight is small. The biggest record we know of is 11 lb. of trout killed by a Stanbury angler in 14 days' fishing. Trout sometimes descend the Ponden Beck as far as Oakworth, when they get choked on entering the Worth. They also come down from the Oxenhope Moors, and are taken as low as Ebor Mills. The Filteringworks, now being made at Oakworth, will no doubt, in time, render the waters here again good and fishable.

The "Manningham Angling Club" (Hon. Sec. Mr. John Cowen, 6, Drewton Street, Bradford) has about two miles of water in the **Newsholme Dene** valley, west of Keighley. The Club also fishes by permission of Messrs. Town & Son, of Goose Eye, a three or four

f

acre reservoir in the same locality. The fish are mostly trout, and though small are fairly plentiful. A single angler will sometimes catch a score trout (from ¼ oz. to 1 lb. each) in a day. The Club dates from 1880, and has a members' roll of about 50.

The "Bradford Angling Association" (Hon. Sec., Mr. George Howroyd, 12, St. Andrew's Villas, Bradford) was formed in October, 1879, and numbers about 50 members. It has the length of the river at **Bingley** known as the Ravenroyd Farm, commencing at the wood above Ireland Bridge and extending westward past the damstones under the railway, including the large field adjoining,—a distance of 1½ miles. The water here abounds mostly in coarse fish, viz., gudgeon, roach, and a good percentage of chub, the latter occasionally raising 1½ lb. to 2 lb. This Club has also a length of water at **Kildwick**, known as Watson's Field, and another at **Bradley** Field, near Cononley. The last-mentioned provides sport with almost every kind of fish frequenting the Aire. It is a splendid trout run, and is especially abundant in roach and chub. At the end of the 1888 fishing season, three members of the Club on two following Saturday half-days killed there over 1 cwt. of nothing but roach. Last year (1890) several pike of 4 lb. to 5 lb. were taken.

The "Saltaire Angling Association" comes next with the three-mile stretch of water from **Baildon Bridge** to **Cottingley Bridge**, excepting the north side of the river between Baildon Bridge and Saltaire. The fish over this length consist chiefly of roach and chub. Formerly a good many trout were taken, but the waters have grown too rancid for this dainty beauty, though last season a few were caught, as well as some perch. But in coarse-fishing the oldest members of this club say they never remember a better year than 1890 has been. We have it on good authority that one angler has hooked and taken from the river not less than 1000 fish, weighing from 2 oz. to 1 lb., during the past season. Of course the smaller fish are put back, it being a rule of this Club that any member found with a trout under eight inches in length in his possession, shall be fined 1s. It is also required that one rod only be used at a time, and no 'dead-line' of any description is to be employed. Chub and roach, as stated, are very plentiful, and of these, one angler, it may be added, last season took 13½ lbs. in a day. By the side of this we may remark that in an angling contest at Bingley in 1885, the first prize was taken with 68 fish (chub principally), weighing together 12 ozs.! The Saltaire Club was founded in 1867, and now numbers about 80 members. The Hon. Sec. is Mr. Henry Sayner, Titus Street, Saltaire.

Below Baildon there is at present no river fishing. The **Leeds Clubs**, of which there are a large number, fish mostly in public waters, canals, &c., in various parts of the three Ridings. Two or three of the Clubs, however, have waters of their own; such are the "Leeds and County," (meets at the *Wheat Sheaf*, Upperhead Row), and the "Royal Exchange," (*Royal Exchange*, Boar Lane), which have private waters at School House Hill, and Killingbeck, and along the Rye. Costa, and other streams in the North Riding. As none of the Clubs have any fishing in Airedale proper it will not be necessary to do more than name them, with their places of meeting. They are as follows. The "Bramley Angling Club," "Old Forge Angling Club" (Wordsworth Street, Kirkstall), "Kirkstall Club" (*Old George*, Kirkstall), "Burley Club" (*Somerby* Inn, Kirkstall Road), "Holbeck Club" (*Gardeners' Arms*), "Wellington Club" (*Wellington* Hotel), "West End Club" (*Hanover Arms*), "Central Club" (*Marquis of Granby*), "Prince Albert" (Newtown), "Anchor of Hope" (Regent Street), "Prince Arthur" (Roundhay Road), "Star Club" (*Star* Inn), "Golden Fleece" (High Street), "White Swan" (Mabgate), and "Woodhouse Carr," the last-named established in 1890, with 42 members. The whole of these Clubs, with but two or three exceptions, are incorporated in one friendly fishermen's society, composed chiefly of working-men, and known as the "Leeds Amalgamated Society of Anglers;" the present Hon. Sec. being Mr. W. G. Royston, of the *Saracen's Head*, Boar Lane.

Owing to the increased pollution of the river below Leeds, the piscatorial 'tale' of the Aire is now a very poor one indeed. But little more than forty years ago, trout, indeed, were caught at Leeds Bridge; and only a few years back, a salmon or two might have been seen as far up the river as Hurst Courtney, above Snaith, and about Carleton Bridge there used to be plenty of various fish observed also, but not a fish has been seen in this locality now for two years at least. A Rawcliffe angler last year (1890) caught a 15 lbs. pike in the Went below Snaith, but this is good water, and does not flow into the Aire. With respect to our own river we may here note an interesting capture of a seal near Rawcliffe, in the Spring of 1888. The animal came up the Aire from the Ouse, and was first observed passing Hooke bridge, whence it was followed a little distance higher up, and shot. It was found to be a very fine, large dog-seal, measuring six feet from nostrils to tail.

Adverting finally to the polluted state of the Aire, the following statistics tell their own tale. They are extracted from the last (1891) Annual Report of the Yorkshire Salmon and Trout Fisheries. From these it will be safe to infer that unless something is speedily done to improve the condition of the Aire at its outlet near Goole, the local salmon industries must ere long be completely extinguished. Since 1883, when the total weight of fish captured was 72,558 lbs., the annual decrease has been actually by 'leaps and bounds.'

Years.	Number of Nets Employed.	Number of Fish Captured.	Weight in pounds.	Revenue.	Yearly Loss.
1888	68	3012	37,784	£332	£73
1889	61	639	8004	£282	£50
1890	25	1102	7989	£110	£172

TABLE OF ALTITUDES.

	Feet above sea level.		Feet above sea level.
Goole, below high-water mark		Bingley Main Street ...	292
Airmyn (Aire outlet)...	0	Norr Hill, Wilsden ...	875
Drax	24	Stockbridge, Keighley	282
Snaith	28	Keighley Par. Church	365
Brotherton Marsh ...	22	,, Tarn ...	1000
Knottingley Par. Ch...	55	,, Moor Res. ...	1200
Castleford	56	Haworth (*White Lion*)	780
Garforth Bridge ...	165	Rumbalds Moor (highest point)	1325
Leeds Bridge	100	Rivock Edge	1180
,, Town Hall ...	135	Silsden (Canal) ...	346
Woodhouse Moor ...	300	Kildwick Bridge ...	320
Moortown (Hill Top)...	525	Eastburn Bridge ...	320
Weetwood, N.E. corner of Iveson Wood, above *Wheat Sheaf* (highest point of the Borough of Leeds)...	534	Farnhill Crag (cairn)...	800
		Carleton Bridge ...	330
		Skipton (High Street)	362
		Highroad near Thorlby	390
Armley, Pasture Hills (footpath)	200	Gargrave Bridge ...	348
		Skirse Gill Bridge (Rylstone)	589
Bramley (Union Mill)	515	Winterburn Reservoir (Top-water level) ...	658
Apperley Bridge ...	168		
Rawdon Billing ...	750	Cold Coniston Church	520
Yeadon Dam	660	Otterburn Bridge ...	505
Idle Hill	750	Airton Mill	585
Bradford Town Hall ...	330	Kirkby Malham ...	614
Heaton Hill (Bradford)	675	Malham, Village ...	640
Undercliffe Cemetery...	660	,, Cove (sum'it.)	1000
Beacon Hill (Gt. Horton)	975	,, Moor (Water-sinks)	1250
Harrop Edge, between Allerton and Wilsden, near Lingbob (high'st point of the Borough of Bradford) ...	1000	,, Tarn (north shore)	1300
		Gordale Bridge ...	808
		Weets	1380
		Black Hill	1536
Clayton Heights (Sheep Hill)	1050	Kirkby Fell	1790
		Ryeloaf Hill	1790
Queensbury (Swill Hill)	1200	Fountains Fell (south end, highest springs of the Aire)... ...	2000
Hope Hill, Baildon ...	925		
Eldwick Hall	730		
Saltaire Park	220	Do. (highest point)...	2170

Length of the Aire (with windings) from Malham Tarn to its confluence with the Ouse at Airmyn... ... 88 miles.

Approximate distance by road ... ... 60 ,,

THROUGH AIREDALE
FROM GOOLE TO MALHAM.

"Now speak I of a flood, who thinks there's none should dare,
Once to compare with her, suppos'd by her descent,
The darling daughter born of lofty Penigent,
Who from her father's foot by Skipton down doth scud,
And leading thence to Leeds, that delicatest flood,
Takes Calder coming in by Wakefield, by whose force,
As from a lusty flood much strengthened in her course,
Who likewise to her help brings Hebden, a small rill,—
Thus Aire holds on her course towards Humber, till she fill
Her fall with all the wealth that Don can her afford."—
Drayton, A.D. 1620.

ABOUT GOOLE AND AIRMYN.

NO English river can possibly present anywhere in its course a greater contrast than the Aire,—that delicatest flood, of our old rhyming topographer,—in the neighbourhoods of its source and fall. Enclosed by hoary-headed mountains, (rising two thousand or more feet in perpendicular altitude), fissured and broken by huge gorge, cavern, and crag, and weathered dome of grey rock, the region of the upper Aire differs as widely as can be, alike in aspect, climate, soil, and vegetation, from the broad, hill-less land of dike and fen and deep alluvial flats that surround the effluence of the river at Airmyn. Whilst the former carries our "hearts to the Highlands," the latter reminds us of scenes peculiar to the school of Rembrandt,—of the rich, and differently interesting terraqueous plains of Holland. And it is evident, too, that the skilful, dike-loving Dutchman once congregated in some numbers in these parts, for in such field and place names as Tokesletts, Dyrtensyke, Weeland, Wrootflete, Tylehouse, Scuttesyke, Airmyn, &c., and in the personal names, Tyson, Gay, Tock, Eckles, Duckels, Barley (van Baerlé), Bunker, Witt, Hey, Burrell (Beharelle), Harley, Platt, &c., we have unequivocal testimony of an early Netherlandish immigration. Many of these original settlers doubtless first "came over" with the "Conqueror,"—not indeed the muscular, ruthless Norman of that name, but a wonderfully clever Dutchman, Sir Cornelius Vermuyden,

NEAR GOOLE.

who was invited by Charles I. to render habitable and fertile the whole of Hatfield Chase, the Isle of Axholme, and lands adjacent, comprising 75,515 acres, four-fifths of which were then laid under two or three feet of water. For the draining and drying of this vast area one-third part of it was to be retained in perpetuity for himself, another third part was to be divided amongst the inhabitants, and the remainder to be held by the King. "This," says Prim, "to the wonderful surprise of the whole nation, and the vast advantage of the whole country round about, which was before but barbarously and thinly inhabited, poor and beggarly, and at the incredible labour and charges of above £400,000, be at length bravely and effectually performed ; whose name deserves a thousand times more to be honourably mentioned and received in all histories than Scaurus's was in those of Rome, for draining a great lake in Italy not a quarter so big as this." Moreover this great undertaking was carried on and completed by Vermuyden and his army of skilled workmen in face of the most violent opposition and open warfare by the inhabitants of the district ; who complained, perhaps often justly, that the new works caused fresh floodings, lands previously dry were "drowned," stacks and barns were spoiled or even washed away, houses were inundated, and altogether much damage and inconvenience sustained. Riots ensued, during which several of the workmen were wounded and killed. In the Court trials that followed Vermuyden argued that the old walls and banks which deponents defended were too low and small and insecure to withstand the extra discharge of waters, whereupon it was agreed that these should be raised to a height and strength sufficient for the future safety of the land and its occupants. The work was completed about 1635, and for seven years there was peace. Then the Civil War broke out, which gave fresh occasion for lawless rebellion against the hapless Dutchmen. The native fen-men generally sided with the Parliament, and when a Royalist invasion was threatened upon the Isle of Axholme, they openly seized the colonists' lands, turned cattle into their fields of rape and growing corn, opened the sluices, broke down embankments, and so flooded the surrounding lands that for a long time they were laid waste, and the fortunes and resources of the thrifty refugees seemed hopelessly crippled. But at last order was restored, not, however, without a long and severe struggle, as appears from the following graphic account in a memorial to the Court of Sewers, wherein it is related that one Nathaniel Reading, Esq., who was appointed in 1655 commandant and justiciary resident for the suppression of the revolt, "after thirty-two set battles, wherein several of his men were killed, divers others wounded, and many lamed, and very many actions and hundreds of indictments against him and his assistants, and several years spent under inexpressible hazards and difficulties, besides loss to his practice and damage to his wife and children, never to be repaired, he subdued these monsters to obedience, and quieted the Crown and participants in their said allotments, repaired the church (Sandtoft), settled another minister, restored the congregation, and thereby made the said Levels and tracts adjacent, quiet, safe, and flourishing."

Although occasionally mentioned in documents as early as the Tudor period, Goole, or Gowle (as anciently spelled) remained a straggling hamlet of no note until the beginning

HOOKE CHURCH.

of the present century. In fact, old Mrs. Dyson, who died in October last (1890) aged 101, tells us that she could remember when, even as a young woman, there was but one house and a couple of fishermen's cottages where the town of Goole, with its growing population of about 6000,* now stands. Both Hooke and Airmyn are historically much

* The present population of the *parish* is estimated at about 12,000.

older, both places having given name to families of consequence in Norman times. Airmyn had its "castle," of which more anon, and at Hooke there was a chapel, of which we find mention as early as the reign of John. The De Hucks and De Armins were notable benefactors to the monasteries of Selby, Drax, &c., and the site of the "castle" or fortified manor house of the former may still be identified in the remains of a moat adjoining the present church at Hooke. There is good reason to believe that the district was much more populous in monastic times than it was subsequently. The fishings, of course, constituted valuable donations to local religious houses, and these, as appears from various early transactions, were jealously watched. The ferries, too, were of considerable importance, alike in a military and civil sense, and date back unquestionably to the very earliest occupation of this country.* We find mention of them as valuable sources of income in our oldest charters. Thus, in the *Monasticon* of Burton is the record of a gift to the Priory of Drax shortly after its foundation about A.D. 1130, viz.: Richard, son of Willm. de Newsom, Clerk, gave the sixth part of the ferry *(in passagio)* of Ayrmin, which was given to him by Adam, son of Adam de Ayrmine by John, called the Carpenter *(carpentarius)*, of York, and Margaret his wife. If a *sixth* part of the ferry was worthy of a special bequest, the value of the whole must have been pretty considerable. It is interesting to note, too, the allusion to a carpenter, from which it may be inferred that the building of ferry-boats would be a trade of some importance at that early period. That the district was extensively drained, and rudely banked, from the foundations of the monasteries is very evident. This would be effected partly for the convenience of the fisheries, and there is no doubt the monks themselves engaged in the work of construction. Frequent, however, were the floods, and frequent the loss of life arising therefrom. Roads there were none or few in these parts, and journeying was done

* At Hemingborough, six miles above Goole, was a Roman fort to guard the Ouse ferry, and some of the stones are still preserved in the church. At Castleford on the Aire, and at Harewood on the Wharfe, similar remains have been found.

chiefly on rafts or barges, which were sometimes upset and their occupants drowned on their passage from place to place. Up to 1493, when license for a burial ground at Hooke was obtained, interments were made by floating the corpse up the river to Snaith, and on these occasions we are told the concourse of mourners, along with the body, were sometimes wholly lost. That floodings and loss of life were once not uncommon, arising mainly from the insecurity of the banks, is apparent from the number of writs of inquisition existing, relating to visits of inspection of these early works. In the year 1322 Sir Thomas de Howke is appointed with others to survey the banks contiguous to the Ouse in Marshland between the Aire and Trent Fall, and this is but one among many other such ancient judicial visits.

Walking from Goole to Airmyn (2 m.) we obtain a characteristic view of the Dike country. On our left is the Dutch river, formed of the waters of the Don, and running for nearly four miles eastwards to the Ouse at Goole, as straight as Dutch ingenuity can make it. Formerly the waters of the Don flowed by Cowick Park and entered the Aire near Rawcliffe. The old channel may still be traced. Here now we have a moderate-sized peninsula formed by the Dutch river and canal and the Ouse and Aire, enclosing the townships of Goole, Hooke, and Airmyn, which comprise some 10,400 acres, of which 528 acres are water.

Airmyn—formerly Armin—(pop. 500) is the point really at which our survey begins, as the Aire merges into the Ouse a little north of the village. As already stated, the family of Armyn or Ayrmine (the name is still preserved in the district) was established here at a very early period. In A.D. 1315 we find a Will. de Ayremynne, Prebend of York, afterwards Bishop of Norwich. In 1310 there was a John de Ayremine at St. Michael's, York, and on the 10th May, 1317, one Adam de Armyn was installed rector of Gargrave, in Craven. A more detailed notice of this family will be found in Foster's "Lincolnshire Pedigrees," and Burke's "Extinct Baronetcies," &c. The village has rapidly grown owing to the development of the port of Goole, the houses being occupied chiefly by artisans employed at the docks. Besides the small church, which has some interesting monuments and stain-glass, a conspicuous object in the village is a handsome clock tower, by a Bradford architect, which was raised by voluntary subscriptions, amounting to nearly £700, and intended as a memorial to George Percy, Earl of Beverley, and lord of the manor, for his many acts of kindness and consideration towards the tenantry on his estates, on the occasion of his succeeding to the Dukedom of Northumberland in 1865. Airmyn Hall, on the south bank of the river, is now the seat of the Hon. A. F. Hood, J.P. Regarding the so-called Castle at Airmyn, which is often

BEVERLEY MEMORIAL TOWER, AIRMYN.

confounded with the one at Drax. we believe this to have been but a small peel or fortified "guard-house" to the adjoining Booth Ferry. Such armed outposts (called by old writers "castles") anciently existed as defences to most of our principal ferries, and it is more than probable that a site so important as this. the "key" of the Aire, would be protected by some such fortification.*

* Possibly an erection of the Paganels. first Norman lords of Airmyn, Drax, &c. (See DRAX). The ferries then became very

It will not be inappropriate to remark here on the origin of our river's name, *Aire*, and also of Airmyn, or Armin, which it suggests. Yet the latter is said to be derived from the Danish Arm or Orm, a chieftain of fame in the old days of the Vikings, whose redoubtable cognomen is interwoven with that of many a north country hamlet and town. At Armley, Ormskirk, &c., such derivations may hold good, but we think not here. The piratical Danes, it is true, found a ready highway into our valley by the Humber and Ouse, and penetrated it with grievous proof, as we shall have occasion to point out, to its fountain head. But the river was here before them and had a name, a very appropriate one too, for the old Britons had christened it *Ara*, meaning *easy, slow*. They also plied upon the river and its tributaries, as is evident from the discovery at Stanley Ferry, below Castleford, some seventy years ago, of a British canoe, about 18½ ft. long by 4 ft. wide, hewn out of a single piece of oak. The Danes, therefore, found the *Ara* and tacked on the *min* or *minde* (Germ. *münde*) *a mouth*, thus Armin became obviously enough the *mouth or outlet of the easy-flowing river.*†

At **Booth Ferry** we may cross to the north side of the river, which here, about one hundred yards wide, winds in

valuable, and were held by the respective lords, a circumstance which holds good of Leeds also, for there was an important ferry there before the bridge was built, and a ferry-house "where the Golden Lion Inn now stands" (*vide* Thoresby), and near by "a castle at Leedes as Mr. Edward Fairfax conjectureth. At the place where it may be thought to stand is now Mill Hill, where by conjecture was the house of Egfrid and Ostryd, Kings of Northumberland, who, as Bede sayeth, lived at Leodys" (*vide* Dodsworth's MSS.); and from which rose, after the manner of Pontefract, &c., the feudal residence or castellated manor house (with fosse) for the protection of my lord's ferry, mill, and the town generally. Leeds, it may be added, was at the time of King John an improving place, for the charter of Maurice Paganel (1207) "expressly notices the then existing trades of the town—namely, corn, wool, hides, and tallow—with the intention of affording protection to the same" (*vide* Wardell's *Municipal History*).

† Spencer, author of the *Faery Queene*, happily hits off the characteristics of the Yorkshire rivers in the following distich:

"*Still Are*, swift Wharf, with Oze, the most of might,
High Swale, unquiet Nydd, and troublous Skell."

graceful curve with willow, ash, and other trees fringing its margin ; and so slowly and placidly does it move along that a stranger to the place would not suspect the proximity of such a breadth of water until close beside it. In the time of Queen Elizabeth there was only one dwelling here, occupied by the ferryman ; now there is a small hamlet, including the beautiful residence of John Wells, Esq., J.P., which was formerly an inn, but is now much altered and improved.

Airmyn to Drax, 3 m. By the Ouse road west. To the side of Drax Abbey the road winds through Long Drax and by Ave Maria Lane. 2 m. The Abbey was founded by William de Paganel, or Paynel, towards the close of Henry I.'s reign. The Paganels were one of the most powerful baronial families that assisted William in the conquest of England, and they became one of the wealthiest, intermarrying with other Norman families of distinction, and acquiring vast possessions in Yorkshire and elsewhere. William Paganel married a granddaughter of the great Robert de Romillé, builder of Skipton Castle, &c., and lord of the honour of Skipton. But a still more powerful family were the De Lacies, builders of the great castle at Pontefract, and founders of Kirkstall Abbey. &c., who obtained their lands immediately of the King, and under whom the Paganels were constituted mesne lords. These Paganels not only founded this Priory of Austin Canons at Drax, but also built and endowed other religious houses, along with fortified outworks or castelets for their protection and defence of river passages as well as for their occasional residence. They were lords of the manors of Armin. Camblesforth, Drax, Leeds, and Bingley, besides many others in Lincolnshire, and had a castle at Drax, and they probably also built the strongholds at Leeds and Bingley, not of the same strength and proportions as that of their superior lords the Lacies of Pontefract, but still sufficiently large and important for all useful or defensive purposes. Though the De Gaunts, their successors, who raised both Leeds and Bingley to the dignity of *burgh* towns, may have been the builders or re-builders of these strongholds. But this is pure conjecture. The Paganels built the church at Bingley, doubtless on the site of a Saxon structure, and gave it with their churches and chapels at Wressle (where the Percies had a castle, still standing) and Roxby, Salteby and Swinehampstead, (the three latter in the county of Lincoln), to this priory. No vestige of the building remains, but according to Burton its site is indicated by a "slight ascent, moated about, on the south side of the river Ouse, nearly opposite where the Derwent enters therein," being on or near the site of the old Drax Abbey Farm. In the original charter of foundation it is spoken of as situated on an island, surrounded by marsh and meadow, afterwards called Holm or Heilam. The castle, too, is stated to have been " strongly situated in the midst of rivers, woods, and marshes," &c., but it also has long since disappeared. It was one of the last castles taken and destroyed by Stephen during the troublous times of the Barons' wars.* A curious coincidence of local nomenclature on the old Paganel property here is the existence near Camblesforth, about two miles west of Drax, of places called Priestshaw, Harden, and Bingley Woods (the latter now a stubble field of six or eight acres), whilst we have a Priesthorpe, Harden, and Bingley, also contemporary Paganel property, adjacent to each other in upper Airedale, which *see*.

Booth Ferry to Howden, 1½ m. From the Ferry Inn take the road *l*. about 100 yds., when leave it and enter a small white turn-stile which leads through fields, and if clear or not too sunny the spires and masts of Goole will be seen three or four miles away, whilst the great church of St. Peter's, Howden, visible along the whole distance, shines white as marble in the bright sun. By corn fields, orchards, and hedges of wild flowers our road continues between a double row of white posts to the town. For miles round Howden a leading topic of conversation (especially in Autumn) is horses; hunters, roadsters, animals for the gig, cab, tram. or 'bus. all qualities and breeds from light hacks of £5 to thoroughbreds of £200, find a well-known market here. The market was instituted in A.D. 1200, and King John, who granted the charter for it, was in all probability an eye-witness of some of these annual gatherings, if he did not actually ride the mettlesome Howdenshire mares on his hunting tours. He often visited the Manor House of the Bishops of Durham here. The Church, which is the tourist's principal attraction at Howden, is, although in a sorry state of desolation and decay, very well worth a special visit for the sake of its ancient and sumptuous architecture, which is mostly 13th century work. The chapter-house, similar though not equal in size to the fine one at York, is considered by many authorities to surpass it as well as every other like structure in England, in beauty of design, symmetrical precision, and the exceeding delicacy of its tracery. Within the interior are several ancient altar-tombs, tablets, and coats of arms to the families of Metham and Saltmarshe. It is said to have also contained a singular tomb of wood to the memory of Osara, sister of King Osred. The church with the manor of Howden was given at the Conquest to William of St. Carileph, who was Bishop of Durham from A.D. 1081 to 1096. In 1267 the church became collegiate, governed by Prebends appointed by the Prior and Convent of Durham. Becoming Crown property at the dissolution, the revenues in 1582 passed into private hands, and the building gradually fell into decay. The choir about 1630 was considered unsafe to celebrate divine service in; accordingly the nave was repaired and fitted up for that purpose. The roof of the choir fell down in 1696, and this part of the church has since remained in ruins.

* It would defend the important Langrick Ferry, where the Derwent joins the Ouse.

RAWCLIFFE.

THE roads from either Goole or Airmyn make "straight" for this famous little place, a distance of about four miles. Rich warp-land producing crops of wheat, oats, rape, flax, and beans of the best quality, raised without manure, is a feature of this locality. There are literally miles of potatoes, about Goole hardly anything else, grown on this constantly recurring new land where formerly were unproductive quagmire and morass. In the season, usually from July to October, land thus warped by special contrivances made for drawing the composite earthy waters from the river, will put on a foot or more of sound loamy soil, and in the neighbourhood of the Humber it is said there are acres of good land which have been raised in this way as much as six feet in three years, and £3 to £5 an acre is no uncommon rental for such lands. Thus the runaway river becomes the unconscious pilferer of one man's property for the benefit of another!

Rawcliffe will always be known for its connection with one of the greatest human oddities that ever lived. James, or "Jemmy" Hirst was born here on October 12th, 1738, and after a life wholly unique in the records of ingenious eccentricity, died here October 19th, 1829, aged 91. After his death the brick house in which he lived appears to have been pulled down and the present old-looking cottage (often mistaken for the original) on its site has since been occupied by a family named Bramley. Relatives of Hirst still reside in the neighbourhood, and one Mr. Woodhouse, a publican, has a curious old silver watch that once belonged to "Jemmy." In the corner of a garden near some cottages as you enter the village from the station, there lay for many years a stone clock-weight which he had fixed to his singular wicker-work carriage (a vehicle of his own construction), and which struck every mile. He appears to have been a man of some natural shrewdness, for on the death of his father, who left him £1000, he began to speculate in corn, flax, and potatoes, and in a few years amassed a fortune of £5000 to £6000, on which he retired for the remainder of his days. Both his habits and garb were characteristic of the man. He wore a red coat with blue sleeves, a waistcoat of drakes' necks with the glistening feathers outside, crimson and white stockings, and yellow shoes with large silver buckles. His hat was of lambskin with a brim nine feet in circumference. In this costume he would attend Snaith market, usually on bull-back. He had trained a white bull for the hunting-field, and on this favourite animal, which he called "Jupiter," could perform "flying feats," it is said, as well as the best Howdenshire hunter. In the winter he gave weekly parties alternately to the girls and old women of the village, summoning and dismissing them peremptorily with a blast of a beast's horn. Long before he died he had made his coffin, which was provided with shelves and a bell. He would exhibit this to his numerous visitors, whom, as it was large and stood upright he would persuade to enter, but would not liberate them without fee; males on payment of a penny, females on forfeiture of a garter. The news of his eccentricities reached the ears of King George III., who expressed a desire to see so remarkable a character, and accordingly he journeyed to London, the innkeepers on the way making "fortunes" out of the crowds who gathered to see Jemmy on his "Royal Progress." Even the nobility and gentry in their carriages did not disdain coming long distances in order to see Jemmy pass. Ushered into the Royal presence, instead of kissing the hand on bowed knee our hero stood up, gave it a hearty shake, saying he was glad to see the king looked such a plain, homely old gentleman, and he would be glad to see him at Rawcliffe whenever he liked to come. The court was convulsed. He afterwards told the king privately, in answer to his Majesty's enquiries, that London was right enough only there were far too many fools about his court for his liking. They did nothing but make fun of him, but he would "lug" some of the powdered rascals before he left; and he did. On his return to Rawcliffe Jemmy wrote some verses, for he was a "poet" whose compositions far outstripped in local popularity even the happiest creations of his Majesty's great poet-laureate. We will conclude with a specimen of his style.

"Who has not heard of Jemmy Hirst
  Of Rawcliffe village gay?
He is a very curious man,
  As Rawcliffe folks do say.

* * * * *

He once to London city went,
  To see King George the Third,
And very much astonished was
  With what he saw and heard.

He says unto the King, 'I heard
  That every London street
Was paved with gold from end to end,
  To put thy dainty feet!

But that, I see, is all a lie,—
  I'll tell it to thy face;
For never in my life did I
  See such a mucky place.'

* * * * *

Old men and women dance and sing,
  When Jemmy Hirst they see,
For well they know he'll treat them all
  With lots of rum and tea.

The foppish youngsters think to quiz,
  As Jemmy passes by;
But Jemmy knows a thing or two,
  And hits them on the sly.

Then shout 'Hurrah!' for Jemmy Hirst,
  Who money has in store;
But if you buy a song of him,
  He'll have a penny more."

SNAITH.

FROM Rawcliffe a three miles' walk through a fertile warp-country and along the "Banks" brings us to the quiet little market-town of Snaith (pop. 1730). The old place seems all corners and gables, whilst out of its narrow thoroughfares peer the red-tiled roofs, with here and there a quaint old house of wood and plaster. Besides the "Downe Arms" there are two or three old inns, but except on market-days the streets wear an aspect of semi-somnolent quiescence, like a decayed town of the Middle Ages. In fact, with a steadily declining population, this is partly what Snaith is becoming. Its markets, we are told, are not what they once were, and are gradually being superseded by those at Goole and Selby. The land round about is a rich alluvial loam, apparently well suited to the growth of corn and fruit, and there is also some amount of flax cultivated. In remote times there is no doubt that Snaith stood upon an island encompassed by the river and an extensive marsh. Its very name *(sneyd,* cut off) proclaims this to have been the case. At anyrate, soon after the Conquest there was sufficient good land here (a carucate) to bestow as a benefaction on the Abbey of Selby for the maintenance of a cell here. This small Benedictine monastery (governed by a Prior and sub-monk) continued in the sway of Selby till the Dissolution, when its revenues were granted by Henry VIII. to John, Earl of Warwick. Since 1624 the interest and peculiar jurisdiction of Snaith have been in the proprietary of the Yarburgh family, now represented by Mr. Bateson de Yarburgh, of Heslington Hall, near York. On the embers of the old foundation rose the present church, a spacious, interesting edifice, consisting of nave, aisles, transepts (with two chapels), elegant chancel, and a square battlemented tower which must have witnessed the sunsets of at least six hundred years. It contains a clock and a remarkably fine peal of six bells, which were re-hung in 1885. The great length of the church (172 ft. by 44 ft. wide) renders the interior very imposing. Separating each aisle from the nave are six pointed arches with hexagonal columns and plain capitals. The great east window (30 ft. in height) consists of five lights, and is a beautiful example of the Decorated style. On the south side of the chancel is the Dawnay chapel, which contains an inscribed Calvary stone (dated 1486) and a large altar-tomb,

SNAITH OLD CHURCH.

bearing shields with coats of arms, in memory of Sir John Dawnay, Kt., who died in 1493. Within this chapel is a magnificent full-size statue by Chantrey of the late Lord Downe (Baron Dawnay of Cowick), who died in 1832. It represents him clad in his robes of state, and is carved out of a block of white Carrara marble, which alone is said to have cost about £500. The total cost was one thousand guineas. There are also preserved, or rather left to decay here, some trophies of the Civil Wars. The distinguished Leeds family of Wheelhouse sprang from Snaith, and in the church there is a neat mural tablet to the memory of Dr. James Wheelhouse, who died June 1st, 1821, in his 40th year.

During the construction of the railway in 1847 some unknown human remains (partly covered in with tiles) were exhumed in the Priory Garth; and on the south side of the street, opposite the church, a very large number of human bones has likewise been found. These, strange to relate, were discovered mostly beneath buildings already occupied. In digging out a cellar in one house (now removed) portions of at least a score adult skeletons were unearthed; in excavating the kitchen of another, three skulls were found immediately beneath the hearthstone. As no battle is known to have occurred in this neighbourhood, it is difficult to account for the presence of these remains in such a place. It is conjectured that during the ravages of the Black Plague which decimated Snaith in 1347-8, this, then an unenclosed area, was used as a burial ground.

Extending about a mile south of Snaith is the noble estate of Cowick Park, now the seat of Benj. Shaw, Esq., J.P., and formerly of the ancient family of Dawnay, Viscounts Downe. Some distance from the house there are the remains of a moated tower, said to have been erected for John of Gaunt, the great Duke of Lancaster.

Snaith to Selby. 7¼ m. Crossing the Aire at Carlton Bridge (¼d. toll). which has a span of 270 ft., we arrive at the pleasant village of **Carlton** (pop. 747). Besides the Parish Church (built by Lady Beaumont) there is a good Roman Catholic Church with convent here; Carlton being the centre of an extensive Catholic population, which has continued down from the Reformation, owing, doubtless, to the lenient attitude displayed by the Crown towards the royal abbey of Selby. Carlton Towers, the seat of the Stapletons, Barons Beaumont, is situated in a fine park (270 acres), with ornamental lake. The house contains some splendid paintings and other works of art, and is occasionally shewn to visitors in the absence of the family. From Carlton to **Camblesforth** is about 1 m. (*see* p. 9). Here is an inn rejoicing in the classic sign of *Comus*, which at first sight would appear to have some poetical connection with the divine lyric of Milton, but no! it is so called from a famous entire horse bred in this neighbourhood, and sire to the winner of some great races. About 3 m. further on, it is fully worth the extra mile which the detour will incur, to take the road *l.* over Brayton Bridge and by the Hall, for a peep at the old Norman

Brayton Church. The porch here retains one of the most exquisite examples of a Norman doorway to be seen anywhere. The arch is of four orders, shewing the usual beak-head, lozenge, and chevron or zig-zag ornament, combined with circular medallions bearing curious figured devices. The interior of the church has two other Norman arches, a single light Norman window in the west wall of the tower, and a plain circular font of the same age. There is also an ancient altar-tomb, with effigies over the bodies of George, Lord Darcie, and his wife. He was the son of the brave, but unfortunate Lord Darcie, who was executed on Tower Hill in 1538 for complicity in the Pilgrimage of Grace. About 1 m. north of Brayton is **Selby** (pop. 6800). It is a busy, attractive little town, with many elegant buildings, its broad main street bordered with good shops and inns, and its market-place conspicuous by an elaborately-carved, though decayed, tall Gothic Cross, erected just a century ago but looking much older. The present wooden bridge over the Ouse was built about the same time (1791). There is no lack of hotel accommodation, gradating from the spacious *Londesborough Arms* to the humblest pot-house. Indeed, all down the Ouse side every other house appears to be a "public." This, with the Market Place. Millgate, Bondgate, and Finkle Street, is the most ancient part of the town, and some curious bits of old architecture will be found in this locality. The "crown and glory" of the place, however, is the **Abbey Church**, founded by William the Conqueror in A.D. 1069. It was originally a wooden structure which stood on Church Hill, and it is only about thirty years ago a number of rough-hewn coffins were discovered here, doubtless the site of an early cemetery. The erection of a castle is said to have been projected during the time of the sixth Abbot Paganel, but was ultimately, for pious reasons, abandoned, The Conqueror, after fighting and wrong-doing, conscientiously enough sought expiation in penitence and prayer, and to consummate his conquest of England and atone for the injuries inflicted on the people by fire and sword, founded Battle Abbey in the south, and that of Selby in the north ; similarly he built the noble church of St. Etienne at Caen, in Normandy (perhaps the purest example of a Norman church extant), in extenuation of the 'doleful crime' of marrying his 'dear cousin' Matilda. According to Camden and the elder historians, the King's youngest son, after-wards Henry I., was born at Selby. There have been other ancient Royal visitors at the Abbey, including Kings Edward I. and Edward II. The Benedictine Abbots of Selby and York were the only Abbots north of the Trent who by virtue of their mitres had seats in Parliament. At the Dissolution, these and Fountains were the richest monasteries in Yorkshire, the gross revenues of Selby being rendered at £819 2s. 6d.; and as there were no particular charges against the character of the establishment, all the Selby monks (numbering 23) were liberally pensioned, and the Lord Abbot (the thirty-third from the foundation) received £100 (equivalent now to £1000) a year for life. In 1618 the Abbey Church was made parochial, and it remains now the only monastic church in the county

C

not entirely or partially in ruins. The splendid old fabric is at present, however, undergoing a thorough and long-needed restoration. The extreme length of the building, including the nave, (139 ft.), is 298 ft., and breadth 58 ft.* The west, or principal entrance, has a very fine Norman doorway, recessed in five orders surmounted by an arcade of nine beautifully foliated arches, above which is a spacious window of three lights. The clerestoried nave with its round, massive pillars and circular arches, is Norman in design, portions of which date from 1090-1170. The walls of the north transept and part of the triforium are likewise early Norman. belonging to the oldest period of the building. The west side of the nave, with the doorway and porch, are late Norman or Transitional, about 1150-70, and the upper part of its south side is of the Lancet or Early English order. When the great Tower fell in 1690, the south transept, with part of the roof of the south aisle, was destroyed, and afterwards reconstructed from the ruins. In this portion of the building, now being restored, an interesting discovery has recently been made of a Norman apsidal chapel extending eastward from the south transept. The south wall of this transept clearly shows, from the foundations exposed, five distinct orders of architecture (proving so many restorations), from simple Norman to last century work. Of the choir (1330-1365), with its beautiful flowing tracery, the late Sir Gilbert Scott observes: "This is in the finest Decorated or middle-pointed style, and of the most perfect design and execution; indeed, it would be difficult to find an example of that style, excepting in some of the finest of our cathedrals, more perfect than that of Selby." It consists of seven uniform bays or arches, elaborately moulded, with clustered pillars having foliated capitals, and curiously carved brackets at the intersections. The roof is of oak. There is here a singularly rich stone altar screen, 10½ ft. in height. In the presbytery are the tombstones of several of the Abbots, and on the south side are the clergy seats of the sedilia, of uniform height and richly canopied. The great east window of seven lights originally contained, says Pugin, "a dome in stained glass, executed in the early part of the fourteenth century, and was, perhaps, the most beautiful example in England." It was taken down many years since to be "cleaned and restored," and with the exception of portions remaining in the tracery, the window is now plain glass. The Norman font is believed to be from the original (wooden) cell. The church contains numerous monuments, and in the burial-ground outside the visitor will hardly restrain a smile over various effusions of the church-yard muse.

Snaith to Pollington 2½ m., **Womersley** 8 m., **Darrington** 10¼ m., **Pontefract** 13 m. Although through a comparatively flat yet rich agricultural country this long walk or drive is not devoid of interest. Leaving the beautifully-wooded Cowick Park away on *l.* the road proceeds through the long straggling village of **Pollington**

* In comparison, Ripon Minster is 270 ft. long, and 87 ft. wide; Beverley Minster, 334 ft. by 64 ft.; York Minster, 524 ft. by 109 ft.; Winchester Cathedral (the longest in England), 554 ft. by 86 ft.

(pop. 387) with its two inns to the road junction (*George and Dragon*)

whence a rise to the left is made over the Knottingley and Goole Canal, a long watery line seen for nearly two miles, its receding surface dotted with barges, and turning now *r.* with Pollington Church, erected by the late Viscount Downe, and Grange on *l.* a straight course of 2 m. is taken, with Pollington Hall away on *r.*, over Balne Moor, passing under the Selby and Hull railway bridge, and ¼ m. beyond crossing the Hull and Barnsley line at Balne Moor Station. Near the red-roofed village of Whitley we cross the Selby and Doncaster highroad (*l.* to Askern 4 m.) and continue thence along a green lane between winding woods to the attractive little village of **Womersley**, approaching which the clustered houses and graceful spire of the old church, peering above the trees and hedges bright in summer time with wild convolvulus and fragrant honeysuckle, present a charming picture. Womersley Park is the seat of Lady Hawke, who is lady of the manor and owns the whole township comprising some 4000 acres. There is no inn here, but visitors may obtain refreshments at one or two houses in the village. Three miles south by rail from Womersley the tourist may alight at Norton station and take the pleasant road by Norton Priory and the Cross, through Kirk Smeaton to Went Bridge for Pontefract or Darrington. From Womersley station to Darrington by this picturesque route, which winds among the crags and woods of Brocken Dale,—a famous picnic and naturalists' resort, it is about 6 m. From Womersley Cross to Darrington direct by Womersley and Stapleton Parks (the latter a domain of about 500 acres, and the seat of Mrs. Frank Hatchard) it is 2½ m. **Darrington** (pop. 523) has a notable old church which was in existence at the time of the Conquest; it was restored in 1880. The registers date from 1563. The early English porch is supported by pillars resting on circular bases with trough-like mouldings, the latter an evident innovation from the East. The interior contains some ancient memorial tablets and brasses, and two recumbent effigies of a Crusader and his lady. There are several old oak "penance chairs," and a richly carved altar-table, formerly a tomb-slab (dated 1604). The rich stained glass deserves notice, particularly the large east window, a very beautiful object, which was erected by members of the Badsworth Hunt, at a cost, it is said, of about £600. Crossing the old coach road from London to York at Darrington we proceed through the park-like domain of **Carleton** (where is a house said to have been the head quarters of General Fairfax during the first siege of Pontefract Castle), and descending Mill Hill are soon in Pontefract.

UP THE "RIVER" FROM SNAITH TO BIRKIN.

TEMPLE HURST 3¼ m.   CHAPEL HADDLESEY 5 m.   BIRKIN 8 m.

 STRETCH of country still tediously flat, yet withal the glow of corn, the presence of foliage, some of it in Autumn rosy with fruit, an abundance of wild flowers, with here and there a spire or tower and red roof, relieve any impression of monotony, and provide a certain charm and fulness of colour reminding us of many an out-of-the-way ramble we have had in pleasant Normandy. The only interruptions of the level scenery which can with any propriety be called *hills*, are a couple of large isolated sandstone mounds observed on the first part of our journey, a little to the north, called Hambleton Haugh and Brayton Barf. In ancient times two such commanding sites as these would doubtless have watch-towers, and it is certain that one of them,—the Barf, was used as a beacon to signal alarm during the threatened invasion of Napoleon in the early part of this century. Similar beacons were erected at this time in other parts of Airedale, of which that (hereafter mentioned) on Elslack Moor, near Skipton, is a notable example. These two hills are being gradually reduced by the high winds that blow against them, so much so that in spring time the farmers working in the adjoining lands have difficulty in withstanding the hurricanes of sand which are torn from the mounds in gusty weather.

Immediately after crossing Carlton bridge our route is by a footpath along the Banks, which leads on to the road turning right through Hurst Courtney to the village of Temple Hurst. The river herealong makes a succession of capital V's and W's, but is hidden by the high banks that border it. High as these are (in some places as much as twenty feet above ordinary water mark), floodings of the adjacent lands are not uncommon. Near Hurst Courtney, six or seven years ago, a heavy river-flood broke a portion of the bank and inundated a pretty wide area of arable and grass lands to a depth of at least six feet, even washing down the walls of the highway. But repeated floodings, from the present polluted state of the river, cannot, as formerly, operate very beneficially on such lands. In fact, the consequences must be the very reverse, for the waters from Leeds downwards have grown so bad that many cattle ailments are beginning to be attributed to the animals grazing off these filth-washed pastures. Moreover, we have observed between

TEMPLE HURST PRECEPTORY.

here and Knottingley, where the lands are open to the river, cows lapping the nauseous river waters in places where the gaseous scum has gathered on its margin almost thick enough to ignite! How such waters, pregnant as they must be with germs of poison, will affect the milk, we shall not pretend to say. But they cannot at anyrate improve either it, or the poor beasts that unconsciously imbibe them.

At Temple Hurst the river comes up with a sharp bend, but passing the *Sloop Inn* we soon leave it and cross under the railway at Temple Hurst Station (on the Selby and

Doncaster N.E. line), arriving shortly in sight of a curious-looking building, having at its east end an octagonal tower, with a low stone roof, and pierced with narrow Norman lights. This is the Temple, or what remains of it, built by the Knights Templars of St. John of Jerusalem, in 1152, and the oldest of their foundations in these parts. They had a similar establishment at Temple Newsam, near Leeds, some eighteen miles higher up the valley, but this was founded at least twenty years later, and has long ago disappeared. When the suppression of the Order was confirmed by Pope Clement V. in 1312, the Temple lands were granted to Sir John Darcy, a monument of whose descendant, Lord Darcy, we have previously noted in Brayton Church. Nothing remains of their chapel here, which stood where is now an orchard, at the north-east side of the preceptory, and is said to have been connected with it by an underground passage. The house (which is now a farm of some 300 acres) still retains many of its characteristic features. The walls, with the deeply-recessed windows, are of great thickness, and look as plumb and as sound as when first built. On the south side of the building the porch retains its Norman doorway, with shafts bearing moulded capitals.

Proceeding through Chapel Haddlesey we pass the curiously rare sign of the *Jug*, which, however, reminds us of two similarly-named inns, the *Foaming Tankard*, and the *Parting Pot*, at Stamford, in Lincoln. The village possesses a neat church, which has recently been restored, and a tower added. It was anciently a chapel-of-ease to Birkin. The rectory, a little further on, is a handsome and picturesque building of wood and plaster; and the rector, the Rev. J. N. Worsfold, M.A., F.S.S., is a gentleman possessed of wide antiquarian knowledge, and who has done useful work in rescuing from oblivion many matters of local history.

Leaving the schools and an enormous wind-mill (with four ten-yard sails), which the owner told us will grind four packs, or over fifty stones of corn an hour, we cross the lock-bridge of the Haddlesey extension of the Selby canal (made in 1778), and going through West Haddlesey there is nothing of interest until in 2 m. we reach Birkin, a quiet, tree-shaded little place, but of no other renown than what attaches to its unique Norman church.

Birkin Church was probably built by the great Ilbert de Lacy, the wealthy grantee of William I. in these parts, not many years after the Conqueror himself had founded Selby Abbey. At anyrate, we are willing to concede a higher antiquity than that usually ascribed to the church, and accepting Mr. Richard Holmes, of Pontefract, as our authority, it would appear that one portion of the building is at least as old as A.D. 1100. This is the blocked south doorway in the chancel, which has a noticeably large transom stone supporting a tympanum bearing simple decorative lines. The main south doorway (protected by a wooden porch) is of somewhat later date, and portrays an example of the architecture of that period of almost unrivalled beauty and skilful design. Somewhat resembling the doorway at Adel (of like age), its mouldings remain, perhaps, even more sharp and perfect than it. The shafts are six feet high, but before the porch was removed and added to the south aisle some two centuries later, they were at least twelve inches higher. The recess is in four orders, three of which are richly sculptured with beak-head, pellet, and chevron ornament. A model of the doorway is kept at the Crystal Palace, London, in the court appropriated to typical examples of pre-Gothic architecture. Most of this tower has evidently been raised in the time of the De Birkins, the last of whom expired in 1230. On its north and south faces may be observed simple shields bearing their arms, a fesse with a label of three points. These arms also adorn one of the pillars on the west side of the porch. The interior, which has undergone a well-judged restoration about six years ago, is extremely chaste and harmonious in its every detail. With the exception of the south aisle, added as a chantry-chapel in 1328, it is pure Norman work. There are three arches, that of the chancel being richly decorated, and resting on pillars with ornate capitals. The chancel has two windows, one on each side, and the apse at its eastern termination contains a Norman light, and some fragments of ancient stain-glass in its east window. Over the pulpit is a remarkably fine sounding-board of the Caroline period. The small Norman font, which is pierced with a view to a dumb well, rests on what is evidently the broken shaft of a churchyard cross. It bears the date 1663, doubtless marking its restoration at the end of the Cromwellian era (a period fraught with many disasters to the people of Birkin), about which time the Birkin chalice was bought, as it also bears the date 1662. A notable feature of the interior is an unknown recumbent effigy occupying a recess in the north wall of the nave. The figure is cross-legged and bareheaded, with loose, flowing robe, and the hands are clasping a heart as if in token of the deceased so offering his heart to God. The figure is thought to represent a Knight Templar from the adjoining preceptory of Temple Hurst, but this is hardly likely, as the manors of Hurst and Birkin were under separate lords, and the church and burial place of the Templars was at Kellington, on the other side of the water. On the south side of the churchyard are two large upright gate-posts, on one of which a heavy, menacing stone ball manages to maintain its equilibrium. These solitary sentinels are all that remain to tell of the departed glory of the great Hall of Birkin.

Birkin to Knottingley. There are various ways of reaching Knottingley on the south side of the river. Either cross it at **Beal** and by road direct (3¼ m.), or by way of Byram Park and Ferry Bridge (4 m.), or leave the road to Brotherton, near a plantation, 1 m. from Birkin, and through the fields to the Bank Dole Lock Ferry, 1¼ m. from Knottingley sta. (3 m.). But to follow the riverside path by this route is very circuitous. To those who know the way the shortest and best route between Birkin and Knottingley (2½ m.) is to ferry the river at Cross Flats and over Brotherton Marsh on to the main road, about 1½ m. from Birkin. Brotherton Marsh, once an extensive swamp, is now drained and converted into remunerative pasture for cattle. There were at one time many pretty large farms in this district, but some few years ago Sir J. W. Ramsden, Bart., of Byram Hall, tried the experiment of small allotments on his Byram estate, and with such success that the small allotment system has now spread to Brotherton, Poole, Burton Salmon, and other portions of his large estate here.

KNOTTINGLEY.

THIS ancient town stands on the magnesian limestone, a narrow belt of rock running through Yorkshire, crossing the western rivers at right angles, and though nowhere attaining a sea elevation of more than 500 feet, is yet ascertained to be very favourable to health and longevity. It has probably yielded a more plentiful supply of centenarians than any other local formation. But from a purely hygienic standpoint, any rocky country where the soil must be drier and the air more bracing, is bound to be more naturally healthy than in districts possessing a deep or impervious soil, especially clay flats. In spite of its smoky canopy and murky waters, Knottingley is not without some attractive features, whilst its broken and picturesque environment provides a stimulus to the mind, of material, if not always regarded, benefit to the inhabitants. Fortunately the town has plenty of open spaces, otherwise that portion of it bordering upon the river, would, in some seasons be simply uninhabitable, for the stench (and we have experienced it) is, on calm hot days, quite strong enough to overpower even a horse.

The town has a history, which has been ably written (1870) by the late Mr. Forrest, dating back to the Saxon era, its name (in ancient charters, Cnutenlai, Cuottingley, &c.,) would appear, like that of Cononley, in Craven, to have been derived from its early Saxon possessor Kunet or Cnut, whence Canute. The town of late years has much increased in size and population, (at present it is estimated at about 6000 souls), and is consequently losing much of its antique character. The oldest portion is in the vicinity of the church and Aire Street, but here we have observed no house of a higher age than about two centuries. The church, however, is a genuine Norman foundation, and up to its restoration, four years ago, looked a very primitive concern indeed, with its old-fashioned fittings, including narrow high-backed pews, arranged in such a curious higgledy-piggledy fashion, that one half of the congregation were obliged to sit with their backs to the communion table. The chancel was also on a lower level than the nave, and was badly lighted. Notwithstanding this stricken aspect, the church seems to have been almost rebuilt in 1757, which circumstance is recorded by the date on one of the south window sills. The church being dedicated to the Anglo-Saxon Saint Botolph, in all probability occupies the site of an edifice erected during that period. In Plantagenet times (A.D. 1203) we find the "Villa Sancti Botulphi in Cnottingley," granted by King John to the Abbey of Meaux or Melsa, in the East Riding. The interior of this building contains many interesting memorials of local families. The old inconvenient chancel was altered and enlarged when the church was restored in 1886, at an outlay of £400, given by the late Mr. J. W. Wasney, of Thornton-in-Craven, as a memorial to his father, who is buried in the church; and the beautiful east window in it is the gift (about £250) of Mr. G. W. Carter, M.A., of Lime Grove. The pulpit in Caen stone and Irish marble, the gift of Mrs. Rhodes, (formerly Miss Moorhouse) is also a very chaste object. The tower (with clock) was only added to the church about eighteen years ago.

Knottingley possesses various other buildings of public note, and amongst them is the Town Hall, (with Mechanics' Institute), built in 1865, and occupying a central position in the town. In East Knottingley there are several good dissenting chapels and also a modern church. The local limestone has of course been brought largely into requisition for domestic building, and there are also a number of kilns where it is burnt for agricultural purposes, and largely exported, as much as 60,000 to 80,000 tons being thus annually sent away. In addition to this important trade in limestone, there are several ship-building concerns, a large brewery, several roperies, tar works, &c., besides the big earthenware manufactory of Messrs. Poulson Bros. The town is uncommonly well provided with the various means of transit by rail, road, and water. In the latter respect, since the opening of the canal to Goole in 1826, the river has fallen into disuse, except as a conveyancer of certain *solid goods* in the form of an unrestricted supply of a compound "essence of factories," (a term that will be readily understood), yet so baleful and unlovely is this to both sense and sight, that its continued presence is nothing less than disgraceful, and a sad reflection indeed on the scientific knowledge of our time. At Cross Flats, on the river, up to the period mentioned, there was a landing wharf, whither trading vessels came and discharged or embarked goods. The river was then not the foul stream it is now, and a sail upon its fish-rippled waters, or a breeze whiffed freshly over them was a delightful and health-giving experience.

But smoke and pollution,—ye gods, how profitable! Here, now the rateable value of property is estimated at about £16,000. Three centuries ago (in the days of good Queen Bess) it was 8s., yet the people, perhaps, were as happy and contented as they are at this day, and Knottingley maintained, too, its relative importance. The fortunes of some neighbouring places, however, have materially changed. Snaith, for example, at that time (the assessment is for the year 1584), was worth 20s., Pontefract, 13s. 4d., Darrington, 8s., Water Fryston, 4s., Carleton, 4s., Broughton, 4s., and Wheldale, 2s. Eighty years later, in the Hearth Tax for 1666, a number of household names crop up which are interesting as illustrating the persistence of families in one district, though many of these have long since disappeared from the locality or altogether died out. Amongst these old Knottingley families at the above period of the Restoration, we find the names Atkinson, Cooper, Crofte, Jackson, Thompson, Roebuck, Smith, Franke, Fugald, Camis, Rouston, Enson, Sikes, Stone, Twisleton, Gages, Clearke, Browne, Towtell, &c.

Resuming now our onward march, a quarter of an hour's walk from Knottingley brings us to

FERRY BRIDGE,

and a pleasant and interesting place we find it to be. The bridge, spanning the Aire, is a broad, handsome structure of eight arches (erected about 1800), over which, in the old posting days, as many as twenty to thirty stage-coaches used to pass daily. The spot is also memorable as the scene of a fatal skirmish during the Wars of the Roses (A.D. 1461), when the "Bloody Clifford" (of whose lordly family we shall have much to say in our chapter on Skipton and its Baronial Castle) fell unawares by a headless arrow whilst defending the river's pass. Many a Craven man under him perished here, too, the land round about being strewn with the bodies of the slain. Bits of old armour and portions of human skeletons have frequently been turned up within recent years, and especially in the neighbourhood of Brotherton Marsh. But pleasanter far in our story of Ferry Bridge are the reminiscences of old coaching days, when the heavily-laden, gaily-coloured vehicles crowded about the old inns, where friends met and parted, "healths" were drunk, news was disseminated, and smart jokes were snapped over the foaming tankard. Away, too, over the old bridge sped bold Dick Turpin on his wonderful ride from London to York, and it was also the point of divergence of the coaches to these famous cities as well as to Carlisle and Leeds. There were four inns here then, the *Angel*, the *Greyhound*, the *Golden Lion*, and the *Swan*. The latter has a singular history. In monkish days it was a chapel of the Priors of Pontefract, erected in the thirteenth century to the memory of Archbishop Walter de Grey. In a report of the Royal Commission appointed by Henry VIII., before the Disestablishment, the following statement is made regarding it: "The Chauntry of our Lady att the end of Ferry Brigg, within the parish of Brotherton, Robert Dey, incumbent, founded by Robert Sutton, April, 1271, to pray for the soul of the said founder, and one Walter Grey, sometyme Archbishop of Yorke, and all Christian souls, and to say Masse in the said Chapell, heaving lands in Lumby, and elsewhere, to the value of £7 4s. 9d.; *de claro* £6 12s..0½d.; goods, £2 12s. 8d.; plate, £1 10s." The old house of God, whose walls had been sacred to chant and song, was eventually "debased" to an inn, and it is now a decayed building, standing in its own umbrageous garden plot hard by the river. A further halo of romance surrounds the old fabric in its being mentioned by Scott in his "Heart of Midlothian," as the place where Jeanie Deans stayed on her famous "walk" to London in

1787 ; the good landlady of the *Swan* being so captivated by Jeanie's simple manners that she generously provided her with a horse and postilion that gave her a good " lift on the way."

Comprising the township and parish of Ferry or Water Fryston are the hamlets of Ferry Bridge, Ferry Fryston, and Wheldale, belonging chiefly to Lord Houghton ; the Earl of Mexborough being also part landowner. A good deal of the low-lying land on Lord Houghton's estate is planted with willows, in fact, much of the marshy land in the valley, all the way up from about Knottingley to near Skipton, is thus appropriated. The osiers do uncommonly well, and were it not for the periodical ravages of the green willow beetle *(Phratora vitellinæ)*, would be a very profitable investment. The risks, however, are such, that not anyone will be tempted into this branch of arboriculture. Whence or how this destructive little pest appears is, indeed, little short of a mystery. The raids are generally local, being confined, in certain seasons, within definite areas. The insects attack the trees from the roots upwards, simply covering them in myriads, and so thick and persistent do they continue, especially in hot weather, that no means yet devised for their destruction has been successful, save by irreparable injury to the trees. They gradually disappear at the end of a second or third season, and then nothing more is seen of the pest, perhaps, for many years. In this district, within the past ten or twelve years, losses to the extent of several thousand pounds have been sustained from this cause, and in upper Airedale, in the neighbourhood of Bingley and Crosshills, willow-growers have likewise suffered relatively severe losses.

We may see some acres of these osiers on the way to Fryston Hall, the seat of Lord Houghton, which well-known mansion contains one of the choicest private libraries in the kingdom. The Hall stands in a beautiful park, which includes, with the surrounding plantations, about 400 acres. The house was restored after a fire in 1876. The late Richard Monckton Milnes, first Baron Houghton, of the old family of that name so long settled here, was a gentleman whom everybody knew and admired, whether in the field of letters or in the stormy arena of politics. As a poet, patriot, and philanthropist, he held a unique position in the affairs of the past generation, and he has assuredly bequeathed an imperishable name in the bede-roll of the best of Englishmen. For nearly forty years he and his father, Mr. Robert Pemberton Milnes, represented the ancient borough of Pontefract in Parliament, and in local affairs he always took the deepest interest. He died at Vichy, August 10th, 1885, in his 77th year, and his remains were brought for interment in the family vault of the old church at Fryston. This church

FRYSTON CHURCH.

at Ferry Fryston is a quaint, old building, which contains several interesting memorials of the Milnes family, besides the large family pew, in which Palmerston, Carlyle, and many another illustrious visitor at Fryston Hall have sat. The tower of the church is curiously built into the nave at its west end, which gives it an odd appearance, not unlike an enormous chimney, when viewed from the outside. According to a writer in the *Gentleman's Magazine* for June, 1798, the church is only remarkable for the singularity of its being situated at a distance of half-a-mile from the nearest parishioner! Not far from here, near Fryston beck, there was dug up in March, 1822, a large uninscribed stone coffin (over a ton in weight), containing a human skeleton of unusual size, with the skull laid between the arms or knees. As it was found in the vicinity of St. Thomas' Hill, where the great Earl of Lancaster, nephew of Edward I., was beheaded and buried in 1322, the remains were conjectured to be those of this 'martyred' earl, and are now preserved as such in the garden of Fryston Hall.

We may now go on to Castleford by way of the old Wheldale Priory Farm, or take the road from Fryston or the Bridge to Pontefract (2 m.) by Stump Cross. The latter has long been used as a township boundary stone, but in mediæval times there is no doubt it formed part of a wayside cross. The roughly ornamented base which held the shaft of the cross is now all that remains of it. A little to the north is St. Thomas' Hill, above mentioned, and near by is a cutting in the road (formerly narrower) called Nevison's Leap, from a tradition that "Swift Nick," the bold highwayman of Charles II.'s time, leaped his horse across it whilst hotly pursued by his would-be captors, a deed of daring, we think, which few horsemen would, however hard pressed, be inclined to follow.

PONTEFRACT.

AMONG the numberless places in our broad shire,—York alone excepted—none have been more conspicuous over so long a period in English national events as the royal borough of Pontefract. "I like Pomfret," says Swift, the chatty and well-informed Dean of St. Patrick's, "because it is in all our histories." And true, from the middle of the seventh to the seventeenth century, there is hardly a reign in which it is not in some

PONTEFRACT CASTLE IN THE TIME OF EARL LANCASTER
(A.D. 1310—1320).

way, alas! but too often bitterly, prominent. Bright, however, was its matin dawn, for the place (then, in the seventh century, evidently of some note) was the chief bridal gift to the betrothed of Edwin, the best of Saxon Kings. This beautiful and virtuous lady, Ethelburgha, or Tata, as was her favourite name, was sister of Ebald, Christian King of

Kent, and the first Christian Princess of Yorkshire, who came hither attended by the Archbishop Paulinus, and received this manor as her dower. The place became known as Tatashall, although when the little temple of Christian worship was built (probably about the time of her marriage) that part of the manor where the church stood was called Kirkby. When the marauding Normans arrived, they, of course, seized this manor, and in Domesday, *Tateshall* (as it is there written) formed part of the 150 manors (in West Yorkshire principally) bestowed by the Conqueror on his arch-confederate, Ilbert de Lacy. Delighted with the locality, then glowing with corn and fruit, raised by the thrifty Saxons, which reminded him of his home in Normandy, the warrior chief selected this as the centre of his great Barony. The royal *Halle*, or "castle" (whatever it may have been) of the Saxons was destroyed, or utilized in the erection of the mighty stronghold which occupies its site. Very soon afterwards (A.D. 1090) the name of the place appears in local charters as *Fractus Pons* and *Pons Fractus* (Broken Bridge), afterwards Pontefract, evidently, thinks Mr. Holmes, from the old bridge at Bubwith, mentioned by Camden, who quotes an inquisition of the time of Edward II., "*juxta veterem pontem de Pontefract*," which was the principal approach to the manor and castle from the north. The stream is now covered in, but in Leland's time (temp. Henry VIII.) this stream, the Wash, was open, and frequently overflowed its banks, rendering the bridge impassable or dangerous to cross. "The ruines of such a bridg," observes old Leland, "yet ys seene scant half a mile est owt of old Pontfract, but I cannot justely say that this bridge stoode ful on Watheling streete" (the old Roman road). However, the place, from the advent of the Normans, has always been called Pontefract, only that portion to the west retaining its Saxon name, Taddensclyf, or Tateshale, now Tanshelf.

Dominating every other interest, historically, is the **Castle**, now but a ruinous fragment of the great building raised by its original owners, yet shewing still, by its massy walls and crumbling towers, something of the mighty fortress that it once has been. Few military houses have

D

witnessed more stirring scenes than this, scenes of valour, treachery, hope, triumph, and despair! Many and many a time of old has the banquet board been spread, the wine has flowed, the jest gone round, and the song of love been heard; yet how often, too, the shout of alarm, the din of cannon, and the clang of arms have resounded within its walls! The grim, old, storied castle is shadowed, also, with many a foul and dark deed of rapine, murder, and deep stain of royal blood. In the *Tragedy* of *Richard III.*, the great dramatist, Shakespeare, thus refers to the latter circumstance:

> "O Pomfret, Pomfret! O thou bloody prison!
> Fatal and ominous to noble peers!
> Within the guilty closure of thy walls,
> Richard the Second here was hack'd to death;
> And, for more slander to thy dismal seat,
> We give thee up our guiltless blood to drink."

Although the murder of Richard II. marks an event of chief local importance, yet many a noble peer besides has been confined a close prisoner within the rooms and dungeons of the castle, or has been laid "shorter by the head" within the shadow of its gloomy walls. We have previously referred to the powerful Earl of Lancaster, grandson of Henry III., who was executed at Pontefract in 1321-2 for the part he took as leader of the rebellious barons against Edward II., a story which is recited in every English history. He succeeded, in 1310, to the castle and estates of the Lacies, by his marriage with Alicia, heiress of Henry de Lacy, and during his "sovereignty" at Pontefract he greatly improved and enlarged the castle, and lived here in a state of almost royal magnificence. He was, moreover, Lord in his own right of Lancaster, Lincoln, Leicester, Salisbury, and Derby, but Pontefract was his chief seat. The castle was then a "power" in the land, of monarchical aspect, unrivalled in strength and security, and, for more than three centuries afterwards, became connected with some of the most notable events in history. It was the place finally chosen for the hiding-away and assassination of Richard II., as mentioned above, that monarch having been removed from the Tower of London, as ordered by Parliament, to a place "unfrequented by any concourse of people," which, at first, was Leeds Castle, in Kent, whence (for his safer custody) he appears to have been conveyed by sea to Yorkshire, and there lodged in the "royal" castle at Pickering, from which he was brought to Knaresbro', and thence, shortly afterwards, in 1399, to Pontefract. It is often supposed, as we have remarked elsewhere, that Leeds Castle, in Yorkshire, was the place of his first imprisonment, and then Pickering, Knaresbro', and lastly, Pontefract; but so "round-about" a journey is incompatible with the geography of these places, and, moreover, if a castle at Leeds, in Airedale, ever existed (and we have shown this to be probable), it is not unlikely to have been destroyed during the sieges of Stephen's time, in this district, more than two centuries earlier. As to the manner of Richard's death, whether by starvation or by the hand of the assassin, this has always been a disputed point. Shakespeare, whom we have quoted, says he was "hack'd to death," and stains of blood are even said to have been at one time perceptible in the apartment where the crime was perpetrated. The deposing King, Henry IV., often came to Pontefract after his royal cousin's cruel end.

The Castle played a conspicuous part in the "Pilgrimage of Grace," in 1536, when it surrendered to the insurgents under Aske. Again, during the Civil Wars 1644—1648), it sustained three important sieges,* bravely holding out for the unfortunate King; even when the news of his execution, on January 30th, 1648-9, reached the garrison, the besieged "proclaimed" his son, Charles II., and they did not relinquish their hold of the castle until compelled by the great loss of life (about four-fifths of their men) to capitulate (March 24th, 1649). Then the Parliament of Cromwell ordered this proud and mighty stronghold, the "Key of the North," as it was called, to be destroyed, and within a few months of the capitulation it was unroofed and rendered no longer habitable, a condition in which it has remained ever since. The expenses of the demolition, and the

* For a detailed account of these sieges, the reader should consult Boothroyd's "Pontefract," or Holmes' "Sieges of Pontefract Castle." *Guides* also may be obtained in the town.

moneys received by sale of material, may here briefly be summarized:

	£	s.	d.		£	s.	d.
Received for lead...	1540	7	2	Charge for demolishing...	777	4	6
,, timber...	201	7	10	Moneys allotted unto the town	1000	0	0
,, iron...	37	2	4
,, glass...	1	0	0	Remr. due to the Commonwealth	2	12	10
	£1779	17	4		£1779	17	4

The remains of the Castle occupy a prominent rocky hill, originally surrounded by a deep fosse. On the west side was the barbican, connected with the outer yard by a draw-bridge, and a similar tower and draw-bridge formed the entrance on the east. Only portions of the outer wall now remain, with its peculiar middle projection, evidently designed with the strategical object of commanding the entire area of the wall. The walls of the ballium, or court-bailey, were high, and had a parapet, and were flanked at equal distances with rectangular towers. But the Castle Keep, the most imposing part now standing, consists of two massive round towers, the bases of which are formed of the scarped rock, built over, which give them the appearance of constructed masonry. A narrow winding staircase in the lesser tower leads down to a small sallyport, branching about midway to what was probably a well, and terminating at another point in a horrible dungeon, not more than six feet square. The diameter of the keep is about 64 ft., and is ascended by a flight of steps. Here are some curious cells and other rooms and apartments of state above. Near the barbican is the Porter's Lodge, of a later style of architecture than the great Round Tower, and other of the early Norman buildings. To be noted, also in various stages of decay, are the King's Tower, Queen's Tower, Swillington Tower, (so called from the seneschal, Sir Robert Swillington) where the Earl of Lancaster was immured before his execution ; Red Tower, in which the murdered king, Richard II., is supposed to have been imprisoned ; Constable's Tower, Treasurer's Tower, and the great Mediæval Hall and Chapel. The latter, eight years ago, was excavated, and a number of bodies found (doubtless victims of the Civil War), whilst more recently the Hall, which, from its fittings, has been obviously used as kitchens, has yielded an excellent mould of one of the siege coins, along with substantial evidences of the coining furnaces. Other relics of the excavations, in the shape of carved stones, are preserved in the outer area, where also a neatly-kept garden-plot marks the place of burial (with an inscription) of the unfortunate beings who perished during the disastrous sieges of the castle.

The grounds, (with the castle) cover about seven acres, and since they were acquired by the town from the Duchy of Lancaster, some few years ago, have been tastefully laid out and furnished with arbours, seats, &c., thus making it an attractive resort. The views from the hill are very fine, extending eastwards as far as the Wolds, thirty miles off, whilst York Minster, and the towers of Snaith and Selby churches are plainly seen, with many another familiar landmark around. The guard-house of the castle has been converted into a museum, where the visitor may inspect a varied collection of relics belonging to the past history of the town.

Pontefract, in addition to the castle, has some other buildings of note. The old parish church of All Saints' was in existence long anterior to the Conquest. In A.D. 1090 it was given by Robert de Lacy, son of Ilbert, to the Priory of St. John at Pontefract. The church remained in ruins from the time of the Civil Wars until 1831, when the transept was restored for public worship, and it has since undergone further repair and embellishment. After the wars, services were conducted in the chapel of St. Giles, in the Market Place, and by Act of Parliament (28th George III.), this was constituted the parish church of the town. St. Giles' is a very old foundation, not without interest, and its peculiar domed-tower may be seen for many miles round. Of the Priory of St. John the Evangelist, above mentioned, no traces now remain, but its site is marked by the Grange Field on Monkhill. It was an establishment of Cluniac monks, which, from its liberal endowments, must have been a place of some importance. At the Dissolution, the last prior, Thwaites, was allowed to retain the Deanery of St. Clement in the Castle; the houses, orchards, and demesne lands of the Priory having been appropriated by the King, were subsequently let on a lease to one Peter Mewtas, at an annual rent of £23 17s. 8d. The Dominican or Preaching Friars had a settlement at Pontefract, (founded by Edmund de Lacy, in 1257), which was situated in a beautifully sequestered spot, now called Friar Wood. At its surrender, in 1539, the monastery consisted of the prior, six priests, and one novice. The Austin Friars and Carmelites, or White Friars, appear likewise to have had houses here, but little is known, (especially of the latter), regarding either their history or sites. Besides these, there was the very ancient Hospital of St. Nicholas, by whom or when founded is not known, but it is very doubtful if there be any older Christian foundation in Yorkshire; it is possibly co-eval with the church. Before the erection of St. John's Priory, in A.D. 1090, it was occupied by the Cluniac monks, and Robert de Lacy, in the time of Henry I., largely endowed it, and gave the wardenship thereof to the monks. After the Dissolution it was perverted to various uses, and in 1673 rebuilt in its present form. Trinity Hospital, founded by Sir Robert Knolles in the reign of the unfortunate Richard II., was also another of the local religious houses suppressed at the Dissolution.

Pontefract has altogether much to interest the occasional visitor. It is one of the oldest incorporated towns in the kingdom, having been constituted a borough, with mayor, in the year 1484, although its first charter goes back some three centuries earlier. The old Market Cross (erected in 1734) superseded the ancient Cross of St. Oswald, (in *Domesday*, written *Osgotcross*) which was the centre of the protective right of sanctuary, and has given name to the wapentake of Osgoldcross. The old Moot Hall was destroyed during the Civil Wars, and the present Town Hall has been erected on its site. The present population of the municipal borough is about 10,000.

Pontefract is celebrated, as everyone knows, for its *Races* and its *Cakes* (the latter made from the juice of the liquorice plant so extensively grown here), but which is the more famous or beneficial, individuals must decide for themselves. Everyone to his taste!

But we must now leave this romantic old town, and

descending the road to Tanshelf station, keep along the pleasant Park side (the Park having recently been rather extensively planted and improved), and through Glass Houghton, under the fine viewing-point of Red Hill (250 ft.) to

CASTLEFORD,

being three miles from Pontefract, and between which towns the visitor, if he prefer, may take 'rail' or ''bus.' Commercially now important as the centre of a busy, smoky colliery and glass-works district, (where upwards of 16,000,000 bottles are annually made) : the place is also of great note historically. Here the Aire was forded by a paved way for the Roman legions passing between Doncaster and Tadcaster, and was a station, as might be expected from its favourable position by the river, of considerable consequence. In the Emperor Antonine's Itinerary it is called *Legeolium*. The paved road ran up the east side of the church, where was the *castrum* or camp, and a numerous collection of buildings (the foundations of which, though now lost, have frequently been dug up) formed the Roman "city," from the ruins whereof it is very probable the church was built. The original fort or "castle," which held the pass of the Aire, doubtless continued as a fortified outwork up to Norman times. At this period there was no bridge here, for in the reign of Henry I., the then lord, Henry de Lacy, bestowed the profits of the ferry on the monks of St. John, at Pontefract.* South of the church is a pasture called Castle Garth, where numerous discoveries corroborative of the Roman occupation have been made. The church, beyond the antiquity of its foundation, (*temp.* Henry I.) has no unusual attractions. It was almost entirely rebuilt in 1866-7, and is now a spacious structure with 600 sittings. Castleford, anciently *Casterford*, is not mentioned in the Domesday Survey, but it appears soon afterwards to have given name to a family of distinction resident in the locality. The well-known early

* We have reason to believe that many wooden bridges across the Aire, built by the Saxons, were destroyed at the Conquest ; the Norman usurpers preferring afterwards to retain ferries instead, protected by watch-towers or 'castles,' as stated on p. 9 *et seq*. This seems to have been the case at Leeds.

historian of Pontefract, Thomas de Castleford, who lived in the time of Edward II., was of this family.

Some few hundred yards above the bridge, the union of the distressed and "blushing" Calder with our nobly-descended, though equally shame-faced, Aire is signalled by mimic shots of gas ; the well-matched pair, in garb classic with all the hues (and bouquet !) this Age of Science and Invention can bestow, continue their "bridal" tour through the fair, inviting landscape ! But we need not enlarge much on the simile. We have already, in our chapter on Knottingley, referred to the deleterious character of this portion of the great stream, and trust that "Science and Invention " (now that these have joined in conclave on the subject) will ere long restore to it its old, good degree of purity and wholesomeness !

CASTLEFORD TO LEEDS.

THE smoke-black skies of Leeds are now at no great distance, yet in the ten miles of country that separates us from big, noisy Woollenopolis, there are scenes as quiet and as fresh, and as wholly removed from thought of cankering city, as one might wish. But this section of our territory, from the southern boundary of the Aire to Wakefield (seven miles), is so effectively described in Banks' *Walks about Wakefield*, and Roberts' *Lofthouse and its Neighbourhood*, that we shall not dwell at any length upon it here. The road runs through Methley, Oulton, and Hunslet, to Leeds.

Methley, however, is such an interesting and picturesque old place that we must make more than passing mention of it. Its fine old church, dedicated to the Christian King Oswald, who died on the field of battle in A.D. 642, has been a recognised beacon of the enlightened truths of Christianity in this district for a full thousand years. It is notable as one of the comparatively few churches enumerated in the great Survey of A.D. 1086. From this famous historic Account we gather that *Medelai* was the property of the Saxons, Osulf and Cnut, and that there was a church and a priest. There must have been a pretty considerable population here at this time, for inasmuch as 800 acres of land were under cultivation (probably three-fifths in corn), and there were 640 acres (a square mile) of wood pasturage besides. Allowing eight of these cleared acres to a family of five persons (a not unfair estimate in this district), the number of people would be 500, and consequently this must have been one of the most populous and richest manors in Yorkshire. Its population and taxable wealth were much reduced by the devastations of the usurping Normans. After the Conquest it formed part of the extensive possessions granted to Ilbert de Lacy, the builder of Pontefract Castle.

Whether he built the original Norman church we do not know for certain. Over the doorway of the south porch there is a rude representation of King Oswald, seated and holding a sceptre in his right hand, and this figure (in an ogee canopy) is probably all that remains of the stonework of the original edifice. The present porch and building are certainly much older, being usually assigned to the time of Edward II., about A.D. 1320. The style is Early Decorated, with a later (Perpendicular) tower and octangular spire. Within the church, which has recently undergone renovation, there are many remarkable objects of interest. Banks says some of the stained glass in the east window is of the time of Edward IV., but this window has been "restored," and no ancient glass is there now. The interior, however, is chiefly remarkable for its grand old altar-tombs, with effigies, which, to the student of ecclesiastical monuments, possess a more than ordinary, if not quite unique, interest. They are executed with consummate skill, and are in an excellent state of preservation. In the Waterton Chantry is the tomb of Sir Robert Waterton, the founder, who died in 1424, and Cicely, his wife. Their effigies, in alabaster, are on a table-tomb, enclosed in a richly-canopied recess. On each side of the tomb are angels bearing shields charged with the arms of Waterton, and of Waterton impaling Fleming; and in the central niche on the south side is a representation of the Almighty in an attitude of benediction, with a crucifix between His knees. Opposite this tomb is another with recumbent figures, also in alabaster, richly gilt and coloured, of Lionel, Baron Welles, who fell in the battle of Towton (A.D. 1461), and Cicely, his wife. This monument is without inscription, but has armorial bearings. There are also several fine monuments of the Savile family; (1) Sir John Savile, Baron of the Exchequer, and founder of the Methley family (who died in 1606), with figures also of his wife and son; (2) Charles Savile, Esq. (ob. 1741), an exquisite sculpture by Scheemakers; (3) John Savile, first Earl of Mexborough (ob. 1778); (4) Sarah, dowager-countess of Mexborough (ob. 1821). The last-mentioned is a very beautiful piece of workmanship, depicting the raising of Lazarus, by R. Westmacott, R.A. There are also several tablets, and in the belfry are two 14th century recumbent effigies of ecclesiastics which should not be overlooked. The inscription is partly defaced.

About Methley are many beautiful residences, the principal of which is Methley Park, the seat of the Earl of Mexborough, and a very beautiful domain it is, well planted and wooded, and containing some fine cedar trees. The original, or oldest portion of the Hall, was built by Sir John Savile, whose initials, and date 1593, appear on one of the stones; the front of the house, which is much higher than the rest, dates only from the beginning of this century, having been built by the second Earl of Mexborough. About two miles nearer Leeds is Oulton, with its quaint manor house, where the eminent scholar and divine, Richard Bentley, was born, in 1661. The house is now occupied by the Blades family, who built the handsome church here (designed by Rickman) some sixty years ago. There are several notable old houses in and about the village, one of these, a good, half-timbered little mansion, and a perfect picture of rustic antiquity, is inscribed on its main gable, "*Edrus Tailor, it. 1611, Apr. 10.*" It was formerly occupied by a family of Quakers, whose ancient burial-ground (now disused) is close by. A mile beyond, and adjoining the road to Woodlesford, is the *John of Gaunt* Inn, which tradition assigns as the place where that princely hunter (about A.D. 1380) slew the last wild wolf in Yorkshire: a distinction which we are loth to deny, either to him or to our valley, and particularly at a spot now almost within hearing of the roar of a great city; yet certain it is that wolves continued to be seen in the wilds of northern England and Scotland even two or three centuries later than this. Whether the animals were actually *slain* or not is another matter; no doubt they were, but of course no one who did anything in those days counted but Dukes!

Returning now to Castleford, we will approach Leeds on the north side of the Aire. After crossing the bridge, the old Roman road (Ermine Street) is followed by Ledstone station, the road running due north, through Aberford to Tadcaster, as stated in our remarks on Castleford. On our left are the pleasantly-wooded slopes of Kippax Park

(J. Davison Bland, Esq., J.P.), and on our right the ancient and picturesque village of Ledsham, with the old Church (restored in 1877) and Ledstone Hall and Park. The Hall (Chas. Wheler Wheler, Esq., J.P.) is a handsome stone mansion, built some three centuries ago, occupied first by the Withams, who, early in the seventeenth century, sold it to the celebrated Sir Thos. Wentworth, the spirited but ill-starred Earl of Strafford, who was attainted of high treason and executed on Tower Hill, in the troublous time of Charles I. His son, the second Earl, sold the hall and estate to Sir John Lewis, of Marr, near Doncaster, who greatly improved both the house and park, and added a beautiful lodge. He died here in 1671, when the property passed, by marriage of his eldest daughter, Elizabeth, with Theophilus Hastings, seventh Earl of Huntingdon, to that noble family. The pious and benevolent Lady Elizabeth Hastings (whose *Life* was written by Thomas Barnard, master of the Leeds Grammar School) was born here in 1681, and also resided here until her death in 1739. A monument, with marble effigies, is erected to her memory, and that of her two sisters, in the parish church.

Ascending now to the village of Kippax (pop. 2540), we pass the extensive and beautiful park (about 250 acres) which surrounds the well-known family seat of the Blands, who have been resident here since the time of Queen Elizabeth. The estate was acquired at this period by Sir Thos. Bland, Kt., son of Richard Bland, of Leeming, in the North Riding, whose son, Thomas Bland, married a daughter of John, Lord Savile, and was knighted by James I., in 1604. His son, Sir Thomas Bland, took a prominent part in defence of Pontefract Castle for the King, during the Civil Wars, and his son, again Sir Thomas Bland, was created a baronet in 1642, in consideration of his own and his father's loyalty and services to the Royal cause. Sir John Bland, Bart., M.P. for the County Palatine of Lancaster, who died in 1743, left two sons, both of whom dying unmarried, the title became extinct, and the estate descended through the female line to Thos. Davison Bland, grandson of Thos. Davison, of Blakiston, in the county of Durham, by his wife, Anne, daughter of the above Sir John Bland, Bart.; and in this family the hall and estate now remain. The old parish church of St. Mary's was restored in 1876, and its tomb-full burial-ground has recently been enlarged to the extent of some four thousand square yards,— the gift of Mr. Bland. An ancient custom prevails here of tolling the large bell in the church, on the death of any person to be interred in the parish church burial-yard, and if the deceased be over 14 years of age, the three bells are then rung 7, 9, 11, respectively, and 5, 7, 9, for anyone under that age. The three bells are dated and inscribed as follows : "*Soli Deo Gloria, 1636 ;*" "*Soli Deo Gloria, 1638 ;*" and "*Fili Dei Misereri Mei, 1638.*"

From Kippax, the tourist may proceed by a pleasantly diversified road to **Swillington** (2 m.), and thence by Garforth Bridge to Church Garforth sta. (6 m. to Leeds), or by Whitkirk and Halton to Leeds, which latter route is 7 m. from Swillington. Swillington Hall has long been the seat of the Lowther family, a younger branch of that of the noble house of Lousdale. The late Geo. Wm. Lowther, Esq., who died, near Cannes, on the 6th of February last year (1890), was a well-known and generous enthusiast of sport, and there was no more familiar group to be seen at the Bramham Moor Meets than that of himself and his four young daughters, each of the latter mounted on a handsome little pony. Mr. Lowther, for many years, drove a "four-in-hand" coach during the season between Scarborough and Bridlington, and his familiar presence at these places will surely be missed. Swillington has a long, but unparticular history. In Domesday Book it is spelled *Swillingtune*, and it gave name to a race of Norman lords. The pedigree of the De Swillingtons, however, we shall not stay to trace here. Probably, if we did, many of our readers would be inclined to agree with the peculiar acumen displayed by a certain country youth, when accosted by some fledgling of distinguished lineage, who began to brag of his ancient descent. "So much the worse for you," retorted the milk-fed peasant, "for as we farmers say, 'the older the seed, the worse the crop.'"

The various places of interest between here and Leeds will be described in our Excursions from that town, and therefore, any present mention of them is unnecessary.

BRIGGATE, LEEDS.

LEEDS.

Area of Borough, 21,572 *acres.*

Pop. (1881), 309,119 ; (1891), *est.* 360,000.

Distance from LONDON, (G.N.) 186¼ m.,(Mid.) 205 m. MANCHESTER, 42½ m. SHEFFIELD, 33 m. YORK, 24 m. BRADFORD, 10 m.

EEDS, the famous and flourishing capital of our Dale, is now one of the foremost towns in the world. To its great trade and commerce are due, of course, this prominence and fame, and these have been of extraordinary growth. For inasmuch as from the wee, small cry of its industrial infancy, the town has risen to commercial manhood almost within living recollection. And to go but a step further, and without, indeed, over-reaching the parallel, were anyone at the present day blessed with the years of old Parr, he might be able to remember Leeds, in many respects, the veritable Norman babe it was seven or eight centuries ago. He would picture a small country town of a few thousand inhabitants, its streets narrow and dirty, some of them bordered with grass and hedgerows, and enclosed with pleasant mead and ample orchard; the houses at night securely fastened against thieves, and either immersed in total darkness, or partially alight with flicker of candle or fitful glare of oil-lamp. A few familiar watchmen patrolled the streets during the dark hours, calling out at regular intervals the time and state of the night, somewhat after the manner of the London watch-men in the days of Queen Elizabeth, who not only proclaimed the hour but rang a deep-toned (curfew) bell, crying, "Take care of your fire and candle, be charitable to the poor, and forget not your prayers."

In Leeds, at the time we speak of, commerce, as compared with now, was but in swaddling-bands. There were no roads, no rails, no canal, and though the river had been in some sort of way navigable from the great Norman Invasion, the means of communication were still miserably poor, and there was but little journey-making. For many long centuries in fact the town remained in a semi-active state, and even by 1753, at the introduction of turnpikes, the people about Leeds seemed so averse to change and "progress," that they declined to support the highway-tolls, and proceeded to pull down the bars, and it was not before several persons had been killed by the military, and many others wounded, that they amended their ways,—in a double sense. At that time the principal streets, Briggate, Kirkgate, and Swine (or Swein) gate, remained pretty much as they were in the days of the Saxon and Norman. The old Market Cross continued to occupy the same site which it had held for centuries in the centre of Briggate, until within living memory. And the streets continued to be lighted with oil-lamps until 1818, when gas first came into use. What a contrast the "busy Leeds" of to-day presents! Now are miles of well-paved streets, rows of lofty and enormous buildings; a teeming, active population; trade, commerce, and communication established with all parts; and in place of the half-dozen watchmen, and the old sombre oil-lamps of a late generation, we have an organisation of 420 able-bodied police, and the town in great part illuminated with the effulgent blaze of the electric light!

Leeds, however, as a town, is of very ancient origin. Though it does not appear on Roman maps, there are abundant evidences of Roman occupation in the numerous relics that have been unearthed in the neighbourhood, and it is also generally thought that a Roman vicinal way passed through that portion of the town which has been known for at least a thousand years as Briggate. When the Saxons settled here, they called the place Leedes, it is said, after one of their towns on the river Dender, in Austrian Flanders, near which also is a village called Holbeck. Some affirm an earlier origin of the name, and that it comes from the British *Caer Loidis Coit*, a town in a wood. The learned Dr. Whitaker, however, claims for it a derivation fom the personal name of *Loidi*, who was the first Saxon possessor of the place. At this period it would be a purely farming village, with a few wattled huts, having a small wooden church, and some two or three hundred inhabitants.*

The town was first enfranchised in the reign of John, but the first charter of incorporation dates from 1626; a second charter was granted to the town by Charles II., in 1661; and a third by James II., in 1684. But with the exception of a short period during the Commonwealth, the borough sent no representative to parliament until the passing of the Reform Act in 1832. The first M.P.'s returned were Thomas Babington Macaulay and John Marshall, Junr. During the great Civil strife between King Charles and the Parliament, Leeds sided with the latter. The town fell into the hands of the Royalists, but on Jan. 23rd, 1643, it was re-taken by Sir Thomas Fairfax, 'Black Tom,' as he was called, the 'Hero of a hundred fights,' who with six troops of horse, three companies of dragoons, one thousand musketeers, and two thousand club-men, entered the town with unsheathed swords, and, compelling the Royalist garrison to surrender, apprehended five hundred prisoners, besides ammunition. Sir Wm. Saville, the Royalist leader, escaped by crossing the river, but others of his followers were drowned whilst making the attempt. The Parish Church registers contain numerous entries of soldiers buried about this time. In July, 1646, when the ill-fated King was journeying to London, accompanied by his gaoler, he was lodged at the Red Hall, then the most sumptuous abode in Leeds. It was built in 1628, by John Metcalfe, Alderman. Thoresby relates a story of how the captive monarch was tempted to escape by the offer of a maid servant of the house, but the King, bravely declining, gave the woman a token, saying that if it were never in his power to reward her, his own son, the future King would. At the Restoration she procured an audience

* The old Moot Hall, or parliament, (from O. E. *motian*, to discuss or dispute, and *alh*, a large room or hall) rebuilt in 1710 and taken down in 1825 at the widening of Briggate, premises a Saxon origin also. The Witenagemot (O. E. *witt*, wisdom) or Council of the Wise, being the supreme court of the Anglo-Saxon nation, was the *prima stamina* of the moot-halls still existing in some old English towns. The Scotch *mute-hill* has, no doubt, a similar origin; in the days before written laws, the Scottish kings gave judgment from some low eminence dedicated to the purpose, and known as the mute-hill.

E

of the King, and presenting the token told him her story. The interview was short and to the point. "Whence did she come?" "From Leeds, in Yorkshire." "Had she a husband?" "Yes." "What was his calling?" "An under-bailiff." "Then," said the King, "he shall be Chief Bailiff in Yorkshire." And so he was. He rose to wealth

RED HALL, LEEDS.

and influence, and built the house called Crosby Hall in the Head Row. The oak-panelled room in the Red Hall which Charles I. occupied, is still known as the "King's chamber," and the piece of land on the south side has since borne the name of King Charles' Croft. Richard Oastler, the "factory king" lived here for some time.

The ravages of war and the disturbed state of the country during the Civil broil, were no doubt largely responsible for much domestic neglect. In 1644 the spring and summer were unusually dry and hot, and the town was visited by a plague of such violence, that no fewer than 1325 persons (or about one-fifth of the entire population) died from its effects. The contagion spread to the lower animals, and it is said that birds even dropped dead in the infected streets. The churches were closed, and the markets, for a time, were held on Woodhouse Moor. The pestilence raged most violently in the poorer quarters of the town, about Vicar Lane, the Calls, and Mill Hill, and many of the bodies appear to have been interred in these localities to avoid the danger of carriage. Many skeletons have been discovered ; and in Nov., 1790, fifty oak coffins containing human bones, were dug up in a field adjoining what is now George Street, the remains, doubtless, of this awful visitation. With the exception of two outbreaks of cholera in the years 1832 and 1848, Leeds has, happily, ever since been free from any similar calamity.

The parliamentary borough, which comprises an area of about 22,000 acres, had in 1801 a population of 53,162 ;* in 1831, (when the first railway was made), 123,393 ; since which time it has probably trebled, and may be reckoned now to contain an average population of 16 souls per acre. The trade of the town and district has proportionately increased. The woollen cloth industry, of which Leeds is the largest emporium in England, began here at a very early date. That it was established in the thirteenth century, is evident from an entry in A.D. 1275, when one Alex. Fuller, of Leedes, was fined for making cloth not of legitimate breadth. It was not, however, as stated, until last century that Leeds began to make any headway in this branch of industry. Previously, it occupied but an inferior position among the clothing towns of Yorkshire. Whilst, for example, Halifax and Ripon at the close of the fifteenth century were each producing upwards of 800 pieces per annum, Leeds sent out barely 200 pieces. Wakefield, at that time, was also in advance of this town. But with the development of the coal and iron trades, and the introduction of machinery,

---

* Bradford at this time had a population of 13,624, or just a fourth of the number of Leeds.

the relative importance of these towns commercially has wonderfully changed. Leeds is now, in point of population and commerce, at the head of all Yorkshire towns. It was at Halton, near Leeds, in 1779, that the first power-loom in England was set up, which was used in weaving bunting for ships' colours. Since that period the town has rapidly progressed. There are now nearly 200 factories in the borough engaged in the various processes of cloth manufacture, and the annual value of goods produced is estimated at from £8,000,000 to £10,000,000. During the past ten or a dozen years, the trade in ready-made clothing has also greatly increased. From about 1870 to 1880, some two to three thousand persons devoted themselves to this particular branch of the trade, whilst to-day probably no fewer than 12,000 to 15,000 persons are thus employed. Many thousands of the inhabitants also find employment at other local industries. The flax trade is one of the most important in the kingdom, and the iron-foundries, machine and tool works, tanneries, glass, and chemical works, &c., also afford considerable fields for employment. There are, in addition, nearly one hundred collieries in the district, having an aggregate output of upwards of 2,500,000 tons of coal annually.

This increase of trade and population has, of course, led to important changes in the general appearance of the town. Almost every trace of ancient Leeds has vanished. The old Norman bridge at the foot of Briggate went in 1760;* wider and more substantial structures have since been erected, and in 1873 the bridge was entirely rebuilt at a cost of £17,500.

Whether Leeds ever had a castle has long been matter of dispute. It is not improbable that some such stronghold existed here in Norman times, and countenance is given to this belief by the discovery, in 1836, of an extensive moat, the remains of which were found near the traditionally accepted site of the castle, on the south side of West Bar.

* Along with the ancient chapel or chantry of St. Mary. It stood on the right hand of the bridge on entering Briggate, and for many years previous to its removal had been used as a warehouse, and from the dissolution of religious houses until 1728 as a school. It was at this school that the celebrated historian, Ralph Thoresby, received his education, under the Rev. Robert Garnett, M.A.

There can be no question, however, that the place of imprisonment of King Richard II., in 1399, as mentioned in Harding's Chronicle (A.D. 1543), was Leeds Castle in Kent. The following is a translation from the *Abbrev. Rotulorum Originalium* (41st Edward III.), upon which antiquaries base their conclusions that the Kentish Leeds was referred to :—

"A.D. 1367.—**Kent.**—The King has granted and demised at farm to Thomas de Burgeis, of Smerdon, a fulling mill, with its appurtenances, which Thomas has constructed in the stream issuing from the outer King's Dam, near the King's Castle of Leeds, and three acres of land, with appurtenances, in the King's Manor of Lewes, through the middle of which land the said water flows ; to hold to him and his heirs for ever, returning thence to the King yearly 33s. 4d."

There appears no documentary evidence of a castle ever having existed at Leeds, in Yorkshire, although, as stated, some such stronghold has evidently been here, not only as exhibited in the immemorial tradition, but in the actual discoveries made. *See* our remarks on Drax, Pontefract, and Bingley.*

After the Civil Wars this ancient southern stronghold came into the possession of the distinguished Yorkshire family of Fairfax, and it was here that in November, 1779, the Hon. Robert Fairfax entertained his Royal master and mistress, King George III. and Queen Charlotte. In the neighbourhood of our Yorkshire Leeds, the Fairfax family had been long established, and at the corner of Wormald Row, in Lydgate, is an old brick mansion (now made into shops) called Fairfax House, built, according to an inscription, in 1727, by N. and K. Fairfax. In the Leeds Parish Church registers is an entry under date "1723, May 8th.—Madame

* Like the manor-castle at Rothwell, &c., the founder or builder may be unknown, yet this spot strongly suggests some kind of fortified outpost, erected to protect the ferry and mill (*see* p. 8), for we have seen that all down the vale of the Aire, from Leeds to Goole, such "castles" existed as defences to the ferries, and, especially in the early Norman period, these passes of the Aire,—the very "keys" to the northern provinces,—were vigilantly held by the Norman chiefs against would-be intruders. No doubt there were minor outposts in the neighbourhood of our river, of which every trace has ages ago been lost.

Fairfax, of Kirkgt., buried." This was the wife of Thomas Fairfax, Esq., the "honoured friend" of Thoresby, the historian.

Within the last few decades, vast sums have been expended in town improvements, and on waterworks, &c., so

LEEDS MUNICIPAL BUILDINGS.

that Leeds now ranks as one of the largest and best built, amplest provisioned, and most accessible towns in the kingdom. It occupies a position equi-distant (sixty miles) between sea and sea, and its enormous railway stations constitute a metropolis to which all the main lines in the country converge. Within the borough are some 240 miles of public roads and streets, maintained at an annual cost of about £90,000. Although the staple building element is brick, with occasional stone-dressings, this is of great durability, and many of the notable buildings, warehouses, shops, &c., display conspicuous structural elegance and solidity. Many of the principal public buildings (of which we give some particulars below) are, however, constructed wholly of Yorkshire stone, and some of these are of very imposing dimensions and appearance. The Waterworks, which originated in 1694, after the third charter of incorporation was granted, are among the best constituted of their kind in England. The water is of great excellence, and well adapted for domestic and manufacturing purposes, being derived principally from a gritstone area to the north of the borough. The present rate of consumption is about 10,000,000 gallons daily, of which about one-fifth is used for purposes of trade. The chief sources of supply are the reservoirs at Eccup (area, 200 acres), 1,280,000,000 gallons ; Lindley Wood (117 acres), 749,000,000 gallons ; Swinsty (156 acres), 961,000,000 gallons ; and Fewston (156 acres), 866,000,000 gallons.

Among a former generation of notable men born in Leeds may be mentioned the following. Ralph Thoresby, b. 1658, antiquary, and author of the *Ducatus Leodensis* ; Dr. John Birkenhout, the eminent naturalist ; Benj. Wilson, painter ; Rev. Joseph Milner, b. 1744, the church historian, and his brother, Dr. Isaac Milner, b. 1751, who began life as a weaver, and became Dean of Carlisle ; Professor Jowett, LL.D. ; Dr. Alex. Leighton, father of the archbishop ; Dr. Jas. Scott, the eloquent divine ; John Harrison, the philanthropist ; Sir Thos. Denison, judge ; the Right Hon. Sir John Beckett, M.P., D.C.L., F.R.S., b. 1775, Judge-Marshal and Advocate-General ; the Rt. Hon. M. Talbot Baines, Q.C., M.P., b. 1799, eldest son of Edward Baines, sen. (whose statue adorns the Town Hall) ; Sir Edward Baines, M.P., J.P., D.C.L., his brother, b. 1800, President of the Yorkshire Union of Mechanics' Institutions, &c.

Leeds is also noteworthy as possessing some of the oldest established newspapers in the country. The *Leeds Mercury* dates from 1718; the *Yorkshire Post and Leeds Intelligencer*, from 1754; whilst among more recent publications are the *Leeds Times*, established in 1833; the *Leeds Express*, in 1857; and the *Leeds Daily News*, in 1872.

The Railway system was generally adopted at Leeds about sixty years ago. An Act was obtained in June, 1830, for the construction of a railway from Leeds to Selby (19 miles, 7 furlongs), when the work was commenced, and the line opened 22nd September, 1834; being the first goods and passenger railway made in connection with the town. The passenger fare for the single journey was 4s., 1st class, and 3s., 2nd class. About a dozen years previous to this time, a coal tram had been laid down from the mouth of a pit at Middleton to Leeds, a distance of 2¼ miles, and it was after an inspection of this novel railway, which was worked by a locomotive engine invented by a Mr. J. Blenkinsop, that the late Mr. Thomas Gray, of Exeter, drew his plans for the first Manchester and Liverpool Railway, afterwards adopted. Mr. Gray, who was a native of Leeds, published his international scheme for largely superseding "conveyance by turnpike roads, canals, and coasting traders," in 1820, but his observations were ridiculed and condemned as the offspring of a monomaniac. The *Edinburgh Review* said that he ought not to be at large: "put him in a strait-jacket," was the recommendation. He lived, however, to see the full fruition of his conceptions, and in 1846 the Exeter City Council presented him with a fitting testimonial for the great and original services which he had rendered to the nation by his labours in this direction. This speedier method of communication soon took the place of the old stage-coaches, and new lines sprang up in every direction. Following the opening of the line to Selby were others locally, viz.:

The Leeds and Manchester Railway, opened 30th June, 1839.
The Leeds and Bradford Railway, opened 31st May, 1846.
The Leeds and Dewsbury Railway, opened 31st July, 1848.
The Leeds and Thirsk Railway, opened 9th July, 1849.

We shall now direct attention to the principal

PUBLIC BUILDINGS IN THE TOWN.

The **Town Hall**, opened with great pomp by Her Majesty, Queen Victoria, on September 7th, 1858, is one of the noblest municipal edifices in the kingdom. The foundation-stone was laid August 17th, 1853. The style of architecture is Roman Corinthian, and the building takes the form of a parallelogram, extending 250 ft. by 200 ft., and stands upon an elevated platform, with a flight of 19 steps, 135 ft. in length. The great tower rises to a height of 225 ft. from the ground, and contains a large clock with four faces, and a huge bell (erected Jan. 3rd, 1860), weighing 4 tons 1 cwt., upon which to strike the hours, which can be heard at a distance of eight to ten miles. The great Hall (comprising a single area), called the *Victoria Hall* in commemoration of Her Majesty's visit, is 162 ft. by 72 ft., and 75 ft. in height. It will accommodate 1800 persons. The magnificent Organ, built by Gray & Davison, in this Hall, is one of the largest, as well as one of the finest-toned instruments in the country, and cost about £5000. The building contains the two Assize Courts, also the Borough Court and Council Chamber, Committee and Reception Rooms, Town Clerk's Offices, &c. Throughout, the interior is handsomely fitted and decorated, and adorned with numerous statues, &c. The total cost of the building, including land, is estimated at £132,000. The **Municipal Offices and Free Library**, adjoining the Town Hall, were erected in 1878, additional premises being required for Corporation work. Here are the Gas, Water, Sanitary, and Borough Engineers' Offices, &c.; also the extensive Lending and Reference Libraries (each containing about 40,000 volumes), Reading Rooms, &c. The total volumes here and at all the branches within the borough numbers over 158,000. The large, well-furnished, and attractive **Fine Art Gallery** was added in 1888; its cost was £9000. The permanent pictures are numerous and valuable, and there are besides special exhibitions of paintings, &c., at frequent intervals. A music *salon*, promenade, and refreshment rooms are attached. Adjoining the Municipal Offices are the Offices of the School Board. The total cost of these buildings is estimated at £85,000. The **Infirmary**, situated in Great George Street, and not far from the Town Hall, was opened 19th May, 1868, by the Prince of Wales. It is a handsome brick and stone building, in the Tudor style, erected from designs prepared by Sir Gilbert Scott, R.A. The interior arrangements are of the best, and were only adopted after many visits of inspection to the principal hospitals in England and abroad. It has accommodation for 300 patients. The entire structure, with additions, has cost about £112,000, and further important enlargements are being projected. The **Coliseum**, in Cookridge Street, is the property of a Limited Co., and was opened by the Prince and Princess of Wales on July 15th, 1885. The great hall is suited for public meetings, entertainments, concerts, &c., and will accommodate 3500 persons. The total area of the building is 14,000 square feet. The **Royal Exchange**, at the corner of Park Row, was opened August 31st, 1875. The foundation-stone was laid by Prince Arthur on September 19th, 1872, the day on which he opened Roundhay Park. It is a large Gothic edifice, with hexagonal tower 118 ft. high. The principal entrance is through the tower, and the main assembly room is a spacious and well-lighted apartment, 60 ft. in diameter. The total cost was about £60,000. **The Corn Exchange**, in Call Lane, is a spacious, oval edifice, containing a superficial area of 2053 yards. The large market room is surrounded with a gallery and offices, and the roof of iron is of singular construction. The original Exchange stood at the top of Briggate, on the site of the old Moot Hall. The present building was opened in 1863, and, with the site, cost £40,000. The market days are Tuesdays and Fridays. Near it was the old **White Cloth Hall**, built in 1710, and, at the extension of the North-Eastern Railway, removed to King Street, where the new building was opened in 1868. Its cost was £20,000. The building, in the Italian style, is rectangular in form, and is 302 ft. long, and 177 ft. broad. The large area contains 1238 stands for the sale of undyed cloth. The **Coloured or Mixed Cloth Hall**, situated near the Wellington Railway sta., is a large brick fabric, 380 ft. in length, and 200 ft. broad, and contains about 1800 stalls, arranged in six walks or "streets," each street and stall being named and attended by their respective owners. The octagonal building at the east end is called the *Rotunda*, and is used by the trustees of the Hall. The building, originally erected in 1758, was acquired with the site in 1889 by the Corporation, for the sum of £66,000.* The **Central Market**, fronting Duncan Street, was erected by a company of shareholders in 1824, and cost £35,000. In 1868 the estate was purchased by the Corporation for £25,000. The interior is chiefly occupied by provision dealers and milliners, and there is also a gallery used by boot and shoe dealers. The **Kirkgate Covered Market**, one of the busiest and most complete erections of its kind in England, was opened in May, 1857, and cost £15,000. It covers an area of 4040 square yards, and is fully provided with shops and stalls for the sale of various goods. It is open daily from 7 a m. in summer, and 8 a.m. in winter, till 9 p.m.; and on Saturdays till 11 p.m. The **New Market**, adjoining, comprises an area of 3¼ acres, and was opened in October, 1876, for the sale of fish, fruit, vegetables, eggs, butter, game, &c., wholesale and retail. Behind the fish market an open space is used for the sale of live stock, birds, &c.; and in Harper Street is the hay and straw market, and a covered pig market, with accommodation for 1500 animals. In the centre of the principal square is a large and costly iron fountain. The amount expended on the construction of these markets is upwards of £40,000. The **Smithfield Cattle Market**, in North Street, was opened in May, 1855, and is one of the best attended cattle markets in the North of England. The ground covers about 5 acres, and is admirably penned with stands for cattle, horses, sheep, &c. Sheds for 600 head of cattle have been erected, and there is accommodation for about 5000 head of sheep. The market for the latter is on Wednesdays. The annual horse fair is held on the 10th and 11th of July, and for horned cattle, &c., on the 8th and 9th of November. Cost of the market was about £14,000. The **Post Office**, in Park Row, was purchased by the Government in 1861 for £6000. It was built in 1811, and originally used as the Court House. It was enlarged in 1844, and again, in 1872, was raised a storey higher for the purposes of postal telegraph; but the building is yet too small for the

* Anciently the markets for woollen cloth were held on the Bridge, where stalls were erected, and the cloth often displayed on the battlements of the bridge. This continued until 1684, when the market was removed to Briggate, where it was held up to the building of the present Cloth Hall.

increased requirements of the town, and a large and handsome Post Office is now being erected on part of the site of the Coloured Cloth Hall. The building will have four floors, and its main façade will front the Royal Exchange. The **Philosophical Hall and Museum**, at the corner of Park Row and Bond Street, was founded in 1819, and is a commodious stone structure of two stories. It was considerably enlarged in 1861-2, and re-opened by Professor Owen. The building contains a large lecture-hall, a library of 16,000 vols., museum, &c. The museum comprises one of the largest and most varied collections in the kingdom. These consist chiefly of animals and birds (British and foreign), and embrace many rare and valuable species. The geological section is especially noteworthy, and includes relics from Yorkshire and other caves, &c. The magnificent collection of Roman, Grecian, Saxon, and other early coins, bequeathed by the late George Baron. Esq., of Drewton Manor, also deserves special attention. The museum is open daily at an admission of 1d. The **Yorkshire College** was formally inaugurated by the Duke of Devonshire in October, 1875. The first portion of the building was completed in 1885, and on July 15th of that year, opened by the Prince and Princess of Wales. The engineering section was opened in the following year (October, 1886), by J. Head, Esq., President of the Inst. of Mech. Engineers. The buildings, in the early Gothic style, have been erected from designs by Mr. Alfred Waterhouse, R.A., and have cost, with site, about £93,000. Towards this the Worshipful Company of Clothworkers have contributed a sum of £30,000, together with an annual endowment of £1800. There are, at present, about 1000 students receiving instruction in the several departments of the College, attached to which are a number of good scholarships. The Leeds School of Medicine, which was established in 1851, was amalgamated with the Yorkshire College in 1884. The **Public Dispensary** is an admirable institution, established in 1824, and is mainly supported by voluntary subscriptions. The present building in North Street was opened in June, 1867, and is replete with all the accessories of a first-rate medical establishment. About 3000 patients are annually treated. **St. James' Hall** and Temperance Rooms, in York Street, was founded in 1877, for the benefit of working people, by W. J. Armitage, Esq., at an original cost of £12,350. In 1884, an additional sum of £14,200 was expended on extensions and improvements. There are spacious dining and refreshment rooms, reading, smoke rooms, &c., and a lecture-hall capable of seating 450 persons. The **Oriental Baths**, in Cookridge Street, were opened in February, 1867, and cost £13,000. Some additions have since been made. The building is in the Moorish style, and excellently equipped. The large swimming bath, ninety feet in length, is open from April to September; the smaller one, all the year round. There are also Turkish, hot, cold, vapour, sulphur baths, &c., open daily. The **Mechanics' Institution**, in Cookridge Street, is a substantial stone building, in the Italian style, opened 1st June, 1868, and cost £20,000. The Institution, established in 1825, was first located at the back of Park

Row, and afterwards in South Parade. It contains a large and well-selected library, and has, at present, about 1250 members and subscribers. Connected with it is the Leeds School of Art. The **Church Institute**, in Albion Place, was opened 16th May, 1868 ; the foundation-stone having been laid by the Archbishop of Canterbury on October 29th, 1866. The cost of the building, a neat Gothic structure of red brick with stone dressings, was about £7300. It has an excellent library, reading-room, &c., and a members' roll of about 700. The Church Sunday School Association, in connection with the Institute, comprised in 1890, 76 Sunday Schools, having 2407 teachers, and 33,043 scholars. The **Leeds Library**, or "Old Library," in Commercial Street, is a commanding stone building, erected in 1808, but since considerably enlarged. This important establishment was founded in 1768, and owed its formation chiefly to the energies of the famous philosopher and theologian, Dr. Priestley, of Fieldhead, the minister of Mill Hill Chapel. The library of 80,000 volumes, is considered one of the most valuable in the North of England. Each member of the Library is a shareholder, and the number of subscribers is limited to 500. The **Grammar School**, on Woodhouse Moor, erected in 1858 at a cost of £16,000, is a beautiful and spacious edifice built in the design of a Latin cross. The school was founded under the will of the Rev. William Sheafield, A.D. 1552, and was further endowed by Wm. Bank and his wife, in the second year of Philip and Mary. The original school house in North Street was built by the pious benefactor John Harrison, Mayor of Leeds, in 1634, " the wonder of his own, and pattern of succeeding ages," whose epitaph adorns the church of St. John, New Briggate. The endowments now amount to about £3000 per annum. The **Industrial School**, at Burmantofts, is an Elizabethan brick building opened in 1848, and cost £14,000. It has accommodation for 400 children.

Chief among the many religious edifices in the town is the **Parish Church**, at the bottom of Kirkgate, re-erected in 1838, at a cost of £40,000. The present building occupies as nearly as possible the site of former churches, the first of which is of Saxon origin. On removing the last building (erected in the time of Edw. III.), several sculptured Saxon crosses were discovered, on one of which was inscribed the words " *Cuni* [Cunung] *Onlaf*," meaning King Onlaf, the Dane, who became king of Northumbria in the tenth century. This ancient relic is preserved in the church. The interior fittings, monuments, &c., are very beautiful and interesting. There are 3000 sittings, of which 1800 are free. The church (180 feet in length by 86 wide), consists of nave, aisles, transepts, chancel, and ante-chapels, and contains a very fine organ, of 70 stops, originally built in 1714, by Price of Bristol, but since reconstructed. The square tower, 140 feet high, contains a splendid peal of 13 bells, weighing 8 tons 3 cwt. by Mears of London. The church registers date from 1572. There are a great many other **Churches and Chapels** in Leeds deserving of notice, which the interested visitor may readily discover for himself. Worthy of attention also are many of the numerous **Warehouses**,

Banks, Hotels, Shops, Clubs, Theatres, Public Offices, Statues, &c., that adorn the various thoroughfares of the town.

No town is better provided with the usual means of conveyance and communication than Leeds. Although the first English Turnpike Act was passed as early as 1662, it was not, as already mentioned, adopted in this neighbourhood until nearly a century afterwards. The last tolls within the borough (on the Leeds and Whitehall road), were abolished on Jan. 1st, 1871. The Leeds Tramway Company was incorporated in 1872; the line from Boar Lane to Headingley having been opened on the 16th September previous. The tramway to Kirkstall was opened in March, 1873; to Hunslet in March, 1874; to York Road and Chapeltown in August, 1874. Since this period the system has extended to all parts of the borough.

The fields for active recreation are both pleasant and extensive. We shall briefly refer to a few of these.

The principal recreation ground is **Roundhay Park**, situate about 3 miles from Briggate (whence 'buses run). This splendid estate, comprising 773 acres, was purchased by the Corporation in 1871, for £139,000. It includes two beautiful sheets of water; the Upper Lake (5 acres) and the Waterloo Lake (35 acres), on the latter there is a small steamer, and boats are also on hire. About half the land is apportioned for villa sites, and the remainder kept permanently as a public park. The natural aspects are very pleasing, the land being undulating and well wooded. A large portion of the park has been laid out with walks, flower gardens, &c. Ample provision for the public enjoyment and convenience is made in the shape of swings, archery butts, refreshment rooms, &c. Fishing is also permitted on the lakes for perch, pike, &c. Tickets, (obtainable at the Town Hall or at the Park Lodge), are, day, 1/-; Sat. aftern., 6d.; Annual, 21/-. **Woodhouse Moor**, (63 acres), purchased in 1855, for £3000. On the south side is the covered service reservoir (3 acres). The ground is pleasantly laid out with asphalted walks, &c., and lighted with gas. There are a handsome fountain and a band-stand, both presentations. From the upper portion the view is of great extent. **Woodhouse Ridge** (17 acres), **Bank Lodge**, in Pontefract Lane, **Potternewton** Recreation Ground, and **Hunslet Moor**, are other attractive places of public resort.

There are public **Cemeteries** at *Woodhouse, Burmantofts, Holbeck, Hunslet, Headingley, Wortley*, and the *Jews' Burial Ground*, in Geldard Road, about three miles from the town.

LEEDS AND DISTRICT
TRAMWAYS AND OMNIBUS GUIDE.

For times of starting see local time tables.

TRAMWAYS. Leeds (Briggate) to **Chapeltown** (Green Light), *Queen;* through fare 3d. From Boar Lane to Headingley (Red Lt.) *Three Horse Shoes,* through fare, inside 8d., outside 2d. From Briggate to **Hunslet** (Blue Lt.), *Thwaite Gate,* fare 1d. From Boar Lane to **Kirkstall** (Blue Lt.), fare to *Cardigan Arms,* 1d., Kirkstall 2d. From Briggate to **Meanwood Road** (Red with White Star). *Buslingthorpe Lane,* fare 1d. From Boar Lane to **Upper Wortley** (Green Lt.), fare to *Crown* 1d., *Star Inn* 2d. From Duncan Street to **York Road** (Green Lt.), fare 1d.

OMNIBUSES. Leeds (*Black Swan,* North St.), to **Aberford** and **Barwick,** Tues. Thurs. and Sat. From *Three Horse Shoes* (Headingley) to **Adel,** morn. and eve., fare 3d. From Briggate to **Armley** *(Rose and Crown),* Mon. to Sat., fare 2d. From Briggate to **Beeston Hill** (Malvern Road), daily, fare 1d.; Sun., 2d. From *Black Swan,* North Street, to **Boston Spa,** through Collingham, every Sunday at 8-45 a.m., return fare 2/-. From *Black Swan* to **Bramham,** on Tues., at 3-30 p.m. From Briggate to **Burley Road,** Mon. to Sat., fare 1d. From *Royal Hotel,* Briggate, to **Dewsbury Road** *(New Inn).* Mon. to Sat., fare 1d. From *Borough Arms,* Kirkgate, to **East Street** *(Cross Green Hotel).* Mon. to Sat., up fare 1½d.; down 1d. From *Royal Hotel* to **Elland Road** (*Waggon and Horses*). Mon. to Sat., fare 1d. From Briggate to **Garforth** (*Miner's Arms*), on Sundays (weather permit). at 2 p.m., fare 1/-; return, 1/6. From *Golden Cock,* Kirkgate, to **Halton and Whitkirk** *(Brown Cow),* daily at 1 p.m. and 5 p.m., fare 6d. From Briggate to **Headingley Church,** Mon. to Sat., fare 2d. From Briggate to **Hunslet,** Mon. to Sat., fare 1d. From *Royal Hotel,* Briggate, to **Ilkley** *(Crescent Hotel),* on Sundays (weather permit.) at 9-30 a.m., fare 1/6; return 2/6. From *Bee Hive,* Vicar Lane to **Kippax,** Tues. and Sat. From *White Swan,* Call Lane, to **Meanwood** *(Beckett's Arms),* Mon. to Sat., fare 3d. From *Bull and Bell,* Briggate, to **Oulton,** on Sundays at 2-30 p.m., fare 6d. From Briggate to **Roundhay** (Park Gates), daily, fare 3d. From *Bee Hive,* Vicar Lane, to **Seacroft,** Tues., Thurs., Sat. and Sundays, fare, weekdays 4d.; Sundays 6d. From Whinmoor 5d. From *Black Swan,* North Street, to **Shadwell** (*via* Moortown and Chapeltown), Mon. to Sat., fare 7d. From Briggate to **Victoria Road** (*via* Park Lane and Burley Lodge Road), Mon. to Sat., fare 2d. From Briggate to **Woodhouse Moor** *(Park Horse),* daily, fare 1d. From *Borough Arms* to **York Road,** Mon. to Sat., fare 1d.

ENVIRONS OF LEEDS.

For notices of Bramley, Headingley, Kirkstall, &c., see text.

Armley, 1½m., owes its name to *Arm* or *Orm*, a Dane of distinction, whose writings, called the *Ormulum*, are yet extant. The name frequently occurs in *Domesday* (see p. 8). The Leeds and Liverpool canal is here cut through the remains of a Danish fortification called Giant's Hill, presumably the *Arms-low*, or hill, that gave the name to the town. **Armley Hall**, for ages the seat of the distinguished family of Hopton, was in its hey-day a grand old mansion (Thoresby says it had 26 rooms), and successively a possession, with the manor, of the Mauleverers and Ingilbys. In 1781 the trustees of Sir John Ingilby, Bart., sold the whole estate. **Armley House** (W. H. Gott, Esq., J P.). occupies the site of an ancient edifice, and is a stately stone mansion with small park commanding a beautiful view of Airedale. The house contains some good paintings. The church of **St. Bartholomew** erected here in 1872 is noteworthy for its fine organ by Schultze; the gift (about £7000) of H. W. Eyres, Esq., who died at Naples in April, 1881. Armley is the site of the **Government Gaol**, which was opened in 1847, and cost £43,000. But in 1857 it was enlarged, and with land, has cost nearly £100,000. It is a massive, castellated stone structure standing well upon the higher ground west of the town. The internal arrangements are admirable, and of interest, but visitors can only be admitted by an order from a magistrate.

Beeston, 2 m. For more than five centuries this was the seat of the noble family of Beeston, who probably obtained the estate from the Paganels, the first lords of Leeds after the Conquest. They were benefactors to the monasteries at Kirkstall, Nostel, and Drax; took part in the wars of the Crusades; Sir William Beeston was wounded at Bannockburn; Miles Beeston fought at Agincourt; and Ralph Beeston was a leader at the battle of Flodden. The last member of the family resident here was Captain Beeston, who died in April, 1641, and was buried in the Leeds Parish Church. (*See Thoresby*). The **Old Hall**, removed early last century, stood on the Cross Hills above Beeston Station, but the last vestige of it, a Gothic arched gateway leading from the street into the village, was in existence about the year 1808. The **New Hall**, anciently called *Stank* (meaning stanch'd or bank'd waters) situated on the Leeds and Dewsbury road, close to the railway, now consists of a number of tenements. On one of the doorways is inscribed C.H. 1616. Christopher Hodgson, attorney, being the first of that noted family that resided here for about a century, when it passed through the female line to Dr. Roger Altham, of Christ Church, Oxford. The "bold Captain John Hodgson," of Civil War fame, was of this family. The Hodgsons also belonged **Cottingley Hall**, on the opposite side of the valley, now a farm house. It had previously (*temp.* Eliz.) been a possession of the Norman family of Clapham. The **Church** of Beeston is of great antiquity, and said to be only second in point of age within the Parish of Leeds. It has several times been restored, and in 1885 was almost entirely rebuilt. It is now a neat edifice, with clerestoried nave of five bays, a porch on the south side, and a tower at the south-west corner rising to a height of 63 ft. The church contains some ancient brasses and mural

BEESTON CHURCH BEFORE 1885.

monuments, and some good stained glass. The fifteenth and sixteenth century church plate is also of interest. The register dates from 1720, but from 1753 until about 1870 there were no marriage celebrations here. The neighbourhood of Beeston abounds in collieries; coal having been wrought here since the time of Charles II. Beeston Park was the scene of a terrible tragedy, when the inmates of a house occupied by a Mr. Leonard Scurr, a master miner, and former minister of the gospel, were foully murdered on the night of Jan. 19th, 1679. The motive was undoubtedly robbery, although Scurr is described as being "a good preacher but a bad man." The men first attacked the mother of Scurr, when the latter, who was in bed, hearing the outcry, seized a rapier and mortally wounded two of the gang. This so roused the anger of the remainder that they at once fell upon the whole household, consisting of Mr. Scurr, his mother, an aged gentlewoman, and a maid servant, whom they ruthlessly attacked and murdered, and afterwards set fire to the house. It was not until two years afterwards that two of the ruffians, named Littlewood and Holroyd, were apprehended and convicted at the York assizes in 1682. Littlewood appears to have been respited, but Holroyd was brought to Leeds and executed, it is said in the presence of 30,000 spectators, on Holbeck moor. His body was then hung in chains upon the spot.

Hunslet, 1¼ m. Anciently *Hundeslit*, named evidently because the royal dog-house was set here when the King's court was at Leeds. That favourite of the Conqueror, Roger de Montgomery, held the manor of Hunslet, which afterwards passed to the Gascoignes and Nevilles, who resided at the **Old Hall**. This historic mansion, with its fine park, occupied a site near the old road between the churches at Hunslet and Holbeck. It was abandoned early last century, and a community called the Hunslet Hallers, grew up around it, whose fame as a race of "sharp" horse-dealers extended much further than their neighbouring trysting place at Leegap Fair.* Some queer stories are told about them, and the following happy character-illustration among the rest. An old Haller whilst travelling in Lincolnshire, fell into conversation with a Fen-farmer, when the latter began to draw comparisons between the productiveness of their two counties but much in favour of his own. "Vegetation," he observed, "is so luxuriant here that if you put a horse into a field at night, in the morning you will only be able to see its head and the upper parts of its body above the long grass." "Ah!" exclaimed the ready-witted Yorkshireman, "but that is nothing to what we can show at Hunslet Hall. If you turn a horse into a field there at night, in the morning dang me if you can see it at all!" The "Leeds Pottery Works," in Jack Lane, cover about seven acres of land. They were established about the year 1760, and for a long period enjoyed a reputation for a class of ware hardly inferior to the productions of the celebrated Wedgwood. It commanded the best markets at home and abroad, and for many years produced an income of £30,000 to £40,000 per annum. This ware is now much prized. Numerous fine examples of it are at Walton Hall, collected by the late Edward Hailstone, Esq. Hunslet was the birthplace of the ancestors of the late Sir Titus Salt, Bart., the noble benefactor and founder of Saltaire. His grandfather, Mr. Titus Salt, after whom he was named, died at Hunslet Foundry, Aug. 21st, 1827. (*See* p. 71.)

---

* Lee, or Leigh (a personal name) Fair is a very old institution; a charter to hold a fair having been granted to the canons of the adjoining village of Woodkirk, whence it originated as early as the reign of Henry I.

F

WALKS AND DRIVES FROM LEEDS.

ADEL CHURCH PORCH.

To Adel, 5¼ m. By the Otley road through Headingley. Or a good route is from the tram terminus,(*Queen's* Hotel) Chapeltown by Alwoodley Lane, and across the moor, descending to Seven Arches, or keep to the road on *r.* leading to Adel, op. the church. This ancient fabric is, though of small dimensions, one of the most exquisite and interesting Norman foundations extant. The visitor will be delighted with the superb Norman porch, which has been so often and deservedly depicted by the artist and engraver. It consists of beautifully ornamented receding arches in five orders, surmounted by a gabled pediment containing a figure of the Almighty, with the emblems of the four Evangelists and the Lamb of God. The interesting interior possesses a similarly beautiful chancel arch, supported on three cylindrical shafts with moulded capitals of singular design. Besides the old font, which has a modern base, the church contains some ancient brasses, mural tablets, and stained glass. Amongst the latter, in the chancel, is the Lepers' window (coincident with the lepers' hospital at Otley),* adorned with an emblem of the Holy Trinity. In a small building adjoining the church are preserved a number of ancient relics, amongst which are three Roman altars.

* A very ancient foundation. In the time of Henry I. these hospitals were to be numbered in thousands, but happily, so far as this country is concerned, the disease for some centuries back has been practically extinct.

one inscribed to the goddess Brigantia. Numerous extensive evidences of Roman occupation have been discovered in the vicinity, **Adel** having, doubtless, been the site of an important town—Burgodunum, (the *Burhedurum* of Domesday) about which, however, little or nothing is known. It was traversed by the Roman road from Castleford to Ribchester, traces of which can be discerned hence in the direction of Bramham and Tadcaster, and westward over Otley Chevin to Ilkley. About fifty yards south of this road, at a point midway between Adel mill and the dam, may be distinguished the site of a camp, about which Roman urns and other vessels, &c., indicative of an extensive settlement have been found. Adel dam will interest the naturalist, botanically and in molluscan fauna.

To Seven Arches and back by the Ridge, 7 m. 'Bus may be taken as far as the *Beckett's Arms*, Meanwood, whence *l*. through fields and wood to Scotland Mill, in the picturesque Meanwood valley. The old mill is now a bleach works, but was formerly a flax mill. Beyond, in the distance, is Meanwood Forest, the haunt, in the Middle Ages, of the wild boar, the badger, and wolf; at the foot of which is the ancient Smithy mill, now used for grinding corn. Above this we come to the **Seven Arches**, a favourite resort of artists. Mr. Gilbert Foster once drew a representation of the view of the valley from this point, which was admirably displayed on the stage of the Grand Theatre in Leeds. The lofty aqueduct was formerly used to convey the town's water across the valley. The return journey can now be made over Woodhouse Ridge and the Moor, wide views being obtainable from the upland walk; the finest, perhaps, being that from the top walk of the Ridge, going towards Batty Wood. It was here that the bold outlaw, Robin Hood, threw down 'the glove' to the lord of the manor and his men, and then, it is said, there was a "merry scene."

To Tunnel Hall Hill and back by Meanwood, 7 m. From Leeds to Chapeltown on the Moorland road to Four-lane ends, (forward goes past Meanwood Hall to Adel); turn *r*. on Moortown lane 200 yds., to a notable wayside fountain, erected Nov. 5th, 1788, being the "100th anniversary from the landing of King William, in memory of which happy era this is by Joseph Oates inscribed **Revolution Well**.* A little higher up the road is the Meanwood Children's Home, erected in 1887, under the auspices of the Church of England Society for providing Homes for Waifs and Strays. The Home has accommodation for thirty children, and possesses a large school-room, dining hall, &c., and a small infirmary for the sick. By taking a path up the field on the far side of the Home, the visitor is soon at the famous **Tunnel Hall Hill**, the 'Teneriffe' of Thoresby. It is a well-timbered verdant mound, commanding a wide prospect. Anciently the name it bore was Penhow, and in later times sometimes called

---

* This anniversary was celebrated all over Great Britain and Ireland. In Leeds the festivities extended over two days, (Nov. 4th and 5th). There was a grand Procession, a Ball, attended by the nobility and gentry of the neighbourhood, and Bonfires at night.

'Peunyfun,' doubtless from the adjoining hamlet of Paenfynaen, the site of an early British settlement, as the name clearly indicates. In Saxon times it was called Tonwaldhow, (from *ton*, a town ; *wald*, waste ; and *how*, a hill), which lapsed into Tunnel How, and since the erection of the tower or 'hall' (now in ruins) on the summit about a century ago, it has been called Tunnel Hall Hill. This building was erected, as the inscription tells, to the memory of Alfred the Great. "the Friend of Science, Virtue, Law, and Liberty," etc., by Jeremiah Dixon, of Gledhow. A descent may be made on the west side of the hill, and through fields to Scotland Mill, and up above the water side through the charming Meanwood valley (*see* p. 67) to Seven Arches. turning up the lane on to the Meanwood and Headingley road, (whence tram). On *r*. the **Reformatory** for Juvenile Offenders will be observed. The institution was established in 1857, and has accommodation for 150 boys. The buildings comprise workshops for wood cutting, shoemaking, and carpentry ; a large swimming bath, (the majority of the lads being capable swimmers) ; besides well-kept fruit and flower gardens, &c.

To Roundhay by Gledhow, 4¼ m. From the tram terminus at Chapeltown take up Back Lane, keeping *l*. down to the park lodge. **Allerton**. For nearly four and a half centuries, Allerton Hall, now the seat of the Rt. Hon. W. L. Jackson, Esq., M.P., F.R.S., was the property and residence of the Kitchingman family, about which much has already been recorded. Interments of this family were usually conducted in the night time, by torchlight, in the old Roman fashion.* The house, the most ancient in Chapeltown, consisting of about 60 rooms, was almost entirely rebuilt in 1730. It is traditionally stated that King Charles I. was harboured here before proceeding to Leeds. (*see* p. 49). A descent is made in view of the fine **Gledhow** woods (*gleed*, *i.e.*, a kite ; *how*, a hill), up the road to Gledhow Hall, (Sir James Kitson, Bart.) This beautiful mansion occupies the site of an older one, owned by the families of Waddington and Dixon. In the reign of Elizabeth it was a possession of the Thwaites' ; Ald. John Thwaites, the last descendant, having died here in 1671. The rambler here turns *l*. a few yards and proceeds through fields to Roundhay Park. (*See* p. 61). **Roundhay** (Norm. *Rund Heia*, *i.e.*, round enclosure), is one of the oldest preserves in England, having been enclosed fully eight centuries. It belonged to the wealthy De Lacies, (whose name so often appears in our pages), who granted lands here to the monks of Kirkstall. The great Duke of Lancaster, John of Gaunt,† frequently visited the estate for the purposes of the chase, and King John (Lackland) is said to have passed three days here in Sep., 1212 ; he and his retinue being royally entertained, the King

---

* The reason for this mode of burial is explained by St. Chrysostom, (A.D. 400), "We attend them with lamps and torches, because being delivered from this life of Darkness, they are gone to the true Light."

† The last wolf recorded as wild in Airedale fell by his hand here about A.D. 1380. In Scotland and Ireland wolves lingered for more than three centuries afterwards. (*See* p. 43).

revelling with the local nobles, whom he joined at the gaming tables, but with ill success: the royal purse-bearer having to pay losses amounting, it is recorded to *fire shillings* in a single night—a sum, indeed, in those days which had the purchasing power of a small estate! Roundhay has yielded many remains of British and Roman origin, notably stone celts, a Roman lamp, (found A.D. 1880, in the Gorge), and a fine Roman altar dug up in front of Elmete Hall, (J. Hawthorn Kitson, Esq.) From the hall a Roman track may be traced in a direction almost parallel with the present road. After enjoying a walk through the park, the return to Leeds (3¼ m.) may be made by 'bus, (which leaves about every 20 minutes), or the walk may be extended from Roundhay church through the fields to Seacroft, and by rail home from Cross Gates.

To Knowsthorpe, 1¼ m. By East Street ('bus), passing Cavalier Hill with the notable church of St. Saviour, erected in 1845 at a cost of £10,000 by an anonymous benefactor (supposed to be Dr. Pusey). The interior has this inscription, " Ye who enter this holy place, pray for the sinner who built it." Before the chancel is a superb oak screen with painted canopy. The interior adornments are of a costly and elaborate description. The services, it may be observed, are "high." Leaving Cross Green, a few minutes' walk brings us to the little village of Knowsthorpe, chiefly remarkable for the old Hall, once the residence of Capt. Adam Baynes, the first and only member of Parliament for Leeds before the enactments of 1832. He sat during the Commonwealth (1654-8); and at the Restoration was compelled to refund the royal manor of Holdenby, in Northamptonshire, which he had purchased of the Parliament for £29,000. He died in 1670 leaving a wife (who d. 1713, aged 88) and a family of sixteen children. An admirable full-length portrait of him by Sir Peter Lely, and another of his wife by Vandyke, are in the possession of his descendant, E. R. Baynes, Esq., of Aylesbury. Knowsthorp continued the property of the Baynes family until recently, but, prior to their purchase of the estate in the seventeenth century it had belonged to a Quaker named Stables. An old burial ground made by this family out of a portion of the orchard is still preserved with its inscribed stones. Before the court are two ancient stone chairs. From Knowsthorpe it is a pleasant walk of 2¼ m.

To Temple Newsam. This magnificent estate with its noble mansion and "ancestral trees," is the site of an establishment that dates as far back as A.D. 1181. In that year William de Villers granted the manor, &c., of Newhusum (likewise so written in *Domesday*) to the fraternity of Knights Templars, an order founded for the protection of Christian pilgrims, and was so called because of its chief settlement at Jerusalem being nigh unto the great Temple. On the suppression of this order by the Council of Vienna in 1307 the estates here and at Temple Hurst were granted "by agreement with the Knights Hospitallers of St. John of Jerusalem," to the Countess of Pembroke for life, and after her death, by Edward III., to Sir John D'Arcy, whose descendant Thomas, Lord D'Arcy, was executed on Tower Hill in 1537 for his share in the "Pilgrimage of Grace." The manor was then conferred on Matthew, Earl of Lennox, who married Margaret, daughter of Margaret Tudor, Queen of Scotland, and during the royal residence here her son, the celebrated Lord Darnley, husband of Mary Queen of Scots and father of James I., was born. The incidents are commemorated in Scott's novel of 'Ivanhoe,' where Temple Newsam is apparent under the name of Templestowe, although there is some ground for supposing this to refer to Temple Hurst, near Knottingley. According to Dugdale, these two houses did not pass to the Hospitallers as might be inferred on p. 22. The present stately edifice here (the seat of the Hon. Mrs. Meynell-Ingram) was built by Sir Arthur Ingram in the time of Charles I.; the whole of the old house having been pulled down with the exception of that portion containing the Darnley chamber. Upon the battlement surrounding the house is the following inscription: "*All glory and praise be given to God the Father, the Son, and the Holy Ghost on High. Peace upon earth, good will towards men. Honour and true allegiance to our gracious King. Loving affections amongst his subjects. Health and prosperity within this house.*" The handsomely furnished interior contains, among other features, a magnificent picture gallery including works by Italian, Dutch, and other masters. The collection contains a full-length portrait, by Mercier, of John Phillips, a noted centenarian and a gentleman of considerable property at Thorner, near Leeds. He lived through eight reigns, ever enjoyed good health, had a retentive memory, and was able to walk about up to within a few days of his death in 1742, aged 117. A memoir of him appears in the *Biographia Curiosa*.

To Garforth and Whitkirk, 7¾ m. By way of Osmondthorpe and Halton. There is 'bus daily to Halton and Whitkirk. **Osmondthorpe** is believed to be the **Villa Regia** of Bede, or residence of the ancient Kings of Northumbria, one of whom, Oswy, built a palace here in the middle of the seventh century. It was then called Oswythorpe, and in *Domesday* (A.D. 1086) is spelled Ossethorpe. The Saxon names of Coneyshaw (King's wood) and Coneygarth (King's field) are still preserved in the neighbourhood, and a few years ago there was to be seen in one of the windows of the old hall here a very ancient piece of stained glass, representing a King with sword, and shield bearing the arms of the Kingdom of East Anglia. Here also was discovered in the year 1774 a gold coin weighing 21 grains, of the reign of Justinian, which, as the Saxons had no gold coinage at that period, further tends to confirm the opinion that Osmondthorpe was a royal residence during the Saxon heptarchy. The present Hall dates from 1814. Passing through Halton (notable as having had the first power-loom in England worked here in 1779) we soon reach the pleasant village of **Whitkirk**, with its fine old church on the hill. It is a fourteenth century edifice (restored in 1855) with lofty machiolated tower, and contains some beautiful monuments to the Scargill and Irwine families, as well as a mural tablet, with lengthy inscription, to John Smeaton, F.R.S., the famous architect of the Eddystone lighthouse. Smeaton was a native of Austhorpe and died Oct. 28th, 1792, aged 68. In about 2 m. the Wakefield and

Bramham road is reached at Garforth bridge, whence *l.*, 1 m. to Garforth station.

To Morley, 4¼ m. By road from Beeston 2 m. Ancient as is the town of Morley, and enjoying as it did a reputation of great consequence in the pre-manufacturing era, it was only in 1886 that it obtained a charter of incorporation. It is now a flourishing centre of industry with some thirty and odd cloth mills, three churches, twenty-five chapels, a Town hall, &c., and an estimated population of about 20,000. Historically Morley (which gives name to the ancient wapentake) possesses special interest. The church of St. Mary-in-the-Wood (with its ancient burial ground) dates from before the Norman conquest. It is mentioned in *Domesday*; and several carved stones and a portion of an arch similar to what exists in some old buildings in Canterbury, (erected in A.D. 1110), are preserved at Osborne House (Wm. Smith, Esq., F.S.A.) from the original edifice. The late fabric (pulled down in 1875) was probably of the time of Edward VI. In the reign of the first Charles it ceased to be an episcopal place of worship by the clauses of a lease obtained for 500 years by a body of Presbyterians, since which time it has been used by various sects, and latterly by the Independents, who erected the present building on its site. The old Manor House (the birthplace of Sir Titus Salt, Bart.), and an old Elizabethan building on Bank's Hill, occupied by Joseph Crowther, a Corporal in the Parliamentary army during the Civil wars, are still standing and of some interest. Cross Hall is another old mansion noteworthy as the home a century ago of the celebrated Miss Bosanquet, afterwards Mrs. Fletcher, the pious advocate of Methodism, whom John Wesley often visited, and with no ordinary pleasure either, for in his Diary under date 1775, Aug. 27th, he writes." How willingly could I spend the residue of a busy life in this delightful retirement."

To Drighlington, 6⅜ m. Rail may be taken to Wortley sta., whence by Farnley wood (the *Silva Pascua* of Domesday Survey) and Moor Top. In the autumn of 1663 Farnley wood was the scene of a political conspiracy against the government of Charles II., led by Capt. Thomas Oates of Morley and other old Parliamentary soldiers. The 'plotters,' however, were quickly surprised, and many of them taken and tried at York. Twenty-two of these luckless conspirators were condemned and executed, and the heads of eleven of them placed upon the several bars and gates of the city. Many other confederates from Bradford, Halifax, Dewsbury, &c., were either fined or imprisoned. **Farnley Hall**, the seat of the Harrington family for six centuries, was pulled down in 1756, and the present elegant mansion erected on its site. Five years later the old Harrington chantry, which stood near the house, was replaced by a small but beautiful chapel-of-ease. The visitor arrived at **Drighlington** and Adwalton (which together form one township in Birstal parish), will find little inviting in the general aspects of the places themselves, but they are of great historic interest. The view also from Penfields, a few minutes walk from the station, is also worth noting, as it commands a prospect extending westwards from the dark-edged

Pennines to the great plain of York in the east, whilst the moors of Airedale and Wharfedale are visible on the north. Adjoining this point is the rough and undermined ground upon which was fought one of the deadliest conflicts of the wars of 1642-4. The Duke of Newcastle having taken Howley Hall after a gallant defence by the Parliamentary garrison, resolved to march to Bradford, when he was encountered on Adwalton moor (June 30th, 1643) by a body of Fairfax's men numbering little more than 3000 strong. Newcastle's army outnumbered the Parliamentarians by nearly four to one, besides a greatly superior force of cavalry. The struggle was hot and deadly, but Fairfax's troops being greatly protected by the natural defences of the ground, held their position until finally compelled by a stand of pike to surrender ; their retreat to Bradford being now cut off, Sir Thomas Fairfax, with his scattered forces, fled to Halifax, whence Bradford was reached the same evening. The number of slain is variously estimated at from 700-900, whilst there were a large number of wounded and prisoners. Within the present century numerous relics of the battle have been found, such as lead and iron cannon balls, portions of swords, pikes, &c., but these have generally been dispersed. No memorial of the battle is preserved here, but in the Drighlington Mechanics' Institute is a large portrait of the Duke of Newcastle, said to have been painted by the celebrated Sir Peter Lely, whose portraits of officers and other personages of that stirring period are now so much prized. A short walk from Drighlington station is **Oakwell Hall** (Ald. Thos. Taylor, J.P.), an old ivy-clad house, occupied during the Civil wars by Capt. Batt, who espoused the cause of the unfortunate King. This historic mansion is celebrated by Charlotte Brontë as 'Fieldhead Hall' in the novel of *Shirley*. (See Stuart's " Brontë Country.")

To Otley, 10 m., **Ilkley**, 16 m. ('Bus, *see Table*). A delightful trip of very varied interest. The road from Leeds may be taken through Headingley, and leaving Adel on *r.* pass through Bramhope and by the Chevin Edge to Otley, Or, from Headingley through Cookridge and by east Chevin down to the Wharfedale capital.* The distance by both routes is about the same, but by the latter more hilly and elevated (for 2-3 m. 600-900 ft.) We have already described Adel on p. 66. Hence 2¼ m. to **Bramhope**, a quiet, clean little village, which until lately formed part of the ecclesiastical parish of Otley. It has produced several centenarians, and notably one Stephen Sharpe, who died here in 1805, aged 107. The new church, which supersedes the old donative chapel built in 1649, was opened in Nov., 1881. It is a small but neat edifice. Bramhope Hall, long the seat of the Dyneley family, is now the residence of Mrs. Lawson. Where the ornamental guide-post now stands was formerly a fine old elm, and prior to the building of the school opposite, the site commanded a wide view of the plain of York, with the towers of the Minster distinctly visible. From here a descent by Staircase Ho. to **Poole** sta. (1 m.) can be made. Proceeding from Bramhope to Otley (3 m.)

* The tolls on the old road were abolished 1st Nov., 1873.

the views over Wharfedale in descending are very beautiful. This side of the river and railway we see old **Coley Hall**, once the home of the Gascoignes, with its large park, now cut in two by the present road, and formerly stocked with all kinds of foreign and domestic animals, including red deer, goats, zebras, wild hogs and Indian axes, or wild deer of the Ganges. Passing the Silver Mills on *l*. (once renowned for their silver-plating trade) we soon reach **Otley**, (pop. 6800 ; market day, Friday). This is the *Othelai* of Domesday, or the *field* of *Otho*, the Saxon, and is not only an ancient but a very pleasant market town. The church (restored in 1868) has both Saxon and Norman remains, and contains many ancient monuments to the families of Fairfax, Fawkes, Vavasour, Palmes, &c. During alterations made in 1851 several curious Saxon crosses were unearthed ; and again in 1867, beneath the south doorway, were found two covered stone coffins, each containing a human skeleton. One of the stone covers had a rude carving of a Roman soldier, and is now preserved in the baptistery of the church. Between the churchyard and the old Vicarage, is the tunnel-shaped monument in Caen stone, (now much decayed), erected in memory of the men killed during the excavation of the Bramhope tunnel, (about 2¼ m. long), from 1845-49. Upon an eminence at the south-west side of the bridge, on the site of the present Manor House, anciently stood the archiepiscopal palace, the manor of Otley having been held by the See of York from the days of King Athelstan. The castle or palace, surrounded by an extensive foss, continued in residence to the time of Archbishop Bowet, of whose lavish hospitality Drake informs us that he annually disposed of four score tuns of rich claret, besides solid viands in proportion. The building was finally abandoned during the Civil Wars. Just above the new cemetery is Gallows Hill, anciently the place for public execution, and near which was an old water-pit, traditionally believed to have been used for drowning *female* thieves in Saxon days. Otley, however, has blessed its maidens with a Maypole for two centuries at least, but the present one, opposite the Mechanics' Institute, dates only from 1872. From the May-day festival of that year no celebrations have taken place here. The modern trade of Otley is various, but in the manufacture of printing machines it has had a long-established reputation, the several works here being amongst the largest of their kind in England. From Otley the road runs close to the Wharfe to Burley, but the pedestrian is advised to cross Otley Bridge and take the north side of the river through Weston Park, Askwith, and Denton, a charming walk to Ilkley, (6¾ m.) **Burley** was the home of the late Rt. Hon. W. E. Forster, M.P. for Bradford from 1861 to 1886. His house at Wharfeside is a very beautiful, snug, and leafy retreat. The deceased statesman was interred in the Burley cemetery on April 10th, 1886, and the epitaph on his tombstone which is an admirable composition, will be read with interest. Mr. Forster was a partner in the firm of Messrs. W. Fison & Co., whose mills at Greenholme constitute the leading commercial industry of the district. Our route is now under the rugged heights of Rumbalds Moor, and passing

Ben Rhydding with the famous Cow and Calf rocks above, Ilkley, the 'Malvern of the North' is entered, where the visitor intending a long or short stay, will find every accommodation among its numerous Hydropathics, Boarding Houses, and Hotels.

To Harrogate by Harewood and Pannal, 15 m. From Leeds through Chapeltown up to Moor Allerton (3 m.) whence along high ground with good views over Adel, Alwoodley and the reservoir at Eccup. At Alwoodley Gates (4½ m.) the Roman road from Adel moor to Brandon and Seacroft is crossed, and **Alwoodley Hall** (a large farmhouse) is passed on *l*. The old Hall adjoining, was pulled down in 1822, but was inhabited until near the close of last century. It was a spacious fifteenth century building on the site of an older

HAREWOOD HOUSE.

one occupied in Norman times by the family of Aldwaldley. The manor is mentioned in Domesday, and the family name, variously spelled, occurs in charters of Kirkstall Abbey. The estate was bought in 1638 by Sir Gervase Clifton, who must have been an especial favourite with the gentle sex, for he had seven wives, the last of whom survived him! From him the manor passed through several hands to Mr. Robert Benson, first Lord Bingley, whose descendant Geo. Lane Fox Esq., Bramham Park, is present proprietor. Continuing alongside the finely wooded Harewood park, which covers about 1800 acres, the pretty village of **Harewood** is reached (8 m.) The trim aspects of the cottages, with their show of flowers, present an attractive spectacle, and as there is much of interest in the locality besides, the stranger might enjoyably make this the culminating point of an excursion (*see* p. 80). The nearest stations are at Arthington, 4 m. ('bus daily; rail to Leeds 9 m.) and Bardsey 3¼ m. (Leeds 11 m.) Formerly Harewood was not the quiet place that it is now; in pre-railway days there were six inns (now the comfortable *Harewood Arms* is the only one), and more than twenty coaches passed through the village daily. Also its annual fair, granted 6th John, and its weekly market, a charter for which was obtained by Lord Strafford in 1633, have long been discontinued. **Harewood House**, the princely seat of the Earl of Harewood, is one of the finest private mansions in England. The site has been well selected and commands a wide prospect of its noble park; the ornamental grounds laid out at a cost of £16,000, by the famous "Capability Brown," cover an area of 150 acres, including a lake of about 50 acres. The house, erected 1759-71, is classical in design, the grand front being 250 feet long, and having a carved pediment supported by Corinthian pillars each thirty feet high. The entrance hall is ornamented with statuary, whence access is obtained to the reception rooms, the large and valuable library, the yellow drawing-room, the white drawing-room, the saloon with its classical ceiling and marble chimney pieces, the gallery with its pictorial and other treasures, the dining-room, music-room, &c. There is a priceless collection of Sèvres and Oriental china, and the paintings include works by Turner, Reynolds, Lawrence, Vandyke, &c. The total cost of the building alone is said to have exceeded £100,000. By the courtesy of its noble owner, the public are admitted to the house during the summer season on Thursdays (from 11 to 5). The manor of Harewood came into the Lascelles family by purchase in 1721. In the fifteenth century it had belonged to the historic family of Gascoigne, and afterwards by marriage to the Wentworths, Earls of Strafford, from whom it was purchased in 1693 by Sir John Cutler, (who by the way is amusingly satirised by Pope in the *Moral Essays*), whose only daughter, married to the Earl of Radnor, failing heirs, the lordship passed to his relative John Boulter, Esq., whose trustees sold the manor with its appurtenances to Henry Lascelles, Esq., father of the first Lord Harewood, as above. **Gawthorpe Hall**, which stood on the margin of the lake, was the family seat before the erection of the present mansion; and here was born (*temp.* Edward III.) the celebrated Sir William Gascoigne, Chief Justice of the King's Bench, who committed the young Prince Henry (afterwards Henry V.) to prison for an insult to himself whilst in court, (*see* Shakespeare's *Henry IV.*, Act 5, Sc. 2.) The ancient and interesting **Church** at Harewood contains a superb altar-tomb to this dignitary, besides other well preserved monuments of the fourteenth and fifteenth centuries. The **Castle** at Harewood now in ruins, is a transition Norman edifice probably of the time of Stephen, although the greater part of the present building is not older than Edward Third's time. Over the principal entrance are the arms of Aldburg, in conjunction with those of Baliol, a fact of some interest, for Sir Wm. Aldburg was King's messenger in the time of Edward Baliol. The interior apartments will well repay inspection;

they were occupied up to about the time of the Civil Wars, when the castle seems to have been dismantled and allowed to crumble away. Camden affirms that there was a Roman fortification here which protected the ford of the river below. The visitor wishing to continue his journey to Harrogate (7 m.) may on leaving the castle cross a field from the road to Harewood Bridge, and passing Dunkeswick on *l.* proceed through Pannal, with its ancient church and grammar-school (2 m.) direct to the famous Spa.

To **Harrogate**, 19 m.; **Ripley**, 20 m., **by Poole and Beckwithshaw**. For this upland expedition clear weather is desirable, as the views from the moors and high ground are both beautiful and extensive. The Otley road may be followed, as described on p. 72, through Bramhope; or rail (N.E.) taken to **Poole**, 10 m. The village stands picturesquely on an acclivity of the Wharfe; having a neat, spired church, houses, and snug inns embowered by various foliage; though situated at the junction of many important highways, its quietude is invaded by a good deal of traffic. One ancient milestone tells us that it is 25 m. to York, another that it is 10 m. to Bradford, and another indicates the direction to Ilkley and Skipton. Our route is over Poole Bridge (a pleasant, open locality), where for many years there flourished in the crevices below the parapets the rare Scale fern (*A. ceterach*), a mural species distributed over Southern Europe and Northern Africa, but somewhat of a rarity with us in the north. In 1888, when the bridge was pointed, it must have got rooted out. From the bridge, a field path cuts across the road, and continues by Leathley Hall (T. L. Ingham, Esq.), emerging op. Leathley church and the odd "five-leg" village stocks. **Leathley** is a charming spot and, lying somewhat off the ordinary routes, is as quiet as it is rurally attractive. But the quaint old church occupies a somewhat exposed situation, and the tall, bent fir-trees and weathered tombstones that surround it, seem to insinuate that beautiful Wharfedale can frown with angry storms when she so listeth. The church is a very ancient structure; the chancel and western archways appear to be Saxon work, whilst the ponderous oaken door on the west side is undoubtedly of high antiquity. The interior of the church contains a few ancient memorials to the families of Hitch, Hopton, and Lindley. The registers date from 1674, and contain entries of the Longfellow family, ancestors of the American poet (*see* HORSFORTH). Ascending the road, with beautiful retrospective views over Washburn and Wharfe dales, Lindley moor is presently reached, whence the road continues at an elevation of 6-700 ft., with rocky Almscliff away on *r.*, direct to **Beckwithshaw** (inn). To the ornithologist this route will afford plenty of scope for observing many of the rarer kinds of moor and other birds; amongst these the greenshank, kingfisher, kestrel, hawfinch, great grey shrike, &c., have been noted, and in June, 1890, a beautiful albino blackbird was caught near Beckwithshaw. The bird, a creamy white, with light pink eyes, has since been caged. The church at Beckwithshaw is a new edifice in the fourteenth century style of architecture, having a substantial tower with six bells. Hence a road branches *r.* to

Rigton, 2 m., the forward one goes to Ripley, 4 m. To Harrogate. 3 m., over **Harlow Hill**. At the summit of the road is the Observatory (for admittance to which there is a small charge), and when near the *Harlow* Inn the prospect before the spectator is of immense extent. To the north is seen the woody Howe Hill, near Fountains Abbey, and a little to the right of it is Ripon Minster; westward are the Nidderdale moors and far-reaching heights of Craven, whilst eastwards the great vale of York, with the towers of the Minster rising from the level landscape, are well observed. Beyond, are the York Wolds and the Hambleton range of hills. Descending the road as far as the *New* Inn, whence *l*. by Cold Bath Road to Low Harrogate, or forward by the Stray to High Harrogate.

To **Bardsey**, 7½ m.; **Wetherby**, 12 m. (By Rail. N.E. 15¼ m.) Going through Sheepscar by the Roundhay road past the ancient little hamlet of Gipton (the *Cepetun* of Domesday), an ascent is made over Whin Moor (400 ft.). This is the Winwidfeld of monkish history, about which antiquaries are agreed was the site of an important battle between Penda, the oft-victorious pagan King of Mercia, and Oswy, the Christian King of Northumbria, in A.D. 655. The pagan monarch was slain, and the Christian conquerors subduing his followers, converted them to the enlightened faith. Passing Red Hall on *l*., and crossing the old Roman road from Adel to Bramham and Tadcaster at Scarcroft Grange (6 m.), a walk of about a mile brings us to the turn *l*. for **Bardsey** (pop. 320). Pleasantly placed as it is, the village has more than scenic attractions. It has a history dating from Norman times, and its old church, built about the time of Henry I., says Dr. Whitaker, is "one of the very best specimens of Norman architecture remaining in the North of England." The inner porch has the same characteristic Norman zigzag and beak ornament as at Adel and Birkin. It is conjectured that the row of piers on the north side of the church are of Saxon origin, being both thicker and shorter than the south row, which correspond with the Norman masonry of the north arches of the nave, and in the chapels at the end of the north and south aisles. The chancel contains sedilia and piscina, and the floor is laid with the remains of Norman tombstones, one of which, engraved with the cross and crozier, chalice and paten, is evidently that of some distinguished ecclesiastic. The registers of the church, which have been carefully transcribed by Mr. F. W. Sheppard, of Bardsey, date from 1538, and are within three years of the oldest in England.* Among the earliest entries are several to the family of Mauleverer. One interesting entry, which has given rise to much disputation, is as follows: "William, the sonne of Mr. William Congreve, of Bardsey Grange, baptised February 10th, 1669." There seems little doubt that this is the baptismal entry of the celebrated court poet and dramatist, William Congreve (*see* Johnson's *Lives of the Poets*, &c.). Though the

* Mr. Sheppard, the obliging cicerone who has been located as schoolmaster, clerk, overseer, &c., at Bardsey for upwards of thirty years, is a native of Trowbridge, having had the honour of receiving baptism (about 1830 at the hands of the Rev. George Crabbe, the distinguished poet and divine.

Congreves do not appear to have ever resided at Bardsey, (there being no other entry of the family in the registers), yet it is not unlikely that the poet's mother, who was a near relative of Sir John Lewis, of the Grange, was on a visit here at the time of the poet's birth. His father, who held a commission in the army, was stationed in Ireland, where the poet was brought up and educated. An undoubtedly genuine entry in the matriculation book of Trinity College, Dublin, agrees exactly with the date of his birth as recorded at Bardsey, and this is as follows: " 1685. On the 5th day of April, at one o'clock in the afternoon, William Congreve, pensioner, son of William Congreve, gentleman, of Youghal, aged sixteen, born at Bardsea, in the county of York, educated at Kilkenny, under the ferule of Dr. Hinton, Tutor. St. George Ashe." The poet, whose best works, "Love for Love," " The Old Bachelor," " The Mourning Bride," and " The Way of the World," are still popular, died in London, Jan. 19th, 1729, and was buried with great ceremony in Westminster Abbey. On his monument there the date of his birth is stated to be 1672, but on what evidence is uncertain. Bardsey Grange, during the Commonwealth, was the residence of the notorious Francis Thorpe, Baron of the Exchequer,* whose signature appears in the registers. Behind the house (now occupied as a farm) is a large green mound, known as the Castle Hill, which commands a pleasing view, and is, no doubt, the site of a once important stronghold, but all that remains of this ancient building are two or three stone steps. Historically nothing is known of it. The tourist proceeding to **Collingham** may take the high-road, (made in 1823), 2 m., or go up through East Keswick, across the Harewood road and Woodhall bridge along the north side of the river to **Linton**, a very beautiful walk of 4 to 5 m. over the Permian strata of rocks, rich in a variety of the less common orders of plants, as well as abounding in many interesting species of birds. The road hence may be followed to Wetherby, 1½ m.

To **Barwick**, 7 m., **Aberford**, 9 m. ('Bus, *see Table*). By the Tadcaster road as far as Seacroft, (4 m.) In rising from Killingbeck bridge, (2 m.), the old Hall of that name is passed on *l*. This was a possession of the ancient Killingbeck family, mentioned by Thoresby as dwelling here A.D. 1335; and the place, no doubt, took its name from the cell of some noted recluse. Proceeding from Seacroft, so called from the great Whinmoor Fight described on p. 77; and leaving Scholes on *l*., the interesting old village of **Barwick-in-Elmet**, with its prettily-coloured May-pole, is reached. This little 'Windsor' of the old British kingdom of Elmete, though shorn of its former pride and importance as the seat of the ancient Kings of Northumbria, still possesses some traces of the extensive fortifications that once guarded the royal town. When the district of Barwick was torn from British rule by the great Edwin, King of Northumbria, in A.D. 620, he is said to have built a noble castle here, and considerably strengthened the defences, which, in Dr. Whitaker's time, were pretty perfect, and covered an area of not less than thirteen acres.

* He died here in 1665, and is interred, without memorial, in the church.

The castle mount, now known as Hall Tower Hill, was encompassed by a double trench, and must have been a seat of considerable strength. When the Normans conquered the country, the manor came to the De Lacies, and afterwards to the Dukes of Lancaster, in whom it is still vested. The benefice is a rectory in their gift, now valued at £800 yearly. The church has some notable stain glass of Henry V.'s time. From Barwick to Aberford the road runs beside a long artificial embankment called Becca Banks (coeval with the fortifications at Barwick), and backed by a series of other entrenchments, and the remains of the old *Watling Street*, still traceable on Bramham Moor. **Aberford** itself lies on this great Roman highway from *Legiolium*, (Castleford) to *Calcaria*, (Tadcaster), (*see* p. 39). It was formerly a market-place of importance, and had an old renown for its trade in pins. The church, with the exception of the embattled tower, spire, and chancel, was rebuilt in 1860. Over its ancient porch is a good sun dial. The surrounding country is beautifully wooded, and there are several extensive parks; the principal being at Parlington and Becca Halls. Some distance east of the latter, on the Aberford road, was an ancient inn known as the *Black Horse*. Here the notorious highwayman, Nevison, often took refuge, and where it is said he baited the mettlesome mare that carried him on his famous expedition from London to York; Aberford, by the way, being on the old coach road from London to York and Edinbro'. The visitor wishing to reach the famous battle-field of Towton from Aberford, (3 m.), may do so by taking a direction eastward, and crossing the historic Cock beck, (which is said to have run red with the blood of the slain) at Lead Hall, proceed to Towton, (2 m.), or go by the old *Crooked Billet* inn to Saxton, (1 m). (For an account of this terrible War of the Roses, *see* Grainge's *Battles and Battle-Fields of Yorkshire;* Leadman's *Prœlia Eboracensia;* and Lumplough's *Yorkshire Battles*).

    Leeds to Bramham, 11 m., **Boston Spa,** 13 m. (N.E. rail to Thorp Arch, 18 m.; 'Bus to Boston Spa, *see Table*). This is a capital outing. By road described on p. 78, to Seacroft, (4 m.) passing through the village and ascending over Whinmoor, (*see* p. 77), past **Kiddall Hall,** (7½ m.) This mediæval mansion, for several centuries the home of the Ellis family, consists of a centre and two gables, ornamented with the rose and Tudor flower, a decoration common to the Perpendicular period. Beneath the sculptured cornice is inscribed in O.E. letters, "*Orate pro bono statu Thome Elys et Anne uxoris sue qui istam fenestram fecerunt Anno Dom.* MCCC MO PRIMO." An older hall doubtless stood here, for it is recorded that Wm. Ellis possessed the house and lordship of Kiddall in A.D. 1216. The family were staunch adherents to the Royal cause during the Civil Wars, and the house is also said to be haunted by the spirit of John Ellis, who was mortally attacked here by the Parliamentary scouts. The last member who resided here was Wm. Ellis, who died at an advanced age in 1725. In a field at Potterton, near here, was found in May, 1886, a very rare example of an Irish stone celt of basalt or volcanic trap, undoubtedly imported in pre-historic times. A number of bronze socketed celts, with hoops and ornaments, were dug up in the same neighbourhood in 1709. About ½ mile beyond Kiddall Hall a road *l*. leads through **Bramham Park** to the village. This beautiful and extensive domain, the property of Geo. Lane Fox, Esq. was formerly a possession of the Manlays and other old families, and was granted in the reign of William and Mary to Robert Benson, Esq., father of Robert Benson, M.P. for York, who was created Baron Bingley, in 1713. Upon his death in 1730, the peerage became extinct, and his daughter Harriet, heiress to a fortune of £100,000, and a rent-roll of £7000, married Geo. Fox, Esq., M.P. for York, who was raised to the peerage in 1762 as the second Baron Bingley, and ten years later, on his decease, again the peerage became extinct. By bequest, the estates went to his nephew, Jas. Fox Lane, Esq., from whom they have descended to the present owner. The noble mansion, built by the first Lord Bingley, was destroyed, with its costly furniture, by fire on the night of July 28th, 1828, when the loss (said to have been uninsured) amounted to at least £40,000. The house has not been restored, and the present family seat, Bowcliffe House, occupies a pleasant eminence at the north-east corner of the park. The latter is adorned with several temples and a large obelisk erected in memory of Robert Fox Lane, Esq. In the chapel adjoining the ruins of the old mansion are also some memorial monuments of the family. The picturesque village of Bramham contains nothing of special interest." but the surrounding district, well known as fox-hunting country, is very beautiful, and affords many delightful walks and drives.† The rambler, who wishes to extend his journey from **Bramham to Wetherby,** (5 m.), may do so by a pleasant route from the Rigton road, through West Wood, and along the rustic old Dalton lane, on to the Collingham road, 1½ m. from Wetherby. By this route, at the right season, the lover of wild flowers will meet with many rare and beautiful species, including white and pink specimens of the hyacinth and milk-wort ; columbine, barberry, meadow rue, and, perchance, the curious and rare fly orchis, which occurs on the north side of the wood. **To Boston Spa,** from Bramham, the road runs through Clifford (1 m.) This attractive neighbourhood owes its existence as a spa to a discovery made in 1744, but it was not until a half-century or so later, that this mineral spring began to attract attention, when its reputation became established, and building operations commenced. The waters, which are saline, are said to resemble most those at Cheltenham, and are good for rheumatism and its kindred disorders. The oldest house is

* Bramham, we may state, was the birthplace of Lewis Whitehead, a noted pedestrian. It is said he could run a fox to death. He once ran four miles over Bramham Moor in nineteen minutes. He died in 1757, aged 104, and when turned ninety his usual pace was four miles an hour!

† To the mycologist the district is particularly rich. At a Fungus Foray on September 25th, 1888, two parties, one led by Mr. Geo. Massee. F.R.M.S., of the Royal Herbarium, Kew, for the investigation of Bramham district, and another led by Mr. H. T. Soppit, of Bradford, taking that of Harewood, collected together 202 species, two of which were new to Britain, and forty-two new to the West-Riding.—*Vide Naturalist*, 1888.

the *Royal* Hotel, built in 1753. Samuel Tate, who was born here, gave the land on which the present Church of St. Mary was built, in 1812, and which handsome edifice was restored in 1873. Connecting Boston with Thorp Arch is the fine stone bridge across the Wharfe. The vicinity is very picturesque, and abounds in many pleasant walks and drives, one of the most interesting rambles being along the south side of the river to Jackdaw Crag, where the lofty limestone cliffs and flowery banks, laved by the waters of the Wharfe, present a rich picture. Formerly large quantites of the beautiful and rare limestone polypody (*P. calcareum*) grew upon these crags, but, as usual, in such exposed places, the fern has wofully diminished, if it has not been entirely rooted out. On the same side of the river a raised beach, about fifty feet above the level of the present stream, may be observed. This proves (if proof were needed) that the river once flowed at a much higher level than it does now.

G

DEPARTURE FROM LEEDS.

THROUGH HEADINGLEY TO KIRKSTALL.

CONTINUING our peregrinations "up the river," it is desirable for olfactory reasons, at any rate, to quit Leeds by as wide a curve from its far-famed gaseous stream as we can conveniently make. So mounting 'bus or tram we have a pleasant run over Woodhouse Moor and on Headingley Lane, and drop down at the old Shire Oak, the alleged *scier-ack* of the Saxons, that has given the name to the wapentake. Some reliance may be placed on the tradition, as the Saxons, like the Britons before them, were accustomed to assemble in conference under groves of oak, the place of tryst being recognised by some tree remarkable for its superior magnitude or personal association. Possibly the present relic, which may be as old as the Roman occupation of Britain, or even as Christianity itself, formed one of a royal grove, under which the Saxon councils were held. But whatever its story, this lingering patriarch is a venerable and striking object, and from time immemorial has given a peculiar interest to the locality. Up to about 1850 portions of the tree continued in leaf. At that time it was enclosed in private grounds, but the land having been acquired by the Corporation, the tree has since been railed off. Ten years ago its main bough fell, which was subsequently sold in fragments for ornamenting neighbouring rockeries. The tree, before this accident, may be seen depicted on the signboard of the adjoining *Oak* Inn. It is a very fair representation, done by a local artist named Pickersgill. At the opposite corner is another hostelry, significantly named the *Skyrack* Inn.

Over the way towers the magnificent new church of St. Michael, unquestionably one of the noblest examples of its style (thirteenth century) in England. Proceeding along St. Michael's Road as far as the Headingley Lodge entrance gates, we turn round by the Leeds new Cricket Field, which is admitted to be one of the largest and finest sporting grounds in the whole country. The cricket sward covers about six acres, and there is accommodation for 25,000 spectators. The cost of the ground, with buildings, &c., has been nearly £30,000. Our walk is now by an umbrageous road between private parks and beautiful villas, descending Kirkstall Lane between the church and Oliver's Mount, which commands an excellent view of the woods and valley below.

Or we may leave Kirkstall Lane by the old house and former hostelry called *Hark to Rover*, the scene of that oft told story of blood and imagination, "Mary the Maid of the Inn,"* whence on the Vesper Lane and down by the Abbey House, we are immediately before the majestic walls of that dark sainted Christian temple, whose mouldering stones for three and a half centuries have been proclaiming how mortal is earthly hope, and how fatal all worldly splendour and ambition! For nearly four centuries before its dissolution the old Abbey

'SHIRE OAK,' HEADINGLEY.

* The reader may refer to the late laureate Robert Southey's short rendering of this tragic story, which he narrates in flowing balladic verse.

was the home and capital centre of a useful order of workers, which for a long time represented the most popular and influential body in Christendom. Weak however is the flesh, and tempting, alas! the golden gewgaws of humanity! The sunshine of fortune smiled upon them, but as "wealth," says Lord Bacon, "bringeth oft pride and foolishness," the old monks heedlessly plucked the apple from the Tree of Life, and then the Light of their lives was eclipsed and the long shadow came! It is said the evil that men do lives after them, the good is oft interred with their bones; yet not of these old monks can it be said that the good bequeathed is held in no deference, and their services remain unrequited by Time. Their churches, for ages, were the scenes of constant benediction and prayer, shrines of pious devotion and self-abnegation; their altars were washed with the tears of the penitent; their houses, moreover, were hospitals for the sick and aged; schools of art, industry, and education; and they offered food, shelter, and entertainment to the needy and way-worn pilgrim! Well might it have been the laudable desire of the great men of the land to live in the good will of posterity, by the erection and support of such noble institutions, and well may it have been, too, their anxious desire to find a last resting place within their sacred walls!

Kirkstall Abbey arose from a vow made by the great Norman baron, Henry de Lacy, in 1147, that if spared, by the mercy of God, from a dangerous and distressing illness, he would erect a monastery to the most pious order of Cistercian monks then lately established in England. Upon his recovery he consulted the Abbot of Fountains, with the result that shortly afterwards a colony of monks and lay brothers were established on lands, confirmed to them by charter, at Barnoldswick-in-Craven. But their life here seems to have been fraught with great hardship and peril; the constant persecutions of the Scots, combined with the rigors of the climate, induced the Abbot Alexander to seek audience of their patron, whose influence with William de Poicton soon obtained for the distressed brothers the delightful site upon which they reared the present temple at Kirkstall. The building was erected and completed in about thirty years, under direction of the first Abbot (Alexander), who died in 1182. It is, perhaps, in architectural design and structural arrangements, the purest example of a Cistercian monastery remaining in England, for owing largely to the financial straits of the institution during a period when great additions and many architectural adornments were introduced by the Order, the Abbey at Kirkstall retained its main features unchanged. The general design is pure Norman, yet all the principal structural arches are in the Early Pointed style. With the exception of some fifteenth century windows, and the tower, originally little higher than the roof, the whole of the buildings are of the same uniform

KIRKSTALL ABBEY.

type, clearly the work of one period and of one hand. Increased riches brought about a relaxation, both in personal discipline and in architecture, and the desire arose for a more lavish style of living and for greater structural elaborations. The lofty tower, which had previously been regarded as a symbol of pride and vanity, was raised to its present height; the magnificent west front, with the transepts and choir, adorned with pinnacles and ornaments, and additions made to the offices and other buildings of the establishment. An improved dietary likewise followed, with greater liberty of action and of speech, and the condition of the lay brethren, who were the workmen, (numbering about 200, or probably about two-thirds of the whole monastery, and included masons, smiths, joiners, tailors, shoemakers, millers, gardeners, ploughmen, labourers, &c.), was on such satisfactory footing that their places were much sought after, and numbers were always awaiting admittance. The amount of food annually consumed was something enormous; upwards of 1000 quarters of wheat, barley, and oatmeal were yearly made into bread, or used for gruel, &c., whilst several hundred sheep, pigs, and oxen were slaughtered in the same period. Besides these, they ate large quantities of venison, poultry, and fish; and in addition to the fruit and vegetables obtained from their own gardens and orchards, they had rice, figs, raisins, almonds, and various spices and delicacies imported from other places. About 800 quarters of oats and barley were annually malted for ale, and when wine came into fashion it is said that nearly 10,000 bottles were drunk in the course of a single year. On special occasions minstrels would attend their feasts, and lecturers recite to them during meals. Although ladies were precluded by the rules of the monastery from these feasts, or indeed at any time within the precincts of the Abbey, except the church, yet it is clearly shown that indulgence was either granted or surreptitiously obtained, for the society of the fair sex. Tempting invitations were issued to them, and we fear were only too often accepted. And so no wonder

> "The monk waxed fat,
> And issuing shorn and sleek,
> Would twist his girdle tight, and pat
> The girls upon the cheek."

At the Dissolution the Commissioners' Reports contained some strange facts. Many of the Abbots were declared to have wives, some more than one; whilst one holy brother, a monk of Furness, had no less than five! With a characteristic exercise of power, bluff King Henry, who himself, in the matter of wives, was not altogether blameless, and might have been expected to have shown some leniency towards the erring monks, ordered to be "tyed uppe without further delay or ceremonie," all such who be "in any wise faultie." Accordingly some of the ill-starred abbots were hanged, and all of them, as we know, ultimately lost their possessions. Kirkstall surrendered in Nov. 1540, when its revenues amounted to about £512 per annum, or over £5000 of present money. The estate was granted to Archbishop Cranmer, and after various transmissions was acquired by the Earls of Cardigan, from which family it was purchased in 1889 by Col. North, of Eltham, Kent, for £10,000, and munificently presented by him to his native town of Leeds.

Last year (1890) the Corporation of Leeds, acting on the advice of Mr. W. H. St. John Hope, M.A., F.S.A., began

NAVE OF KIRKSTALL ABBEY.

certain work which was thought necessary towards the better preservation of the ruins. Of the value of this work from the historical and archæological view points there can be no question, but the upturned soil caused by the excavations, the destruction of the ivy and removal of some fine trees, have obliterated a wonted picturesqueness, which time will take long to assuage. The ruins are open to the public on all days except Sundays, (when the grounds only are open), from sunrise to sunset. The admission is *free*.

DESCRIPTION OF THE RUINS.
(See Plan.)

1. **West Front.**—The spacious Norman doorway consists of five recessed arches of exquisite design. Over it is a double window, surmounted by a smaller one, with pediment resting upon the stonework of a semi-circular arch. The embellished turrets are fifteenth century additions.
2. **Nave of Church.**—In Cistercian houses this was always in the form of a Cross built east and west. Here the direction of the church is somewhat north of west, probably for the reason that the line points to that part of the horizon whence the sun rose on the day of dedication. Its greatest length is 224¼ ft., and breadth 118¾ ft. Being tolerably perfect, its aspect is very grand and impressive. Some time ago Sir Gilbert Scott, R.A., estimated the cost of restoring this portion of the fabric complete for service, with organ and fittings, at £34,250.
3. **Aisles of the Nave.**—Each of the two aisles consists of a row of massive columns, eight in number, supporting pointed archways, and terminating with an upper row of small Norman arches. At the west end of the south aisle a circular staircase ascended to the turrets and roof of the church.
4. **Choir.**—Portions of the groining remain. Formerly the roof of the choir, transepts, and nave was of oak protected by lead, which was removed at the Dissolution. A piscina, for holy water, and ambry, for alms, occupy each side of an arched recess that formerly contained the seats of the sedilia.
5. **High Altar.**—This was dedicated to the Virgin. The table is said to have been of white marble. The grand east window is a substitute for a former Norman light, but like most of the Tudor work of the abbey buildings it is in a very ruinous state. During the late (1890) excavations a stone cross was found here, probably belonging to the original altar.
6. **Transepts.**—These have no aisles. Against the south transept is the Vestry. Here a staircase led on to the monks' dorter, and formerly it had a landing with an entrance to a small vaulted safe or treasury on the right of the transept. The north transept has a doorway; and above stands the remains of the lofty Tower, a Tudor addition originally supported by four majestic arches. When this enormous structure fell in the winter of 1779 an interesting discovery was made. Firmly embedded in the mortar were found several smoking pipes proving apparently the fact that the old monks smoked something long before Sir Walter Raleigh introduced tobacco in the reign of Elizabeth.

7. **Side Chapels.** Three in each transept, with windows, and roofs of barrel vaults complete. In the south wall of each are a piscina and ambry.
8. **Cloister Court.** In the form of a quadrangle 143 ft. by 115 ft. Here the monks were interred and the rich laity of the neighbourhood also, who freely exchanged acres of productive land for two yards of this coveted ground of sepulture. Several unknown tombstones have been removed, and some bones have been dug up. There was also a general cemetery east of the church reached from the cloister by a vaulted passage on the south side of the chapter-house. The doorway is now blocked. Originally the cloister area was surrounded by a covered arcade or ambulatory, whence access was obtained to the church and other apartments that opened into it. A beautifully wrought lavatory of the fourteenth century adorns the south side.
9. **The Archivium,** where the church plate, books, records, &c., were kept. Above it was the treasury.
10. **Chapter House.**—The most beautiful apartment of the monastery. Its area is 65 ft. by 30¼ ft. Here the chief abbots were buried, and several stone coffins still remain unopened and walled up. The business of the abbey was transacted here, and here the church processionals were formed. The building was enlarged eastwards, and some small modern windows replaced the "dim religious lights" of a former age.
11. **The Study,** where novices were initiated, &c. Adjoining this was the day stairs to the dorter, under which a small room or cell with an east window has a doorway to the south.
12. **Cloisters or Ambulatory.**—Length 172½ ft. by 29 ft. wide ; consisting of a double-arched walk of eleven bays (now destroyed), at the south end of which was the Frater of the Lay Brothers. Extending above this was their Dormitory, arranged with a double row of beds separated from each other by a wooden partition. A doorway in the middle of the east wall enabled the brethren to descend by a covered staircase to the arcade and so under shelter to the church.
13. **The Refectory and Monks' Day Room.**—Here were kept all table utensils, cloths, glass, and all the silver except church plate. In the Day Room fires were kept burning where the monks might meet and converse.
14. **The Cellarer's Offices,** where all the provisions and liquors of the establishment were kept. Adjoining was the brewhouse, &c.
15. **The Locutorium,** or parlour and reception room.
16. **The Frater,** or monks' dining-hall. This was one long apartment with its north end against the cloister court, whence it was entered by two doorways. In the fifteenth century a second story was added, also used as a dining-room on fast-days.
17. **The Library and Scriptorium.**—Here was kept the *Liber diurnalis*, the ledgers, missals and church books ; and here also the scribes were employed in the writing and illuminating of histories, &c. Gifts of land, &c., were often specially made for

carrying on this valuable work under direction of the learned Precentors.
18. **The Domus necessaria** of the conversi.
19. **Passage and Staircase** to the Monks' Dormitory, which extended to the south transept, where was a convenient gallery for sick or feeble monks unable to sustain the fatigue of

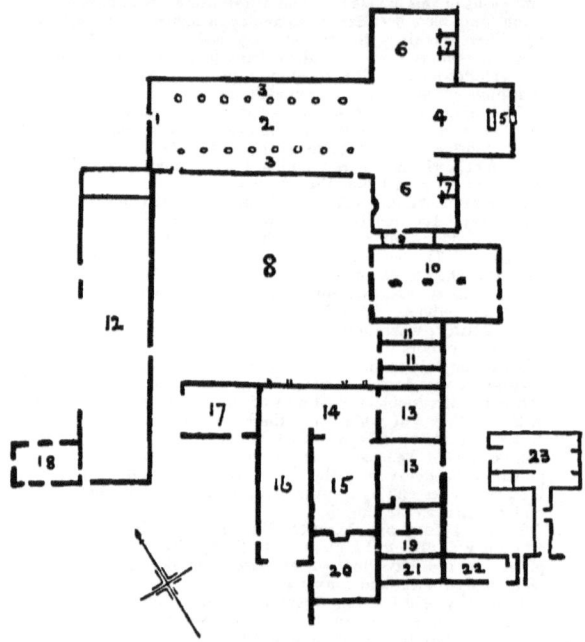

GROUND PLAN OF KIRKSTALL ABBEY.

descending and ascending between the church and dormitory. Every midnight, in all seasons and in all weathers, the monks were signalled by the Watch to attend service in the church.
20. **The Great Kitchen.**—The old bee-hive ovens, and smoke-stained flues, together with other indications of a culinary nature

remain here. No coal was ever used, the ovens having been heated entirely by wood obtained from the neighbouring forests. The original kitchen was on the west side of the Frater (16).

21. **The Abbot's Kitchen.**—The Kitchens were always placed nearest the river, so that the refuse might be discharged without offence to other parts of the house.

22. **The Lord Abbot's Residence, &c.**—This part is in a very ruinous state, and consists of several rooms and offices, with a chapel formerly on an upper story. In one of the rooms is a noteworthy fireplace with an ancient ' herring-bone ' backing.

23. **The Monks' Infirmary.**—This and Fountains are the most complete and perfect Cistercian infirmaries remaining in England. The Kirkstall one includes a large hall and numerous other apartments of which only the foundations are now standing. Contiguous to this building was no doubt the abbey prison.

The whole area included within the boundary walls and the river was about thirty acres, and within this spacious **Clausum**, or close, were also the **Hospitia** (or guest-houses), **Corn Mill, Granaries, Stables, Orchards, Gardens and Fish Ponds**. The principal entrance was from the **Gate-House** to the north-west of the church, a large handsome building still standing, and containing a spacious vaulted room panelled with beautifully carved old black oak. To the west of this Abbey House stand the remains of the ancient walls and the **Vesper Gate**, with stone dated 1152.

Routes to the Abbey.—From **Leeds**, Mid. Rail., 3d.; Tram from Boar Lane, 2d. From **Bradford**, Mid. Rail., 7d. From **Calverley**, ascending past Horsforth cemetery by road, 3 m. From **Bramley** (G.N.) 2 m. From **Stanningley** (G.N.) through Whitecote by road 2¾ m. From **Horsforth**, see next page.

From **Bradford** pleasure parties of ten or more passengers are booked per Mid. Rail. to Kirkstall and back, 3rd class, 9d.

KIRKSTALL TO HORSFORTH.

HIS is a nice upland walk to a place famed in the annals of Kirkstall, for the old monks had lands at Horsforth, and were on terms of good fellowship with the illustrious lords of the royal manor, some of whose members doubtless resided at the old Hall.

Leaving the main road at the *Vesper Gate* Hotel we pass the old Vesper Gate, with portions of the ancient enclosure walls clinging to it, and continuing up to the villas, are tempted to turn aside a few yards for a peep at Mr. John Wood's famous flower gardens. Though barely an acre in extent, they contain perhaps a greater variety of plants and rarities than it has ever been our privilege to discover in a similar sized piece of ground. Mr. Wood, who is an authority on matters horticultural, and a well-known contributor to several gardening magazines, kindly conducts us through the flowery maze, and points out to us the specialities of the place. These include Indian thistles, Himalayan and other roses, beautiful though curious 'thunder-bolt lilies,' Madeira Isle orchids, " flaming " plants, whose juices are of peculiar gaseous nature, and under certain atmospheric conditions will, when ignited, emit flames as large often as an ordinary gas jet; hundreds of Alpines, &c, from all latitudes; and here also in fine flower we see the much-prized *Wulfenia carinthica*, "the rarest plant in the world," for it has been found but on one spot only, and that on a mountain of Carinthia, in the Austrian Alps, where it has been known to flourish for about a century past. Altogether about 2000 species of plants, British and exotic, are included within this small garden, and we cannot but express astonishment at the wonderful results of acclimatization which Mr. Wood has achieved; many of whose tender nurslings have been coaxed into bloom and beauty, despite Leeds skies and oft malodorous breezes. In early November, even after the first snows, he has had as many as 180 species of herbaceous plants in flower together!

Now returning and following the road r. over the hill, taking a last look of the tower of the Abbey, rising in proud ruin behind us, we continue to the end of the way and make a descent, with a beautiful view northwards, by the wood side on to the road to the *Bridge* Inn. Hence it is a walk of about a mile to the ancient, albeit now modernized Saxon village of

HORSFORTH,

which stands high, and on its south side commands, especially from its pleasant cemetery,* a wide view of Airedale. Horseforde, as it is called in *Domesday*, was a royal manor which, after the Conquest, was held of the De Lacies by the ancient family of Paytefin, of Headingley, from whom it subsequently passed, with the estate at Kirkstall, to the illustrious Archbishop Cranmer, whose heirs disposed of it to Edward, Lord Clinton. In the eighth year of Elizabeth (1565), John Stanhope became joint purchaser, in whose family it has since remained. The Hall, now the seat of Surr W. Duncan, Esq., is a handsome Georgian building, doubtless the offspring of an edifice that has stood here for a round thousand years. For so important and valuable a place as Horsforth, held as it was by several Saxon thanes, would have its manor house, although the earliest recorded mention of it we have met with, is in a deed of gift made in the twelfth century, by one William de Povile, (Poole), to the monks of Kirkstall. These De Poviles must have been people of substance and fashion in their day. In a marriage gift of lands at Horsforth called Huelot Royd (which afterwards also went to the monks at Kirkstall) made by Walter, son of Nigel de Horsforth, William de Povile receives an annual acknowledgment of a pair of white gloves at Easter. The De Lellays were also another notable family here in pre-Reformation times, having been territorial benefactors to the order of Knights Templar, as well as to the Abbey at Kirkstall.

* The cemetery is open from sunrise to sunset, but on Sundays only after 1 p.m.

Perhaps the most interesting association of later times belonging to Horsforth, is the circumstance of its being the family home of the distinguished poet, Henry Wadsworth Longfellow,—an "Immortal," be it said, who was not only possessed as a poet and philosopher of unique gifts, but as man too, simple and good, he lived a life as near unto the angels as it was possible for anyone to do on this earth. The Longfellows were settled in this part of Yorkshire at an early period, (at Otley there are records of them in 1486), but it is to one William Longfellow, of Upper House, Horsforth, a clothier of means, that we may clearly trace the poet's ancestry. This William, who died in 1704, aged 84, had a son William, who migrated to New England, and was drowned off Cape Breton during an expedition against the French and Indians in 1690. His son, Stephen Longfellow, was the original "Village Blacksmith," of Newbury, whose son, also named Stephen, graduated at Harvard in 1742, and was grandfather of Stephen Longfellow, LL.D., father of the poet, who died at Cambridge, Mass., in March 1882, aged 75. The poet's mother was Zilpah Wadsworth, a descendant of John Alden, and of "Priscilla the Puritan maiden." Nothing being positively known of the American William, or his descendants, at the time of the father's death at Horsforth, in 1704, the property was left to his daughter Mary, who was married to a Mr. Hardy, and living in London. Another daughter, however, wife of Timothy Stables, seems to have come in for a share, for after her father's death we find her in free occupation of the farm and residence at Upper House.* In October, 1805, John Stables, a descendant of Timothy, committed suicide whilst suffering mental aberration, caused by the loss of his brother William Stables, who had been murdered in his bed in the July previous. Upper House Farm had been purchased by

* After many enquiries on the spot we are persuaded this old home of the poet's ancestors stood somewhere in the neighbourhood of Tom Royd Hill, at Woodside. The house was long ago pulled down, and the site partly quarried and since partly built upon. A great many Americans have visited Horsforth, but so far as obtaining relics and local knowledge of the poet, they cannot we fear have been very successful.

Edward Longfellow, father of the clothier, of a James Caubert, early in the seventeenth century, after which the following interesting additions to the family property were made by William Longfellow:

1. Bought land at Tom Royd Hill. Sold in 1680, apparently to raise money to send William to America.
2. Bought of Michael Green one cottage and land at Horsforth.
3. Bought of the same, Thornton Cottage.
4. Bought of the same, Dawson Croft.
5. Transfer of Upper House and land from Edward to William Longfellow, in 1647.
6. In 1663 bought of Mary Thornton half of Clay Flatts.
7. In 1669 bought of Grace Scott a quarter of Clay Flatts.

Numerous entries of the Longfellow family may be found in the registers at Otley, Ilkley, Guiseley, Leathley, &c.; and at Horsforth, where they have been resident for at least three centuries, some members bearing the family name still linger. Horsforth has some good houses and schools, several commodious chapels, built of the excellent native stone, and a church founded in 1758. The population is now estimated at about 8000.

The celebrated pedestrian, Foster Powell, was born here in 1734. He was an attorney's clerk, and did some wonderful feats during his lifetime of sixty years. One of his achievements was in 1786, when he accomplished a walk from London to Canterbury and back, (112 miles) in 23 hours 53½ mins., thousands of spectators witnessing its completion. Another great exploit was a walk of 400 miles, being from London to York and back, which he completed in 5 days 15¼ hours. He was also invited abroad, where his powers won him additional fame and favour.

Horsforth to Adel, 2¼ m. From above the station either of the roads over Cookridge may be taken. Cookridge, with its large and conspicuous Convalescent Home, connected with the Leeds Infirmary, occupies for the most part high ground, (6-700 ft.) and the air is exceptionally pure and sweet. Numbers of the rarer kinds of birds haunt its bushy uplands, and among these the common buzzard, missel thrush, and several of the warblers have been noted. In May, 1886, a nest of the fieldfare, containing four eggs, was found here by the Rev. J. Beanland, B.A., Curate of the Bradford Parish Church, an interesting and notable record, as the bird is not known to have nested here since the year 1824. After crossing the Leeds and Otley road, a field path leads directly to the church-gate at Adel. (*See* p. 66).

From Horsforth it is a short mile down to

NEWLAY,

leaving the Leeds and Guiseley road by a field path past Newlay Hall and Newlaiths Grange, the ancient seat of the Greenwoode family, who trace their ancestry far back to Norman times. There are a few other pleasant villa residences, but this neighbourhood, on the whole, is not now very attractive, and so we will cross the old toll-bridge over the Aire up to Bramley, a long up-hill mile, passing the Aire Vale Dyeworks, (Messrs. Whitaker Bros.), which were burnt down in August, 1890, at an insured loss of £20,000. This bridge was built in 1819, by a Mr. Richard Micklethwaite, at a cost of £1500, and up to 1889 was subject to ½d. toll. For many years it produced a revenue of £600 per annum. It has since been acquired by the Midland Railway Co. and the Horsforth Local Board, and a new free bridge takes its place. All the way from here to Kirkstall, and crowding the slopes between the 'Midland' and 'Great Northern' highways, the visitor will be struck with the wide fields of broad-leaved rhubarb, which is grown here with much success. In the course of a season 50 to 100 tons of the plant are despatched weekly from Kirkstall station to various parts of the home countries and abroad. Large quantities are forwarded to the continent, to be used, we are told, in the manufacture of "champagne," &c.; and in America, too, where it is largely imported, it is considered a rare delicacy, the climate there being too arid to grow it. Ascending the lane through Bramley Whitecote, and crossing the Leeds and Bradford highroad, a rise of about half-a-mile brings us to

BRAMLEY,

the village being about ten minutes' walk from the station (G.N.) beyond. There is not much to attract us about here now in the way of picturesque detail, although in ancient times,—before the age of steam and smoke,—the country around was fresh with the clear brook, blooming corn land, and wide stretches of waving woodland that covered abundance of game. In the Norman Conqueror's time, we gather from his great Survey, that there was wood pasture at Bramley Fall exceeding three hundred acres in extent, and that, too, there were several hundred acres of other land in Bramley in a state of profitable cultivation. So that Bramley has been a settled centre of civilization from a very early period. In the thirteenth and fourteenth centuries the Abbots of Kirkstall belonged the greater part of the land here, where they grazed large numbers of their sheep and cattle, which at one time might have been reckoned in thousands. It is generally thought that they had a grange at Swinnow, where their hinds were located, and, although our evidence is slight, it is certainly singular that during the construction of the Pudsey railway in 1877, the foundations of some such building were discovered near the watercourse then being diverted from its old channel at Swinnow. Some of the stones were of immense size, several at least four feet long and half a yard thick, being in good condition, well cemented together, and so firmly laid that it was deemed advisable to cut through them rather than excavate. The stone at Bramley Fall, whence these blocks were quarried, has an old and deservedly excellent reputation, having been used in the building of Kirkstall Abbey, in the walls of the Castle at York, and in many modern buildings and works requiring strength and durability in our large towns, both inland and seaport. The stone used in building the celebrated Martello Towers, on the coast of Kent, erected as a means of defence in the troublous times of the French Wars, also came from Bramley Fall.

The church at Bramley is an ancient fabric, believed to have been built on the site of an older one in the reign of Charles the First. The registers, however, date only from 1717. There is a sundial, erected in 1729, in the churchyard ; and the oldest gravestone, which is noteworthy, is one to the memory of the wife of William Vevers, of Bramley, who died 23rd March, 1673, and bears this salutary epitaph, " *Houses and riches are the inheritance of fathers, but a prudent wife is from the Lord.*" It is to be hoped that this oft-contemplated laudatory tribute would provoke emulous desires among the good wives of Bramley in olden times. Some of them, however, must have been terrible scolds, for the public Ducking-stool here was brought into frequent requisition. In one year (1710) the Constable's account shews that a single payment of 3/4 had been made for repairs to this instrument of female punishment, a rather heavy amount, considering that skilled workmen at Bramley earned barely a shilling a day at that time. The Stool was evidently over-strained by its "heavy weights."

BRAMLEY IN "THE GOOD OLD TIMES."

By the requirements of modern business life Old Bramley, like other similarly-circumstanced places, is fast receding into the invisible Past. Houses centuries old have come down, new ones are taking their place, thoroughfares are widened and the whole contour of the village changed. Stocks Hill for example wears a very different aspect now to what it did within the recollection of old persons still living. There stood here a plain stone pillar about eight feet high, which is said to have been erected in 1644-5 and used as a market-cross during the prevalence of the plague in Leeds, when the markets were sometimes held in the outlying districts. The old column got broken, and finally was utilized in building some sixty and odd years ago. Opposite the *Globe* Inn a May-pole was erected about the year 1830 when the old Loyal Friendly Society, established in 1765, broke into two rival sections, and celebrating their festivals on the same day (the first Monday in May), instituted what has become known as the "Bramley Clash." The Manor house at Bramley disappeared about 1845 ; but portions of the old Hall in Town Street still retain their original character, although now in a very dilapidated state. The house, which is close to the *Star and Garter* Hotel, was for many generations the seat of a wealthy local family named Hiles, the last representative who lived here (an eccentric miser named Oliver Hiles) having been brutally murdered in his bed on a wild winter's night towards the close of last century. The old bow-windowed room in which the horrid deed was perpetrated is still existing, the gory marks of guilt are yet, it is said, visible, and (of course) the spirit of the murdered man occasionally visits the spot. As the ancient dilapidated hall is one of the few remaining relics of Old Bramley we may conclude our notice of it with its story of

THE HAUNTED CHAMBER.

Oliver Hiles was pretty well descended from a stock of well-to-do yeomanry, who by diligent work and careful habits had acquired enough of a competency that would have enabled them to live in comparative affluence and style if they had desired to do so. But they cared little for show or company of any kind, and friends were rarely ever seen or known to visit them. Although they owned plenty of land at Bramley, and were undoubtedly rich, yet their habits of seclusion and penuriousness were so engrafted that they descended to the last generation. They asked nothing of anybody, and never gave anything in charity. Indeed they never paid their just debts without a sigh or a murmur. In the old Town Book at Bramley the very first entry we find, dated Nov. 17th, 1684, records a list of about a score persons owing together a sum of seventeen shillings to the township, of whom Tho. Iles is separately mentioned as debtor in the sum of 2/4, *which he refuses to pay!* No one exactly knew what they did with their money, but there were rumours of unheard-of treasure stowed away in great chests and secret places of the house. But there is no doubt that Oliver Hiles, the last of the family that occupied the house, inherited great riches, yet he lived very frugally and kept but one servant. In his old age his miserliness knew no bounds ; neither allowing himself nor his servant barely sufficient to eat, and fire only when real necessity compelled it. No one had ever seen lights burning in the lower rooms ; only in an upper chamber had the villagers sometimes been attracted by the soft glare of yellow flame reflected through chinks of the closely-drawn shutters, whence might have been heard faint utterances of impassioned joy, a crazy, meaningless chuckle, mingled with the distinctly audible sound as of the crinkling and tumbling of great heaps of gold. But other eyes and ears had been watching these proceedings besides those of the simple villagers, and one dark and stormy night in the winter of 179—, when as we might be sure no one of good intent was abroad, a ladder was firmly laid against the upper story at the back of the old hall, where a short, coarse-featured man, in low cap and roughly clad, quietly lay secreted. Furnished with the appliances of his sin-born craft he quickly ascended the ladder, and undoing the fastenings of the window, as quickly entered the apartment where old Hiles lay in deep slumber. The intending murderer had previously taken off his boots, and approaching the bed side with stealthy step, his lantern cautiously turned upon the wrinkled visage of the old man, revealed him in his last sleep. With pitiless and disdainful look the ruffian quickly laid his hand upon the sleeper's mouth and with one stroke of a sharp knife did the deed of horror. Searching then the old man's clothes he found his keys and proceeded to examine the chamber. His eye quickly fell upon a large oaken chest, with heavy iron fastenings and securely locked. This he soon opened and raising with difficulty its ponderous lid, his lantern light revealed its glittering and precious contents. There was gold loose and gold in bags, silver also, and even copper, in one of the divisions of the box. Bending now forward to raise some of the bags of coin, the murderer was surprised in the act by the sudden clash of a bell, and turning round beheld the bleeding figure of old Hiles crawling towards him. A second loud clash of the sonorous bell so startled the victim of deceit, that the heavy lid dropped upon his arms and held them as in a vice. He tried in vain to extricate them but his efforts only caused increased laceration, and by their peculiar position he could not raise the lid. Meanwhile the sounds of the bell roused Hiles' old servant, who appearing with a light, and finding her master speechless and motionless in a pool of blood upon the floor, with the savage-eyed fellow on his knees before the chest, apparently unable to free himself, quickly locked the chamber door and went for assistance. This soon arrived, and the man was taken into custody, when it was found that one of his arms was broken above the wrist. He was afterwards tried at York, and suffered the full penalty of the law. Old Hiles died and was decently buried, his money going to a relative; his faithful servant, it is said, shortly afterwards left the old hall, which has since been broken up and used as cottage tenements. The room where the murder was committed is still kept entire, and where, as we have said, the ghost of the unfortunate Oliver Hiles is still believed to hover.

BRAMLEY TO CALVERLEY,
(Distance 3 miles.)

ESCENDING the main road towards Rodley, there is a far-reaching prospect of the country northwards, but the large gasometer which occupies such a central feature in the vale at Calverley Bridge by no means lends "enchantment to the view." High moors, waving woods, and the distant shining river, which here sweeps southwards to the canal in the form of a large letter U to Newlay, meet our gaze, and then, approaching the busy foundries, soon "Rodley greets you." These were words of welcome displayed upon one of the triumphal arches erected at the opening of the Recreation Ground here, in October, 1889, and may they long remain a symbol of good wishes between Rodley folk and the visitor to their thrifty and improving village ! Instead of descending to Calverley station over the Aire bridge, (a short mile), where a larger new road bridge is to be built at a cost of £12,000, (the County Council paying half), in place of the present narrow stone one, which has been here since 1776, we leave the Leeds borough boundary at Rodley and proceed by the open highroad direct one mile to

CALVERLEY,

which, singularly, has its railway station in the township of Horsforth, about a mile off. The village is the centre of a pretty extensive parish, which includes Farsley, Pudsey, part of Stanningley, Idle, &c., and occupies a delightful site above the south banks of the Aire, the tower of its old church standing out picturesquely from many points of view. This venerable fabric well merits attention. It is of Norman origin, but since rebuilt, and in recent years several thousand pounds have been expended upon its restoration. The interior contains some choice ancient and modern stain-glass ; the east window of five lights being especially noteworthy, its upper tracery portrays three angels bearing emblems of the Passion, viz., the hammer and nails, sponge and scourge, and the two lower ones censers. At the base of each light is a shield. A curious and interesting architectural feature of the nave (which is in the Norman style), is the inclined position of the apex of its west arch, which was apparently so constructed to symbolize the leaning of the Head upon the Cross. In the chancel is a superb and costly reredos, in English oak, presented by T. H. Gray, Esq., of Brookleigh. There are also some monumental inscriptions of interest. The valuable registers, which date from 1574, have been carefully copied and printed in convenient volumes by Mr. Saml. Margerison, of Calverley Lodge. In the churchyard are some notable tombstones, one of which reads:

"In memory of Benj. Cromack, son of John and Mary Cromack, of Idle, who departed this life the 25th of September. 1826, aged 25, and who took a coffin 7 ft. 11 in. long. Also Elizabeth Cromack, the mother of John Cromack, who died June 4th, 1827. in her 100th year."

The neighbourhood has a very park-like aspect, with a fair sprinkling of villa residences. Amongst them Calverley House, (S. Milne-Milne, Esq.), occupies an attractive and luxuriant domain, but should not be mistaken for Calverley Hall, the seat of the old Calverley family. This was formerly surrounded by an extensive park, and is not far from the church. Norman in point of age, it has several times been rebuilt, but has long since lost every semblance of its ancient grandeur, being now divided into cottages, whilst the adjoining chapel has been converted into a workshop. But for upwards of six centuries (*ca.* A.D. 1150-1754) the old hall sheltered one of the foremost of English families. The Calverleys, who originally bore the name of Scott, were descended from the Earls of Northumbria, the dauntless and spirited opponents of the equally fearless Conqueror. In the time of Edward III., John de Calverley was knighted by the King's hand, and his son, Sir John, was appointed one of the squires to Anne, Queen of Richard II. His nephew, Sir Walter, who succeeded him as lord of Calverley, caused the church to be rebuilt, and had his family arms—six owls—carved on the woodwork. His successor, Sir John Calverley. Kt., fell along with young Hotspur, at the battle of Shrewsbury, (1403) whilst fighting under the banner of the King. Early in the sixteenth century Sir William Calverley was created a Knight Banneret for his distinguished services during the Scottish Wars ; and his grandson, Sir William, Kt., who died in 1571, filled the important office of Sheriff of Yorkshire. The Calverleys were ever staunch adherents to the Romish faith, and in the reign of Elizabeth suffered considerable penalties, which obliged them to sell large parcels of their estates to pay the heavy fines imposed upon them, simply for their

CALVERLEY OLD HALL.

unwavering adhesion to inherited principles. Although they were a wealthy family—their estates producing near £2000 per annum, (at least £12,000 of present money)—yet these grievous and repeated sacrifices were undoubtedly a burdensome concern, and sensibly increased the family cares and responsibilities.

We now come to a painful episode which sadly defames the career of this illustrious race. In Queen Elizabeth's time Walter Calverley, who had married Philippa, daughter of the Hon. Henry Brooke, fifth son of George, fourth Baron Cobham, proving for many years childless, at last became the happy father of a son and heir. In due time a second and a third son were born, when Calverley, who was a man of strong passions and indulgent habits, began to suspect his wife's fidelity,—suspicions, as it proved, that were totally groundless. A brooding madness preyed upon him, he drank copiously, and in a fit of intoxication seized his eldest born, a child of five years, whom he slew with a dagger; then rushing with the bleeding body to the apartment of its mother, threw it before her, and seizing the second child, killed that likewise, afterwards attempting the life of the terrified wife. He then rode off to where his third and youngest child was at nurse—in a cottage some three miles away—intending to murder it, but was overtaken by his servants and secured. Stow in his "Chronicles," 1604, thus relates the circumstances. "Walter Calverley, of Calverley, Esquire, murdered two of his young children, stabbed his wife in the body with full intent to have murdered her, and instantly went from his house to have slain his youngest child at nurse, but was prevented. For which fact at his triall at Yorke hee stood mute, and was judged to be pressed to death. According to which judgment he was executed at the Castell of Yorke, the 5th August."* His only surviving son Henry, succeeded to the estates, and the mother some time afterwards became the wife of Sir Thomas Burton, Kt. Among several accounts of the crime that appeared was one entitled "A Yorkshire Tragedy, not so new as lamentable, by Master Shakspeare; acted at the Globe, 1608. London, 1610. With a portrait of the brat at nurse." Although the play was published in Shakspeare's lifetime, with his name attached, there is little to support the belief that it was the production of his master mind. A single passage will suffice :

Wife—Good Sir, by all our Vows I do beseeche you,
    Shew me the true cause of your discontent.
Husband—Money, money, money; and thou must supply me.
Wife—Alas, I am the least cause of your discontent;
    Yet what is mine, either in rings or jewels,
    Use to your own desire; but I do beseeche you,
    As you are a Gentleman of many bloods,
    Though I myself be out of your respect,
    Think on the state of the three lovely boys
    You have been father to.
Husband—Puh !——

* The body is said to have been secretly conveyed to Calverley and buried in the Calverley Chapel, and on removing the plaster work here at the restoration of the Church a quantity of bones were found, supposed to be his remains.

Sir Walter Calverley-Blackett in 1754 sold the manor and estate of Calverley to Thomas Thornhill, Esq., of Fixby, in whose family it still remains. Sir Walter was created a baronet by Queen Anne in 1711, the title becoming extinct in 1777, on the death, without surviving issue, of his son Sir Walter Calverley-Blackett. The old hall dates from about the time of Henry VII. The room in which the murder was committed is still existing, although the interior arrangements of the house were long ago altered to their present uses. The park extended a considerable distance eastwards, and before the present roads were made there were a number of very fine chestnut trees adjoining the hall, only one of which is now standing.

Calverley to Farsley, 1¼ m. The direct route passes the *Thornhill Arms* Hotel (formerly the *Old Leopard*) and several handsome houses to the Farsley Baptist Chapel (erected in 1868 at a cost of £4000). Or a pleasant round walk (1¾ m.) is up Shell Lane, and when at the top turn down past old **Wadlands Hall** (now a farm) on *l.*, a very ancient edifice that belonged in the fifteenth and sixteenth centuries to the Bollings, of Bolling Hall, and to the Tempests, of Bracewell and Tong.

Farsley (pop. with Calverley, 6680) is a thriving place with some fine big mills. It is notable as the birthplace of the Rev. Samuel Marsden, the celebrated missionary and the first exporter of Australian wool to England. A stone in Turner's Fold commemorates his birth there in 1764. He died at Sydney, Australia, in 1838, whither he had migrated in his 30th year. In 1808 he came to England with a cargo of the Botany wool, and obtaining an audience of King George III., his Majesty ordered a suit of clothes to be manufactured from the wool, which was taken and woven at the old Park Mill at Rawdon. Mr. Marsden laboured hard among the native tribes of Australia and New Zealand, teaching them religion, agriculture, and sheep farming. Upon his death a handsome memorial to him was erected in Sydney at a cost of £6000, and in his native village of Farsley (where he had originally worked as a blacksmith) a beautiful tribute to him adorns the chancel of the church of St. John the Evangelist, and there is a granite monument also erected to his memory in the churchyard.

CALVERLEY TO APPERLEY BRIDGE.
(*Distance* 1¼ *miles.*)

 BROAD extent of ancient woodland sweeps down to the vale below Calverley, and these fine woods were once continuous with the present Buck Woods below Thackley, and circumvested the hills of Wrose, Frizinghall, and Bolton to Bradford, forming a green and unbroken mantle many miles around. Where these woods have been cleared evidences of their former existence are still preserved in the *carrs*, *woods*, *hirsts*, and *holts* of the surrounding places, and in the names of the trees peculiar to them, such as Buck (*buch*, *i.e.* beech), Hollin (holly), Esholt (eshe, *i.e.* ash), and possibly also Apperley (for *abele*, the grey poplar, from the city of Arbela, in Nineveh, whence it was imported, a tree rather rare in the district now). In the middle ages, these woods contained thousands of oaks, which in season provided a staple article of food for the herds of swine that pastured in them. Foxes too, as in other parts of Airedale, were here once very numerous, and up to about the middle of last century as much as a shilling a head was awarded, according to Act of Parliament, by the parish authorities for their capture and destruction. Entries of such payments are frequent in local town-books.

These extensive woods give a stately feature to the landscape, and are the old haunts of many uncommon birds. Some birds of prey, including the kite and sparrow-hawk, which feed on small game, and being especially partial to young ducks and chickens, must have been a trouble to the farmer at one time, still nest here. But they are very rare now and do no harm, preferring the recesses of the woods where the small birds are kept in subjection by them.* Then

---

* But two centuries ago these birds of prey, were, like the foxes, so common in Airedale, that they were included in the awards settled by the Act for their destruction.

there is the cunning magpie, with his shiny black bill and feet, and long glossy tail of banded purple and green ; also the curious tree-creeper may sometimes be noted here, holding on to the tree trunks or running up them with the alacrity of a mouse. The sedge-warbler, too, makes alive the Calverley woods with his full song ; he has rich, varied, and fluent notes, and is often mistaken for the nightingale, when it pleases him to " trill to the silent moon his sweet lonesome lay." The cuckoo, too, pays them an annual visit, and the *crake, crake* of the landrail may also be heard in the vicinity in the long evenings of summer.

Our walk is by a green lane near the schools and by the field-side adjoining the carriage drive of Ferncliffe, the beautiful residence of Briggs Priestley, Esq., M.P. The house, erected some 35 years ago, is in the Italian style, and surrounded by extensive grounds, where art mingles with a natural wildness among boulder, and moss, and fern. Mr. Priestley, who represents the Pudsey division in Parliament, has the interests of the working people at heart, and every movement calculated for their benefit has his support. In 1870 the Factories' Half-day Holiday Committee presented him with a handsome illuminated address as a token of his labours in their behalf. A little way below the lodge the wood is entered on *l.*, and the famous quarries of Rough-rock past, and down by the old Tomling Well on to the wood bottom, we continue our pleasant walk between the canal and the flower-spangled wood as far as the Underwood farm, where the road is entered at the castellated archway of Thornhill Lodge, whence *r*. down to the Aire side at

APPERLEY.

The view from the bridge is very pleasing ; beautiful woods, stately halls, and fertile meads are to been seen from this coign of vantage. It moreover possesses singular interest in being the scene of a great "religious" gathering in the year 1824. John Wroe, a native of West Bowling, and a so-called "Prophet of the Lord," was the recognised leader of the Southcottian movement in this district. The famous Johanna herself, who, according to her own declaration, was to have been the mother of Shiloh, and to have lived for ever!

disappointed her believers by dying like ordinary mortals, in consequence of which event, had it not been for the timely influence of "Prophet" Wroe, whose steadfast faith and eloquence and insinuating prophecies roused her followers into new belief, the movement here might have suffered an ignoble collapse. But as there have always been bigots and fanatics ready to support doctrines however plausible or strange, so in Wroe's case, apostles of help rallied around the new "hero of light," and with no small success either. Their cause, however, suffered a disastrous shock, when on the last day of February, 1824, the "Prophet" declared his intention of walking upon the waters of the Aire, near Idle Thorpe, and glory-making sunbeams were to illumine his head during the act! This at any rate was the popular impression. On the same occasion his public baptism was solemnly announced upon a printed placard, whereon was stated: "At which holy ordinance appropriate hymns (accompanied by a select band of music) will be sung, and immediately after, William Twigg, *one of the witnesses mentioned in Rev., chap. ii.*, will preach the everlasting Gospel, as revealed by the Redeemer of the World." Many thousands of people followed the "Prophet" and his disciples, the former of whom, appropriately attired, rode upon an ass, down to the Aire at Apperley, where it is said by one o'clock fully 30,000 persons had assembled. Every available vantage was secured, the bridge, roofs of houses, and branches of trees were crowded with people anxious to obtain a sight of the promised miracle. There is a tree standing upon the north side of the bridge, from which, we are told, a branch fell into the river with a youth astride it, who narrowly escaped drowning. Another tree also gave way entirely, and precipitated some of its occupants into the river. However, the grand design of this great meeting, as might have been expected, was a gross *fiasco*, a blasphemous imposture; the sun certainly shone a little, but the Aire, of course, flowed on in a natural way, and the "Prophet," who greatly imperilled his life by the venture, presently very prudently retreated. Indeed he escaped with difficulty, protected by his people, followed by the crowd armed with stones and sods, and there was something of a riot. Crowds continued to visit the place for several days afterwards, and there were some of the 'Prophet's' faithful ones who devoutly believed he would "do it yet." Wroe, himself, we doubt not, if eccentric, was actuated by a good heart, having an unshaken faith in his own peculiar doctrines, and no doubt inspired good in others. His house, in Park Road, West Bowling, is still standing. He was born here in 1782, and died in Australia in 1862, not less to the chagrin than surprise of his numerous followers in the salubrious colony, to whom he had publicly announced his intention of living for ever!

The bridge at Apperley is of remote origin, and in the Middle Ages was no doubt a plain wooden structure, suitable for foot passengers; used doubtless also by the wild four-footed creatures infesting the neighbouring forests. During the reign of Esholt Priory the bridge was maintained by this establishment, in consideration of fishing-rights over certain reaches of the Aire. There are traces of an ancient paved ford a short distance below the present bridge, and the inn near by, enlarged in 1704, as its Latin inscription inside relates, was in all probability the ford-house. The present bridge was erected after the great flood of 1776, and situate at a somewhat important junction on the old coaching road from Manchester, Bradford, Halifax. &c., to York, Durham, Newcastle, and the north, is a solid and substantial stone structure of two wide-spread arches. Just above the north side of it is the old toll-house.

Apperley is in the townships of Eccleshill, Idle, and Rawdon, each of which now forms a distinct ecclesiastical parish. The country around is an attractive one to the visitor, being beautifully wooded and adorned with villa residences of the Leeds and Bradford gentry. John Wesley called it the Caprera of Yorkshire.

Apperley to Esholt, 2 m. Many people coming from Bradford for a morning or afternoon's out take this walk, and it is a favourite one with the local residents too. The walks about Esholt Springs are very delightful, although the woods are private. Esholt Avenue, which is reached by a lane opposite Apperley sta., or from the *Stansfield Arms*, is a charming long promenade composed principally of Dutch elms, the vista being bounded by the thick woods around Esholt Hall. Neither the avenue nor the long road beyond is provided with seats, a desideratum to ladies especially who visit this long and favourite walk, unable to find a convenient resting-place. From the end of the long walk on the Guiseley road it is good ¾ m. to Esholt village.

Apperley to Idle, 1 m. To those who wish to reach Bradford or intermediate stations on the G. N. railway this is the most convenient route. From Apperley Bridge go up Milman Lane and cross the canal direct up the New Road to Idle sta.

RAWDON

may be reached from either Apperley (the nearer) or Calverley stations. From Apperley Bridge it is an uphill walk of about 1¾ m., obtaining on right a view of the pleasantly-placed Woodhouse Grove Wesleyan School, established in 1812, and passing near to the road Upperwood (T. A. Firth, Esq.), where the distinguished authoress of 'Jane Eyre,' &c., Charlotte Brontë, was for some time governess in the family of the late John White, Esq. Charlotte Brontë's mother was a Miss Branwell, niece of Mr. John Fennell, who at the time of her marriage (at Guiseley church in 1812) with the Rev. Patrick Brontë, was head master of the Woodhouse Grove School. For forty years (1820-61) the home of the Brontë's, as everyone knows, was Haworth Parsonage. Above Upperwood is Acacia, formerly seat of the late Sir H. W. Ripley, Bart., and above the lodge a road winds pleasantly through the Buckstone estate on to the Leeds road at Rawdon.

Here we are at an elevation of 6-700 feet, and every visitor who comes to Rawdon on a fine day ought to ascend the Billing, an eminence (750 ft.) crowning the north side of the village, which commands, undoubtedly, one of the best views in mid Airedale. We have been able to distinguish upwards of twenty village churches from this summit, besides the double tower of York Minster, and the thirty-mile distant hills of upper Craven and Wharfedale.*

For many centuries Rawdon was the seat of the ancient family of that name, the manor having been granted by the Conqueror to Paulyn de Roydon, or Rowdon, for his successes at the battle of Hastings in A.D. 1066. During the Civil Wars George Rawdon, a Royalist officer, was created a baronet (A.D. 1665) for his eminent services in Ireland. Sir

* See the Author's " Pleasant Walks around Bradford."

John, fourth baronet, was created Baron Rawdon of Moira, in 1750, and Earl of Moira in 1762, both in the peerage of Ireland. His son Francis, the second earl, inherited the baronies of Hastings, Hungerford, Botreux, and Molines, and was created Marquis of Hastings in 1816. He was born in 1754, and died in 1825, having served with distinction in the American wars, when he rose to a generalship. In 1813 he was appointed Governor-General of India, which office he retained until 1823, when, in his 70th year, he changed for the less onerous Governorship of Malta. He was a

RAWDON OLD HALL.

brilliant statesman, a wise and high-principled governor, generous and cultured, and made the government popular. During his tenure of office in India he did a great deal for the amelioration of the poorer classes, and by his action also the ruling power of the provinces was greatly improved and strengthened. Nearly the whole of his prize-money, amounting in the ten years of his Indian administration to upwards of £100,000, he ungrudgingly devoted to the public use. Some idea of his inner life and public activity may be gathered from the *Private Journal of the Marquis of Hastings*, edited in 1858 by his daughter, the Marchioness of Bute. His grandson Paulyn Reginald Serlo, dying celibate in 1851, his brother, Henry Weysford, succeeded to the marquisate, but he died in 1868, at the early age of 26, having by his excesses on the turf brought himself almost to the verge of bankruptcy. He was fourth marquis, and with him the titles expired.

It was George Rawdon, grandfather of Sir George above mentioned, who built the old Hall yet standing, and his initials, with those of his wife, are to be seen above the large entrance porch. It is a roomy old Elizabethan mansion, retaining both in its outer and inner aspects much of its original character. The present tenant, Major Harrison, possesses an excellently mounted collection of natural history objects, consisting chiefly of foreign birds. The last of the Rawdon family that resided here was Priscilla, sister of Sir George, but the house, with some forty acres of land, is still held by the Hastings family, and a branch of the old Rawdon family still remain lords of the manor.

All the high ground extending from Rawdon by Yeadon to Hawksworth, Baildon, and Rumbalds Moor has undoubtedly been in the occupation of the ancient Celtic tribes driven to these wild heights by the conquering invaders. This is not only evidenced in the derivative British names of the places so situated, but in actual discoveries made, and remains still existing of a remote age. Of these we shall have more to say in our chapter on Baildon. On the Billing at Rawdon there was dug up, rather over a century ago, a magnificent example of a British torque or collar of pure gold, consisting of two plain rods twisted together, and valued intrinsically at £18 sterling. What has become of this highly-interesting relic we have not been able to make out. It was claimed by the lord of the manor. In 1849 two similar gold collars were found in a tumulus at the Grottes de Roch-Guyon, near Plouharnel, in Brittany.

Sloping southwards to the Aire the sunny and sheltered acclivities of Rawdon have been admirably chosen for villa residences, and for institutions requiring a healthy and retired situation. The Baptist College, removed from Horton Lane, Bradford, in 1858, is a handsome and commodious erection here well suited for purposes of study. It is a Tudor structure, by a Cardiff architect, admirably fitted, and among other features of interest is a beautiful stain-window to the memory of a former student, the Rev. John Mackay, who was killed, whilst engaged as a missionary in India, at the siege of Delhi. Not far from the College is the Woodlands Convalescent Home, founded by the late Sir H. W. Ripley, Bart., formerly M.P. for Bradford, and opened by the Marquis of Salisbury on Oct. 10th, 1877. The grounds cover about 12 acres, and the pleasant walks within them and in the vicinity afford unequivocal proof of the advantages of the Home to inmates, who are aided during convalescence by the pure air and beautiful scenery.

Rawdon to Bramhope (*see* p. 72), over the 'Toughs' and Moor Top by the Bleach Works and None-go-by farm (4¼ m.). To **Otley** (*see* p. 73), by the Yeadon Moor high-road, passing the Dam on *l.* and the stone pillar (Long Stoop) to the four-road ends (3 m.), whence *l.* over the Chevin (925 ft.) down to Otley. From Rawdon, 5¼ m. Both these are delightful walks over high ground, undulating, and commanding rich prospects.

Proceeding now from

RAWDON TO ESHOLT,
(*Distance* 2½ *miles*),

we take the road to Little London, and crossing the Apperley road follow a field track down to the railway, emerging under the bridge on Gill Wood Lane, a charming locality, rich in wild flowers and surrounded by woods alive with the songs of many birds. A little to the right is Yeadon Low Hall, a seventeenth century building, which has been in the occupation of the Barwick family for at least twelve generations. In a picturesque and sheltered locality, its gardens and conservatories contain a large variety of choice and many very old plants, and are often visited by kind permission of the present owner, J. M. Barwick, Esq. Our turn is to the left by a pleasantly shaded walk through Esholt Springs to the ancient and semi-deserted village of

ESHOLT,

a "Sweet Auburn" in its loveliness and decay, for the erst "busy mill" is silent now, and moss and grass are spreading over the stonework of its many deserted cottages. Trade here for some reason or other cannot be remunerative, for the people have sought employment elsewhere. Those houses that are occupied lie snugly amid leafy surroundings and gardens teeming with roses and fruit trees. Native woods also spread away to the horizon, and shelter them from the north winds. What a delicious retreat this must have been for the small company of Cistercian nuns who had their habitation here from the middle of the twelfth to the

YEADON LOW HALL.

sixteenth century! This secluded Nunnery was dedicated to God, St. Mary, and St. Leonard. But nothing remains of the design of the structure now, for when Sir Walter Calverley built the present large and handsome Hall in the early part of last century, it is generally thought to have been wholly removed then, and some of the material used in the erection of the Hall, which occupies its site. Several pointed arches and ancient carved stones are noticeable in the building, which countenance the supposition. Behind the mansion lay the nuns' burial ground, where several of the old Calverley family were buried, as well as other local notabilities. Numerous bones have been dug up here. The **Old Hall**, near the church, in the village is a substantial and well-preserved building of fifteenth century age. It is now divided into cottages, and is gabled, with mullion windows and curious projecting gargoyles. The cellars are vaulted, and contain ancient wells. Around the house are distinct evidences of a moat. Prior to the erection of Esholt Hall the Calverley family resided here, and the manor and estate were also for a time the property of the ancient Catholic family of Sherburn, the last male descendant, Sir Nicholas Sherburn, Bart., dying at Stonyhurst, near Blackburn, in 1717, bequeathed the Esholt, Guiseley, and other estates in Yorkshire and Lancashire, to his daughter Mary, Duchess of Norfolk.

Shortly after the erection of the new mansion now known as **Esholt Hall**, a dispute arose between the above Sir Nicholas Sherburn and Sir Walter Calverley about a dam and cut which the latter had made for conveying water to the house.* Sir Nicholas contended that the piece of land through which the cut was made was his property, while Sir Walter took an opposite view of the case, enclosed the land, and claimed the right of way. An interesting record in the *Diary* of Sir Walter Calverley shews how the dispute terminated. It is dated 15th Aug., 1705, and is as follows :

"1 went from Esholt to go to Sir Nicholas Sherburn's, of Stonyhurst, and took with me Mr. Emott. Mr. Rawson, of Bradford, met us at Skipton, and we went that night to Gisborn, and lay there, and the next day to Stonyhurst ; and after dinner had discourse about the dam and cutt I had made for bringing the water, and Sir Nicholas seemed very courteous, and said I would not ask anything which he would not grant, and for any small acknowledgment yielded, I should not only have that, but liberty to make any other cutt, and particularly over Simpson and Tiddiswell Crofts, and to get stone, &c., and I thought it had been fully agreed that I should give Sir Nicholas some small consideration, and for that should have liberty granted to me and my heirs, to maintain, repair, and continue the said dam and cutt as I should think fit. Sir Nicholas yielded that it might be with a proviso not to prejudice the right I had to the wast, below or under

* " There was about two tuns and 32 stone of lead used in making the pipes, which with charge of workmanship and laying, and with cocks, &c., cost above £40."—*Diary*, 8th Sept., 1703.

the cutt I had already made; and pursuant to that agreement I ordered a paper to be drawn up next morning in manner of articles to that effect, but when I came to shew it, Sir Nicholas wanted the way to be inserted for leave for his tenants to go down my grounds, in consideration of granting me the libertyes above, and proposed that if I would grant that liberty to him and his heirs, he would pay a yearly acknowledgment, and likewise that his tenants should be at the charge of repairing the way, but I told him that I could not condescend to that, for that the libertyes he proposed to grant me were no ways equivalent to what he desired me to grant him. * * * I always insisted upon it, that the parcell of ground over which the cutt was made belonged to me, and that I could make better proof thereof than what Sir Nicholas could make appear for himself about it; whereupon it was proposed by one Mr. Hornby, who was with us all the time, and appeared as agent for Sir Nicholas, that Sir Nicholas should grant me the libertyes, as above, to me and my heirs, and that in consideration thereof I should grant Sir Nicholas the liberty of the way during my life; to which proposal Sir Nicholas seemed to comply on his part, but I refused to accept thereof, upon which the treaty of accommodation broke off, and we came away."*

The Hall, above mentioned, has been the home of the Stansfield family since 1775, when Sir Walter Calverley-Blackett sold the estate to Robert Stansfield. He having no issue, gave it to his sister Ann, wife of Wm. Rookes, and at their deaths it was again transmitted, in the female line, to their daughter, Anna Maria, who married Joshua Crompton, Esq., of York, whose eldest son, Wm. Rookes Crompton, took the name and bore the arms of Stansfield. The mansion, which is built after the design of the old residence of the Calverleys, at Wallington, in Northumberland, is surrounded by a fine park, and forms a noble back-ground in the vista from Esholt Avenue, which was planted by Sir Walter Calverley when the house was built. The interior of the hall contains some rich wainscotting and curiously carved oak. Historical documents of the family and of the extinct Esholt Priory (many in curious Norman-French) are likewise preserved here.

The Aire, which here makes a beautiful curvature under Idle Hill, was in pre-mercantile days specially famous for the size and quality of its fish. They were considered finer than, and in several respects differed from, those in the

* *Vide Diary of Sir Walter Calverley, Bart.* (Vol. 77 of Surtees Society's Publications).

Wharfe, but the two sorts sometimes got singularly mixed. The Aire trout were accustomed to ascend the springs above Esholt woods to spawn, which were also the source of the brook flowing through Hell Hole Ghyll, under Otley Chevin, into the Wharfe, whither fish from the latter river would come for a similar purpose, and forgetting their respective ways would descend the opposite rivulets. Fine sport was obtainable in the river bordering Esholt Park, and in 1821, Mr. Crompton, jun., hooked a 7 lb. trout here, which is probably the largest fish of that species ever taken from the Aire.

The walks to and around Esholt are very attractive; from Shipley to Esholt, 2¼ m., and from Esholt to Guiseley, 2¼ m., or Yeadon, 2¼ m., or Hawksworth, 1¾ m., being favourite short excursions.

From

ESHOLT TO IDLE,

(Distance 2¼ miles).

is also a nice walk, and we accomplish this by leaving the west end of the avenue, and crossing the suspension bridge over the Aire, ascend the Thistle Holme and over the canal, up through the fields, from which we have a charming prospect over the vale behind, and so on to the road that takes us up to the high-situated and prosperous village of

IDLE,

whose strangely-spelled name is, indeed, a standing calumny on its character for thrift and industry. Mr. J. Horsfall Turner, the local Thoresby, resident here, maintains, and we think rightly, that the present spelling is a corruption of the older form of Idel, Idill, Ydell, &c., met with in documents of pre-Reformation times, and that it plainly indicates the hill or elevated land of its Saxon possessor *Ide*, or *Ida*, precisely as Adel, near Leeds, is admittedly the *hill of Ada*. There is also a small property in the township called *Idlaw*, doubtless so called from having been held by the Ides in ancient times. This family is included in the Poll Tax levied on the township by the spendthrift King Richard II., in A.D. 1379. There were about 62 inhabitants in Idle and

Windhill subject to this tax, who paid a groat, or fourpence each, afterwards raised to three groats on every person above fifteen years of age ; with what result the sad rebellion of history recounts.

The most important family resident in Idle in olden times was the Plumptons, who acquired the manor from the Lacies, with a number of others in Yorkshire some time after the Conquest. Nigel de Plumpton, about 1210, gave to the nuns at Esholt an essart or 21½ acres of land in Idel, and his grandson Nigel likewise bequeathed a meadow, and (with his corpse, to be buried at Esholt), "all his lands beneath the essarts (or clearings) called Eholm, Strangford, and Aldrodrode in this territory." About a century later Sir Robert Plumpton was a dauntless foeman to the King, and had married a sister of Richard Scrope, the famous Archbishop of York, by whom he left a son, Sir William, who was beheaded with that prelate for joining in the allied plot against the King (Henry IV.), in 1405. The Plumptons, who were always staunch Catholics, continued to reside at Idle and at Roecliffe up to about the time of the Reformation. The Roecliffe portion of the manor went by marriage to Sir Ingram Clifford, who, dying without issue, left it to his nephew, George, Earl of Cumberland, father of the celebrated Countess of Pembroke. Lord George had the manor of Idle surveyed in 1583-4, on which occasion it is stated of the Manor House, then called Idle Hall, that it "be greatly decayed," yet "in convenient repaire for the use of the tenants who dwell therein." The hall is believed to have occupied the site of the Post Office buildings, being "at the north-east corner of the town, near unto a well." It was surrounded by a large park, and had "a pretty lodge wherein the keeper dwelt when deer was kept there." A portion of the boundary wall of the park still remains near Hill Top, and its existence is also preserved in such local names as Park Hill, Park Lodge, &c. At this time the township, which included the hamlets of Thorp, Wrose, and Windhill, was thickly wooded, there being not less than 250 acres of forest, and common or waste lands equivalent to 236 acres.

How different the Idle of to-day, with its every acre enclosed, its mills, and schools, and many houses, and 8000 of a population! The old Chapel would be in existence then, although the present building dates from 1630, and is now used for the Church Institute. The Church here, built by Government, dates from 1830, and there are also some splendid Chapels, notably the Wesleyan, erected in 1871, at a cost of about £10,000.

The visitor ought to, if the weather be fine, ascend **Idle Hill** (750 ft.) which is 1 m. from the station. The summit is occupied by a reservoir belonging to Bradford, but the promenade round it is open only on Saturdays and Sundays from April 1st to Sept. 30th, on Sundays all day and on Saturdays after 1 p.m. It occupies a singularly commanding position at the junction of Bradford dale with Airedale, and the view embraces the country as far as the Pennines westward, the moors of Wharfedale northward, and to the south and east the L'enholme and Thornton moors and low lands below Leeds. Some Roman coins and a human skeleton were discovered near the summit about a century ago, when the ground was first ploughed, and there is little doubt that it was the site of a Roman camp, and at a later period one of those "bekyns" ordained by the Commissioners for signal-fires in times of national alarm.

The G.N. railway from Laisterdyke to Windhill (Shipley), opened in 1875, has a station at Idle, so that the visitor who may wish to run into Bradford, may do so by train quickly. From Bradford to the stations at Eccleshill, Idle, Thackley, or Shipley, the 3rd cl. fare is 3d. The distance by road from Idle to Bradford (descent) is 3¼ m. There is also a 'bus about every hour between Bradford (Mid. Sta.) and Eccleshill (Mechs. Inst.), whence Idle is 1 m.

THE EXCHANGE, MARKET STREET, BRADFORD.

BRADFORD.

Area of Borough, 10,776 acres.

Pop. *(1881)*, 194,491 ; *(1891)*, est. 240,000.*

Distance from LONDON, 193 m. MANCHESTER, 40 m. HULL, 65 m.
SHEFFIELD, 40 m. CARLISLE, 104, m. GLASGOW, 207½ m.

AIREDALE has many side valleys, but none more important in a modern historical sense than that which strikes southward from Shipley to Bradford, a distance of three miles. Like its neighbours, the Harden and Worth valleys, it has its tributary beck, which, notwithstanding the large sums annually expended in filtration at the works at Frizinghall, about midway in the dale, still flows in fetid blackness to the Aire. Yet there are persons still living who can remember trout and other fish sporting in the beck in the heart of the town! That very haunt of Salus is now a covered-in drain, over which the roar of traffic passes daily!

Bradford owes its name to this invisible stream. Three other important tributaries, coming from Thornton, Eastbrook and West Bowling, unite in the town, and form what is commonly called the Bradford Beck, which then flows on to the Aire at Shipley, as above stated. Many other minor open streams and watercourses fretted the hill sides around the town, and these after heavy rains so augmented the main body of water in the centre of the town (the present Forster Square) that in order to ascend Church Hill from the west the stream had to be forded, a method of passage which doubtless originated in pre-Roman days. Following or

---

* The borough of Bradford is much more thickly populated than that of Leeds; the former, on the estimated population of 1891, averaging about 22 souls per acre, and the latter 16.

co-eval with the original ford was a long line of stepping stones, and this particular spot was known up to the recent street improvements as *Broadstones*, a name that will be found in any late directory of the town. Thus Bradford was the *broad ford*, the *Bradeford* (A.S. *brade*, broad), of Domesday.* Draining, mining, and cultivation subsequently reduced the flow of water to the dimensions of a comparatively small beck, over which a one-arch bridge was constructed, yet so disastrous occasionally were the floods at this part, even up to our own time,† that the bridge here appears repeatedly to have been swept away. This was notably the case in 1768, when the town, such as it was at that date, suffered immense damage. In the Brigantian, or earliest period of its settled occupation, and probably long after, there is little doubt that the great basin in which the town lies would after unusual floodings present the appearance of a wide-spreading lake, surrounded by luxuriant forests of oak, beech, alder, maple, &c., in which numerous beasts of chase and other smaller animals ran wild. Near the Ive bridge, at the foot of Ivegate, in ancient times was a verdant piece of land called the Holme, a name plainly indicative of lake-like environs. We make no doubt that so favoured a situation, commanding the several valleys and passes which gave access to the town, was the chosen haunt of the native tribes who in course of time settled into a rude form of civilization, with all the accompaniments of an established domestic community. The huts or dwellings of these people, which we have elsewhere described, would occupy the eastern acclivities of the broad stream which washed the foot of Church Hill, and from which an abundant supply of pure water was readily obtainable. Around these homes of the early Britons ranged the primeval forest (mentioned in *Domesday*) extending from Bradford northward by Bolton, Frizinghall, and Thackley, along the slopes of Airedale, and of which the most extensive lingering

* Of like Germanic origin is the name of the town (with castle) of Bredevoort (*i.e., broad ford*) in Gelderland (Holland), on the border of Westphalia.

† In 1859 for example, damage to the amount of over £40,000 was done by floods in the centre of the town.

remnant is Buck Wood. Over the forest ground about their dwellings, too, spread the fruitful bramble, hazel, wild rose, and fragrant honey-suckle, of which the Britons are said to have been especially fond. Herds of domestic swine browsed on the acorns that fell from the tall oaks, then most abundant in these woods, and in times of scarcity these acorns also provided an important food for the people. When the Romans came about the dawn of the Christian era, these rude tribes would no doubt take refuge on the higher hills, a forced migration that we shall speak of more fully in our chapter on Baildon. Such positions they continued to hold with greater freedom from molestation until united by family relations with the later conquering races. Bradford, however, no more than Leeds, does not appear to have been a Roman settlement, but merely a passing place on the great roads between Manchester, Dewsbury, and Ilkley, and between Castleford and Colne. If it was a Roman station, all traces of it have been lost. Cleckheaton, however, would appear to have been the chief seat of the Roman householders in the neighbourhood of Bradford, for in the early part of last century, that painstaking investigator of the antiquities of this district, Dr. Richardson, of Bierley Hall, discovered here extensive remains of Roman villas as well as numerous coins ; likewise, near Bierley, heaps of iron scoriæ covered by a considerable depth of mould,—the remains of rude smelting works, unquestionably also Roman.

We need not trace the vicissitudes of the Bradford people down to the Norman period, at which time the town was the capital *vill* of the manor, which included six berewicks or hamlets—probably the two Hortons, Manningham, Haworth, Oxenhope, and Stanbury. Bolling, (or Bowling as now called) it may be remarked, was a separate manor, merged like that of Bradford in the great Honour of Pontefract. In Saxon times there were some 1500 acres in the Bradford Manor in cultivation, (probably half of it in corn), and a flourishing settled population, but when the merciless Conqueror came with his band of trained warriors, fire and sword decimated this industrious population, and laid the country in ruins. In was then given to one of the "heroes" of this mighty conquest, the great Ilbert de Lacy, (*see* PONTEFRACT), and the wretched, simple record of Bradford in *Domesday*, (A.D. 1086) is, "*Ilbert has it, and it is waste.*', In all probability, —Mr. James, in his *History of Bradford*, uses the word "undoubtedly,"—a castle stood here at the capital of the manor, but by whom or when erected and demolished we are left in ignorance. Like the fated fabric at Leeds it is a mystery, in so far as actual historical knowledge is concerned. We have, however, in the Leeds division of our work, and in the chapters on Airmyn and Drax, (pp. 8-10) sufficiently explained the probable existence of many castles or castlets along the valley of the Aire, of which all record appears to have perished. But if ever Bradford had its castle, we may be sure it would not be far from the church and the ford. James supposes it have stood somewhere to the north-west of the present Parish Church, where was an enclosure called Baily Croft, and that the "Aula" or Manor Hall, mentioned in an Inquisition of the lands of the Earl of Lincoln in A.D. 1311, was built out of the ruins on its site. This is where the Hall Garth lay, and after the above Inquisition was taken the meadow lands to the south of the Hall were called Hall Ings, a name by which one of Bradford's busiest streets, in this ancient domain of the Lacies, is known at this day. It is interesting to note that the land here at that time, now in the very heart of the town, was valued at 8d. an acre. In our time £30 and upwards has been paid for a single square yard of it! At the early period referred to, the lord of Bradford had a valuable corn water-mill here (worth £10 yearly); a fulling-mill (thus shewing "the Bradford trade" was already established) of the annual value of 20s.; and a market dating from A.D. 1251, the tolls of which yielded annually the sum of £3. The market was long held on the *Sabbath*, in or near the churchyard, a custom which prevailed in England up to the time of Elizabeth, especially in country districts having a scattered population, which necessitated the people coming often long distances.

The early history of the Bradford manor is coincident with that of Pontefract already described. From the Lacies it passed to the Earls of Lancaster, and in the reign of Edward III. descended, by marriage of Blanche, co-heiress of the great house of Lancaster, to the powerful John of

Gaunt. This famous prince used to rest in Bradford during his periodical "progresses" through his extensive dominions, and as before pointed out, Airedale was the scene of many a lively and gallant chase by him and his retainers after the bounding stag, savage boar, or even an occasional wolf, which infested the wilds of the valley. A curious appurtenance of these "royal hunts," which is said to have been originated by him, lingered in Bradford until the present century. This was the blowing of a horn in winter on the occasion of the great Duke visiting Bradford, and in requital a grant of land was made to one John Northrop, of Manningham, and his heirs, who, in addition to this interesting duty, had to wait upon his august chief, and his heirs, with a lance and hunting-dog for thirty days; receiving for yeoman's board, one penny for himself and a half-penny for his dog. A piece of land was afterwards granted by the said "heirs of Northrop" to one Rushforth, of Horton, to hold the lance while Northrop's man blew the horn. This horn is now preserved in the Bradford Public Museum, although it is deprived of its original ornaments.

On the death of John of Gaunt, the Bradford manor was seized by Richard II., and on his unhappy end in 1399, (*see* PONTEFRACT) it passed to the Crown, and after various transmissions through private owners, it has since 1795 been held by the family of Rawson. No event of striking importance marked the town's history for a couple of centuries—up to the time of the Civil Wars. During this bitter and unseemly struggle, when Englishmen pitted against Englishmen deluged their country with their own best blood, Bradford in common with the two other principal trading centres in this district, Leeds and Halifax, sided with the Parliament. The first action in the north, says General Fairfax in his *Memoirs*, took place at Bradford, on Sunday, Dec. 18th, 1642, which ended in a sortie and repulse of the Royalists. During this and subsequent engagements, the parish church was garrisoned by the home troops and the tower hung round with wool packs to protect it from the cannonade of the besieging army, which was stationed on the eminence of Barkerend, some few hundred paces from the church. In the following summer, after the daring stand made by

Fairfax against the overwhelming forces of Newcastle on Adwalton Moor, the town sustained a second siege, and was only spared from destruction and ruin by the timely intervention, tradition says, of a female apparition before the sleeping Earl of Newcastle in one of the rooms of Bowling Hall, where he had taken up his abode for the night. Evidently, the story goes, deeply impressed by the appearance of this gentle spirit and its weeping plaintive appeal, "*Pity poor Bradford, Pity poor Bradford!*" the gallant Earl rescinded his horrible order to slay every man, woman, and child, and give instead quarter to all. Fairfax, however, retreated by way of Apperley Bridge to Leeds,* and a sufficient garrison being left in the town by the victorious Royalists, Newcastle withdrew his army soon afterwards to the Midlands. We need not follow the oft-told story of the War further. In and around the church, and about old buildings taken down in the town, various relics of the memorable conflict have from time to time been found. The tower of the church, says Lister, the contemporary historian of the "Sore Calamities that befel Bradford" during the war, received "many a sad shake," but from the size and calibre of the shot found none appears to have been larger than eight pounders, so that the damage to this sturdy edifice could not on the whole have been great.

From the time of the War for upwards of a century the town remained practically stationary. Its population in 1781 numbered but 4200 persons, and in 1801 it had increased to 6393, whilst the borough at this time totalled 13,624. The advances made by the town during the present century have, indeed, been marvellous. With an estimated population of 240,000 persons the borough has now attained a magnitude and importance exceeded by few other towns in the kingdom. Though inferior in population to Leeds, yet in actual wealth it is not, for in prosperous years the town has paid income tax on as much as ten millions sterling, a sum we believe not exceeded by its great industrial neighbour.† We have before

* The bridge at Kirkstall having been blown up by the Royalists.

† Compare again the present (1890) ratable value of property and population in Bradford with other large towns : Bradford, (240,000)

alluded to the "sleepy" character of Leeds in past ages, and in the time of Henry VIII. old Leland, the topographer, who visited both places, observes this circumstance as follows : " Ledis, two miles lower than Christeal Abbey on Aire ryver, is a praty market, having one paroche chirche, reasonably well builded, (that is the town) and *as large as Bradeforde, but not so quik as it*." Again he speaks of Bradford as " a praty *quik* market tonne."

This epithet "quick" has been more than justified, especially by the rapid expansion of the town during the current century. A century ago there was a fair amount of wool-combing, spinning, and weaving carried on in the neighbourhood, but this was done by hand in the homes of the inhabitants, and from wool grown often at the very doors of the houses where it was wrought. The first spinning-jenny was set up in Bradford in 1790, and in 1798 the first mill chimney inaugurated with monumental prominence the era of local prosperity, on which the town has founded a world-wide reputation as the great centre of the wool and worsted trades. As offering some idea of the vast strides made by the town during the last fifty years, a few facts may be adduced. At that time, say 1840-42, the population was about one-fourth of what it is at present. There were then sixty-five mills employing some ten thousand of the inhabitants. The waterworks of the town, now one of the most elaborate and extensive systems in the country, comprised a small reservoir in Westgate, holding some 15,000 gallons, and a number of bore holes from which the water was pumped, and conveyed in barrels to be sold at the doors of the houses of the principal streets. The suburbs and outlying districts derived their supply chiefly from pumps and open wells. The town now possesses 13 supply reservoirs, having a total capacity of 1,786,240,000 gallons, and 6 compensation reservoirs with storage for 1,292,036 gallons. The ratable value of property was in 1841 about £135,000 ; it now reaches a million sterling. Land which at that time in the town was worth 5s. to 10s. a square yard has fetched in recent years £40 to £50. There were then only a dozen

£1,025,000 ;   Leeds. (360,000) £1,190,000 ;   Sheffield, (330,000) £1,073,000 ; Nottingham, (240,000) £907,000.

places of worship in the town; now there are about 170. In postal matters things were equally "primitive," the town being served by four carriers, who had on an average some 10,000 letters, &c., to deliver per week.* So far as Scotland was concerned, Bradford was *near* Manchester, all postal communications coming *viâ* this city, and from Glasgow occupying a day and a half in transit. The post office was a small rickety building situated in a gloomy ginnel, off Kirkgate, known as the Union Passage, where it continued to be used as such even so lately as 1867. What a marvellous contrast to the present stately edifice in Forster Square, whence some quarter-million letters and book-packets are despatched and delivered weekly!

There is now no town in England better built or architecturally more attractive. Its noble Town Hall, Exchange, and various public institutes, banks, shops, hotels, warehouses, &c., all constructed of excellent native stone, present in solidity and style a most effective appearance; whilst the recently enlarged and admirably-appointed railway stations of the Midland, Great Northern, and Lancashire and Yorkshire Railway Companies are amongst the finest of their kind in the country. Several of the open spaces in the town are ornamented with statues, viz.: of Sir Robert Peel, Bart., Mr. Richard Oastler, Sir Titus Salt, Bart., the Rt. Hon. W. E. Forster, and in Manningham Park, Mr. S. Cunliffe Lister.

Bradford has been so "improved" and modernized of late years that of the old town very little now remains. The principal ancient streets or "gates" of Saxon origin, are Kirkgate, Westgate, Ivegate, and the Turles, or Tyrrel Street as it is now called. These however, have been altered past all recognition of their former aspects. The old Manor Hall (where Viscount Cranbrook was born), Market House, Piece Hall, the Exchange and Assembly Rooms at the junction of Piccadilly and Kirkgate, the Infirmary in Darley Street, and many another remembered edifice in the heart of the town, have each and all succumbed within quite recent

* In 1838 (two years before the introduction of the penny post) the number of letters, &c., delivered in a week was about 3600.

years to the greater necessities of our progressive times. One of the oldest and most notable bits of bygone Bradford remaining to our own day was the Toll Booth, Prison, and Hall of Pleas, at the corner of Ivegate, Kirkgate and Westgate, which was in existence here in the time of the Plantagenets. The Abbot of Kirkstall, Sir Walter Calverley, and other dignitaries of the grand Duchy, presided here in the justice room where the Courts Baron and Leet were held. In connection with this ancient court-house occurs in 1420 the first mention of the Rawson family, of Bradford (who

TOLL BOOTH, PRISON, AND HALL OF PLEAS.

originally came from Ferry Bridge), who built Bradford Hall in 1502, and who afterwards acquired and still possess the manor. In that year (1420) one Robert Rawson made application at this court for "a parcel of ground, now waste, lying by the lane called Goodmansend, leading towards Horton Kirk Gate, agreeing to pay a rent of 1s. a year, besides the usual service of court every three weeks." Goodmansend here mentioned was where the old tithe barn stood (near St. George's Hall), and was doubtless so called from its being on the site of the residence of the ancient vicars of Bradford. Here and

K

about the church were the oldest parts of Bradford, and whence diverged the several ancient thoroughfares of the town. In coaching days the old road to Leeds went by way of Church Bank and Barkerend, and it is recorded that owing to the great steepness of the Bank, the ponderous vehicles were to lower into the town by aid of ropes. This and Ivegate were as now the two steepest roads in the town. Ivegate was possibly called from a small chapel dedicated to the famous Saxon Saint Hiev, to whose immortal memory many such chapels or cells were erected in various places and parts of England bearing her august name.* We have however no record of a pre-Norman chapel in Bradford,† but about the middle of the fifteenth century a chantry was erected on this spot in honour of the Holy Trinity and the virgin Saint Sitha. In a single deed of this later period the street is called *Avegate*, but this is obviously but a suggested innovation or corruption of the older Saxon name.

Bradford, as we have said, contains some splendid public buildings, and some of these we will now proceed to particularize.

The **Town Hall**, unlike that of Leeds, is, whilst lacking "elevation" and massiveness of proportions, unsurpassed in decorative architecture by any similar building in the provinces. The architects were Messrs. Lockwood and Mawson, of Bradford.

---

* Mr. James, in common with other authorities, affirms that "all places having the term *Ive* (A.S *Hefe*) or some root or derivation of it in their names, lie on steep acclivities." This however is not always the case. The town of St. Ives, in Huntingdon, for example, is quite on the flat, only a few miles from the Fens, and its name was certainly derived from such chapel or cell as we have cited. According to Dugdale (Vol. II., p. 631), at the Dissolution of monasteries the last Prior of this cell received a pension of £12 "over and besyds the chappell and chamber stondyng upon the brygge at Seynt Ives during his lyffe." The local legend however in this case is that the body of a certain Persian Bishop, St. Ivo, was found here and translated with much pomp to the neighbouring Abbey of Ramsay, and the "chappell on the brygge" shortly afterwards founded and named in his honour. We have long thought there might be some connection with our mediæval chapel in Ivegate and the mysteriously-named Black Abbey, which are separated from each other by a very ancient, direct thoroughfare of one mile.

† Excepting in the name Kirk Gate, meaning in Saxon the *gate* or way to the *Kirk*.

The design of the structure is Mediæval, divided into three main gables, with high-pitched roof, and surmounted by a tower modelled after the much-admired campanile of the Palazzo Vecchio at Florence. The length of the grand façade is 275 ft., the height of the building 70 ft., above which rises the tower an additional

TOWN HALL, BRADFORD.

height of 135 ft. The total area of ground comprised by the site is about 2000 square yards. On either side of the principal entrance to the hall are statues of Queen Elizabeth and Queen Victoria, and in canopied niches there are also full-sized statues of the sovereigns of England from the Norman Conquest, including Oliver Cromwell.

Over the doorway is a large and handsome oriel window, 37 ft. by 17 ft., surrounded by a machiolated cornice and parapet, at the angles of which are four griffins bearing the arms of Bradford, Leeds, Halifax, and Wakefield, on shields. The tower contains a clock with four dials, a carillon machine chiming 21 tunes, and said to be one of the finest peals in the world. The largest bell weighs 4½ tons. The entire cost of the building, including site, was about £110,000. It is constructed entirely of local stone obtained from the Cliff Wood quarries. The foundation-stone was laid by the Mayor, Mark Dawson, Esq., on Aug. 10th, 1870. and it was opened with great rejoicings (the day being marked as a general holiday) on Sept. 9th, 1873. by the Mayor, Sir (then Mr.) Matthew W. Thompson, Bart. The **Exchange** was originally located in rooms acquired in 1867 for the Post Office at the bottom of Piccadilly. The present handsome building (*see* frontispiece view) was opened March 13th, 1867 ; the foundation-stone having been laid by Lord Palmerston on the 9th of Aug. 1864, only a few months before his death. The architects were the same as for the Town Hall, St. George's Hall, &c., Messrs. Lockwood and Mawson. The building (which cost over £40,000) has its main frontage in Market Street, and includes a spacious hall, 80 ft. by 72 ft., and news-room, 68 ft by 28 ft. In the hall is a fine marble statue of Richard Cobden, which was unveiled by the Rt. Hon. John Bright in 1877. The statue was erected at the expense (about £1500) of the late Geo. Hy. Booth, Esq., a Bradford merchant. At the eastern extremity of the building rises (150 ft.) the great tower (with clock), adorned at its lower angles with statues of Bishop Blaize, the patron saint of wool-combers, and King Edward I. (said to be), who granted the second trading charter to Bradford in 1294. It was however Henry III. who granted the first great charter in A.D. 1251, to his favourite "beloved valet," Edmund de Lacy, for the holding of a weekly (Thursday) market at Bradford. Through this princely courtier, who was lord of the manor of Bradford, the same monarch likewise conferred other privileges on the town which raised it to a degree of importance as a market town, at this time (*temp.* Henry III.), not inferior to Bingley or Leeds. Indeed Bradford then paid more *tallage* or property tax than Leeds. Is it possible that Bradford has raised a statue to the wrong King ? At the junction of Bridge Street and Hall Ings is **St. George's Hall**, a lofty, spacious building used for public meetings, concerts, &c., and containing one of the largest public halls in the kingdom. It will seat 3800 persons ; the gallery alone possessing accommodation for nearly 2000 visitors. The raised large orchestra contains a fine organ. The building, which belongs to a limited company, covers an area of 1600 square yards, and the total amount expended upon it has exceeded £30,000. The foundation-stone was laid by the Earl of Zetland on Sept. 22nd, 1851, and the building was opened in Aug., 1853, by a grand musical festival lasting three days. Adjoining this edifice in Hall Ings, is the **Old Court House**, erected in 1834, and then considered the handsomest public building in the town. Its cost was about £7000. Here until 1868, the hustings were erected on the occasion of parliamentary elections.

The building is now wholly appropriated for West Riding Court purposes, but previous to the erection of the Town Hall the Borough Courts were held here also. In the court-yard are preserved the old town-stocks. Occupying a central position in the town with a frontage to Bridge Street, Market Street, and Tyrrel Street is the **Mechanics' Institute,** a large, handsome, well-lighted building, erected at a cost (with site) of £35,800, from designs of Messrs. Andrews and Pepper, of Bradford. The foundation-stone was laid by the first Lord Houghton in Jan., 1870, and it was opened by the Rt. Hon. W. E. Forster, on Oct. 2nd, 1871. The institute has an amply provisioned news and reading-room, a large lecture-hall, and a library of 18,000 volumes. There are various well-attended day and evening classes, including schools of Art and Science, in connection with the Science and Art Department, South Kensington, successfully carried on. The Institute, founded in 1832, now numbers about 1500 members. The **Church Institute,** dating from 1843, occupies elegant and commodious premises in North Parade. The foundation-stone of the building was laid by the President, Sir (then Mr.) M. W. Thompson, Bart., in June, 1871, who contributed a third of the entire cost (£6000) of its erection. It was opened in 1873, and contains a good news and reading-room, lecture-hall, and an increasing library of about 4000 volumes, which had a circulation in the year 1890 of over 17,000. The **Subscription Library** and Literary Institute, originally founded in 1774, has since 1854 been located in the premises formerly occupied by the old Dispensary in Darley Street. The library, which includes many old and scarce works, is a very valuable one, and numbers over 20,000 volumes. The **Central Free Library,** at the junction of Darley Street and Godwin Street, is a large and well-appointed building opened in 1878. It possesses a spacious news and reading-room, which received in 1890 958,330 visits. The lending library contains about 18,000 volumes, and the reference library about 19,000 volumes; including the eight branches, the total number of volumes is 65,670. A movement for the establishment of a separate Art Gallery and Museum in the town has been projected. This since 1879, has occupied a single upper room in the Central Library. From that year the visits paid to the Art Museum have grown from about 26,000 to 328,756 in 1890. The **Grammar School,** of uncertain origin, but mentioned in A.D. 1553, in a deed relating to certain lands and messuages which "*antiently* belonged to the living and sustentation of a schoolmaster teaching *grammar* within the town of Bradford," was re-erected under the provisions of the new Act in 1871, on the site of the old school at the top of Manor Row. The building, a handsome and commodious structure, erected at a cost, with master's residence, of about £9000, was formally opened by the Rt. Hon. W. E. Forster, on July 2nd, 1873. The school is one of the most successfully conducted in the whole country, and having been largely endowed by private munificence now possesses many valuable scholarships. The **Girls' Grammar School,** in Hallfield Road, formerly occupied as a private school by the late Mr. M. Watson, was acquired for the sum of £5000, and opened by Lady Frederick

Cavendish on Sept. 29th. 1875. The **Technical College**, one of the finest as well as one of the most useful buildings Bradford possesses, is situated in Horton Road, and is admirably fitted with all the appliances for affording instruction in the local industries. The building, with furnishing, cost about £30,000, and was opened by the Prince of Wales in June, 1882. The site of the **Post Office** in Forster Square was purchased by the Government in April, 1884, for the sum of £37,650, and the present handsome building was publicly opened in Sept., 1887. It occupies a triangular plot of ground, with a frontage to Forster Square 227 ft. long, and 78 ft. at its greatest width. It is classical in design, and built of Bradford stone. The **Covered Markets**, comprising the general goods market, (opened in 1872) having entrances in Kirkgate and Godwin Street, and the butchers' and fish markets (opened in 1878) in Upper Godwin Street, are large airy buildings, covered by lofty octagonal domes, ventilated by glass louvres, and resting on substantial ornamental iron pillars. The interior fittings and decorations are of a superior kind, and there are altogether some 300 shops and stalls. The cost of the buildings was about £80,000. The **Temperance Hall**, Chapel Street, Leeds Road, was the outcome of a local movement initiated in 1830, and is remarkable from the fact of its being the first public edifice erected in the United Kingdom from funds wholly applied to the promotion of temperance. It is a large, plain building, completed in 1837, and cost about £1500. The **Infirmary**, an imposing Tudor structure, (from designs of Mr. W. Rawstorne), occupies an extensive area between Lumb Lane and Westgate, 1 mile from the Town Hall. The site cost £3750, and the building, opened in 1844, about £6000. In 1864 an additional £7000 was expended on enlargements, and recently a new wing has been added entailing a further outlay. On the Westgate side is the Dispensary, erected in 1873 at a cost of £6000. The whole of the buildings are among the best appointed of their kind in the country, and there is a large and efficient staff. In Hallfield Road, a short distance from the Infirmary, is the **Eye and Ear Hospital**, a handsome Gothic edifice, erected in 1865, at an expenditure of £6000, and which has recently been enlarged. The **Fever Hospital**, another of Bradford's useful institutions, stands upon an elevated site at the top of Penny Oaks Lane, Leeds Road. It was opened in Jan., 1872, and cost £22,500, towards which Sir Titus Salt, Bart., contributed £5000, and Alfred Harris, Esq., £4400. The **Blind Institution**, in North Parade, was opened in 1868, and is likewise a very useful and deserving establishment supported by voluntary contributions. The **Nutter Orphanage** is a neat, long building of two stories, pleasantly situated near Horton Park. It owes its origin to the munificence of the late Mr. John Nutter, who bequeathed the sum of £10,000 for the purpose of providing an institution "for the assistance of helpless boys of his native town," his own early struggles having prompted this generous deed. The building was opened by the Mayor of Bradford, William Moulson, Esq., on June 19th, 1889, and has accommodation for 40 boys. Of the 170 Churches, Chapels, and Mission Rooms in Bradford, many of which display considerable architectural pretensions, all (with two or three exceptions) have been built within the last fifty years. Our space, however, precludes more than a brief reference to the oldest of these, viz.: the **Parish Church**, built in the time of Henry VI., when masons' wages were about threepence a day and meal a penny a stone! It is probably the *third* of these foundations in the town; the first being a Saxon structure, and the second erected after the Conquest. A list of the Vicars is preserved from A.D. 1293. The registers date from 1596. The church has been extensively restored and has now about 1450 sittings, 600 of which are free. It contains some excellent stain-glass, numerous monuments to local families, a handsome reredos, (the gift of Sir M. W. Thompson, Bart.), and a superb marble sculpture, consisting of a personification, in three figures, of Age and Youth, by Flaxman, to the memory of Abraham Balme (ob. 1796), a member of an old Bradford family that is named in the registers as early as 1571. Among other local buildings and institutions of interest may be noticed the various **Clubs, Theatres, Banks, Hotels, School Board Offices, County Court, Tradesmen's Home, Airedale Independent College, Orphan Girls' Home, Children's Hospital, School of Industry, Workhouse, Female Refuge**, etc.

Bradford, despite its buildings and smoke, enjoys a reputation for salubrity; its sanitary arrangements, though costly, are excellent and the outlay has apparently been well justified, for statistics of mortality shew that for many years past the general health of the inhabitants is exceeded but by few other towns in the kingdom. Unquestionably not a little to do with this happy state of things is the ample provision of Public Parks, in which respect Bradford enjoys advantages superior to most other English towns. By their extent, variety, and admirably-chosen sites they form very important attractions in the various suburbs of the town. The following are their names, with the dates of opening, and areas. Peel Park (1863) 56 acres; Lister or Manningham Park (1871) 53½ acres; Horton Park (1878) 39½ acres; Bowling Park (1880) 53 acres; Bradford Moor Park (1884) 15 acres.

The borough of Bradford includes the following townships, with their acreage. Bradford (1595), Bowling (1561½), Horton (2033), Manningham (1318½), Allerton (1849), Bolton (712½), Heaton (1324), Tyersal (137), Thornbury (246); parts of the two latter are included respectively in the townships of Pudsey and Calverley. In the immediate neighbourhood of Bradford are Manningham and Heaton, with their old Halls, the former having been the seat of the Lister family (a branch of the noble house of Ribblesdale) for three centuries; Undercliffe, standing high and healthily, —the Montpellier of Bradford; Horton, with its old Hall, the ancient seat of the Sharp family, now represented by Francis Sharp Powell, Esq., M.A., M.P. The celebrated John Sharp, Archbishop of York, was of this family, and was born (Feb. 14th, 1644) at a house (now removed) in Ivegate, Bradford. Bowling, with its baronial-looking mansion, the seat of the old manor lords Bolling, and afterwards (A.D. 1502) for many generations of the Tempests of Bracewell, Tong, &c.; and Bierley, with its ancient Hall (the scene of the scientific labours of the celebrated Dr. Richardson, F.R.S.) and famous cedar tree (the first planted in England) are also within easy access of the town.

Few if any of our inland towns can compare with Bradford in the varied attractiveness of its environs. These are strikingly picturesque by a natural diversity of hill and dale, affording from many points fine prospects, and abounding in many scenes and places of high historic interest. We have however already pretty exhaustively dealt with this part of our subject in our volume "ONE HUNDRED AND EIGHTY PLEASANT WALKS AROUND BRADFORD," so that it would be mere repetition to enter upon it again here. That volume must be regarded as supplementary to this section of our work.

SHIPLEY.

THE Aire, which takes a general direction from east to west, here breaks almost north to Esholt, and the country is remarkable for the striking contrast it presents on its north and south sides. Above, all is wild moor, and wood, and health-giving breezes, whilst south of the water line we have a region of manufacturing towns and villages; of busy mills, pits and iron works; and a teeming, industrious population engaged in all the variety of pursuits for which the district is famous. The thirty and odd square miles of country lying south of the Aire between Bradford and Leeds is, for the simple reason of human dependence on its great coal field, assuredly the "busiest" along the whole course of the river, and contains a population of not less than six hundred thousand souls.

Shipley occupies its north-western angle at the junction of Bradford dale with Airedale, and is sheltered on the east by the lofty crags of Windhill and Wrose, and on the north by the early-inhabited moors of Baildon and Hawksworth. As a place of residence the district is naturally favoured, and judged by the average mortality for the past ten years (under 18 per thousand of its population) the town may well have thriven and increased. Shipley, however, up to the institution of its Local Board in 1853, had been little more than a moorland village amid wastes of grass and gorse. Gas, however—the harbinger of commercial progress,—had been introduced into the township in 1846, the same year that the Leeds and Bradford (Midland) Railway was opened, with a small station at Shipley, situated below the Oddfellows' Hall on the Frizinghall road. The population of the entire township was then about 3000, and the ratable value of property about £12,000. The present annual estimate is £60,000 with a population of about 20,000. Owing in great measure to its splendid situation, its industries, which are allied with those of Bradford, have during the past forty years developed with remarkable rapidity. Vasts sums have been expended on street improvements, and lighting, sewerage, and waterworks, a scheme of progress which has raised the mortgage debt of the Board to a round £200,000. The town is now the head of a Parliamentary Division, is well provided with schools, clubs, institutes, and places of worship, which present in their architectural aspects a wonderful contrast to the town as it looked even a generation ago. On the 31st May, 1890, a public park was opened by Mrs. Titus Salt, of Milner Field, when amidst the general festivities, a choir of about 400 voices, chosen from all the church and chapel choirs in the district took part, and speeches were delivered by Mr. Joseph Craven, M.P., Mr. Chas. Stead, Chairman of the Local Board, and other gentlemen concerned. The park is on the Crowgill estate, near the parish church, and comprises some $3\frac{1}{2}$ acres, nicely planted and laid out with walks, alcoves, band-stand, &c. The lower portion is to be laid in grass as a play-ground. The central situation of Shipley has greatly impelled the facilities of transit since the era of industrial progress set in. Numerous Acts for the construction and improvement of highways have been obtained ; the Leeds and Liverpool Canal, with a branch to Bradford, passes the town ; the Gt. Northern Railway, from Bradford *via* Laisterdyke, has a terminus at Windhill ; and in place of the station " shed " of " pre-Reformation " days the Midland Co. has now a spacious stone-built "junction" through which run a daily average of 340 trains, and there is a muster of pass-holders (chiefly from Bradford) numbering 500. A joint proposal of Shipley and Windhill for obtaining a Charter of Incorporation has been moved, but there is some lukewarmness among the inhabitants on the ground of a possible increase of cost. The Shipley township rates total now (1890) 5s. 6d. in the pound.

The Manor of Shipley is thus reviewed in *Domesday*. " In Scipleia, Ravenchil had three carucates [about 300 acres] of land to be taxed, where there may be two ploughs. Ilbert has it, and it is waste. Value in King Edward's time, *ten shillings*. There is a wood pasture half-a-mile long and half-a-mile broad." This was in A.D. 1086, and after a lapse of 600 years, it is interesting to note the significant advance from "waste," for the Shipley Town's Book records an assessment of lands in the township for the year 1688, of 46 oxgangs, (about 550 acres) at 69s., equivalent to 1s. 6d. an oxgang, or about 1½d. an acre! What an interesting comparison with the present day : land selling in Shipley at a guinea a yard, with an average assessment in the township (comprising 1330 acres) of nearly £50 an acre! That wealthy Norman foeman, Ilbert de Lacy, ultimately disposed of the manor, and early in the fourteenth century we find it in possession of the Knights of St. John of Jerusalem (not the Templars, but the Hospitallers, who acquired most of their property), who retained lands here for several centuries afterwards, but the only visible evidence existing of their former proprietorship is the stone lantern, peculiar to the Order, at the top of the lodging house (once Dixon's old Hall) opposite Rosse Street Chapel. In 1551-2, William Gascoigne obtained from Leonard West and Barbara his wife, the "Manor of Shepley and 20 messuages and 12 cottages with lands there and in Heyton Roodes in the parish of Bradford." By the marriage of the daughter of William Gascoigne, in 1570, to Wm. Rawson, the manor and estates remained with the Rawsons until the middle of the eighteenth century, when the widow of Wm. Rawson married Dr. Cyril Jackson, of Stamford, who thus inherited the property. From the Jacksons the manor was purchased by John Wilmer Field, Esq., of Heaton Hall, for £24,000, and one of whose daughters having married in 1836 Lord Oxmantown, afterwards Earl of Rosse, their son, the second Earl, is now proprietor.

Before the introduction of the woollen industry into Shipley fifty years ago, the chief manufacture of the district was cloth. Cloth weaving must have been carried on here at a very early period, (in Leeds we have noticed it in the time of Edward I.), when hand spinning and weaving busied the homes of the scattered peasantry. In monastic times there were evidently works for the dressing of cloth in Shipley, and the personal name Walker, (*i.e.*, *fuller*), located here in the fourteenth century, pre-supposes the existence of walk or fulling mills in the district ; the Walkers being included in the Shipley Poll Tax of Richard II., A.D. 1379. In the first of Elizabeth (1559) we find that one Thomas Pollard obtained from Wm. Gascoigne, Esq., lord of the manor, a "messuage and *two fulling-mills* with lands in Shipley." These mills subsequently came with the manor as already stated to the Rawsons, and in the assessment of 1688, above mentioned, Rawson's Mill (one oxgang) is rated at 18d. Members of the old Dixon family of Heaton, referred to, were long resident at Shipley, and ran the corn and fulling mill near Saltaire Bridge, known as Dixon's Land and Mills up to the founding of Saltaire. In the same assessment this property (comprising five oxgangs and one-third) is rated at 8s.

THE OLDEST HOUSE IN SHIPLEY.

The Dixons built the substantial old Hall (opposite the Manor House) now in a dilapidated state, and occupied as a common lodging house, and their initials, J.D., A.D., with the date 1593, are still discernible on a stone in front of the house, which is now the most ancient tenement in Shipley. The Manor House, in Church Lane, appears to have been built in 1630, and enlarged in 1673, and was the residence of the manorial lords Rawson. In Dr. Jackson's time the house was let as a farm with 120 acres of land extending in the direction of Shipley Moor. Subsequently it was let off in separate dwellings, and in 1880 was leased to the Shipley Local Board, and is now occupied by that body as Public Offices. An inscribed stone kept in the yard states that "The site of this Lock-up was given by William, Lord Oxmantown, Lord of the Manor of Shipley, &c. in 1839." The old Lock-up referred to was in Chapel Lane, and was demolished for street improvements when the present West Riding Police Office was erected. Among the few ancient residences remaining in the town must be mentioned Shipley Hall, or the Low Hall as it was formerly called, which faces the Bradford road. It had a large park and gardens that covered part of the site now occupied by the Midland Railway Station and line, extending eastwards as far as the beck, which, once sparkling stream, would provide many a dainty dish of trout long after the Gascoignes and Rawsons ceased to live at the Hall. The date of its erection is uncertain, but it is evidently older than the Manor House, whither the Rawsons removed in the seventeenth century. In the garden is the trunk of an ancient yew tree, fully ten feet in circumference; and as the yew had a religious symbol and was also used in the making of bows for archers, this site in all likelihood would be selected for the dwelling of a knightly family in the Middle Ages. The Wainmans, of Carr head, were a long time proprietors of the Hall and adjoining property, which in 1845 was bought from them by the Midland Co. for £24,000. and the Hall was afterwards separately sold to Mr. Thomas Arton. It is now occupied by Dr. Ellis Another noteworthy old building, now occupied as two separate residences, is the Old Hall, which is now somewhat hidden by the handsome premises of the Bradford Old Bank. It is an imposing Georgian structure, and was occupied by the Lascelles family during the building of Harewood House, (1759-71.) It belongs, with the estate, to the Walkers, an old family settled. as we have shewn, at Shipley many centuries back. The hall and land were, some years ago, sold by the Walkers, and are now the property of the family of the late Mr. Joseph Hargreaves, of Shipley Fields.

Conspicuous among modern public buildings is the church of St. Paul, one of the last and handsomest churches erected under the *Million Act*, in 1826. With subsequent alterations its cost has been about £12,000. It has nave, aisles, chancel, and a square battlemented tower, and will seat 1000 persons. The Baptists are about the longest established body in Shipley, having been located at Bethel since 1758. Their new chapel in Rosse street, opposite the old Manor House, is a very tasteful structure, opened in 1866, at a cost of nearly £6000. There is provision for about 1000 worshippers. The Primitive Methodists have also a large and well-appointed place of worship in Saltaire Road, with accommodation for 1000, which was built in 1872 at a cost of over £5000. The Independents, Wesleyans, New Connexion Methodists, and Roman Catholics are also well represented in Shipley. The public schools in the town are likewise notable; on the Central and Albert Road Board schools a sum of over £30,000 has been expended. Shipley has now, if a modern, a very serviceable look about it, a sum of £100,000 having been spent on street improvements since the formation of the Local Board in 1853.

Such an important junction as Shipley is naturally a good starting point for exploring the adjacent hills and dales. Many persons, however, prefer to commence their walks at Saltaire, on the rustic skirts of the town. From either place it is a nice walk up to Baildon and the Moor. From Shipley southwards, Heaton Hill (1½ m.) may be reached, whilst eastward, Wrose Hill and Idle (3 m.) can be ascended by way of Windhill and Carr Lane. From either of these summits the view extending forty miles northward, and east over Leeds, is very fine. An enjoyable half-day may also be obtained from

Shipley to Guiseley and Otley Chevin, 6 m. 'Bus leaves Shipley station every hour up to 2 p.m., and every half-hour after, for Charlestown (1d.) and *Shoulder of Mutton* Inn, on Otley Road, (2d.) Hence to Esholt ¼ m., or Guiseley 2 m. From Baildon Bridge is a nice field walk by the Buck Mill Bridge to Esholt (3 m.) From the village to **Guiseley** through Esholt Springs is 2¼ m. This pleasantly-situated old place is mentioned in *Domesday*, and has doubtless been the centre of a Christian population from the dawn of the faith. An emblematic Christian cross of Saxon age was discovered in the north wall of the church at its restoration in 1831, and on excavating at the removal of the old school which stood near the entrance gate to the churchyard, several stone coffins were unearthed. These are now preserved in the church-yard. The church, dedicated to the Saxon King Oswald, (*see* METHLEY) is a semi-Norman structure, having circular arches in its south aisle resting on clustered columns. The choir and transept are of the time of Henry III. The tower (which has a fine peal of bells) has evidently been rebuilt and raised, as the stone-work between the plinth and clock seems to be of more recent date than the parts above. The interior has a private chapel to the Stansfields, with piscina in the south wall. There are also memorial tablets to this family, as also to the Rawdons, Pollards, and other local families. The registers date from 1556, and a list of the rectors has been preserved from A.D. 1234. In the churchyard are some old quaint inscriptions. One such reads.

" If on this stone you cast a weeping eye,
Know underneath doth Wm. Baildon lie,
His body's dead and in the grave doth rest,
His soul's alive and free from death's conquest."

To " Prudence Baildon, wife of the adjacent Wm. Baildon, of Esholt," is a stone dated 24th Sept., 1682. On another bearing date 1711, it is pleasing to read ; " Here lyes interred ye body and ye dust of Gracious Prudent, and one of ye most virtuous humble of women— Mary, ye wife of John Marshall, of Yeadon. whilst in life."

Since the opening of the railway from Leeds to Ilkley, with a station at Guiseley, in 1865, building operations have considerably increased. In 1867 the Town Hall was built. chiefly through the munificence of Sir M. W. Thompson, Bart., of Park Gate. The cost was about £3000. At the top of the main street is the base of the old Town Cross, and the remains of the Parish Stocks. Ascending Moor Lane from here, a mile walk brings the rambler on to the York Gate Road, which, as previously pointed out. was a Roman road from Ilkley over Bramhope Moor to Adel and York. The road here runs at an elevation of nearly 900 ft. and **Otley Chevin** top (925 ft.) is soon reached. This is a favourite and delightful trysting point on a fine day. the view over Wharfedale being extremely beautiful. whilst the hills that bind the area of vision enclose a prospect of not less than 8000 square miles. Northward the road is seen climbing up from Leathley over the moor to Beckwithshaw and Harrogate. Eastward we can discern Leeds Town Hall clock, and the Grammar School and spires on Woodhouse Moor ; to the N.E. Almscliff, Arthington Viaduct, Harewood House, and the towers of York Minster are visible. South are the hills of Denholme, Swill Hill, and the smoke-enveloped Bradford dale. Looking west is Rumbalds Moor, Flasby Fell above Skipton, and the Craven mountains ; Great Whernside peering above the lower Wharfedale hills is usually distinguished in the Spring time by his snowy cap when all other hills are clear. Like a veritable Lucerne. indeed, at the foot of this Wharfedale Righi is the picturesque old Saxon town of Otley (*see* p. 73), whither the rambler may descend and train home.

BAILDON.

CLIMBING the hill from the Otley road out of Shipley we come to Baildon, with relevant reflections, perhaps, on the ages that have passed since the tattooed and skin-clad Britons climbed this very hill,—of those long populous idolaters here, of whom nought survives now but the ghosts of them in their charred remains! That Baildon has been, so to speak, a metropolis of Celtic Paganism is abundantly testified in the purity of its ancient place-names, and in numerous remains of primeval dwellings, earthworks, temples, and burial mounds. There are or were recently old inhabitants in Baildon who could remember the High Plain covered with upright stones, mounds, trenches, and stone circles more or less perfect; and many of these, as will be indicated in our itinerary, still (though imperfect) exist. The very name of Baildon would seem to denote a scriptural origin in the place being chosen by the High Priests for propitiating sacrifices to their god Baal, when in honour of the all-giving Sun *baal* or *bel* fires were kindled on the hill tops, just as the festal fires are in Ireland and elsewhere at the present day.* Up to the time of the Conquest the place appears to have been called *Beldune* (*i.e.* Hill of Baal), and evidence of Celtic or Pagan occupation is, as we have said, found in names coupled with *bil*, *beal*, and *bel* along all the higher ground in Airedale from Rawdon Billing to Bell Busk, as well as in the level country below Leeds, as Beal, &c. It is needless to say that relics in plenty of these early races have been turned up also over the same area. In Norman times the place was called Hope Town, and a family of Hope resided in Baildon at this period, and figured in the capitation tax of Richard II., A.D.

* Such also for example as the *Sommer Gewinn* of the Thuringian Forest, and the *Beltane* Feast in France.

1379. The name is also still preserved in the principal eminence, Hope Hill, and in Hope Farm, &c.

" Hope and Hopetowne,"

> " With all the bounds, both up and downe,
> From yerthe to heven, from heven toe hel,"

were, if we are to trust an old copy of a Norman deed bestowed by the Conqueror on Paul de Royden (*see* RAWDON). But the first authentic record touching the manor is of one Essulf, a Saxon, who was seized of lands in Baildon in the last year of Henry I., A.D. 1135. In 1181 John, his son, bought an assize of *mort d'ancestor* against William de Lelay then lord of Baildon, from whose descendants the manor was purchased by the Stapletons in the last year of Edward I. (1307). From them it passed to the Fitzwilliams, and in 1615 was sold to the Hawksworths, who conjointly with the Baildons retained possession until 1704, when Henry Thompson, Esq., late of Escrick, purchased it, and it remained in this family until 1849 when the estates were divided and sold. When the first manor house was built we have no record, but the present Hall was rebuilt in 1553 by Robert Baildon, who was one of King Henry Eighth's attendants at the Field of the Cloth of Gold, and Groom of the King's Chamber and Wardrobe in 1526. Francis Baildon the last male heir, enlarged and improved the house in 1664. He married a daughter of Sir Richard Hawksworth, and died at Baildon in 1669. He was probably born at the Old Hall in Westgate, occupied and perhaps built by his father William Baildon, who died in 1627. William Baildon, grandfather of Francis, died at the Low Hall in 1628. The family, which had been settled at Baildon soon after the Conquest, expired in an heiress, Mary, d. of Francis Baildon, who married in 1665 Bradwardine Tindall, Esq., of Brotherton, and left an only child, Lucy, wife of Edward Thompson, Esq., of Marston. who died in 1715. Her last descendant, and consequently the last descendant of Francis Baildon, was Lucy Sarah, wife of the Rt. Hon. Thos. H. S. Sotheron-Estcourt, (Home Secretary in 1859) who died without issue in 1870.

The Church at Baildon is a very ancient foundation : mention being made in a grant of land to Esholt Priory (*ca.* A.D. 1240) of a *priest* at Baildon, and in another charter, dated 1265, Henry de Baildon is described as *deacon* of the same place. The old chapel was destroyed by fire and its books and records unfortunately lost in the time of Cardinal Wolsey. It was rebuilt, according to a stone over the vestry door, in 1549, and again in 1848. The church (which has 280 free sittings) contains some choice memorial glass, and the pulpit and reading-desk are of carved black oak saved from the previous edifice. The Moravians are an old-established body at Baildon, having had a license to preach here since the time of the foundation of their settlement at Fulneck in 1749. They have now a very neat building here, opened in 1868. The Wesleyans and Primitive Methodists have also several good houses of worship at Baildon, where they have continued to flourish since early in the present century. Of other buildings mention may be made of the Mechanics' Institute, which includes the Board Offices, &c. It is a commodious structure erected at a cost of £2000 in 1862. The township, which is divided into five parts, viz.: High and Low Baildon, Baildon Wood Bottom, Baildon Green, and Baildon Bridge, contains many handsome private residences; the locality having an old reputation for its salubrity, and has probably produced more long-aged natives than any other township included within our work. One such patriarch, old Joseph Halliday, who died in Aug., 1890, aged 95, used regularly to walk from Baildon to Bradford and back, up to within a week of his death; and old Mr. Thomas Lupton (aged 80), living at Baildon, is still able to *run* from his house in five minutes to Baildon station, a distance of half-a-mile.

Before the era of turnpikes, Baildon was a notable stopping place on the old pack-horse road to Ilkley and the north. In fact it is supposed that a market was held here before the charter for a market at Otley was granted in the days of King Athelstan. The Town or Market Cross (which now serves for a lamp-post) is a plain stone column about 14 ft. high, on a square base of two steps. On the north side of it stood the village stocks; and the beck ran close by, bordered with trees, and near to the present memorial fountain. This part is called the Town Gate.

So far our history. Let us now see what fine walks these

healthy uplands can yield, without, indeed, journeying very far, although it would be quite possible to keep this altitude on to Rumbalds Moor and along the "backbone of England" to the very borders of Scotland, were the traveller so inclined. But we shall desist from this experiment at present, and so, having lately intimated that this locality was the probable theatre of Baal worship, we will commence our *tour d'exploit* with

A RAMBLE AMONG THE ANTIQUITIES OF BAILDON MOOR.

Abundant and various as these are our observations will be confined to what can be seen in a day. Leaving Baildon then by the Old Hall we go on West Lane by an elevated and airy walk under Hope Hill, passing the beautiful residence of Mrs. Hird, and the pretty mediæval mansion of Mr. Edwin Speight, whose windows command a fine and uninterrupted view of the hills and woods of upper Airedale and as far as the Lancashire moors ; emerging shortly at the rocky top of **Shipley Glen.** This is perhaps the most popular of the pleasure resorts around Bradford, but forty years ago, before the railway days, its existence was hardly known outside the immediate locality. It appears to have been called Shipley Glen only since the Rev. Peter Scott, the well-known and respected Baptist minister of Shipley (from 1831 to 1847) first drew public attention to its natural attractions. It had always before been called Brackenhall Green, and being wholly comprised in the township of Baildon, and in the parish of Otley, no part of it is within a mile of Shipley township. It is now annually visited by thousands of pleasure-seekers, for whose entertainment there is a varied and ample provision. The Glen itself, running in a northerly direction towards Eldwick, is clothed with natural wood, and, geologically, very strikingly illustrates, by its deep and precipitous banks the extraordinary erosive power of water and weather. Along its eastern edge the rocks are bared to a great depth, and present every variety of size and figure. In former times vast quantities have been taken and broken up for building purposes and for repairing roads, and doubtless the same fate has befallen many of the druidical altars and rock idols of the High Plain. This district, at the period of its earliest human occupation was covered with forests of oak, remains of which may be found embedded in the turf at the summit levels of Hope and Penythorne Hills. When the Roman conquerors drove for a time the Celtic tribes off these partially cleared hills, or subdued them fc. their civil service, the growing woods were further felled or burned, (that they might better see their way about) so that often for months together the sky was a-glare with the light of burning forests, and some of the wood was converted into charcoal for the smelting of iron, traces of such operations being discoverable here at the present day. The Romans also drained the swampy flats, and repaired the old British 'highways' which crossed these elevated tracts, and otherwise 'improved' or utilized the existing camps. The once extensive but now rather shapeless earthworks on the north-west side of the High Plain. are no doubt referable to this Celtic-Roman period. For long after the treaty of submission in the reign of Vespasian, A.D. 70, we know that the Brigantes continued in revolt, and sure enough battles would be waged and attacks be repeatedly made upon these sturdy hill-tribes. The peculiar character of at least one of these earthworks would seem to mark an irruption of the Picts and Scots here in the fourth or perhaps a later century. Possibly the Runic stone at Bingley is a memorial of a great battle fought somewhere in this locality. when the armies of Eadberht. the Saxon, and Ongus, King of the Picts, were victorious in A.D. 756. Anyway it is highly probable that this was the last conquered portion of the British kingdom of Elmete. And though destruction was rampant among the foreign hordes that overran the district, a superstitious respect seems ever to have been shown by them for the graves of the dead, many of which remained unmolested even to our own day. The altars and temples of the Druids had long ago been thrown down. but in some places their rites were remembered and practised, and human sacrifices continued even into the Saxon era.

The oldest rock sculptures on our moors are usually attributed to the British Druids. There are here a number of examples. After crossing the stream from the Glen gate, and going about thirty paces, we come upon such an **incised stone**, whereon are a number of circling lines and cup-like cavities—one at each corner, with a long line branching off to the north-east ; but this stone unfortunately has got broken, and lying on the main path is much defaced.* Such carvings are now commonly designated "Cup and Ring marks," They are to be found (often covered with peat) on other parts of these high moors once occupied by pre-historic races. and in similar places elsewhere in our islands and on the Continent. That they are of like symbol and of remote artificial origin is obvious from their similarity of design over such wide areas ; the peculiar vermicular character of the lines or "rings " being apparently a pattern of the well-known 'labyrinth' that originated in the east, and of which such fine examples still exist among the old sun-worshipping nations of Babylon, Persia, India, and Crete. The absence of any written record leaves us in darkness as to their precise meaning or purpose. Some suppose them to typify the mystery of the Deity, all circles being regarded by the ancients as symbols of eternity and of endless faith. The advocates of Baal worship premise them to have served as ducts on the altars of sacrifice, and at other times for retaining oil for anointing, or fats that lit their holy-fires on the great Druidical festivals. (*see* Genesis xxviii.) In various parts of Scandinavia such

---

* It is a great pity that the notable stones on these moors have been so much damaged, and many of them removed or totally destroyed. Something ought really to be done to ensure their better preservation. A notice board at the entrance to the Glen would, perhaps, do something towards this.

stones are still in use as altars, upon which corn, herbs, and green woods are burned as thank offerings to the beneficent Giver. But we incline to the belief that these ' cup and ring ' stones were used for the simple purposes of instruction in astronomy, for as is well-known, the Druidical priesthood, who were the " wise men " of their time, took especial care in imparting knowledge of their deities, and these round cavities and involved lines may have been used to illustrate the position of the sun, moon, and stars, (the cups with rings round. the planets) and their various movements in the heavens. The accompanying illustrative sketch depicts a fac-simile of one of these stones on Rumbalds Moor. They are generally met with in ' high

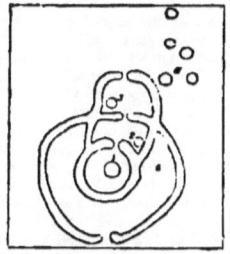

places,' and often in proximity to Druids' circles. Sir Richard Hoare, Bart., agrees in thinking that these circles served an astronomical purpose also, and observes that "by looking along the edges or sides of two opposite stones in any of the circles, certain determinate points, either in the horizon or at certain elevations above it, might at fixed times be marked out, whence an observer might ascertain precise points in the elliptic or zodiac, and the varying distances of the planets from certain fixed stars, and might by such means better observe their motions." Many of the Druids' circles were doubtless so constructed and recognised. There is a circle situate near the top of Cader Idris, in Wales, which to-day goes by the name of the Astronomers' Stones. In Iceland they are called "domk-ringr," or judgment rings. Here, where we now stand, a little beyond the farm-house and the 'cup and ring' stone, there are parts of an **ancient circle**, but whether it has been constructed on astronomical lines, or as a place of judgment or sacrifice, would be hard to determine now. Many of the stones have been removed, but sufficient remains to indicate its extent and former importance. It comprises portions of an earthwork (which was perfect a few years ago) raised between two concentric circles, whose greatest circumference is 137 yards. and diameter 50 yards north to south, and 39 yards east to west, but with the exception of a few stones on the west side the outer ring is quite effaced.* There are unmistakable evidences about it of intense fires. A tenon hole in one of the upright stones apparently indicates the former existence of a gate or of a simple cromlech, or *trilith*, such as is seen in such perfection at Stonehenge. We know of no cromlech existing here now, unless that be considered one at the upper end of the Glen, but this may be, and probably is, an accidental disposition of the rocks. If Baal worship prevailed

* This must consequently be of lesser antiquity, for *single* circles of stones are accounted the most ancient, according to Borlase's *Antiquities of Cornwall*.

here there must have been such cromlechs, for Cæsar in his 'De Bello Gallico,' expressly states that these were the altars on which the sacrifices were offered. Between this double or aisled circle and the 'cup and ring' stone is part of another circle, where were formerly two upright stones, about a yard apart, having similar tenon holes. One only of these stones is now left and it is broken. At the top of Trench Wood, on entering the Glen there is a large stone with a bowl-shaped cavity, called from time immemorial **Robin Hood's Seat**. This designation is, of course, purely mythical, many such curious stones and other remarkable objects in our part of the country being associated in some fanciful way or other with 'this famous mediæval outlaw. It may just as well have been the judgment-seat of some Druid priest or chief, or even (if credence may go so far) a holy basin for the retention of water in which leaves of the sacred oak were dipped and borne, as we are told, in processionals to the festal altars.* Similar stones are found elsewhere in our district near Druidical temples. Continuing our walk, it is worth while turning aside for a peep at **Walker's Old Farm**, on Brackenhall Green, which stands on what appears to be pavestones of a Roman public way, running from north-west to south-east. At the north entrance there is a stone recess containing a shallow basin like a piscina, and the old oak doors are noteworthy, one having a curious handle and is pegged with wooden nails. An old oak chest bears the initials and date, J.B., 1688, and on the woodwork inside are the same initals, (probably of the Booth family), with date 1701. The house is dry-walled, and must be at least four centuries old.† The Walkers lived at Bracken Hall and at Hope Farm in the time of Charles I., and are returned as pew holders in Baildon Church after the Restoration. Behind the farm we ascend under Hope Hill by a drinkable iron spring, and come upon what we might naturally expect to find in this locality, the remains apparently of a **British Village**, consisting of a number of circular, bowl-shaped pits, eight to ten feet in depth, fifty to sixty in circumference at the top, and running east and west in an alternate double column all the way up the present wall side under Crook Farm. A similar cluster of these pit-dwellings is to be found near Eldwick, and they also abound on other parts of the moor. and often in surprising perfection, as the land they occupy not having since been cultivated or built upon. The presence of coal about here has originated the idea that they are abandoned coal workings, but their number, arrangement, even formation, and proximity to each other, at once disproves such belief. Some coal has certainly been won here, but such pits are isolated and of different construction. Being near the surface, the ancient Britons themselves would no doubt be acquainted with the coal, and possibly use it, but as there was plenty of wood this would be their chief fuel.‡

* Our Christmas mistletoe is a survival of this Druidical custom.

† Should this house ever come down or its foundations be disturbed, a careful look out should be kept for ancient relics.

‡ That coal was known to the early Britons is evident in the British origin of the word *Kol* or *col*; in Cornwall still called *colan*, and by the Irish Celts, *ocual*.

A considerable area around their dwellings was evidently cleared of growing timber, and piles of the felled trees would be used as defences against the encroachments of enemies. (The more advanced Celts of South Britain called their northern contemporaries *Caoill daoin* (*i.e.*, people of the woods); obviously the root-words of ancient Caledonia.) In the woods around them roamed the wolf, boar, wild deer, and other native animals, which they hunted, both for the sake of the flesh and for the skins, which provided clothing and material for bedding, &c. Besides domestic and wild flesh, their diet consisted largely of various native fruits and acorns, which abounded in the adjoining forests. Their huts, which rose bee-hive fashion in wattles of rough thatch, were usually lined with impervious deer-skins, and the rain which fell from the slanting roofs upon the land-slopes was drained into trenches, or simple open gutters, now filled up and imperfect, though in places are still tolerably well-defined. Several of them (possibly all) originally appear, moreover, to have been protected by raised banks sloping towards each other and the trenches. On the open space above their dwellings would be kept a few cattle, and some amount of grain would also be grown here. This was ground into meal by stone hand-querns, examples of which are occasionally found in the district. We cannot, however, go into all the details of their life here, but we are able to discern by the number of dwellings, earthworks, and tumuli, that it was a considerable settlement. Climbing the hill again, we come upon an old coal-pit, where the shale is exposed by cutting the road, and above is an ancient paved causeway, evidently a **British**, and subsequently a **Roman trackway**, that ran by Crook Gate northwards across the moor to Golcar Gate by Faweather, on to the main Roman road over Otley Chevin to Ilkley. Parts of this causeway still exist, and it is doubtless a continuation of the road which came from the Roman station at Dewsbury and along Tong Street over Eccleshill Moor to the ford at Baildon. Having gained the top of our first ascent, a tolerably perfect **Barrow** is observable. It is of circular form, 90 ft. in circumference, and does not appear ever to have been disturbed. Just above this is the **High Plain**, and the farm called **Dobrudden** (*i.e.*, in Celtic, *a plain below a hill*), and here we can discern traces of former cultivation in the grass-grown ridges or balks characteristic of the old open-field system. Hence the top of **Hope Hill** (925 ft.) is soon attained, and the view in every direction is well worth noting, reaching as it does far over the Haworth moors into Lancashire, eastwards over the thick woods of Esholt and Calverley towards Leeds, where the dome of the Town Hall is seen, and north and west are wide stretches of heath, and hidden valleys, bounded by the Craven and Wharfedale hills. At the summit of the hill bits of decayed tree roots and **fossil stems** six to nine inches through are met with, and before quarrying began here stone circles, earthworks, and cairns must have been numerous, as their mutilated remains cover a large area. Most of these have no doubt been dug into in the hope of finding treasure, but only rude urns (often broken, and in ignorance tossed aside), containing ashes of the dead, have been discovered. The stones that covered them had doubtless previously been carted away. Right at the top (facing the shooting-house) there are, however, several apparently untouched barrows, but there are no cairns or monoliths. The site of one of these is still preserved in the name Rerehowe Cross, and the stone, we are told, was standing less than a century ago, though its character and purpose seem now to have passed out of knowledge.*

Descending upon **Acre Howe**, several "cup and ring" marked stones are observable; and at the summit of the broad road from Baildon to Bingley, on the north side, close to the road, is a very remarkable earthwork and circle, the latter about 150 ft. in circumference, and originally 8 ft. high enclosed with upright stones. The circle is bounded on its south and east sides by a singular entrenchment in the form of an angle or reversed letter ⌐ extending about 80 ft. on the east and 36 ft on the south side. It consists of a fosse with a double agger, the breadth of the fosse being 27 ft., and depth 40 in., the entire width of the entrenchment from the outer edges of the aggers being nearly 50 ft. The interior of the circle had at some time been excavated before it was again opened in 1843 by Mr. Colls, who discovered two broken urns, slightly ornamented, and containing burnt human bones, and in one of the urns was a flint arrow-head. Details of this discovery were narrated in a letter to the late Edw. Hailstone, Esq., of Walton Hall, which was printed in Vol. 31 of the *Archæologia*. No similar burial mound has been found elsewhere in England, although several in Scotland are said to resemble it. Proceeding now westwards we get on to **Penythorne Hill**, at the top of which is a mutilated earthwork of circular shape, 150 ft. in circumference, and consisting of portions of a stone circle. A barrow here was opened, and at a depth of two feet was found to contain a rude urn (*see engr.*) of bowl shape 12 in. in diameter and 10 in. deep, ornamented with diagonal lines on the upper part, and containing charcoal, ashes, and the cremated remains of what upon medical analysis proved to be a young subject of 9 to 13 years of age. Under this

---

* An effort to solve the whereabouts of this Cross has led to the discovery that it was situate about 50 to 60 yards left of the road going from Baildon to Eldwick, and a short mile from the former place. It was a craggy ridge on Acra or Acre Hill, and the only bit of "crag" about here, and there was one large, flat stone on which the traditional Cross stood. Our aged informant (Mr. Thos. Lupton, of Baildon) says no one now living remembers it. The "crag" was demolished when the reservoir was made. On the right of the road, and separated from the Cross by a distance of about 100 yards, was a large and copious spring of very cold, clear water, called Acra Well, probably once a Holy Well, connected with this early Rerebowe Cross. The well is now covered in; the water from it, as well as from the Spink and Birch Close springs higher up, being conducted in pipes to the reservoir.

hill are also a number of pit-dwellings. Descending hence towards
 Faweather we enter (by permission) a field at Birch Close farm, and here find evidences of an extensive stone circle, some of the large unhewn stones having been built into an adjoining wall. In the next field is a rock sculptured with the previously described "cup and ring" marks. Retracing our steps now under Penythorne Hill along the old British pathway, before mentioned, towards Eldwick, about midway, close to the pavement, but also abounding (formerly in very large quantities) in the adjoining fields, are abundant fragments of iron scoriæ, used from time to time in repairing the roads. These indications of **early iron smelting** were first noted by the late Mr. Edward Hailstone, F.S.A., who shewed them to Mr. J. E. Preston, the antiquary, of Littlebeck Hall, Gilstead. Mr. Preston, whose guidance and writings on the archæology of the district have considerably aided our investigations, informs us that he has since found pieces of calcined ironstone elsewhere in the district; and some few years ago was discovered on the north-west side of Hope Hill a **mould** in one of the gritstone rocks in the shape of a hammer or axe-head, lined with iron, and which has evidently been used in the casting of these articles. In August, 1890, Mr. Preston's son (Mr. W. E. Preston) dug up in a plot of previously unbroken garden at Littlebeck several pieces of iron
 slag, weighing from two to four pounds each, very impurely run, which are probably of pre-Roman origin, for the early Britons, as is known, manufactured weapons and articles of iron and bronze long anterior to the Roman occupation of this country. At Eldwick, about 1865, several bronze spear-heads were unearthed, but they were probably Romano-Celtic. In this locality also a very fine flint spear-head of Neolithic age was dug up in May, 1882. It is 4½ in. long, and 1¾ in. at its greatest breadth (*see engr.*). At Littlebeck also, a few weeks later was found a very perfect flint knife or scraper, 2 in. in length (*see engr. next page*), along with a number of flint arrow-heads, and there is little doubt that if the ground was broken in the neighbourhood of the pit-dwellings mentioned other relics of like prehistoric interest would be found.* Many such objects, however, attributed to the handicraft of the remotest ages, are often proved to be of Roman or even of later date. The Saxons,
indeed, centuries after the introduction of iron and bronze, are known

* Since the above was written a most interesting discovery has been made by Mr. W. E. Preston, above mentioned, in singular corroboration of these remarks. Only a few inches below the surface large quantities of broken mediæval earthen-

to have used stone implements, and to have fought many of their battles with weapons of flint and stone. They overran Airedale in the seventh and eighth centuries, and have left a very remarkable memento of their visit to Bingley, which is preserved in the parish church. Coming to **Eldwick**, these Saxons would find most abundant proofs of the antiquity of this place, and so probably called it *eald wick* (i.e., old village), a name that is still recognised.* On the Common, at the north-east side of Eldwick are remains of more pit-dwellings, which have been cut through by the road from the Glen up to Cropper Fold farm. We have now conducted the visitor over such pre-historic relics as yet remain on these moors, where, in the apt words of the poet,

"The Pagan's myths through marble lips are spoken,
And ghosts of old Beliefs still flit and moan,
Round fane and altar overthrown and broken,
O'er tree-grown barrow, and grey ring of stone."

The route from Eldwick may be taken to Bingley, 1¼ m., or to Saltaire, 2¼ m.

Baildon to Hawksworth and Ilkley, 7 m. Crossing the Common, descend through Spring Wood by a picturesque road to the four-lane ends, (2 m.) **Hawksworth** is on r., occupying a terrace on the south side of Hawksworth Moor, and commanding a wide and very beautiful view. The Hall and Manor Cottage (the latter was an old thatched building up to its restoration three years ago) are identified with a family of historic consequence since early Norman times. Upon the completion of *Domesday*, Walter Hawksworth appears as first lord, and the proprietary continued in that name until 1786, when Walter Ramsden Beaumont Hawksworth assumed the name and arms of Fawkes, pursuant to the will of his relative Francis Fawkes, Esq., of Farnley Hall, who dying *s. p.* left him his estates. The old ivy-gabled Hall is a roomy building containing a splendid collection of carved oak, amongst which is a bedstead of unique design that is

ware have been found, consisting of handles and other pieces of jars, vases, bowls, and vessels of various kinds, partially glazed, but unfortunately none hitherto found are perfect. Some of these have been submitted to the authorities of the British Museum and pronounced "unquestionably mediæval." Below these again, at a depth of three to four feet, and apparently extending over a wide area, similarly large quantities of Roman red ware have been dug up. These include unglazed specimens of pieces of various domestic pottery, and several slightly ornamented Roman amphoræ. The fragments are literally in thousands, proving this to have been a great earthenware manufactory through successive long-past ages. A careful examination of this ground will probably disclose other coeval relics.

* The name, however, may have been based upon the older Celtic *El*, a height, or *Hel*, a hollow, and *gwic*, a village. In *Domesday* it is spelled Helguic, and later Elwic. Near Belford and Beal (in Northumberland) there are some pre-historic earthworks and a village called *Elwick*, which exactly coincides with the early spelling of our Airedale Eldwick.

said to have found its way here from Skipton Castle. King James I. is declared to have slept here during a "Knighting expedition" in the north, on which occasion he was the guest of Richard, afterwards Sir Richard Hawksworth, Kt. One of the rooms bears the royal arms with the date 1611. The Hall was occupied by the Fawkes family until 1825, and shortly afterwards was leased to the late Mr. Timothy Horsfall, J.P. (a member of the old manufacturing firm of Horsfall Bros., of Bradford), who resided here until his death, in March 1877. It has not since been let by the present owner, Ayscough Fawkes, Esq., of Farnley Hall.

Pursuing the road northward we reach **Burley Wood Head**, (4¼ m.), whence the village of Burley-in-Wharfedale may be visited, where, in the winsome notes of Stephen Fawcett,

> "O'er sleepy, chiming wood and wave,
> The voice of joy, in choral stave,
> Sings, "Pleasant are the streams which lave
>   The primrose banks of Burley."
> Far over Greenholme's cascades sough,
> Mellifluous strains the stock doves coo,
> What fragrance flings the cedar bough,
>   When morning shines so clearly."

The words of an observant naturalist surely! At Burley lived the Rt. Hon. W. E. Forster, M.P. for Bradford from 1861-1886. On April 10th, 1886 he was interred in the beautiful little cemetery here, and the stone upon his grave bears an admirably expressed epitome of his public virtues. On the road to Burley Wood Head is a small hostelry called the *Hermit* Inn, after an eccentric character, known as "Old Job Senior, the Wharfedale Hermit." He lived more like the ancient Britons described in the last route than a civilian of the nineteenth century. His cave or hut, which might have been seen by crossing the Coldstone beck and ascending the moor path, a short distance above the plantation, was a primitive structure of his own erection, just big enough to turn round in, and roofed with rough stones on which sods of grass and heather grew. He presented a striking appearance himself, having a ruddy and not unintelligent countenance, but his head being bald, excepting where the grey locks hung over his ears, and his body bent almost double, and clad in parti-coloured garments patched together with strings and loops, a stranger meeting him might have thought he had encountered an escape from a menagerie. He hobbled on two bent holly sticks, and when he was not puffing his weed his pipe was usually in his hat. He had an unnaturally powerful voice, and hundreds of people use to be attracted to the neighbourhood of his hermitage in the hope of hearing him give what he not inappropriately termed his "blast." He would entertain his audience by singing hymns, which could be heard in the valley at an uncommonly long distance. Having married an old woman of 80 who had "a bit of property," his life, after her death, was spent in vagrancy, and he died at Carlton workhouse on Aug. 6th, 1853, aged 77, and was buried in Burley churchyard. One of his old walking-sticks is preserved at the *Hermit* Inn. Continuing along the elevated moor road, with charming views over Wharfedale, and passing under the famous Cow and Calf rocks, Ilkley is reached in a walk of about two miles.

Baildon to Ilkley by Gaping Goose, 6 m. Cross the Common to the little bowery hamlet of **Sconce**, where a new industry was started a few years ago, for the artificial hatching of eggs. Sometimes the feathered population here has reached 1000. The present occupier has a large number of canaries and breeds a good class of birds for exhibition. Our road is now straight to the stone mine at **Faweather**, where a seam of excellent flag and roofing stone is worked at a depth of 90 ft. The mine was opened in 1889, and now goes a good way underground. In monastic times the canons of Drax Priory received tithes in all the cultivated lands here belonging to the abbey of Rievaulx. The monks had a grange at "Fawdre on Rumblesmore," and also an essart of land called *Aughetwait*,* where they had iron mines. At the farm beyond the stone-pit turn sharp *l.* and cross the beck up an old rustic lane, called Wood Lane, banked with hawthorn, honeysuckle, and red and white roses, and where also in season bloom the sweet blue speedwells, golden saxifrage, woolly campion, sweet-cicely, with its odour of aniseed, red valerian and wild geraniums, whose brilliant-hued foliage is so conspicuous in the sear of autumn. This lane emerges on the Keighley and Guiseley moor road near the **Gaping Goose**, as the solitary house on our right is called, from its having been the sign of an Inn, and a noted haunt of cock-fighters, poachers, &c., and where also many a man-battle for big stakes has been fought in the "good old days." Here a path strikes into the heather, parallel with the wall for some distance, and by keeping a sharp look out the naturalist will observe the pretty swamp-loving butterwort, one of the three insectivorous plants indigenous to Britain; perhaps too a flower of Parnassus; and among birds the golden plover, ring ouzel, mountain linnet, wheatear, whinchat, &c. may be met with, whilst this is also the home of that curious silk-producing insect, the emperor moth, whose 'royal' wings measure sometimes three inches across. Passing an old stone stoop in a northerly direction the conspicuous **Shooting House** is reached at an elevation of about 1200 ft. Here the view over Wharfedale, &c. is very beautiful, and somewhat the same as from Otley Chevin. Ingleborough is well seen. A rough track continues again northwards and joins the main road from Saltaire, 2 m. above Ilkley. *See* p. 163.

---

* A name derived from Haugh, (Hough, How), a burial hill, and thwaite (from A. S. *thweotan*, to cut down) a wood clearing; presumably Baildon, where iron mines were worked in early British times.

SALTAIRE.

 CHARMING diversity of hill and dale, of woodland, water-side, and moorland walks, easily accessible to even feeble pedestrians, have made this undoubtedly the chief open-air resort to half-holidayists of Bradford and district. But if Nature is mainly responsible for so much health-and-pleasure-giving popularity, human achievement has given to it even a wider fame, for citizens of all parts are annually attracted to the 'model town,' which has in reality become, through the genius and philanthropy of its noble author, a famous industrial shrine.

Saltaire forty years ago was not known by its present name. The site and surroundings of the town were all in field, and moor, and forest, remaining pretty much as it was in the days when the now forgotten Priory at Esholt, three miles lower down, was in its prime. A quickset lane led down to the river, where was an old ford and stepping stones that led into the thick woods opposite, reminding us not a little of the beautiful Wharfe at Bolton Abbey at the present day. Where the mills now stand was a waving corn-field, and there was also an old corn-mill, also used as a fulling-mill, on the piece of ground now occupied by the dyeworks and spinning-mill of the Saltaire firm. This locality was known as Dixon's Land and Mills, from the family of that name, who built the old Hall at Shipley, in 1593, and were living at Heaton Royds in the reign of Elizabeth. So 'out of the way' was the place considered, that up to the removal of the old mills in 1850 there were two houses near, suggestively known as the 'Whistle Jacket houses,' where malt liquor was brewed and sold without a license, or if there was one it was of the old type of 'pious smuggler' age.

The estate comprises about fifty acres, the first purchase (some 6½ acres) having been made by the late Sir Titus Salt, then Mr. Salt, of the proprietor of Esholt Hall, the late

Mr. W. R. Stansfeld, in 1850. About 26 acres are now occupied by some 900 dwellings and other buildings; the mills have absorbed 9½ acres, and the remainder is laid out in a public park. The lofty-mindedness, good taste, and unsparing philanthropy of the noble founder of this model working-town are indeed apparent on every hand. Sir Titus did nothing meanly or by halves, and his architects, Messrs. Lockwood and Mawson, of Bradford, acting upon his instructions, had the fullest liberty given to them in the

SALTAIRE FROM THE NORTH-WEST.

carrying out of the appointed work. The town is built in the Italian style, and is marked by a symmetry, breadth, and chasteness of design, conjointly with a solidity which the excellent native stone has given it, certainly unique in this country. The colossal mills, opened with great pomp on the founder's 50th birthday, (Sept. 20th, 1853), comprise a block six storeys high, having a maximum length from east to west of 548 feet, being 50 feet wide, and having a total height from the Midland line of 73 feet. The Warehouses are each 330 feet in length, and adjoining the canal are 90 feet high. On the east and west sides are the weaving and combing sheds, the former containing at one time 1200 looms, and when in full work producing 18 miles of alpaca or mixed goods per day, or equal to 5700 miles per year! To drive the machinery of these enormous works there are two miles of shafting, and engines with a register of 1800 horse power. The chimney is a solid and ornamental structure in the form of an Italian campanile, 250 feet high, the same height as the larger one at Manningham Mills. Since the decline of the alpaca trade the firm, which is now designated Sir Titus Salt, Bart., Sons & Co., Ld., and employs some 3500 workpeople, has been producing soft-wool goods, plushes, velvets, and a variety of "specialities." Alpaca was, of course the foundation of the firm's success, but we must refer the reader to Dickens' *Household Words*, for the story so happily told of its 'discovery' and successful treatment by young Mr. Salt, in 1836.

Sir Titus Salt had an especially quiet, gentle, and unassuming disposition, and found his greatest pleasure in doing good. His benevolence was unbounded, and it is said that during his lifetime he distributed in public and private charity not less than half-a-million of money. Though raised to the baronetage in 1869, and urged by his admiring townspeople to a seat in Parliament, (from which he soon retired), he sought neither titles, honours, nor fame. Of him it might be said, as Virgil (who, by the way, was himself so modest, that he would go down the by-streets of Rome to escape the popular applause) said of his flocks in the *Pastorals, Sic vos, non vobis, i.e., not for yourselves but for others you live*. His pious, just and generous spirit is perceptible in his dedication of the Saltaire almshouses, " In grateful remembrance of God's undeserved goodness, and in hope of promoting the comfort of some one who, in feebleness and necessity, may need a home." At Lightcliffe, on Dec. 29th, 1876, at the age of 73, Sir Titus Salt fell asleep. Some two years before, a costly statue of him was unveiled in Bradford ; but though we may there scan his portrait and outward semblance shaped in marble in the busy heart of the town, yet if we would see the monumented *character* of the man (of far greater import) we must go to Saltaire. It was the noble wish and desire of the founder that if there could be anything elevating or improving in erections combining structural beauty with utility it was to find expression here. There was to be nothing mean or cramped, nothing scamped. On the little town he expended over £120,000, exclusive of cost of land. Amongst the chief buildings may be mentioned the Institute and High Schools (before the formation of the Shipley School Board used as Factory Schools), the Baths and Washhouses, the 45 Almshouses, with their neat Chapel and Infirmary, and the handsome Congregational Church, to which is attached the family mausoleum. The latter, built in 1859, is an exquisite example of pure Italian art, and if there can be such a thing as poetry in stone it is surely expressed here. In grace and elegance of composition this building would be hard to surpass. In addition there are the new Science and Art Schools, erected at a cost of £7000 in 1886, as a memorial to the late baronet. They were opened by the Princess Beatrice on May 6th, 1887, and are modelled after the best schools of their kind in England. The Park, beautifully situated on the north bank of the river, was opened in 1871, and occupying, as it does, an open yet sheltered and unvitiated site, many kinds of trees and botanical rarities flourish here uncommonly well. A portion of the fourteen acres comprised is set apart for cricket, lawn-tennis, &c. The gates are open daily from sunrise to sunset.

Saltaire is a favourite starting-point, as we have said, with the half-holidayist, and whether in the direction of the Glen, Gilstead or Eldwick, Baildon, Cottingley, Heaton, or Bingley, the walks are always interesting, and there is besides ample provision for boating here. Saltaire is in Shipley township : the two stations being a half-mile apart. There is also tram service from Bradford to Shipley (3d.) and Saltaire (4d). The following routes are especially noteworthy.

Saltaire to Bingley by Seven Arches, 2¾ m. By the highroad over Cottingley bridge it is also 2¾ m. By a tree-shaded sweep of the canal a mile walk brings the visitor to the famous **Seven Arches**, a very picturesque spot, and attractive to the scientist too. Owing to the great heaps of boulder-gravel having prevented the straight eastward flow of the river, it here serpentines round them, and is crossed on separate arches by the railway and canal. This, whilst one of the most interesting, was one of the most costly of the engineering difficulties overcome in the 129 miles course of the Leeds and Liverpool Canal. The 'arches' were constructed at the end of last century by Mr. James Rhodes, whose son William, at that time was steward of the Wainman estate at Shipley, and lived at Dixon's old Hall, opposite the Rosse Street Chapel. James Rhodes, his son, was also a large contractor, and constructed the well-known Hollingworth Lake, near Rochdale. The canal was opened in Oct., 1816, with a grand aquatic procession, and as the gaily-decked boats passed over the long line of arches, many people who had assembled in the vicinity gave them ringing cheers! By the circling, shady river below, is the haunt of many less common birds and wild flowers. Following the pleasant bend of the canal by the church of Holy Trinity to the old Dubb Bridge, Bingley may be entered by crossing the bridge and on Mornington Road past the Technical College, into Park Road.

Saltaire to Bingley by Cottingley Bridge, 4 m. The route here indicated is not by the highroad but takes the canal bank to the first lock. Here the bridge is crossed and **Hurst Wood** entered by a cart road on *r*. The road is followed down to the railway viaduct near Seven Arches, an umbrageous walk abounding in a variety of trees, mosses, and wild flowers. In Spring the cuckoo may often be heard here, whilst the wood is blue over with the odorous wild hyacinth, a peculiar "anomaly of Nature" in our woods and hedgerows, for whereas other flowers at this season are pale and fair of hue, the "blue-bells," clustered blossoms are, singularly, of the deepest dye! Crossing the stream the south bank of the Aire is now followed to the picturesque Cottingley Bridge, on the way noting the various kinds of birds that frequent this part of the river, including the finches, the little blue-tit with its short sharp bill, the sandpiper, and lively wagtails with their glossy plumage and erect tails. Occasionally also an otter may be seen. Ascending the flight of steps the village of **Cottingley** may be visited round by the toll-house, erected when the road was made in 1825. The old coach road from Bradford north came over Shipley High Moor and through Cottingley Park, (where the bridge it crossed may be seen from the present highway), to the *Sun* Inn. Here in a bygone age the 'village court' was held, whose last presiding Justice was one Colonel Wickham, of Cottingley House, who died in 1804. He was a gentleman well-known and of good note in his day, and lived in great state at Cottingley. Every Sunday, when 'at home,' he and his family might have been seen driving to Bingley church in a finely-equipped coach-and-four with postilion. The Wickhams were a very old family and claimed a distinguished descent. James, the historian of Bradford, traces their lineage to the famous Bishop Wykeham, of Winchester, founder of the College there and of New College, Oxford, in the 14th century. Colonel Wickham's sons held high offices in the Church and State, one being a Privy Councillor and Chief Secretary for Ireland in 1804; another was Prebendary of York, and father of the late Mr. H. W. Wickham, M.P. for Bradford from 1852—67. After the family left Cottingley House it was occupied by the Ferrands and Thorntons, and here in 1838 was born Richard Thornton, a geographer of high promise, who died at the early age 25, whilst on an expedition with Dr. Livingstone in Central Africa. A notice of him will be found in 'A Popular Account of Dr. Livingstone's Expedition to the Zambesi'; also in *Good Words* for 1865. The old Hall at the top of the village, was built by the Ferrands in 1659, but was pulled down some twenty years ago. In 1865 a Public Hall was erected, where the Mechanics' Inst. (founded in 1852) is now located In 1886 the Church at Cottingley, which had previously been a Mission in the parish of Holy Trinity, Bingley, was re-opened and liberally endowed by Henry Mason, Esq., of Bankfield. Resuming now our walk along the pleasant Beck Foot Lane, we arrive at the old farm with its small lantern turrets denoting an ancient proprietary here of the Knights of St. John of Jerusalem. Crossing the rustic bridge the lane is followed on to the Harden and Cullingworth road, or a field path over Hesp Hills may be taken to Bingley. Around Beck Foot the scenery is beloved by artists, and here too the lover of birds, wild flowers, &c., will likewise be delighted. Mr. H. T. Soppitt, the mycologist, enumerates several uncommon species of fungi that occur about here, and notably the St. George's mushroom, (*Tricholoma gambosus*), a much prized comestible. Here is the haunt of that rare and beautiful bird the pied-flycatcher, also of the spotted species, and of the tree-pipit, white-throat, &c. Here, too, on many a still summer's eve are poured forth the rich, mellifluous strains of the song-thrush and the blackcap, each vying with the other for rivalship with that prince of songsters, the silver-tongued nightingale.

Saltaire through Shipley Glen to Ilkley, 7 m. The first portion of the route may be varied Either along the Park road and by Trench farm into the Glen, or keep straight on until the entrance gate to Milner Field (Titus Salt, Esq., J.P.) is reached, whence a narrow foot road leads up to New Scarbro', (pleasure grounds) and forward *l.* to Littlebeck, or *r.* to Eldwick. The Trench farm is a roomy old 17th century building, where tanning and dressing of leather used to be carried on a century or more ago. In a wall in the farm-yard is an enormous grey bone of some extinct animal, which has been roughly squared and used as a wall-stone. When the grounds of Milner Field were laid out and the fish-pond made, about 1869, a single large tooth of a bison was unearthed. This speaks of a time when wild animals roamed in Airedale much the same as they do now in the remote forests and mountainous regions of Asia and America. Evidences of the existence of the bear, wolf, hyæna, &c., have been found in other parts of the Aire valley, and in Lothersdale of the lion and mammoth.

From Saltaire the usual route to the Glen is upon rounding the Park to turn up through Trench, now called Glen Wood. Leaving the station a descent is made over the handsome and costly bridge near Saltaire Mills. Before the erection of this bridge, which was rebuilt in 1869, the river was crossed by stepping-stones, often impassable by the heavy floods that washed over them, particularly in winter-time or after the melting of the snows in spring. It was at such a season—the night before Good Friday, 1843—that the Airedale poet, John Nicholson, lost his life in the attempt to cross them. The stones were clear, but still wet and slippery from the recent passage of water. The poet had all but succeeded in crossing them when he appears to have fallen into the river, near its brink, from which, however, he managed to extricate himself, but in a wet and exhausted condition. On the following morning he was found dead in the meadow hard by. The spot is still pointed out. At that time a footpath ran along the north bank of the river past here from Baildon Mills. Continuing hence up through the wood, bright with moss, and shrub, and wild flower, **Shipley Glen** is soon reached. We have already described the antiquities of this locality on pp. 147-154. To the lover of Nature the Glen abounds in many striking bits of woodland scenery, whilst the hanging rocks above, tumbled together in many a curious position, provide scope for youngsters' games of hide-and-seek, &c., and quiet corners, too, for "foolish couples." The scientifically inclined will find the Glen *a paradise*. Not only is it the haunt of many rare and beautiful birds, such as the great and blue tits, nightjar, missel thrush, tree-creeper, redstart, &c., but of some uncommon plants, insects, and molluscs also. Here the botanist will find the golden saxifrages, the dead nettles, red and yellow, the climbing fumitory, tutsan, and that peculiar insectivorous plant, the round-leaved sundew. In molluscan fauna several rarities have been met with. About ten years ago, Mr. Wm. West, F.L.S., discovered here a variety of *Limax cinereo-niger*, which had not before been found in Yorkshire. In August, 1889, Mr. J. W. Carter, a well-known Bradford entomologist, took here a fine example of *Bembidium nigricorne*, a beautiful species of beetle, likewise an addition to the county fauna. In moths and butterflies the neighbourhood of the Glen is fairly rich. Altogether the naturalist will find this a happy hunting-ground. From the Glen the route over Rumbalds Moor to Ilkley may be taken either through Eldwick, or without crossing the beck a path ascends the fields by way of Cropper Fold farm, whence the well-known road to "Dick Hudson's" is entered. Behind the inn the path enters upon the wide, heathery moor, which it traverses for 3¼ m., and at its highest point, near the Druids' Circle, 1¼ m. above Ilkley, attains an elevation of 1220 ft. Here the view is truly magnificent, extending northwards over Wharfedale to Simon's Seat and Beamsley Beacon,

eastwards away over Otley to the Vale of York, with its famous landmark the two-towered Minster (*see* Otley Chevin, p.143). Looking westward the conical summits of Flasby Fell are seen, with Malham Moor, Ryeloaf, &c., behind, and due N.N.W. the conspicuous flat top of Ingleborough 40 miles off, limits our vision, as represented in our sketch of the view. Ilkley lies below, and a precipitous descent is now made to the handsome spa-town.

BINGLEY.

NO place in Airedale better deserves the title of Little Switzerland, now-a-days so often applied to English scenes of romantic beauty, than old Bingley. Despite modern encroachments, the same high craggy hills, wide open moors, and towering steeps clothed with dense forest, still unite to form a variety of majestic landscapes. Though the grinding glacier no longer rears its frozen walls against the slopes, vestiges of that remote icy period are still here abundant. Enormous mounds of coarse boulder gravel fill to a great depth the narrow valley, and which at one time here must have dammed back the onflowing waters into an expansive lake. The town of Bingley is built wholly upon such a drift-hill consisting of rounded, water-washed grit, sandstone and limestone boulders and pebbles of varying size. Fragments of decomposed quartzose grit, friable yellow sandstone, and 'petrified' animal remains are also found. Much of the limestone has, at some period, been extracted and burnt, traces of old kilns and cinders being abundant on the Cemetery hill, which likewise is composed wholly of such drift stuff. By a subsequent redisposition of these glacial deposits the river has cut a channel on the west side of the town, and it here flows between steep banks clothed with luxuriant wood, reminding us in some respects of the far-famed scenery of Matlock in Derbyshire. When the railway was made in 1847 its progress was greatly impeded by the deep swamp left by the old river expanse or lake, and we are told that several thousand tons of stone and debris chiefly from excavations at Shipley were tipped here before a permanent foundation could be obtained. Sometimes carts left high and dry over night would be found up to their axles in water the next morning. When the present Vicarage was built in 1837 log piles were laid down in addition, a method of construction similar to that which is adopted in maritime towns in Holland. Huge joists laid transversely also formed the surface foundation of the railway from the station all the way on under the canal-locks. Some five acres of this site are now planted with willows, which have from time to time sustained similar devastations from the rapacious little willow-beetle to those described in our account of the neighbourhood of Ferry Bridge.

It is not unlikely that there was a British settlement at Bingley, dependent subsequently upon the Romans. Portions of British stone querns, or hand corn mills* have been turned up, and one of these querns, now in the Bradford Public Museum, is an exceptionally fine example, being almost perfect. At any rate Bingley in Saxon times must have been a place of some note. The unique and very valuable Runic stone preserved in the church is, whilst suggesting a wide field of inquiry, plainly indicative of the gathering here in the eighth century of Pictish and Saxon hosts, assembled with their kings, princes, and chiefs, to consummate either a union of arms or a treaty of peace. The reading of the stone has been variously rendered, in substance, however, it is the same:

"Eadberht, son of Catha, King, uttered a gracious ban (with) Ongus (King of the Picts), visited (again) Bingley."

At the Conquest the place was held by Byng or Bingel, a Saxon, and given by the Conqueror to his follower Ernegis de Burun. Afterwards it was granted by Henry I. to William de Paganel or Paynel, of a celebrated Norman family, who held 45 lordships in Yorkshire, and divers manors and lordships in Lincolnshire, Devonshire, and Somersetshire. But of this distinguished family we have already spoken in our chapter on Drax. Wm. Paynel, early in the 12th century, built the church, which he gave to the abbey of Drax, also one of his foundations. The Paynels were lords of the manor of Drax, Leeds, and Bingley, and, though mainly resident in Normandy, they had numerous residences and strongholds for the defence of their property here. They had a castle, as we have seen, at Drax, protected by its surrounding marshes; possibly one also at Leeds, and it is likewise probable they built the castle at

* As used by the primitive races of Africa, India, &c. at the present day.

Bingley, of which the foundations were observed by Dodsworth in 1621. The site of the castle at Bingley is still known as Baily Hill, and the land adjoining as Castlefields.* Furthermore, the fact is suggestive, that a local benefactor to Drax Priory was one William de Castelay, who held a toft here " lying on the south side of the church between the road and the river Ayre." In the reign of John, the manor passed by marriage to the De Gants, a wealthy and powerful Norman family, who owned over 50 lordships in East Yorkshire and elsewhere, and who were the founders of the magnificent Priory at Bridlington. It was to Maurice de Gant that King John granted, in 1212. a charter for the holding of a weekly market at Bingley, or five years after he had obtained the same privilege for Leeds. This Royal concession must have raised Bingley, like Leeds, to a town of chief importance at that time. Though in a state of feudalism, with its (presumably) strong-walled castle, church, ale-houses, and thatched cots, cultivation must have considerably extended, and a more generous dietary likewise resulted. It may be noted that there was no market at the now very much larger town of Keighley for nearly a century afterwards. What a picture feudal Bingley must have presented every Sabbath when its market was held ! Droves of oxen, sheep, and pigs were brought together in the main thoroughfare much as they are now : the husbandmen and herdsmen with their Norman caps and blouses, and the women with their coloured hose, buckled shoes, and short gowns, assembled with baskets of fruit, honey, eggs, butter, and pastry cakes which bore an imprint of the sacred cross ! Among the motley throng of buyers and sellers moved the martial freeman, villein, and monkish visitor, staff in hand, with youths who came from

---

* How long the castle, noted by our great antiquary, had lain in ruins; whether destroyed by Stephen during the Barons' Wars, or razed by the Scots after Bannockburn, we cannot say. Indeed, after several visits to the Record Office and the British Museum, we have hitherto been unable to authenticate by written evidence the existence of this castle. It is a matter of regret that Dodsworth furnished so few particulars. Possibly the building may be pre-historic, yet, from the fact of the eminence upon which it stands being called Baily Hill, from the Norman *ballium*, or court-baily, there is presumptive evidence of a later origin.

the monasteries or parish schools to see and learn the business of trading. On the days of the hunt, too, what a scene of gay animation! Assembled, as we may imagine them, in the baily or court-yard of the castle, protected by river and moat, or marsh, the lordly baron with his retinue of armed retainers, and sprinkling of handsomely-mounted ladies, summoned "the yeoman tall," who

> "The iron studded gates unbarr'd,
> Rais'd the portcullis' pond'rous guard,
> The lofty palisade unsparr'd,
> And let the draw-bridge fall."

Then with bow and barbed arrow they rode forth to moor or forest, rousing the wild game with keen-scented dogs, and returning at day's close with the trophies of the chase. In later times attached to the Bingley manor house was an extensive park in which deer were kept, but no traces of this park are seen now. For more than two centuries the manor belonged to the noble family of Astley, and at the end of the 16th century was sold by them to the Walkers, and resold to Hugh Currer, Esq. of Marley, from whose grandson the manor and market rights were purchased in the time of Charles II. by Robert Benson, father of the first Lord Bingley. The manor is now vested in his descendant, Geo. Lane Fox, Esq. of Bramham park; the market rights having, in 1882, been bought for £800 by the Bingley Improvement Commissioners.

The Norman Church was, with the exception of portions of the tower, replaced by the present structure about the time of the Reformation. From its foundation up to the Dissolution it was the property of the Canons of Drax and dedicated to St. Lawrence; since that time to All Saints. It was completely restored in 1870 at an outlay of £3000. The interior contains some especially rich, ancient and modern stain-glass. The large east window by Powell & Sons, London, is an admirable composition of five lights, typifying Charity, Purity, Love, Truth, and Humility, and was erected in June, 1890, by Dr. Cheadle, son of the former Vicar, as a memorial to his wife, Anne, daughter of Wm. Murgatroyd, Esq. of Bankfield. There are also other notable windows and tablets to the families of Busfeild, Ferrand, Leach, Sunderland,

Harris, General Twiss of Harden Grange, &c. The Riddlesden chapel, (where the organ is placed), is, like the Ryshworth chapel opposite, coeval with the church. The latter, "in pious remembrance of his ancestors," was restored by J. A. Busfeild, Esq., of Upwood, in 1870. The font, with oak canopy, (a handsome memorial to Mrs. Emily Busfeild) is from designs by Mr. Norman Shaw, R.A., and is of Mansfield stone, erected in 1881. The silver plate belonging to the church comprises six pieces, a plain chalice, two flagons, and two patens, the gift of Henry Hoyle, Esq., in 1705, and a handsome ornamental chalice presented by Wm. Busfeild, Esq., in 1725. The registers of the church date from 1577, and are well preserved, as are the old churchwardens' accounts of the parish. From these we abstract a few of the earliest entries, which throw some light on the life and aspects of the district at that period :

A.D. 1651.	Spent upon our first meeting to consider what children was fitt to be placed apprentice and with what masters	1s. 6d.
	Paid to John Hudson for 4 orchan* heads......	4d.
	,, ,, Tom Shackleton for a bawson* head...	4d.
	,, for a fox head to Thomas Leach, and another to Thomas Blakey..................	2s.
	,, to Wm. Oldfield for relief when he went to the Spaw Well [Harrogate]	6s.
	,, Martha Wallis for 20 gallons of wyne for Easter Communion £4, with bread 3s. 1d.	£4 3s. 1d.
1653.	,, to Matthew Thomas for 2 stone of iron, and working it into bands and cotterells for two of the bells...........................	11s.
	,, for Ringing of eight o'clock bell each night from Martinmas to March	10s.
1666.	,, for 8 Ringtayles* heads to Mr. John Bynnes	1s. 4d.

Some of these entries reveal the fact that many destructive animals abounded, though not to the same extent as in the upper reaches of the valley. In the churchyard are some

* *Orchan*, a hedgehog; *bawson*, a badger; *ringtayle*, a hawk.

quaint epitaphs, and one, to the good-hearted old sexton, Hezekiah Briggs, who died in 1844, aged 80, supplies this bit of musical biography:

> "Here lies an old ringer beneath this cold clay,
> Who has rung many peals both for serious and gay,
> Bob majors and trebles with ease he could range,
> Till death called a Bob brought round the last change."

The same epitaph we find repeated on another stone here to Isaac Rhodes, who died in 1842, aged 76. Beneath a stone erected by the lord of the manor, Mr. Lane Fox, lies the body of the Airedale Poet, John Nicholson, who died, as described, from exposure at Saltaire in 1843. He was a native of Weardley, near Harewood, but spent most of his life in the neighbourhood of his beloved Bingley, the 'Throstle Nest of Old England,' as it was poetically called. Though one of Nature's "uneducated poets," he has left, perhaps, the happiest descriptions of local life and scenery that have yet been furnished to us.

The old Grammar School at Bingley, where Nicholson obtained a year's schooling, under the learned and estimable Dr. Hartley, was founded in the year 1529, for the sons of resident householders in the parish. The new School at Castlefields, built in 1853 and enlarged in 1877, is governed under the new Act, and has separate wings for boys and girls. The endowments now amount to about £900 per annum.

The powers obtained by the local authorities for street improvements, have of late years altered the old-world look of Bingley very materially. The stone Butter Cross erected in 1753, when the market-day was changed from Sunday to Tuesday, and the old parish stocks, so long located in the churchyard, have been removed to the new Park. The old whitewashed Workhouse, with its couple of dingy prison-cells, was pulled down when the new Court House was built in Myrtle Place about 1860. Many of the old chapels and schools, too, have been replaced by modern structures of larger and more imposing character. It is two and a quarter centuries since Nonconformity was established at Bingley; the Rev. Oliver Heywood having assembled a congregation privately, at Marley Hall in Sept., 1667, some three years after the Conventicle Act was passed, proscribing every other form of worship but that practised by the Anglican Church. The Rev. John Wesley was also a frequent visitor at Bingley last century, and used to preach in the old chapel, opposite the market place, which has now a counterpart in the magnificent chapel in Mornington Road.

Bingley being an old coaching town has some very old inns; doubtless inns, or public guest-houses, have had an existence here from the days of the Anglo-Saxons. Up to a late period they were the authorised courts of the justiciary, where cases were tried, and parochial business was transacted.

MAIN STREET, BINGLEY.

Here at the *Brown Cow* is a large room where the petty sessions were held, subsequently used as a school-room. At the *King's Head* the lord of the manor held his great Court Leet, and at the old *White Horse* many a poor delinquent has had to render an account of himself before the sitting judge, in a room where the Royal Arms may still be dimly traced on the dark oak chimney board. This house, singularly constructed, contains a vaulted cellar, the span of the arch being about five yards, with a leaded window, now blocked. It may have been used as a prison at some time.

The flow of commerce into the district has raised a

number of modern buildings of interest in Bingley. The new Technical College, in Mornington Road, is a handsome building fitted up with all the latest requirements of industrial training, and cost about £5000. The corner-stone was laid on Oct. 27th, 1888, by Alfred Sharp, Esq., of Carr Head, near Crosshills, who subscribed about one-fourth of the entire cost. The Mechanics' Institute, in Main Street, was opened in 1864, at an expenditure of £3000. It is from designs of Mr. Alfred Waterhouse. The Free Libraries Act having lately been adopted in Bingley, the building has been leased for its purposes. In a beautiful situation at Ferncliffe is the new Cottage Hospital, a memorial of Her Majesty's Jubilee, opened July 26th, 1890. It is a neat one-storey building designed for the benefit of the sick poor of the town and district, and completed at a cost of about £3000. Enclosed by an extensive piece of ground it is very well suited for convalescents.

Bingley also possesses as pleasant a public Park and Cemetery as are to be found anywhere in Airedale. The former, commenced in 1863, occupies an elevated area of about 18 acres, on the north side of the valley, and commands magnificent views over the dale westward. The Cemetery, opened in 1870, occupies a dry and sheltered position on the Castle or Baily Hill. It is beautifully laid out, and variously planted with Alpine and other foreign specialities. A new walk is being constructed along the south side above the river, composed chiefly of limestone *debris* from the old kilns formerly worked here.

The soil of the district seems well constituted for the production of a good quality of vegetables and especially some classes of bush fruit. The largest gooseberry seen in Airedale since 1805 was grown here in 1890. It was exhibited at the 15th annual show at Bingley on Aug. 22nd, (open to England) and weighed 31 dwt. 3 qr. Not the least important event of the year is the *Tide* or Feast, sometimes called the "King of Feasts," which is held annually at the end of August. The two half-yearly cattle fairs here are an old institution, and there is also a weekly market (now held on Fridays) dating, as already stated, from the time of King John.

THE VICINITY OF BINGLEY.

It was the opinion of Dr. Whitaker that "in extent of view, richness of scenery, and wild and rocky distances, every situation in Airedale to the north must yield to **St. Ives.**" It is admittedly to the natural beauty and extent of this private estate that Bingley owes not a little of its attractiveness. Up to 1855 the family mansion of the Ferrands, who have been so long seated here, was known as Harden Grange. In that year the old hall of St. Ives, in the Harden valley, occupied by Walter Dunlop, Esq., was rebuilt, and exchanged names with the present St. Ives. The Monks of Rievaulx having acquired lands here early in the 14th century from the Canons of Drax, this was probably a grange to these monasteries. A chalice and paten are cut in one of the stones. We have already offered an opinion as to the meaning of St. Ives on p. 130. Here is preserved a stone table from Harden Hall, (one of the oldest mansions built [in 1616] by the Ferrand family in this neighbourhood), on which General Fairfax is stated to have written his despatches while the Parliamentary troops were encamped here during the Civil Wars. For several hundred years from the Norman Conquest, the Ferrands were Officers of the Lords of the Honour of Skipton, but of the four branches into which the family came to be divided, that of St. Ives now alone retains its seat. In 1805, Sarah, daughter and sole heiress of John Ferrand, of Harden Grange, married Mr. Currer Fothergill Busfeild, B.A., of Cottingley Bridge, and brother of Mr. Wm. Busfeild, M.P. for Bradford from 1837 until his death in 1851. The eldest of a family of five sons and five daughters, was William Busfeild (born in 1809), who added the surname of Ferrand, the late Squire of St. Ives. He represented Knaresborough (1841-7) and Devonport (1863) in Parliament, was a J.P. and D L., and for many years Chairman of the Bingley Bench of Magistrates. He died in 1889, devising the estate under the entail to his nephew Mr. Wm. Busfeild. **Ryshworth Hall**, on the Keighley road, a mile north of Bingley, is a large old house of unknown date, but in 1672 it was bought by the Busfeild family, and occupied by them for nearly two centuries. Adjoining it was a large park encompassed by well-stocked woods. An excellent print of the Hall from an engraving made in the fourteenth century is to be seen in the British Museum.

Priesthorpe, on the north or Park side of the town, was the abode of the ancient Vicars of Bingley. The site, still known as the Vicarage, is now occupied by Priesthorpe Hall. The Canons of Drax belonged "the whole township of Priesthorpe," and in a document of A.D. 1312, mention is made of one Robert, son of Ralph, villayn of Bingley, who gave, (with his body, to be interred in the Priory), "to the Canons residing at Pristhorpe, two acres of arable land in the territory of Bingley; of which one abuts upon Brigflat on the one part, and Brerilands on the other. The other acre lies in Northfield; all which Simon, his son, confirmed." The ancient family of Dobson were, some two centuries ago, proprietors of land here and at Marley and Cottingley, where they resided. The Bingley registers shew a marriage between Wm. Dobson, churchwarden, and Ann Farrands, in 1665. The oldest house at Priesthorpe is that now occupied by Mrs. Craven, and divided into cottages which are partly in ruins. Over the door is inscribed X.H. I.H. 1632. The house possesses nothing of special interest, except a magnificently carved black oak sideboard, bearing upon its panels two owls and other sculptured figures, and the date 1671. Another oak cupboard bears the initials and date E.B. 1711. The owner has also in her possession a good small silver lamp used by the late Dr. Hartley, before the streets of Bingley were lighted with gas.

Gawthorpe Hall, on this side of Bingley also, was the seat of the lords of the manor in the Middle Ages. It is difficult to determine the precise age of the present building, notwithstanding that additions and alterations have been so adroitly made about it from time to time. Its terrace commands one of the richest private views in Airedale, having the lofty woods of the Druids' Altar in front. with the silvery, far-reaching river below. The Bensons, Lords of Bingley, long resided here, and in 1867 Mr. Lane Fox sold the property to Mr. John Horsfall. It was recently purchased from Major Salmond, of Bradford, by Mr. Robt. Wetherhead, who has been lately thoroughly restoring the old mansion.

We shall now indicate some of the many pleasant

WALKS AROUND BINGLEY.

A very nice round is the following: From the station cross the bridge at the **Canal Locks**, one of the wonders of the Leeds and Liverpool Navigation Co's. system. Ascending here in two combinations of Locks of three and five 'stairs' each, boats of 45 tons burthen may be raised or lowered perpendicularly 96 feet. From the top Lock there is a level run on the Canal to Holme Bridge, Gargrave. a distance of sixteen miles. This reach of water passing through a fine open country is often used in summer by steam barges for the conveyance of picnic or school parties to places of resort in the district. At the end of Plevna Road turn l., and up the fields past **Gawthorpe Hall** (see above.) Hence a green lane leads in about 100 yds. by a well-known medicinal iron spring. The water is very clear and said to be good for 'nerves.' A convenient stone receptacle with canopy, (inscribed T.G., 1871) now encloses it. From here the main road is soon reached, and a walk may be taken through the beutiful **Park** up to **Gilstead.** Here are the visitworthy Filter-Beds, constructed in 1885 by the Bradford Corporation for the cleansing of the low-level supply to the borough from Barden Moor. The six 'filters' (situated at a sea-elevation of 571 ft.) are each 300 ft. long, and 110 ft. wide, with a water capacity of 1¼ million gallons. The beds are laid on the solid rock, over which is a floor, a foot in thickness, of Portland cement, and above this lie seven feet of filtering material, consisting of a bottom of fine sand graduating to loose rubble at the surface. The cost of the works has been about £40,000, and were carried out under the direction of Mr. A. R. Binnie, C.E., now Waterworks Engineer to the City of London Corporation. Gilstead Moor, (spelled in Norman deeds *Gildested*) has been, since the passing of the enclosure scheme, largely built upon, and some of the land laid out in public pleasure gardens, &c. Littlebeck Hall here, a modern house in a mediæval style, was designed and built by the late Mr. John Preston, the well-known artist, and brother of Mr. Ben. Preston, of Eldwick, poet, and author of the inimitable dialect poem "Natterin Nan." This locality, referred to on pp. 153-4, has been undoubtedly, from the number of relics of the stone and bronze ages discovered, an important centre of a stationary population of the ancient Celtic tribes. From Gilstead the route may be taken by **Eldwick** and **Shipley Glen** (p. 147) to Saltaire, a round walk from Bingley of about 7 m.

To the Druids' Altar, 1¼ m. Ascending the Altar Road from Ireland Bridge the open moor is gained (680 ft.), whence

strike r., along the moor-edge some 250 yds., when the great Altar Rock is reached. It is a huge mass of disintegrated gritstone; its largest diameter being 18 ft., circumference about 52 ft., and height 24 ft. Whether it has ever been appropriated for the purpose its name implies will always be doubted,* but no doubt can exist that from the earliest period right up the steps of time to the great Feast of the Royal Jubilee in the late year of grace 1887, the stone has beaconed forth huge fires both of Joy and Alarm,—how often, alas! too, the one but a portent of the other! The site commands a very wide view, and in a direction north-west, above the pointed summit of Flasby Fell, the crest of Inglebro' is discernible on a clear day, and were it not for the balking double-cairn'd crown of Kirkby Fell (1790 ft.), the rugged flanks of Penyghent, and possibly also Whernside, could be seen; in fact this summit is responsible for the loss of what would be a magnificent and uninterrupted view of the mountains of upper Ribblesdale, and as far even as the confines of the Lake District. On the other side of the dale are the heather-vested heights of Rumbalds Moor, with Riveck Edge, and the village of Morton conspicuous in the foreground. In the valley below winds the bright and gentle Aire, of no consequence to us at this elevation what foulness it may bear down upon its lucent tide. When the late Lord Beaconsfield was a visitor at St. Ives, Mr. Ferrand brought him to this spot, which so captivated the great statesman-author's fancy that he introduced a description of it in his novel of *Sybil.*

* "The beautiful valley beneath, favourable to the growth of the oak, and eligible for their sacred groves, *place it beyond all doubt* that the valley of Bingley was once the residence of the ancient priests of the Britons."—NOTE TO NICHOLSON'S POEMS.

To Harden and Goit Stock Waterfall, 2¾ m. No road was more familiar to the Bard of the 'Throstle Nest' than that which leads from the old town to the charming Hallas Woods. Nicholson, who for a time lived at Harden Beck, close by, loved to wander here, where his gifted and oft too brooding spirit found solace and inspiration in their choirful recesses. At all hours,—even when the midnight moon, 'sweet regent of the sky,' chequered the bright forest walks with leafy dance as of mimic fairies,—he has stood by the silvery fall and said,

"Oh that I could meet tribute pay,
 As 'tis upon my heart impressed ;
 My song of friendship here would stay,
 When waves the grass above my breast." *

Beautiful and attractive almost at any season, it is a sad reflection on these (necessarily) much-travelling times, that some restraint has had to be put upon the public visiting these woods. Access, however, will not be denied to any respectable person, on applying to the Steward of St. Ives. The visitor on leaving Bingley crosses Ireland Bridge, and turning *l.* along

'A lovely road
As e'er the foot of minstrel trode,'

arrives in 1¾ m. at **Harden.** This district was no doubt the scene of several fatal skirmishes during the Civil Wars (*see* p. 172). On the moor above Harden is a now enclosed piece of ground, marked by numerous earth mounds, where it is said some 200 soldiers lie buried. The troops crossed these high lands on their way to Otley (which is near the home of Sir Thomas Fairfax), and various mementoes of their contested passage have been found. Only in the Spring of last year (1890) a Morton man, while rambling on Rumbalds Moor, stumbled upon an ancient sword partly embedded in turf. It has a recurved blade, and an iron hand-guard, and is 36 in. long ; evidently dropped or lost by some Parliamentary or Royalist adventurer. Harden formerly lay on the old pack-horse road to Keighley and the north (the old *Malt Shovel* Inn, where the manor courts were held, being a still existing *sign* of those times) ; the substantially paved Roman way over Harden Moor having been utilized by these traders. Brass Castle, at Harden, doubtless occupies the site of one of the Roman Watch-towers that guarded the road from *Mancunium* (Manchester) to *Olicana* (Ilkley). Evidences of Roman occupation are likewise suggested in the heaps of iron slag abounding here, the refuse of undoubted primitive smelting. Harden Hall is entirely built upon such scoriæ. The Roman horse went up old Dolphin Lane, by Catstones † quarry, and portions of it may be seen near a farm called Casty Wood, on the way to Hainworth. The

* Lines written at Goit Stock.

† From the Celtic *Cath* or *Cad*, a battle or defence. Near here are the remains of a large earthwork.

beautiful forest of Harden (*not* Shakespeare's, dear reader, although 'books in the running brooks,' and 'sermons in stones,' may be read here just as well,) being now entered, the visitor comes to the waterfall at **Goit Stock** after a delightfully shaded walk. Here he may list to the sonorous voice of the rushing waters, disturbed or alarmed by no cries of wild four-footed prowlers as in the days of the old Romans; the only "foreign" life being the troops of little feathered

GOIT STOCK WATERFALL.

migrants which attract attention by their winsome ways and song. Amongst these may be noted, when the greenery of moss and leaf is at its best, flitting from bough to bough, or perched upon some rock or twig above the water's spray, the little gold-crest, the smallest of all European birds,—hardly bigger than a man's thumb, uttering its sharp, sweet 'tweet-tweet,' out of harm's way. It comes from the snowy regions of the northern hemisphere, and for a brief season makes the Goit Stock woods its home. Mr. E. P. Butterfield, of Wilsden, who knows all the birds in these woods, pointed out to us this feathered gem, and also shewed us another rarity, in size and colour not unlike an English jay, called the garrulous rover. This handsome bird is an African migrant, and as there is no record of its having been seen in West Yorkshire before, steps were taken to secure it, and it is now in Mr. Butterfield's possession. The waterfall at Goit Stock does not pretend to the grand or sublime,—it is but 20 ft. high, yet the volume of water, combined with its rocky and forested environment, create a very pleasing impression. On the stream a little higher up is a smaller cascade.

One of the pleasantest walks in this neighbourhood is from **Harden to Wilsden**, by the public foot-road through Hallas Wood on the north side of the waterfall to Hallas Bridge Mill. Then crossing the bridge and skirting the wood top to Hewenden for the station at Wilsden; or from Hallas Bridge ascending to the village. Not so far from the station, on 'Manywell Heights, is an eminence called **Moot Hill**, and near a house called Moot Hill Farm. This was undoubtedly the scene of the open-air parliaments held in the time of the Anglo-Saxons, as described on p. 49. Wilsden was evidently one of the chosen centres of the Anglo-Saxon government (*Witenagemot*), and had in all probability a castle or fortified manor-hall. Mr. Æthelbert Binns, of Wilsden, has kindly furnished us with an exact description of this important site. "About the Moot Hill," he says "are scattered a number of hillocks, and one of these, formed of millstone-grit boulder, extends some sixty yards to the north-east, terminating the hill in this direction. On the south side of this hillock there is a U-shaped hollow in the ground large enough to assemble a couple of thousand people. The open part of this hollow faces the north-east or Hewenden Vale, whilst the opposite or enclosed part is to the south-west. At the north-western angle of the hollow is an enormous singularly-placed grit-stone, forming a kind of platform about eleven yards long and four yards at its widest diameter. Anyone standing on this raised stone could very well be seen by the entire assembly occupying the hollow." There is another large flat rock on Wilsden Banks, known within the recollection of the oldest inhabitant as **Orange Rock**, but why so named is not locally known. It was, however, doubtless so called from its having been one of the scenes of the centenary celebration of the landing of the Prince of Orange which took place at various places in Airedale in 1788 (*see* p. 67).

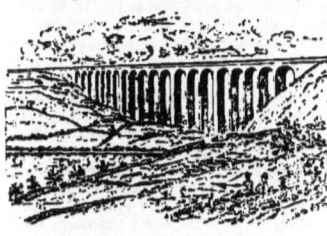

HEWENDEN RAILWAY VIADUCT.

Probably there was a gathering here and a bonfire at night. Close to it is another stone called **Nicholson's Seat**, where the poet used to sit and compose. He would be here some mornings by sunrise, noting all that he saw around him of Nature's life and moods. It was here that he penned those beautiful lines on 'The Return of the Swallow,' and where also much of his long poem on 'Airedale' was conceived and written.

Bingley over the moor to Ilkley, 6 m. The best known route is of course that by way of Morton and Upwood. Another is this: Crossing the spa-lane opposite Gawthorpe Hall (p. 173) ascend field path and wood above Greenhill Hall (G. H. Leather, Esq.), and emerge on the road at Greenhill Grange, a very old farmhouse, occupied for several generations past by the Wild family. From the promontory of the road just beyond there is a grand view northwards of the Aire valley towards Cononley. Continue up the road to the summit (850 ft.). The rock formation here exposed by quarrying shews a top bed of ordinary brick clay, divided from an underlying bed of pipe clay by a thin seam of black shale, the series resting upon a substratum of bluish marl. The clay is worked for fire-bricks and drain-tubing by the Bingley Sanitary Tube and Lime Co., Limited. Here the rambler may cross the patch of heather on to the Gilstead and Morton Road, following it about ¼ m. under the plantation of Drake Hill (Edward Holden, Esq.) on to the Otley road. On r. opposite pass through a turnstile, and by wall side follow the path over the heathery moor about 1¼ m. until the long wall is reached. Here diverge r., keeping the rough track, and not trespassing, about ¼ m. and over stile at top. passing an old boundary-stone inscribed WM 1789, and shortly another stone. WM 1855, where the main road from Eldwick to Ilkley is entered near the Druids' Circle, and the moor edge is soon reached, with Ilkley and the Wharfedale hills in full view (see p. 163).

From

BINGLEY TO KEIGHLEY,

we can vary our walk by going along the highroad (4 m.) past Ryshworth and Riddlesden Halls, or by taking a shorter route along the river side, through Marley, the ancient home of the Currers. East Riddlesden Hall, about a mile out of Keighley, is now a farmhouse, but in past centuries it was a notable seat occupied by the Ryshworths, Paslews, Murgatroyds, and other old landed families. The manor of Riddlesden is surveyed in *Domesday*. Sixty years ago the rich sward of this estate helped to nourish that wonderful animal known as the Airedale Heifer. She measured 11 feet 10 inches long and weighed 41¾ stones per quarter, and was to have been publicly exhibited, but happening an accident had to be slaughtered. Shortly before this piece of ill-luck Mr. Slingsby, her owner, had the sum of 400 guineas bid for her !

The aspects hereabouts are pleasant and retired ; the river gliding placidly along through fresh, verdant meads, and with many a lazy bend as if in no haste to leave such rustic abodes. In the words of the late Abraham Holroyd, another of Airedale's true-hearted sons of song, we may aptly exclaim,

A BEND IN THE AIRE NEAR MARLEY.

Flow on, gentle Aire, in thy course to the sea.
By the hall, and the cot, the woodland and lea ;
And long may thy banks, which know not a slave,
Be the home of the free, the fair, and the brave !

But perhaps the nicest route on a clear day is to ascend from Bingley to the Druids' Altar (p. 174), whence follow the path along the moor edge and direct through the fields, making no descent until Long Lee Lane (720 ft.) is entered at Currer Lathe. Opposite the farm enter a stile, and continue, crossing over Thwaites Lane opposite Fairmount, and under the vicar of St. Mary's new house, whose windows frame a panorama extending from Riveck Edge over Flasby Fell to Ingleborough. A rapid descent is now made through the

Park wood (a remnant of the Keighley Manor Hall park), by the quarry into the town, which is seen spread out below.

Coming *from* Keighley the best way is from the station over the fine broad bridge (built in 1876 by the Midland Co. at a cost of nearly £60,000), down by Low Mill and under the railway viaduct on Pitt Street, and up Quarry Street through the Park wood, as above. Low Mill, it may here be stated, was originally built by Messrs. Ramsden, of Halifax, as a cotton-mill, and is the oldest cotton-mill in Yorkshire. It was opened in June, 1780; the machinery for running it having been made under the personal supervision of Sir Richard Arkwright, to whose works at Cromford, in Derbyshire, a body of operatives from Keighley were deputed for a time to learn the mysteries of the craft. It is now a large concern appropriated by several firms engaged in the worsted industry, but until recently was owned and run by the old-established firm of Messrs. J. & J. Craven, who have lately disposed of the property to the Great Northern Railway Company, whose extensive goods yard adjoins.

KEIGHLEY.

EIGHLEY, like Bradford, has been "quick" to sow the seed and reap the harvest of commercial prosperity. Now a corporate borough of some 40,000 population, it was even less than forty years since but an overgrown village, wearing a mediæval look, having little or no modern architecture, and the ears of its inhabitants accustomed to the nightly tolling of the eight o'clock bell, a relic of the Norman curfew. In postal matters, up to 1854 it was *near* Leeds, and all letters were sorted in that town. It had no Local Board until 1855; no Petty Sessions or Police Force of its own till 1857, and though the railway was brought here in 1847, its little station was primitive, indeed, in comparison with the large, spacious and comfortable structure of to-day with its annual million of passengers! Brimming as it were, over the neck of the Worth valley into Airedale, the expanding town stands uncommonly well, and is surrounded by purple and benty hills, and deep rugged glens, which within an hour's walk are comparable indeed with the heathery and brawny land of the Scot.

Resembling Leeds in variety of trades, its progress has been steady and continuous. Though its principal industry is now in worsted goods, it has large works producing almost every kind of machinery, viz.: for worsted drawing, spinning, washing, &c., and for sewing machines, bicycles, tricycles, &c. There is also a good business done in leather and in furniture made chiefly for export. Consequent upon this development, mills, shops, and dwellings, have gone on increasing and crowding upon each other, in many cases it is to be feared, with but scant room. And though its main street can hardly be said to be a model one for a town of such increasing size and importance, yet there are some buildings, notably in

Skipton road, that stand out to advantage. The Mechanics' Institute and Technical College is a particularly handsome building, and amongst the numerous places of worship there is abundant evidence too of architectural taste and discrimination. Keighley now possesses three public parks, numerous social and philanthropic clubs and institutes, and the inhabitants may regard it, doubtfully perhaps, as an indication of their status among West Riding towns that the borough debt now stands at some £310,000.

To the commendable action of the Duke of Devonshire, who as Earl of Burlington is lord of the manor and chief landowner, must be attributed not a little of the unrestrained progress of the town. His Grace has dealt with a free hand, and in various ways has been a liberal benefactor, believing, no doubt, in the fair words of the Saxon song:

"Earls that seek a lasting throne
Must make the people's weal their own."

His last notable acts have been a free gift of nine acres of land in 1887, for what is now the Devonshire Park, and a substantial contribution in 1891 towards the new vicarage of St. Peter's.

Although so extensively modern in a commercial sense, Keighley has been a market town from the time of Edward the First, A.D. 1305. From that year until 1833, when it was removed to its present site, the market was held every Wednesday on the Church Green, adjoining the churchyard, where bulls used to be baited in the "good old days." The charter was granted to Sir Henry de Kygheley, or Kighley, Kt., which important personage was Master Forester of Blackburnshire from 1288 to 1294, and had residences at Inskip and Keighley. He appears also to have won military renown. The family, which took its name from the place, was settled at Keighley at a very early date, but the earliest mention we have is of one Ralph de Kyghley who gave the church of Keighley to the prior and canons of Bolton in the time of Henry I. The manor passed to the family of Cavendish in the reign of Elizabeth, by the marriage of Anne, daughter of Henry Kighley, Esq., the last male descendant of the direct line of this old family which had flourished here fully five centuries. Albeit they must have lived here in some splendour, yet so fleeting in the roll of years appears all earthly greatness that the very site of their ancestral home is forgotten, and of the once extensive deer park that surrounded it nought now survives but the name. An interesting reference however, is made to the manor-hall by an unknown writer in the year 1667. He says : " I then inquired for the Manor House of Keighley, belonging to this family, and was shown a poor cottage, where a simple schoolmaster lived, where they informed me stood formerly the hall and great large buildings, but now converted into meadows, orchards, and gardens."

At the Conquest four Saxon thanes held the manors of *Chichleia* (*ch* pron. as *k*) *i.e.*, the lea or field of Chichel or Kikel, a Saxon. In one Norman deed we find the name written Kiggellay, the sound being imitated rather than the original spelling. The Saxon guttural was variously preserved in the *gh*, as in the patronym above, and up to the present century the name was commonly spelled Kighley, as may be seen on old gravestones in the churchyard and on old milestones, &c., in the district.

Keighley Church, (St. Andrew's) so closely connected with the history of the parish, is a Norman foundation, (*ca.* 1100-1135) and has been twice rebuilt within the present century. The present building, consisting of nave, aisles, chancel, and square tower with clock and eight bells, was raised by voluntary subscriptions amounting to upwards of £6000, and was opened in August, 1848. Up to the Reformation the patronage of the living was in the gift of the Priory of Bolton, and a list of the Rectors has been preserved from A.D. 1245. The registers date from 1562. In the north aisle are two ancient tombstones bearing armorial devices, (a cross, a sword and two shields), and on one of them is inscribed : " *Gilbertus Kyghlay de Utlay et Margaria uxorse*, A.D. MXXIII." The much-worn date (1023) appears to have been carelessly restored, for this same (presumably) Gilbert de Kyghley died in 1383-4. Among other interesting memorials in the church are two beautiful monuments : one of them dedicated to the Rev. Theodore Dury, for 26 years Rector of the Parish, who it may be stated, was at Harrow

School with Lord Byron, the poet, and the late Duke of Devonshire, and who died in 1850; the other is in memory of the Rev. Wm. Busfeild, M.A., of Upwood, who died in 1878, after a faithful rectorship of over 30 years. Before the church was rebuilt in 1805, there was an epitaph (copied by Dr. Whitaker in his *History of Craven*) to the Rev. Miles Gale, M.A., Rector from 1680-1720, and a name always to be cherished in the annals of Keighley. He was father of the famous learned Judge Gale, and was a man of some scientific attainments, and author of a short history of this parish. Mr. Gale married a daughter of Dr. Stone, Chancellor of York, and died in Jan. 1720-1, aged 74. Turning now to the ample churchyard we cull some admonitory epitaphs. One stone, inscribed to William Weatherhead and dated 1808, bears the following pathetic lament:

"Farewell vain world, I've had enough of thee.
I'm careless therefore what thou sayest of me,
Thy smiles I court not, nor thy frowns I fear.
My cares are past, my bones lie quiet here.
What faults thou foundst in me take care to shun.
Look well at home enough's there to be done."

Of a more hopeful tone is the following to John Greenwood, who died in 1807, and whose exemplary life's-work is thus confessed:

"Blest with a cool and comprehensive mind.
His Soul by Grace to Virtue's path inclin'd,
Music, Mechanics, and the Builder's Art,
Each in his Talents had a noble part,
Indulgent Mercy smil'd on all his ways,
Crown'd them with wealth and clos'd in peace his days."

The oldest Dissenting body in Keighley is the Friends, whose meeting-house in Mill Lane is now the oldest Nonconformist place of worship in the town. The Briggs' were the chief original promoters of the movement locally, and Thomas Brigg, whose initials, and date 1637, appear on one of the stones of the doorway, "freely gave" the piece of land adjoining the chapel for a burial-ground "to future ages." The house was rebuilt in 1877, and since 1823, when it was bought back, the burial-ground has been used as a private sepulchre by the Brigg family.

The environs of Keighley possess a very various field of interest, abounding in many remarkable objects, and deserving of more than local recognition. We enumerate all the best trips. It is evident that Keighley was once encompassed by broader and other waters than now exist; the district name of Lawkholme (an *island* in a *lake*), abutting upon the Aire, plainly suggests this, as do the names Damems, Laycock (anciently Lacoc, *little lake*), &c., in the vicinity.

TRAMS RUN BETWEEN

Keighley (Church Street) and **Ingrow** (for Haworth, &c.), fare 1d., and **Utley** (for Steeton, &c.), fare 1d., daily, about every 14 minutes; on Saturday p.m. every 10 minutes.

The Tramway Co.'s scheme also includes a line from Coney Lane along East Parade to Marley Street; and another from the Railway Bridge along the Bradford road to Stock-bridge.

'BUSES RUN BETWEEN

Keighley (*Victoria Hotel*) and **East Morton** on Wednesday (fare 6d.) and Saturday (fare 4d.) afternoons; and between
Keighley (Skipton Road end) and **Stock-bridge** (fare 1d.), and **Granby Lane Bottom** (for Morton), fare 2d., on Wednesday and Saturday afternoons.

EXCURSIONS FROM KEIGHLEY.

To Haworth, 3¾ m. The Worth Valley Railway was opened April 13th, 1867, and cost nearly £100,000. It is a single line, 4¾ m. long, and took three years in making. It was purchased from the originators by the Midland Railway Company in 1881, and has since been worked by this Company. The visitor may, if preferred, take train or tram to **Ingrow** (1 m.), and walk through the hamlets of Hermit Hole and Cross Roads to Haworth: or from **Oakworth** follow the path up the Worth valley, under rich woods, in Autumn bright with the red-fruited ash and knots of blooming heather; —crossing the stream at Ebor Mills on to the Haworth road. **Oakworth Hall** (Isaac Holden, Esq., M.P.), six minutes' ascent from the station, is one of the largest and handsomest private residences in the county. By the generous permission of its owner the magnificent grounds and conservatories are open to visitors on Saturdays in the summer months, on application at the Secretary's Office, near the Hall.

Haworth (Pop. 6873) includes in its township Stanbury and Oxenhope, and is enclosed by high, wild hills reaching on the Lancashire boundary (about three miles west) an elevation of 1700 ft.

These desolate moorlands have at one time apparently been a centre of Druidism, for on Crow Hill, at 1500 ft. above the sea, is a huge cromlech or altar-stone, weighing fully five tons, which is laid horizontally upon two upright blocks, now half concealed in the turf. On Stanbury Moor there is also a great heap of stones known from time immemorial as Oakenden Stones. The name Haworth (*Haugh Howe*, a burial hill) is suggestive of very early occupation, but there is no historic record of the place until A.D. 1296, when Godfrey de Haworth is mentioned as joint possessor of four oxgangs of land in Haworth. This patronym occurs locally no later than the time of Edward III. The **Church** at Haworth is possibly of Norman

HAWORTH OLD CHURCH.

origin, but it is foolish to suppose that it dates from A.D. 600, as several stones in and about the steeple have been inscribed. These must have resulted from the misreading of the word **TOD**, which terminates a Latin inscription on the tower of the time of Henry VIII. The recent building was probably of this period. The registers date from 1645, but there are transcripts at York that go back to 1600. The church, with the exception of the tower, was rebuilt in 1879, but not before a stout stand had been made against its destruction by lovers of **Bronte** literature in all parts of the country. The Rev. Patrick Brontë was incumbent of Haworth from 1820 until his death in June, 1861, and at the old Parsonage his gifted family created and fashioned their imperishable works These, which include *Jane Eyre*, *Shirley*, *Villette*, *Wuthering Heights*, and the *Tenant of Wildfell Hall*, will be read and remembered as long as the English language endures, and it is to this circumstance that hero-worshippers of all nations annually make their pilgrimages to this secluded Yorkshire shrine. Next to Stratford-on-Avon there is, perhaps, no home of genius in England that has had a larger visitors' roll. William Makepeace Thackeray, who was no unknown guest at the familiar house on the moors, says of Charlotte Brontë's creations : " Who that has known her books has not admired the artist's noble English, the burning love of truth, the bravery, the simplicity, the indignation at wrong, the eager sympathy, the pious love and reverence, the passionate honour, so to speak, of the woman."* Such testimonies are numerous ; yet this is but one thread in the mantle of fame worn by the great novelist, of whom, and her gifted sisters, it is needless here to spin out eulogies. Branwell Brontë, whose unhappy genius, alas ! broke into hopeless insanity, was no less wonderfully endowed than his sisters ; indeed it is remarkable,—perhaps unique in English letters, that all the members of this marvellous family should have fed the same desires, cultivated the same tastes and sympathies, nourishing like thoughts and aspirations, and culminating nobly in the same potential glow of imaginative fiction ! How the sisters loved and wrote, and walked and talked together is now matter of history. Yet the loving fervour of their lives was all too quickly spent, as the simple annal preserved in the church sadly tells. Their memories, however, will be always with us. The interest taken in every belonging of this famous family has recently produced at Haworth a **Bronte Museum**, near the church, the result of many years' patient collecting by the brothers R. and F. Brown, sons of the old sexton of Haworth during the Brontës' lifetime, and cousins of the late Martha Brown, the family's faithful domestic. Among the objects exhibited are : 21 *Pencil Drawings and* 10 *Water-colours by Charlotte Brontë, the latter including a sketch of her favourite dog, Floss. A clever portrait in oil of William Brown, sexton, by Branwell Brontë. A lock of hair of Charlotte Brontë taken after death by Mr. Nicholls, and given to Martha Brown. A letter from Miss Nussey authenticating an accompanying lock of Charlotte's hair. An antique cashmere shawl worn by Charlotte, and a silk patchwork counterpane worked by her with her usual astonishing minuteness. A silk needlework picture from her hand, and a purse made by her in* 1842 *whilst in Brussels. Old Mr. Brontë's spectacles, fob chain, and snuff box. Branwell's pocket-book. Several autograph letters ; scrap book, relating to Brontë matters; other volumes ; and miscellaneous household relics.*

Haworth now-a-days is a busy, progressing, commercial place, but in the Brontës' lifetime it had a strange fame. The " barbarities " of the place have been portrayed by many writers. Less than a century ago the cruel sport of bull-baiting was indulged in, and the bull-stoop still remains near the old *New* Inn at Stubbins. Near here too was the Ducking-stool pond (now contracted into a well), where scolds had their ardour cooled in a very practical manner.

Haworth to the Bronte Waterfall and Wuthering Heights and back, 6¼ m. The visitor in order to appreciate

* *Cornhill Magazine* for April, 1860.

fully the interest of these wild moorlands should first acquaint himself with the Brontë novels. At Ponden Kirk, the scene of *Wuthering*

BRONTË WATERFALL.

Heights, Charlotte Brontë wrote most of *Jane Eyre*, and here the sisters used to come and picnic in summer. Leaving Haworth by

West Lane,* when the last houses are past, just where the road dips, a gravel cart-road enters the moor on *l.*, with the village of Stanbury away on the grassy summit *r*. Some 200 yds. beyond the moor house the roads divide; take *r.* along wall-side, and follow on 1 m. past a few cottages, still keeping on the road, when the deep-wooded clough in which the **Waterfall** is situated is seen on *r*. Follow the path down into the clough, when the waterfall will be seen descending at right angles into Sladen Beck below. The fall is about 80 ft. down a 'stair-case' of weathered gritstone, each side decked with grasses and various species of fern. Two only trees—a birch and mountain ash, springing from the same root-bed—suggestively mingle their graceful foliage above the foaming cascade, like those heath-loving sisters in their solitude! Above all is wild moor. Crossing the foot-bridge the path leads by a farm on *r*. into a lane on to the cart road across the moor. Turn *l*. and when just past the ash-tree farm leave the road and strike along the moor edge in the direction of the gully at top of which shines the **Ponden Kirk** waterfall. The walk of ¾ m. descends by a narrow and precipitous path, requiring care—the Precipice Walk at Dolgelly in Wales, is a mean comparison with it. It should not be attempted by ladies or any but the sure-footed. The path leads into and across the chasm, (down which the fall of 100 ft. leaps,) and traverses the opposite side by an abandoned farmstead up to a gate at the top. From here (1180 ft.) the white house (Two Laws; an old bar) is seen on the moor-road to Colne; but returning to Haworth we descend the hill *r*. to a lane leading into the main road at the village of **Ponden** (760 ft.), whence along the north bank of the picturesquely-formed (fishing) reservoir (30 acres) is a walk of 2½ m. to Haworth. The natives of these parts have a saying: "Let's go to Ponden Kirk, where they wed odd uns," which has its origin in an old custom of passing parties through a hole, capable of admitting only one at a time, that exists in an enormous boulder called 'Ponden Kirk,' near to the waterfall so named. The belief is that if you pass through it you will never die single! Not far from the rock is a spring called Robin Hood's Well. No one knows how the rock acquired its name, but the Saxon *Kirk* suggests a temple of worship possibly extending back to Druidical times. A melancholy interest attaches to this place from the fact of it terminating the last long walk which Mrs Nicholls (Charlotte Brontë) made from Haworth, from which she developed a fatal cold in the Spring of 1855.

Keighley to Colne, 12 m. Ascend Oakworth Road to **Exley Head** (610 ft.), 1 m. Here it is said the markets were held when the plague was ravaging Keighley in 1645, and here in 1794 the last bull-baiting scene was witnessed in the parish of Keighley.† Passing

---

* The old Open Field system still prevails in this locality. The Town Field in West Lane being divided into thirteen 'gates' or 'deals,' which are owned by six parties in very unequal shares. A 'gate' contains 1¾ day-work, that is a little short of an acre, which is given as 1½ day-work. The balks are fairly discernible to a stranger, but clearly identified by the farmers, who take certain 'gates' along with other enclosed fields and on the same terms.—*Yorkshire County Magazine.*

† The last in Airedale is believed to have taken place at Knottingley.

through **Oakworth** (725 ft.), 2 m. (*see* p. 184), the road continues on high ground, with a fine open view of the surrounding landscape. Haworth and its high-up church are away on *l.*, and crowning the hill *r.* are seen the tower, &c., of **Tewit Hall**, built and occupied by the late Mr. Israel Thornton, of Bradford, who

HAWORTH.

likewise set the extensive plantation adjoining the hall, when it was built some thirty years ago. Passing Pickles Hill, the *Grouse* Inn, and **Hare Hills**, where, in pre-board-school days, there was a small free school (still standing) dating from 1743. On the slope *l.* a little further on, and opposite the village of Stanbury, seen on the hill below the moor beyond, is **Oldfield House**, for many years the property and habitation of an eccentric old gentleman of the name of Mitchell. He died in 1835, and was buried in his own grounds, in the presence of several thousand spectators. According to his wishes a rough stone, about a ton in weight, was rolled down the hill on to his grave, which is now enclosed, with an inscription. Continuing, the junction of the Haworth and Keighley roads is

passed (6 m. from Colne) at **Two Laws Bar**, just beyond which are the old stones marking the boundaries of Lancashire and Yorkshire. Here, at this bleak lonely spot (1100 ft.) the source of the Worth river, the Keighley Corporation has a large reservoir covering some 35 acres, and a fine sight it is, in the semi-gloom of a stormy day, to see the white waves leap up against the strong-walled banks, where the wild birds skim and dart over the water's surface! The top of Pendle is conspicuous from this point, and at **Camhill Cross** (the keeper's house) ¼ m. further on, a good view is also had of Boulsworth Hill, with the rock called the Abbot's Seat crowning its summit (1700 ft.). Crow Hill is on this side, with the gully down which the torrent of mud and water rolled enormous stones into the Ponden valley on the occasion of the singular eruption of the Crow Hill Bog on September 2nd, 1824. The bog, situated at an altitude of 1360 ft. above the sea, consisted of the accumulated waters of centuries, which being disturbed by a violent storm, burst its feeble banks, with the result that the waters of the Aire, even as far down as Leeds, could not be used for manufacturing and other purposes for some length of time. At Camhill (Celt. *cam*, a bend) here, a pilgrims' cross doubtless stood in the early days of English Christianity. In the valley below may be observed numerous drift mounds left during the Ice Age by the Pendle glacier. The limestone has been extracted from them and burnt for agricultural and other purposes, leaving traces of such operations in the old kilns that abound. Half-a-mile beyond Camhill Cross the road-summit is reached at the **Herders Inn**, whence, at an elevation of about 1350 ft., the view north and west is truly magnificent. Pendle Hill looks well, with the whole of Colne lying at the feet of the spectator. Beyond the Ribble, Longridge and Easington Fells appear, whilst northwards are the limestone crags of Craven, whence the glacial debris just mentioned has been partly derived, as far as Ingleborough. Colne (4 m.) can now be reached either by way of Laneshaw Bridge (the most direct) or by old Wycoller Wall and Winewall.

Keighley to Hebden Bridge or Hardcastle Crags, 11 m. By rail to Oxenhope, 4¾ m. The moor road over Cock Hill (1300 ft.) being excellently laid, those who prefer to drive may obtain a conveyance at Greenwood's, Upper Town, Oxenhope. From the station the road ascends between the new Wesleyan Chapel and Messrs. Greenwood's Corn Mill. A "cut" can be made by ascending a lane past the church and West Croft Farm on to the new road under the plantation of Aberdeen. On the low side of the road is the high-up pleasant little cemetery of Oxenhope, opened in 1887; and in the lap of Haworth Moor (850 ft.) beyond lies the Lee Shaw Compensation Reservoir, constructed by the Bradford Corporation, and covering some 21¼ acres. Over the wall on *r*. the substantial conduit of this waterworks may be seen. A little above **Dyke Nook** (inn), 1¼ m. from Oxenhope, the open moor is reached, and a wide retrospective view of Airedale is obtained, with the high gap through which runs the Lancashire moor road to Colne, conspicuous to N.W. A good level run of nearly 4 m. is now enjoyed over this high and far-ranging moor, the haunt of grouse, pewits, and scattered flocks of lonk sheep. Following the continuous line of semi-white stone stoops, which beacon this wild way in all weathers, the few houses of **New Delight** (doubtless so-called from the prospect afforded from this point) are passed, and those desirous of visiting the beautiful scenery of Hardcastle Crags may descend the fields through a gate at Bent Head Farm, near here. The road continues above the wooded Crimsworth Dene to **Pecket Well** (inn), with splendid views of the country southwards as far as Salisbury Plain beyond Rishworth; Heptonstall Church being conspicuous on the hill in front, as is also the monument on Studley Pike above Todmorden. In descending to Hebden Bridge, just before the wood is reached, the visitor will not fail to admire the rich prospect up the Hardcastle Crag valley.

Keighley to Sutton by Goose-Eye, 5 m. The rambler may go either by way of Braithwaite and Laycock, where until lately

"Lads and lasses danced the Pole around,
And Whitson ales and May-games did abound;"

or what is a nice (and nearer) walk on Oakworth Road and Fell Lane to **Goose-Eye,** 2 m. The peculiar name of this romantic little place is simply a corruption of the O.E. *hee*, a height, originally Goose-high, from the elevation on which these dainty creatures sported. Turkey Mill, an old-established paper manufactory, owned by Messrs. J. Town & Sons, employs the bulk of the inhabitants. In February, 1879, there died, aged 38, an innkeeper here who was renowned as one of the biggest 'fat men' of his time. He drew the scale at 24 st. 10 lb., and was 6 ft. 2 in. in height. Only a few years before his death he was known as a gaunt, tall, young fellow, the reverse of stout. A stiff ascent must now be made towards Sutton Moor, with Haworth church and the Brow Road conspicuous away southwards. In the early part of the century there were over 1000 acres of unenclosed land on Sutton Moor, but in 1815 an Act was obtained and the land divided amongst the different proprietors. Keeping straight on, a descent to the village is made over **Sutton Brow,** with an immense and beautiful prospect of the country northwards; Pendle Hill, the conical top of Flasby Fell, the summits of the Craven and Wharfedale hills, and the line of railway winding round the Gibb under Cononley Moor, vary the panorama.

Keighley to Cowling by the Hitchingstone, 7¼ m. Route as above to Goose-Eye, whence a charming walk of about 2 m. through **Newsholme Dene** to Slippery Ford. The path through the glen runs along the top side of the quarry some distance up. Newsholme alternates beautifully between native woods, water, and verdant meadows (land here being worth about £60 an acre), and that it was a 'paradise' even 800 years ago is evidenced by the tax on a 'carucate' of land put upon one William de Newhuse by the Conqueror in 1086. A family of the name of Shackleton was living here in the time of Queen Elizabeth, one of its members, Roger Shackleton, being Lord Mayor of York in 1693. A ¼ m. above the bridge at **Slippery Ford** (*anc.* Slitheryfore) a lane is entered near a line of trees opposite the farm, leading up to a solitary store-house on the moor. Round the building sharp *r.* to field-gate (not to open). when follow wall-side ⅜ m. due W. to the prominent **Hitchingstone** (5¼ m.), a huge isolated block of gritstone standing about ¼ m. due S. of Wainman's Pinnacle, from which it is plainly seen. The rock measures 28¾ ft. by 25 ft. and is 21 ft. high. Its cubical contents are therefore 15,100 ft., and weight 1060 tons ; and so far as Yorkshire is

HITCHINGSTONE, KEIGHLEY MOOR.

concerned we may venture to say it is the King of Boulder Stones. Scientifically speaking, however, it is not a boulder, or ice-borne block, but a portion of the rough rock disintegrated from the strata on which it stands. It will be observed that the rock is weathered much more on the north than on the south side, and it is also much fissured, though no glacial smoothings or striæ are now apparent. A hole runs right through it, caused by the weathering out of a large tree (*Lepidodendron*). What looks like an artificial recess in the stone near the west corner is called the "Priest's Chair," and is believed to have some connection with Druidical worship, to which tradition assigns a place on these moors. The view hence (1180 ft.) commands a wide stretch of country, including the hills of Boulsworth, Pendle, and Ingleborough, the limestone scars of Malham and Settle, the peaks of Flasby above Gargrave, Embsay Moor and Airedale to Farnhill Crag. Below the Hitchingstone is a permanent swamp. therefore the rambler had better follow the cart-road west, descending in sight of the Lumb Head cascade, and Cowlafton glacial 'scars' (*see* p. 212) on to the Colne road at the Bar Chapel, Cowling. From Cowling the tourist may either go on to Colne (5 m.), or return by Kildwick sta. (3¼ m.) to Keighley.

Keighley to Steeton by the Tarn, 3¼ m. Through the town up West Lane past the Primitive Methodist Chapel (1879) to **Calversike Hill.** Just above Messrs. Briggs' mill is Guard House, the ancient residence of the Brigg family, founders of the local Society of Friends two-and-a-half centuries ago (*see* p. 183). Below is one of their old burial-grounds. Ascending over Black Hill to the **Tarn** (1000 ft.), 1½ m., the view embraces the Haworth and Lancashire Moors, Swill Hill, Idle Hill, Hope Hill, Farnhill tower, Silsden Nab, &c. The Tarn, originally a swampy flat, was constructed in 1865 by the Keighley Skating Club, and occupying a high, open site, usually after frost affords early sport. It covers about seven acres. The house adjoining was built by the club in 1873 at a cost of £300. Above the road-ends here *l.* is a house called Whorls, remarkable as the habitation of Wm. Sharp, alias '**Old Three Laps,**' the son of a respectable farmer, who died here in 1856 after lying in bed, in the enjoyment of good health, a period of 49 years! A disappointment in love, at the age of 30, was the cause of this self-inflicted confinement, and from that time forward he obstinately refused to leave his bed or to hold converse with any but his immediate attendants, an instance of human resolution and endurance, we should think, that has rarely had a parallel. He was interred in Keighley churchyard. Proceeding, a descent is soon made by a plantation and farms called **Redcar,** and some little distance lower down is a place of like salubrious appellation.—**Brighton.** These 'watering-places' were so called on account of the crowds that used to come up here from the surrounding villages fifty years ago to enjoy the invigorating breezes, excellent waters, and baths that were kept open at a small charge. With the spread of railways, however, people went to the real Redcars and Brightons, and the baths and buildings were removed. A quick descent is now made through Whitley Head and by the picturesque Steeton Gill to the village.

Keighley to Gill Grange (Holden Wood), 4 m. On the Bradford road to Stockbridge (282 ft. above sea), and by field-path *l.* across first canal bridge up Willow Bank by **West Riddlesden Hall** (J. N. Clarkson, Esq.). In Elizabethan times, when this hall was built, it was occupied by an old Airedale family named Maud, descendants of the Montaltos, of Norman renown, resident here. Robert Maud, of Riddlesden, removed to Ireland, where he died in 1685, and was succeeded by his son, Anthony Maud, M.P. for Cashel, grandfather of Sir Cornwallis Maud, Bart., afterwards Baron Montalt, and in 1791 created Viscount Hawarden. The last of the West Riddlesden Mauds had a family of seven sons and one daughter, and the way in which the estates were acquired by the Leaches, their kinsfolk, is certainly curious. The daughter danced at the marriage-feasts of her seven brothers in succession, everyone of whom died childless; she survived them all, married a Leach, and carried the property over to that family. The last heir was William Leach, who died here in 1854. Should the rambler prefer he may continue along the canal bank past Mr. Carter's house, which, some twenty years ago, was the *Woodpeckers* Inn, and cross the next canal bridge *r.* up to Wood Nook House (where the bramble is very profitably cultivated ; large quantities of the fruit being annually disposed of to Keighley and other dealers) for **Holden Gate** (2¼ m.). From Willow Bank the path ascends through a small wood past two old, mossy-roofed farms, respectively, Lower Wood Head and Higher Wood Head, to Holden Gate Farm (920 ft.). This was evidently a gate-house to the preserves of the Cliffords, of Skipton Castle ; and from a deed of Cromwell's time we gather that deer then ranged over Holden Wood, which formed the northern boundary of their great park. The house appears to have been built in 1619, and additions made to it in 1641. Leaving the main road, ascend to the wall top above some large rocks, conspicuous amongst which is one called **Robin Hood's Chair.** It is an enormous block of gritstone, measuring 14 ft. by 18 ft. and 20 ft. high. The prospect from this point is very fine, reaching as far as Pendle and Ingleborough, with the vale of the Aire below, above which rises the long road over Glusburn Moor. Descending past the farm, follow the road to the *second* gate on *l.*, when a path goes down *r.* towards the head of the romantic **Holden Gill,** and crosses the old, narrow stone bridge above a picturesque cascade up to Gill Grange farms (1030 ft.). This is a very attractive resort for visitors and picnics in summer, and teas and refreshments may be had at Mrs Lambert's. For large parties two days' notice should be given ; address, *near Silsden, viâ Leeds.* A little above Gill Grange are the curious "Double Stones" (*see* p. 203). The visitor may either return to Silsden, 2 m., or along the Gill top to Steeton sta., 3½ m. On the edge of Holden Gill may be observed deposits of iron scoriæ, doubtless the remains of Roman smelt-works (*see* p. 153).

Keighley to Ilkley, 6 m. By Eastwood Park over Stockbridge to the old octagon bar-house (1¾ m.) Here cross the canal and ascend to **Morton Banks,** winding *r.* up to the Silsden and Bingley cross-roads, 3 m. from Ilkley. A good gravel carriage road now runs past the plantation at Upwood (Col. Busfeild) and Bradhope Ho. (refreshmts.) adjoining Brass Castle, the site of a Roman watch-tower erected beside the Roman *via vicinalis* that traversed Rumbalds Moor to Olicana (Ilkley). The late Mr. Busfeild, M.P.. took up at different times nearly a mile of this road, which ran through his property. In some places it was covered by a foot depth of soil. From the moor top, about 1200 ft., the view over Wharfedale is charming (*see* p. 163), and a descent is now made past **Cowper Cross** and the Semon Convalescent Home into Ilkley. Cowper Cross (from *couper,* to deal, to barter), has evidently been a market-cross brought hither at some time. A Calvary cross has since been made of it by breaking off some three feet from the top and setting it upon a pedestal. Originally it appears to have been about 7½ ft. high. In the vicinity are some rudely-sculptured rocks and British pit-dwellings, (*see* p. 150).

KEIGHLEY TO STEETON.

PURSUING our journey north, a tram run on the Skipton road passing the beautiful Keighley cemetery (9½ acres), brings us to Utley, 1 mile. This ancient little territory remained a separate lordship for some centuries after the Conquest, and was undoubtedly a residence of the Norman de Kyghleys, previously mentioned. A careful examination of the place renders it, however, not possible to discover the exact site of the original manor-house, although in High Utley there is a substantial building bearing the initials and date EAS. WB. 1677, called the Manor Farm, which from its position, well suited for defence, is not unlikely to be on or about the site of the original manor-hall. The oldest dwelling recently existing here was that owned by Mr. Zacchens Keighley in Low Utley, and pulled down in 1887 when the present building now occupied by him was erected in its stead. Up to about 40 years ago it was a well-known rendezvous, called the *Fisherman's* Inn. It was a 'single-decker' with two large arched windows, having no upper chambers, and drywalled, portions being cemented with clay, over which an old ivy-tree had spread a luxuriant mantle. The building was no doubt of Plantagenet age, and in taking it down an old copper coin was found in an inner wall. Its ancient name, Keelham Hall, is of Anglo-Saxon origin ; *kil* meaning a well or spring, and *ham*, a home or dwelling.

A lane past Keelham leads down to the Jowhole, as this locality is singularly called, where the foundations of an ancient foot-bridge may be seen in the bed of the Aire, opposite Low Holden Farm. One of the most splendid proofs of the presence of the old Roman legions in this neighbourhood was discovered on March 7th, 1775. A farmer, whilst digging a drain in land belonging to Elam Grange close by, came upon a copper chest containing about 100 lbs. weight of Roman denarii, and which included coins of nearly every Roman emperor from Nero to Pupienus, (A.D. 14-238), besides a silver image and a variety of reverses. Found barely two feet below the surface, it had evidently been hurriedly concealed in an hour of peril, by some carriers on the Roman road from Ribchester to Ilkley, (which here crossed the river at Longlands Ford), and had lain undisturbed for a period of nearly sixteen centuries! Its intrinsic value was about £400.

Continuing, our route runs with a nice open view along the highroad to Steeton, (2 m.), passing the old bar-house, (where no tolls have been taken since 1877); and the pleasant district of Hawcliffe, where is a wood in which we have been told is a cave reaching to Bolton Abbey!

STEETON.

Of Gamelbar, the Saxon, from whom the great Norman Plunderer wrested lands here at the Conquest, we have but scant knowledge, save the record of his enormous wealth in *Domesday*. His name, however, is bequeathed in the district in a farm called Gamelsgill or Gamsgill. As an instance of the medley of races enjoying the fruits of their toil here at an early period there are some strange survivals in local field-names. Here are a few : Kelk, Barfside, Great Maw Redding, Larelands, Trankers Butts, Whamdole, Two Bracelets, Penny-piece, Yawmire Legs, Yeomorend, Great and Little Barrows, Scallum, Pudden, Nar Moor, Stone Groves, Blind Pool, &c.

The name of Steeton, says Dr. Whitaker, is derived from Styveton or Steveton, the town of Steven,—the Styvetous being mesne lords of the Percies in the Norman centuries. But we think it just as probable to have originated from the Roman Stræton, or Street-town, seeing there is indubitable evidence of the passage of Roman cohorts at this place, whence also their roads to Colne and Lancaster diverged. An old lane leading from the south end of the village was, until the new road was made, called Wood Street.*

* It should, however, be observed that for six centuries, from the Conquest to the Commonwealth, the name was almost invariably spelled Stiveton or Steveton, and so late as 1695 in the Keighley Quaker Registers we find it written Steven.

The De Stivetons were undoubtedly a very notable family in Yorkshire, and of high military fame, who resided at Steeton. Sir Robert de Stiveton died in 1307, and it is his effigy in the garb of a Knight Templar that adorns the nave of the parish church at Kildwick. Almost immediately after this date this military religions Order was by law suppressed. The uninscribed recumbent statue in Birkin church, previously mentioned, is usually regarded as that of a Knight Templar also, but it differs very materially from this one. The Birkin effigy is plainly that of a layman, clad in a double tunic, closely buttoned at the sleeves, a mode of attire not adopted until nearly half-a-century after the suppression of the Templars in A.D. 1310-12, (*see* p. 69). Sir Robert de Stiveton had three sons, all of whom fought with bow and battle-axe at the terrible carnage of Bannockburn in 1314. About the end of this century the manor was acquired by the Plumptons, and some time after the death of Sir Robt. Plumpton in 1523, the manor was divided and became freehold. The largest freeholders were the Garforths, who were living at Steeton in the time of Edward IV., and whose descendants are still represented at the old Hall. Richard Garforth fought at Flodden in 1513: and Thomas Baynes Garforth, "Squire Garforth," whom the oldest inhabitants may yet remember, early in this century officered the so-called 'Flower of Craven,' an army of volunteers mustered by Lord Ribblesdale when the French war broke out, and when there were threatenings of an invasion. He lived in grand state at the Hall, and kept a pack of hounds, &c., and was moreover a generous and true-hearted English country gentleman. As he was a 'Justice' when the courts were held at the old *Goat's Head*, we may be sure, if his judgment erred, it would be on the side of leniency.

The Hall, rebuilt in 1662, was greatly improved by him, and he also enlarged the grounds and planted, and erected or strengthened the embrasured wall round the garden, whence the ladies used to view the exploits of the chase. The stone in it, marked IBG 1781, was brought from another building. This old ivy-clad Manor or High Hall, now so called in contradistinction to the later handsome Low Hall, occupied by Mrs. Craven, has several dated stones and the Garforth arms (six goats) about it. We lately much admired the luxuriance of its sheltered garden, where the tall sunflowers rested their golden discs upon the lofty wall nine or ten feet from the ground. The chesnuts and sycamores attain fine proportions about here too.

The highroad through Steeton was cut in 1780-2, at which time the Aire was crossed here by a wooden bridge, superseded by the present stone structure in 1806. It was built by the county; its exact cost being £3529 7s. 10¾d. A century ago carts and waggons had to ford the river near the 'streams,' or if in flood go round by Kildwick bridge. Floods used once to be of common occurrence and much damage was done from time to time, but this has been greatly remedied by the Act obtained in 1861, whereby the river bed was deepened and fresh courses cut, ensuring a straighter and more rapid current. But before the alterations were made at Steeton bridge the water used to overflow the highroad, and the adjoining lands in winter afforded grand sport to skaters. The land is now worth about £100 an acre, but near Steeton station a parcel of six acres recently sold fetched nearly double that price.

In coaching days the main road came down the Old Bank to the *Pack Horse* Inn, (now done away with), and at the top of this road, near the Victoria Tower, are portions of an ancient pavement, laid down for the heavy and various traffic that has passed along this road from time immemorial. The coachman's horn has often awaked the echoes of Airedale from this point !

The handsome and far-seen tower here was erected as a memorial of the Queen's Jubilee in 1887, by Mr. Butterfield, of Cliffe Castle. It is a square, battlemented stone structure of four storeys, 70 feet high, and bears upon the four sides of its summit the inscriptions, 'V.R.,' '1887,' 'H. I. B.,' and the Butterfield Arms. It is now occupied as a keeper's residence. The view from here is mentioned in Carey's Atlas of 1793, as one of the principal sights in Yorkshire. Pendle and the Lancashire hills, Malham and Settle hills, Rumbalds Moor, and the valley of the Aire from near Skipton to Windhill, Shipley, present a very wide and half-wild, half-luxuriant panorama.

The traveller coming south might agreeably take this route to Keighley (2½ m.), ascending the Old Bank, as above, and on Spring Gardens Lane behind Cliffe Castle, and past the pleasantly-situated Devonshire Park into Keighley.

'Buses to and from Silsden (1¼ m.) meet all trains at Steeton Station daily, from 8-0 a.m. to 9-0 p.m. Fare each way 2d.

On Sundays 'Buses leave Steeton Station for Addingham at 9-0 a.m. and 1-55 p.m. Fare from Steeton, 6d.; from Silsden, 4d.

Steeton to Addingham, 4¾ m. Crossing Steeton Bridge (*see* above) to **Silsden**, (pop. 3329). This township, comprising 7060 acres, has for the past six centuries been included within the barony of Skipton, now held by Lord Hothfield. In the reign of Henry VI., or nearly two centuries after the establishment of the first burgess Parliament, there were nearly 700 acres here of bond-land, that is

SILSDEN OLD HALL.

land held by servile tenure, the rents of which were paid partly in money and partly in hand-service, such as in reaping the lord's corn, conveying his wood, &c., repairing the Castle and Moot-hall at Skipton, &c. Such bondmen or *nativi* were part and parcel of the estate and might be sold away with it, or disposed of like cattle to any buyer. This species of slavery, or tenure in bondage as it was called, continued up to the reign of Charles II. when it was abolished by statute. There were, of course, besides a large number of Free tenants on the estates, and at the death of every tenant the lord claimed the best chattel (living or dead) of the deceased, as a heriot. This might be, as sometimes happened, either a table or a cow. That there was a corn-mill at Silsden in the feudal ages appears by a grant of the mill and lands here to the Canons of Bolton in the 12th century. We have no record of a church, oratory, or notable family seat at Silsden at this early period. A chapel, erected in 1712, received a small endowment from the "good Earl Thanet." and this was rebuilt in 1815, and again restored and enlarged at a cost of £2000 in 1876. There are no registers kept here prior to 1768. The incumbents of the church did not reside here until 1837, when the vicarage was restored. This had previously formed part of some buildings called **Jennings Hall**, mentioned by Dr. Whitaker in the 'History of Craven.' The hall was pulled down when the church-yard was made, with exception of a portion on the north-west side. The Jennings family had a considerable estate here, sold in the early part of last century to the Earl of Thanet, when they removed to Ripon, and became the representatives of that important

REV. J. FLESHER'S HOUSE.

borough in several parliaments. The old three-gabled hall (now a farm) at the top of the town was probably built by them. Over the door is inscribed H I 1682. A daughter of Edmund Jennings, of Silsden, married Gilbert Dean, of Sattonsall, whose son, Richard, was Dean of Kilkenny, and afterwards Bishop of Ossory, who died in 1612. In this year we find certain property at Steeton being made over to trustees by one Wm. Laycock, yeoman, of Silsden, for the benefit of his nephew, Wm. Jennings. In Kildwick church is a brass plate to Edm. Jennings, A.M., who died in 1623, aged 25. He was the son of Peter Jennings, of Silsden, whose will was proved in London by his grandson, Edward Jennings, in July, 1651. In Bradley Lane, near to the Old Hall, is a house in the occupation of a family named Longbottom. It was erected by them in 1793, and is remarkable for two enormous gate-pillars. They are of local grit, in single blocks 8 ft. high, 5¼ ft. round, and weighing nearly 1½ tons each. The two stone balls that surmount them weigh at least 200 lbs.

each. Many old buildings about Silsden, reminding us of feudal times, have had to come down in the march of modern progress. One of these, a picturesque old thatch, with diamond leaded panes, was removed some seven years ago when the Mechanics' Institute was built. Another old house near the beck bridge is notable as the residence of the Rev. John Flesher, a son of the village schoolmaster, and declared to be "the best grammarian in the West Riding of Yorkshire." He was the founder of local Primitive Methodism early in the century, a body that is now represented by one of the handsomest buildings in the town. Among other modern architectural adornments may be mentioned the beautiful new chapel of the Wesleyans, who have been established here since 1808,—longer than any other local body of Dissenters. The worsted industry occupies the bulk of the inhabitants, but farming is extensively carried on in this, an essentially rural township. Descendants of the old villeins and yeomanry class have been settled on these lands many generations. A piece of land here comprising about three acres, has been in the possession of one such family named Lambert, a branch of the Lamberts of Civil War renown, from the time of the Commonwealth. To an artistic member of this old family, Mr. W. H. Lambert, we are indebted for several of the pictorial sketches appearing in these pages.

The neighbourhood of Silsden is highly picturesque. Holden Gill, Throup Gill, Swarthadale, &c., are all within easy access, and abound in many choice bits of rock and wood. In the Middle Ages they were the lurking places of wolves, wild boars, red deer, foxes, badgers, polecats, and various birds of prey.

The road now ascends under the Nab, and presently a good view is obtained of the Bradford Corporation reservoir in the Cringles, the deepest (78 ft.) of all the Bradford reservoirs, where the water following the irregular outline of the beautifully wooded dene adds to its picturesque interest. At the road top a descent is made past the houses of Marchup (whence there is a short route to Bolton Abbey, (*see* p. 204), in full view of Beamsley Beacon, direct to Addingham.

Steeton to Ilkley, 7½ m., or **Addingham,** 7 m. **by Holden Gill.** This is a charming 'round about' trip. The visitor from **Silsden** may go through Brunthwaite and up the road direct under Crag Wood Quarry to Gill Grange 2 m. From Steeton directly after the Aire bridge is crossed go over a narrow stone bridge across Silsden beck and through the fields in the direction of Holden Wood. When the lane is entered at Holden Ho., turn *l.* a short ½ m. and enter a stile on *r.* where path leads up to the canal, which here goes over the Holden beck on a single arch. This is a pleasant spot, and a favourite one with naturalists. Turn *r.* and cross the canal bridge up to the Park farms, where teas and refreshments may be had. From these houses the road may be ascended to the top of the open moor at Robin Hood's Chair, near Holden Gate, or at its divergence *r.* there is a private gate-way into **Holden Wood,** and no objection, we understand, is offered to visitors who properly adhere to the path by this private way to the Gill Head, described on p. 195. The woods form part of the Skipton Castle estate, and on the stream that courses through the deep and narrow gill are several high and picturesque cascades. Ferns, flowers, and several uncommon grasses clothe the sides of the luxuriant forest, revealing here and there scenes of rare beauty. A short distance above the two farms at Gill Grange are the famous **Double-Stones**, a striking combination of

WATERFALL IN HOLDEN GILL.

denuded millstone grits, which, from their unequal hardness, have weathered most fantastically. The larger one consists of a stout stone column, some 60 ft. in circumference, supporting an overhanging cap, and suggestive of a gigantic stone mushroom. The smaller rock from one point of view bears some resemblance to an upturned boot. The caps of both stones bear artificial incisions; the larger one having three basin-shaped cavities (15 in. to 24 in. across, and 9 in.

deep) united by a deep groove, and surrounded by upwards of a score
cup-markings. The lesser stone has small cup-markings only. Like
the Druids' Altar, Bingley, and the demolished altar stones on Baildon
Common, &c., they have been probably associated with the mysterious
practices of the early races inhabiting these commanding moors.
The altitude at this point of the moor is about 1200 ft. At the
Double-Stone Farm close by, a violent robbery was committed in the
winter of 1844-5. At that time the house was occupied by Mr. Abm.
Flesher. After an obstinate resistance, during which it is stated
Mrs. Flesher wrestled with and severely punished two of the men,
the small household, consisting of Mr. Flesher, his wife, and maid-
servant, were completely overpowered. The track of the thieves,
however, was immediately discovered by their footprints in the snow
down to Addingham, where they were apprehended and afterwards
convicted. To **Ilkley** from the Double-Stones the road continues
northward to another farm, and along the moor edge whence the
town is seen. To **Addingham** either by the road westward to
Seamoor* Ho., descending under the moor edge to the four-lane ends,
whence r.; or by the road under the Double-Stones wind to the
moor top (1260 ft.), and descend path through the rocky pass, from
which a view of Arcadian loveliness bursts upon the vision, rendered
all the more captivating by its complete suddenness. Wharfedale,
with the hills to Ingleborough, are now revealed in grand array, and
a descent l. may be made to the Slaid Farm seen at the junction of
the road to Addingham, or r. (nearer) to Hodgson Farm, whence
there is a track down to Addingham.

Steeton to Bolton Abbey, 7 m. A very attractive route.
Walk or 'bus to Silsden (1¼ m.) and down to the two way-side houses
at Marchup (p. 202). At the first gate on l. on leaving these a path goes
up to the road, which cross, and over stile to Cross Bank Farm.
From the road the Cow and Calf rocks, at Ilkley, and Otley Chevin
overhanging Wharfedale are well seen. Going through the farm fold
descend the field r. in the direction of Beamsley Beacon, below which
lies the town of Addingham. From no other view-point does the
majestic Beacon, with its heathery purple cape and skirts of forest
green, look better than from here. Crossing the beck bottom ascend,
and on the Skipton road 50 yds., when over stile and past Hag Head
farm and lathe, on to the road forward. The prospect from this
elevated road is of great beauty, and in richness, extent, and
proportion of its several parts, is perhaps unequalled in upper
Wharfedale. Below us are the green and spreading meads wherein
cattle are grazing by the quiet farmsteads; woody knolls are seen by
the beautiful river here flowing away under Bolton Bridge, there are
the ruins of the venerable Abbey with the Deer Park beyond, and
the Cavendish Memorial Fountain surrounded by lofty hills!
Descending towards the wood at Lobbart the grouping of the hills

* **Seamoor,** so called from an extensive sheet of water that lay here before
the land was drained. In a Survey of the boundaries of Silsden Manor in 1681 we
find it referred to as *Seamer Tarne*. The site is now planted.

appears perfect, and the whole chain from Beamsley Beacon (1330 ft.) to Simon's Seat (1474 ft.) forms a graduating and noble perspective. From Lobbart under the railway viaduct Bolton Bridge is soon reached, whence the road to the Abbey is well known.

Silsden to Kildwick, 2¼ m. Ascend Skipton road, leaving the extensive village of Silsden lying compactly in the hollow under the Nab, and still ascending, the southward view of Airedale is very rich, embracing the Harden moors and the belt of native wood which extends almost uninterruptedly from above Riddlesden to Gill Grange, a circuit of nearly three miles. Passing the ivy-clad house (C J E 1818) at Low Cross Moor (750 ft.), a descent is made past the time-stained sixteenth century home of the old Bolton monks, **Kildwick Grange**, occupying a snug situation among other houses just above the road, and commanding an excellent prospect.

"Towers and battlements it sees,
Bosom'd high in lofty trees,
Where perchance some beauty lies,
The cynosure of neighbouring eyes."—L'ALLEGRO.

It now forms two separate dwellings, and is the property of Mr. J. P. Smith, (see p. 206). At the junction of the road near Kildwick Hall, descend steeply Priest Bank, where we hope the visitor will escape the fury of the life-size lions from the gate of the old Hall which are said to come this way to the canal to appease a raging thirst, *on hearing the noon bell!* At the top of Priest Bank is the disused manse of the ancient vicars of Kildwick. The house consisted of three ground-rooms; the two south ones being divided by a black oak panel, and the roof supported by a thick oak beam. In the south mullion are two diamond panes, having a coloured design with the initials E R. The west end, with porch and arched windows is now used as a barn. The village is now entered at the church.

Steeton to Cowling by Sutton, 5m. Through Eastburn (p. 206), crossing the bridge and *l.* by the beck to **Sutton**, a township covering 2348 acres. At the date of *Domesday* (A.D. 1086) there were 200 acres taxed as King's lands. The old-established worsted mills of Messrs. T. & M. Bairstow and Wm. Hartley employ a large proportion of the population, which is semi-agricultural. The Church (St. Thomas) is a very handsome structure, erected in 1869 by bequest of Mr. Thomas Bairstow, of Royd Hill. Leaving the village south-ward, an ascent of ⅜ m. brings the visitor to the picturesque **Sutton Clough**, a romantic wooded gill, the joint property of Captain Sutcliffe, of Hebden Bridge, and Mr. John Clayton, of Bank Foot Farm here, to whom application must be made to visit the clough. At the farm parties are accommodated with refreshments. A path by the stream side leads up to the Gating Stone and waterfall, and there is also a dropping well which is said to petrify. The gill used to abound in a great profusion of choice ferns, but these have so far diminished that gathering of them is now strictly prohibited. Crossing the footbridge in the wood bottom, ascend to the farm at Bank Foot, which commands, perhaps, as charming and as complete a natural picture as is to be found anywhere in Airedale. The conical summit of Flasby Fell forms a fine background. Proceed along Sutton Crag to Stubbin Hill. In 1888 the pleasant house here, for many years the home of the Misses Clough, was almost wholly destroyed by fire, and much valuable furniture was lost. The field path forward passes several farmhouses, and under the **Wainman Pinnacle** (1050 ft.) by a cart-road down into Cowling (p. 212). Various reasons are assigned for the origin of this famous landmark, but the most likely one is that it was erected by Lady Amcotts, the young wife of one of the Wainmans, in memory of her husband who fell in the Royal cause during the Civil Wars. This story is supported by the fact that to this day the proprietor of the Wainman's estate pays 1s. per annum as rent for the ground on which the Cenotaph stands. It was originally about 50 ft. high, and 10 ft. square at its base, but has been much shattered by lightning.

STEETON TO KILDWICK.

(Distance 2 miles.)

Walking along the highway we observe the grass-grown old road, which ran close to the stream by Steeton Hall before the present Station road was made in 1826. The good, nicely situated house on our left is the Shroggs (T. Clough, Esq.). Passing through **Eastburn** (1 mile) we cross the county bridge, perceiving that for a considerable distance on either side the road is raised on stone arches above the surrounding low-lying land. Eastburn was a royal manor at the time of *Domesday*, but how long a bridge has existed here we cannot tell. One was rebuilt after a destructive flood in 1642, and again rebuilt in 1738. When the road was constructed, about 1782, the bridge was greatly improved. Coming to the junction to Colne, (9 miles), that portion of the road forward to Kildwick was cut in 1825, and the present hotel built by the Stirk family, who still occupy it. The Stirks are descended from an old stock of Craven yeomanry, and have been resident in this neighbourhood from a remote period. We have met with the name in Latin deeds relating to the transfer of property here as far back as the reign of the First Edward

At the *Junction* a sheep fair is held annually in September. Hence the visitor may turn left for the station, or cross the line for the ancient village of the 'Lang Kirk.'

KILDWICK.

ALTHOUGH this ancient parish includes some populous townships, the old village of Kildwick itself contains barely a score habitations, and in point of population at any rate, remains much the same as in that remote day when Saxon yeomen called it *Childeuuic*.

The Church is historically notable as one of the oldest foundations in England, being mentioned in *Domesday*, and was given with the Manor by the great landed family of Romille to the Priory of Embsay, afterwards Bolton. The present edifice was built in Henry VIII.'s time. It is often called the Lang Kirk of Craven, from its being the longest church in the Deanery, as well as one of the longest in Yorkshire. Its length is 176 feet and width $48\frac{1}{2}$ feet, just 4 feet larger each way than the church at Snaith. It was thoroughly restored in 1868 and the porch replaced in 1873. A west gallery erected in 1825, necessitated the removal of a splendid antique oak canopy to the font. This canopy was the gift of the Canons of Bolton, and having been cast aside was afterwards cut up and wrought into chairs and then sold by auction! The Norman font luckily remains, and the gallery has been removed. Before the restoration the present oak ceiling was covered with a flat plaster roof erected as a preventative against damp, caused by the old system of 'mossing.' Icicles in winter and rain in summer, dripping from the roof, cannot, to say the least, have promoted a pious ardour among the worshippers in the sacred edifice. Such items of expenditure, as 'stopping drops and sweeping snow out of church,' are of frequent occurrence in the old parish accounts. At one time colonies of bats infested the recesses of the roof, and even yet are occasionally seen fluttering about their old haunts. The interior contains a good deal of fine old carved oak, notably the Eltoft pew dated 1632, various memorial windows and tablets, and a magnificent recumbent monument in Hazlewood stone, of Sir Robert de Stiveton, who was interred here with great pomp in A.D. 1307, (*see* p. 198), as appears by the contingent expenses in the Bolton Abbey cash book.

Kildwick, at no distant date, must have been a literal 'Back Woods,' judging from the many sums paid for the destruction of beasts and birds of prey plaguing the district. In no parish accounts in the dale have we seen more of such entries. From 1669, when the churchwardens' accounts begin, for nearly a century afterwards, there are hundreds of entries of small amounts disbursed for the slaughter of foxes, badgers, otters, foumarts, hedgehogs, kites, hawks, &c., and in 1673 we find 3s. 10d. awarded to three persons for 150 crows' heads!

Appended are a few suggestive extracts from these old parish books:

A.D. 1746. Sept 1. To Thos. Witherop, the Sexton, for his first half-year's wages for looking to the clock and bells, and ringing night and morn .... 10s.

,, To same for first half-year's wages for Whipping the Dogs... 2s. 6d.

,, To same for weeding the church steps the whole year... 1s.

,, Paid for a cart load of turf and leading .... 10d.

,, Nov. 5th. Paid to the Ringers for Ringing on Oct. 9th, being the Thanksgiving Day after the Rebellion .... 1s. 6d.

1746-7. Jan. 15. To Joshua Hill for mossing and pointing the school .... 5s. 3d.

In 1673 we find 1s. is paid for an "houre-glass," an instrument by which the parson timed his sermon before the days of pocket watches. We also find that the old enactment of 1531, for publicly whipping vagrants naked in the street was in full force here up to the Stuart period. The stocks preserved near the entrance to the church were put in use so recently as 1860.

But if there have been reprobates, we have only to turn to the churchyard for many a tale of local worth and virtue.

Mark the concentrated goodness implied in this lament of a dearly-beloved spouse :

> "She was,—but I forbear to tell you what,
> Think what a wife should be and she was that."

Very different from the following, observed elsewhere :

> "Here lies my wife, poor Molly, let her lie,
> She finds repose at last, and so do I."

But a good Jack, 'tis said truly, makes a good Jill, and this may lie at the root of both epitaphs.

Kildwick Hall, the seat of John Brigg, Esq., C.C., J.P., is a picturesque old Elizabethan manor-house, added to from time to time, and contains many trophies of the Civil Wars. In 1728, during the occupancy of Haworth Currer, lord of the manor, a box containing gold medals of the time of Charles I., was accidentally discovered whilst digging in an adjoining outhouse. They were of the value

KILDWICK HALL.

of £150. The village and manor of Kildwick were purchased by the Currers over three centuries ago, and are still owned by their lineal descendant, Sir Mathew W. Wilson, Bart., of

P

Eshton Hall. Their pedigree is given in Dr. Whitaker's *History of Craven*.

Kildwick Grange, (p. 205), erected by the monks

KILDWICK GRANGE.

of Bolton who were proprietors of the church and manor up to the Dissolution, wears a truly captivating look of genuine antiquity. It has a curious stone balconied portal, and its cosy interior appears to have undergone but little change since the days of its original owners. One of the upper rooms has an ornamental plaster ceiling, and has evidently been used as a private chapel. There are indications of a small altar, and on the outer wall is a cupboard which has apparently been used for the vestments. The panellings are of black oak, and the banister of the same material has at its foot the hinges of a door or gate which once closed the staircase. The house (in two parts) is tastefully cared for, and is in the occupation of Mrs. Smith and the Misses Weatherhead.

Not the least interesting local monument of antiquity is the **Aire Bridge** at Kildwick. An expenditure of £21 12s. 9d. was made in the probable rebuilding of it by the Canons of Bolton in 1305. It is the oldest bridge over the Aire of which we have any written record; reference is made to one at Bingley a few years later, viz. : in an agreement between the monasteries of Drax and Rievaulx in 1312, but both places being important manors with churches in early Norman times, it is more than likely that bridges connecting them with outlying parts of the parishes existed some centuries before this. Mention is made of a bridge at Eshton, near Gargrave,* and Briggate, Leeds, likewise suggests a much earlier foundation than our first notice of the bridge in 1376, (*see* p. 39). The structure at Kildwick consists of two pointed and two rounded arches, and was originally only about half its present width, as may be seen by an examination

KILDWICK BRIDGE.

of the piers underneath it. The widening took place in 1780, when the four east arches were all made round.

But glancing up at the church clock we are warned to "Redeem the time," so now to our pleasant walks.

'Buses run between **Kildwick** and **Cowling** (*Bay Horse* Inn) about four times daily, meeting the trains. On Sundays from Cowling 8-55 a.m. and 7-50 p.m.; from Kildwick 9-15 a.m. and 8-10 p.m. Fare 3d. each way.

* Written 'Essheton Brigge' in MS. at Bolton Abbey.

Kildwick to Colne, 8½ m. From the station southward through the thriving and well-built village of **Crosshills** (pop. 1629), which less than a century ago had but two or three thatched houses, to **Glusburn** (⅞ m.), passing the large, old-established worsted mill of Mr. J. C. Horsfall, and the good old Glusburn Hall (now farm cottages) with its gables of sturdy gritstone, projecting gargoyles and miniature tower. Over a door are the almost effaced initials P S 1587 J S, standing no doubt for Peter and Jane Scarborough, for in the Feet of Fines of the Tudor Period, we find that in A.D. 1589, Peter Scarborough, gent., and Jane, his wife, were parties to the conveyance of "three messuages and a cottage with lands and a third part of a water-mill at Glusborne." The Scarboroughs were a noted old local family, and there are memorials of them in Kildwick church. Crossing Glusburn bridge we pass through **Malsis** (*vulg.* Mawsis), looking in vain for any signs of what may be termed a village. But Malsis is named in *Domesday* as part of the Royal manor of Glusburn, and was no doubt a place of ancient importance. The manor and hall of Malsis were sold in 1625 to Richard Horsfall, Esq., and the old hall occupied its site opposite the present inn until the new park surrounding the stately seat of James Lund, Esq., J.P., D.L., was made about 1865. Mr. Lund purchased some 600 acres here of the Spencers, of Raygill (*see* p. 214), who resided at Higher Malsis, now in the occupation of Mr. John Bancroft. Keeping along the pleasant open road with Carr Head Hall (*see* p. 214) away on *r.*, and Wainman Pinnacle (*see* p. 206) up on *l.*, we reach **Cowling** (pop. 1901), 3½ m. Anciently called *Colling*, no doubt from the presence of coal, which was worked up on the Moss in old times. Some years ago an extensive boring for lead was made in the Gill Bottom, but the search did not prove successful. The township is supplied with gas from Kildwick, and some little time back it was proposed to light the road thence to Cowling. But the farmers met and decided that the benefit would be but partial, one of them pithily remarking, "What'll he t'use o' gas to me, I shall hev to milk i't dark as usual."

At **Cowlaughton** on the Ickornshaw moors, a mile to the south of Cowling, are a number of grass-grown, rounded hillocks from 10 to 30 yds. in circumference, and 10 to 30 ft. high. They are composed of the drift of pre-existing glaciers, and where cut into form fine sections locally known as 'scars.' Many of them have been destroyed for the limestone fragments they contain. The mounds were formerly much more numerous, and lay in a line from N.W. to S.E. The altitude is about 1200 ft. Near the farm here, (Mr. Timothy Bancroft), are visible traces in the grass-covered furrows of the ploughshare, the strips or reins being from three to four yards wide. A tottering house hard by, displays to the elements a chamber wall with ornamental plaster work dated 1671. This was no doubt at one time a notable farmstead. As some evidence of the character and capabilities of the soil at this elevation, may be mentioned that at the adjoining **Wreck** and **Fleet** farms (the latter bought by Mr. John Moorhouse in 1882 for the sum of £2275), two fine ash trees were lately cut down whose trunks were 8 ft. to 10 ft. in girth. In the gardens here, we have noted in flower, red and white roses, pinks, peonies, marsh mallows, &c., and in fruit, the hardy gooseberry, red and black currants, and a few strawberries. At **Cowl Head** is a narrow cave which penetrates the gritstone under the 'scars' to an unknown distance. At **Lumb Head**, below Cowlaughton, is a deep gill with a cascade having a plunge of over forty feet, but the spot lacks the charm it would derive by planting. The view from these high lands is very fine, and includes all the higher hills of Craven.

From Cowling to Laneshaw Bridge is 3 m., passing about midway the county boundary, a little beyond which on *r.* is Barnside Farm, tenanted early in the century by a singular couple, a woman and her son. The face of the mother, it is said, was covered with hair, and

THE ORIGINAL "VILLAGE" OF CROSSHILLS.

the nails of her fingers so long that they looked almost like the talons of an eagle. The son strangely became enamoured of a girl, whom he betrayed and then mysteriously murdered, and some time elapsed before the body of the missing woman was discovered in a neighbouring field, by the accidental appearance of her apron corner above the ground. The house, it is said, was haunted by her disturbed spirit, and remained without tenants for a long time. At last it was taken by a farmer named Tillotson, and presumably the 'ghost' being 'laid,' has been occupied ever since. From the junction of the road at Lidget, the tourist now enters Colne,—the Roman Colonio, with the tower of its ancient church appearing like the keep of some mediæval castle.

Kildwick to Lothersdale, 5 m. Past Malsis Hall, as last route, and at the division of roads turn *r.* down to the picturesque Lumb mill, and forward by the gates of Carr Head (Alfd. Sharp, Esq.), turning *r.* a little further on past Old Carr Head (Robt. Harrison, Esq.), formerly called Colling Carr. In the reign of Elizabeth it was owned by the Laycocks, and afterwards by the Bradleys, but by the marriage in 1740 of Elizabeth, daughter and heiress of John Bradley, with Richard Wainman, of Bolling, near Bradford, the property came into the Wainman family, and has remained in their possession since. The house consists of a centre with mullions and two gables containing arms and initials, and is said to be an exact reproduction of the old building taken down in 1884. Passing Mr. Cannan's house a pleasant rural walk of about ¾ m. brings us to the Owl Cotes farm. Here a lane on *r.* goes down to the beck in view of Lothersdale church and village. Follow the path up the Bottoms to the mill, and emerge opposite the inn. **Lothersdale** (*anc.* Lothersden). is a deep grassy valley with swelling hills marked by a boldness of outline which cultivation has not deprived of a certain wild charm. It was one of the earliest seats of Nonconformity in Craven, and was frequently visited by the celebrated Rev. Oliver Heywood, whose sister Esther, in 1650, married William Whitehead living at Bent Hall here. A strong body of Friends was at one time congregated in the dale, and many stories are related of their sufferings and confiscations for non-compliance with the rites of the Established Church. From Dale End the tourist may proceed through Whitting or Wedding-Hall Fold by the road to Raygill (1 m.) and forward to Colne (6 m.), or return to Cononley (p. 222), 2¼m. **Raygill** has a wide renown for its barytes mines and great quarries of limestone, where the lofty cliffs of contorted strata present a sight of enormous geological interest. The rocks at the west end dip at an angle of 70° to 80° against perfectly horizontal beds to the east, and are overlaid by the Yoredale grits and shales. The quarrying sometimes reveals peculiar beddings in the strata shaped like a V or S, shewing the curious lateral and long-continued pressure the rocks underwent during the process of consolidation. Occasionally bits of 'Blue John' or amethystine fluor, so much prized by lapidaries, are met with. At an angle of the quarry is situated the famous and unique bone-cave known as the Raygill Fissure, which descends the mountain limestone in a southerly direction a distance of 114 ft. When opened some ten years ago it contained drifts of blue and laminated clays and sand, with numerous teeth and bones of the mammoth, hippopotamus, bison, bear, antlers of roebuck, wild ox, and what is of rare occurrence, the molars of a lion. As the mouth of the cave was choked with glacier drift it looks as if the bones, which represent a tropical or sub-tropical fauna, had been washed in during or before the subsequent Ice Period. Many of these remains are now preserved in the Leeds and Bradford museums. The quarries are the property of the trustees of the late Peter W. Spencer, and are now managed by Mr. Wm. Spencer, of Raygill, whose house-front here is curiously ornamented with the barytes spar, which has a striking and pretty effect, especially after rain. The estate was acquired by the marriage of Wm. Spencer, of Malsis Hall (*see* p. 212), successively with Mary (in 1820), and Hannah, daughters of Peter Aldersley, of Raygill. The Aldersleys appear to have settled here about two centuries ago, and to have worked the quarries subsequently, and many of the old kilns and hillocks of debris adjoining the 'new' quarries are still noticeable. A tradition exists that the family was a powerful one of Welsh extraction, and that one Anthony Aldersley joined the Monmouth Rebellion against King James, which was annihilated at Sedgemoor, the last battle fought on English ground, in 1685. To escape the tyranny of the 'Bloody Assize,' presided over by Judge Jeffreys, Aldersley fled to Yorkshire, where many of his relatives had been long settled, and here in the fastnesses of Lothersdale he ultimately found a secure abode. The Aldersleys appear to have been a respectable, well-to-do family in this part of Yorkshire, and we find their name amongst the earliest entries in local registers. They had estates in Yorkshire, Lancashire and Kent.

Kildwick to Elslack, 6 m. For sweet air and good views this is a capital outing over Glusburn Moor (800 ft.) Leaving the station on the south side by a short field path on *r.* ascend the moor, having Mr. Petty's turreted mansion hanging above Airedale on *r.*, with Robin Hood's Seat and Flasby Fell away in the distance. Descend past Upper Leys farm to the four-lane ends, where just above the plantation is a large artificial earthwork in the form of a circular camp. It is probably Danish. Keep straight up Baby Ho. lane over Carlton moor by a narrow band of mountain limestone, which ascends to Park Head quarry, where glacial drift is seen resting upon the limestone at an altitude of 1030 ft. The road passes the quarry to a second four-lane ends. Here there is an old dated (1730) milestone: to Skipton 4 m., to Colne 8 m., &c., and the prospect from the (Elslack) moorland eminence just above is one of immense variety and extent, including Pendle, Boulsworth, Embsay Crag, Rylstone Fell, due N. the cones of Flasby, and beyond them the flat top of Ingleboro. Under the second eminence of Pinnowe, about ½ m. on the Colne road, is a gravestone to the memory of a man named Robt. Wilson, who perished on the spot on a stormy night in Jan. 1805. He was one of three of the Elslack Beacon guards who were stationed here during the threatened invasion of Napoleon to signal fires in case of alarm. Along this road are a series of ancient encampments which lie above the Roman road from Skipton to Colne and Clitheroe. In the Standrise plantation here a good example may be seen. Crossing these moors are also several very old paved paths which will well repay examination by the studious enquirer into these ancient trackways. A descent is now made upon a beautifully wooded valley to Elslack, crossing the trout beck near the old White House, for nearly a century and a half the home of the Moorhouse family, and past Elslack Hall (p. 239) to the station, whence train may be taken to Skipton.

Kildwick to Skipton by Bradley, 4¼ m. The canal path may be taken below Farnhill Hall, or the road ascended past the church to

Farnhill (pop. 561). After the Conquest this became a mesne manor in the parish of Kildwick, and the manor house, now **Farnhill Hall**, probably occupies its original site.  The last mention of the first lords discovered by Dr. Whitaker occurs in an award made in 1318 by the Canons of Bolton to Willm. de Fernhill, for a destructive raid upon his property by the Scots, after their triumph at Bannockburn. Later than this, however, a John de Fernhill was witness to a deed dated at Glusburn, 14th Edward III. (A.D. 1340); and in the 40th Edward III. the family of Coppley appears, from whom early in the next century the Eltofts acquired the manor and retained possession until 1636, when it was bought by the Currers. Its subsequent transmission is well-known. Farnhill Hall (F. E. Slingsby, Esq.) with its ivied front and towers standing amid a framework of ancestral trees, is an interesting feature in the view from the railway between Kildwick and Cononley. Remem-

FARNHILL HALL.

brances of the marauding Scots probably led to its erection as a seat of defence, the outer walls having an average thickness of six feet, and in some places are over eight feet thick. The cellars are hewn out of the solid rock, and from which there is a passage (now blocked) that is said to have communicated with Royd House on the opposite side of the valley. The interior dwelling appears well preserved, and there is a look of solidity and airiness about the rooms, which are large and lofty for a building so conspicuously ancient. On an outbuilding appear the letters and date EE 1560 AE., the initials of Edm. Eltoft and his wife. In 1590 we find Edward Walmysley, gent., and Robert Walmysley, gent., obtained from Edmond Eltoft, Esq., and Thomas Eltoft, his son and heir, conjointly with four others, " Ten messuages with lands at Farnhill, to be held at an annual rent of £20, payable on the 15th day next following the feast of St. Martin the Bishop, and the 15th day next following the feast of Pentecoste, in equal portions at the south porch of the parish church or chapel of Cliderowe, in the co. Lancaster." The Eltofts were a very wealthy family having extensive possessions in Airedale and elsewhere. The tourist may now ascend **Farnhill Crag** to the Jubilee Cairn by a path past some houses over the moor. The Cairn (800 ft.) is 12 ft. high and surmounted by a stone cross bearing the initials VR. and the insignia of the Union, a rose, shamrock. and thistle. The view is one of the best in upper Airedale. embracing northwards the Malham moors with Gordale Crags, Ryeloaf, Ingleborough, Norton Tower on Rylstone Fell, the three-peaked Flasby Fell, and the chimneys at Gargrave. Descend the moor-path on to the road, and by the Lidgate down into **Bradley**, (pop. 513), the township including the two hamlets of Higher and Lower Bradley, which by the way is 1½ m. from the nearest railway and telegraph station at Cononley. The old Hall here is a substantial three-gabled building, with projecting gargoyles and three rows of mullions. Over the door is carved IBD 1678. A curious feature of the south front is the four small square loop-holes (now glazed) between the west and middle chamber windows, and suggestive of an era when it was at times desirable to obtain a cautious peep at an approaching visitor before admitting him. The house for a long time was the property and residence of the Greenwoods; the late Mr. R. Greenwood, clerk to the Skipton bench of magistrates for 47 years, being of this family. West of the house may still be seen the old water-mill mentioned in ancient charters. The Canons of Bolton had lands with the tithes of corn here. Passing the south end of Bradley Gill an ascent and shortly a descent is made to the *Bay Horse* Inn at **Snagill**, whence the canal path may be followed to Skipton, (1 m.), emerging at the woods under the Castle walls, or the high-road may be taken to its entrance upon the High Street, Skipton.

Kildwick to Draughton (for Bolton Abbey), 6 m. Up Priest Bank and on the Grange road about 200 yds. (*see* p. 205) to a lane on *l* which ascend to the four-lane ends at Snake Hill (850 ft.) Here follow the Addingham road about 1¼ m. past a second four-lane ends and several farms down to **Cowburn Beck**. Just beyond the farm here an old lane ascends *l*, up to Bank End farm, and at the summit of the watershed (985 ft.) a little above, the southward view embraces the Haworth and Lancashire moors, with Pendle Hill, &c., whilst descending on the opposite side Chelker reservoir (57¼ acres) lies down on our right, with the rolling heathery heights of Wharfedale from Beamsley Beacon to Simon's Seat, in full range. Approaching Draughton Height farm (935 ft.) the beautiful Abbey woods are seen extending far up the valley, with the old Tithe barn conspicuous, and Otley Chevin, Langber, Hawbank, Embsay Crag, the rocky top of Cracoe Fell, Kirkby Fell beyond Malham, Stank Fell, and in the far distance due N. the top of Gt. Wham (1900 ft.) on Grassington Moor, whilst further north over Burnsall Fell may be descried the long back of Gt. Whernside (2263 ft.) above Kettlewell. Just below the house here, built in 1878, a path on *l.* descends fields into the road near the *Matchless* Inn, Draughton (*see* p. 244). To Bolton Woods an old lane at the top side of the school goes by Haw Park and comes out op. the Devonshire Hotel (2 m.), a nice walk.

KILDWICK TO CONONLEY.

A field path on the south side of the railway emerges in a short mile on the road under Glusburn Moor, and a descent is made past **Royd House**, a famous old farmstead with grey-green roof, overshadowed by majestic yews. The great Cromwell is said to have passed a night here during the residency of Master and Dame Maymond, whose initials appear on the old stone-seated porch fronting the road. Access to the interior is gained by a short passage through an inner doorway that enters upon a further oaken door opening into the spacious oak-raftered kitchen. The walls are over a yard thick. For about a century after the Commonwealth it belonged to a notable local family named Coates, and the initials and date R.C. 1678 M.C. are cut over an outer door. Roger Coates, who died in 1725, and lived at Royd House, belonged Kildwick Grange, and had also other property in Airedale and at Addingham, in Wharfedale, &c. The father of Roger Coates, also named Roger, lived at Kildwick Grange, and died in 1728. His two daughters married respectively Roger Swire, of Cononley Hall, and Christopher Hartley, of Marton. Another Roger Coates, who died in 1660, is buried in the chancel of Kildwick Church, where his gravestone may be seen. Royd House is now the property of Major Whalley, of Lancaster, and for the past 120 years has been occupied by the family of Speak.

Pursuing the road we drop on to Cononley Flush, a locality which, before the high bank of the railway was made near the south side of the river, was subject to extensive periodical floodings. At such seasons the people, and pack-horses with their sacks of spar, &c., from Raygill, used to have to leave the road and climb the high way still traceable in the fields above. The obtaining of the Airedale Drainage Act of 1861 has however considerably amended matters. The river courses here and at other places between Skipton and Bingley have been deepened and straightened; a sum of nearly £14,000 having been expended in these contracts. Law and other expenses have added another £4000 to £5000, and the money borrowed on the security of the rates has, according to the provisions of the Act, to be paid off, with interest, on the 22nd of July, 1891.

A short ascent is now made past the Club houses into Cononley.

CONONLEY.

ONONLEY, in *Domesday* Cutnelai, or the field of Kunet or Canute,* is another township in the extensive parish of Kildwick. During the monastic sway of Bolton Abbey the Canons had here one of their principal estates, comprising some 250 acres, an account of which appears in the *Compotus*† under 'Conedley.' In more ancient times a good deal of the land was held by the Knights Hospitallers of St. John of Jerusalem.

There are a number of notable old houses in the village, chief of these being Cononley Hall, long the seat of the Swire family, whose pedigree is given in Whitaker's 'Craven.' The house is now the property and residence of Geo. Turner, Esq. A considerable addition was made to the old building about a century ago, consisting of a square plain-built edifice of three stories, which from its dimensions, gives it rather a chapel-like appearance. Only the west end remains of the old hall, with the original mullions, and in the kitchen an old-fashioned open fire-place of unusual dimensions. It is about four yards wide. Adjoining it is the 'oak room,' panelled all round with black oak. In the new portion the rooms are large and lofty, and a striking feature is the handsome, spacious staircase, with oak steps and banister winding from basement to attic. Upon a stone on the south wall is carved   S E S   standing for Samuel and Elizabeth Swire, R 1683 S, and their son, Roger Swire, who died in 1705, at the early age of 35, having married

---

* We have on page 25 ascribed a similar derivation to Knottingley. Possibly, however, the latter may come from the older British word *Nott* or Knot, a rocky knoll, as in the case of Nottingham, &c.

† According to this authority the Nevilles had a private chapel here, *temp.* Edw. II.

Rosamund Coates, daughter of his father's cousin, Roger Coates, of Kildwick Grange, who survived her husband 35 years. Other old habitations 'grey with storied Time' are Milton House (long the residence of the Balme family), Pear Tree House, with its original oaken pegged doors and round arched doorways; and opposite the Beck bridge Tillotson's farm (inscribed TT 1632), the property of Mr. Lund, of Malsis Hall, who is the principal landowner.

Club Row, as the long line of houses so conspicuous from the railway is called, was originally built for hand-loom weaving, the upper rooms being specially well lighted and constructed with recesses, into which the backs of the looms were fitted, whilst the operatives sat close to the windows. By this arrangement as many as four looms could be placed upstairs, whilst the ordinary furniture of the bedroom occupied the centre.

The chief local industries at present, besides agriculture, are the two worsted manufactories of Messrs. Turner. Formerly the lead mines on Cononley Moor, owned by the Duke of Devonshire, were very productive, and employed a large section of the male population, besides a goodly number of skilled miners from Cornwall. They have, however, been long since abandoned, as the increased importations of foreign leads have so cheapened the home markets. The metal in many of the Spanish mines is, we are told, so rich in silver that this alone pays for the cost of getting. At Cononley, however, the lead is far from exhausted.

The male and mining population have had their wants met by a suitable provision of societies and clubs, formed for mutual benefit and amusement, the male persuasion being usually well looked after, or rather taking care to look after itself in this respect. At one time, however, it was declared here that the welfare of the opposite sex had been somewhat neglected. *Apropos*, an amusing incident happened at an early meeting, held in 1875, of the movement for a Mechanics' Institute, when one earnest worker on behalf of the sex warmly remarked: " Now look here, my boys, we've hired a room, which is to be specially fitted up for the purpose of embracing females." A statement that was received with mingled laughter and applause, but as it was Christmas time the proverbial confusion inseparable from that festive season may be reasonably advanced as an excuse for this *lapsus linguæ*.

Cononley to Dale End (Lothersdale), 2¼ m. Ascend past the church above the picturesque Cononley Gill, watered by a purling beck, which before the lead mines began brimmed with trout, until a wooden seat is reached appropriately inscribed 'Rest and be thankful.' Whilst taking advantage of this generous provision the visitor may enjoy the extensive panorama around, in which the cairn on Farnhill Crag is a noticeable feature. At the top of the road (820 ft.) turn *l*. past **Stone Gappe**, the ancient seat of the Laces, who have had a residence here from the time of the Norman Conquest. In a deed 14th Edward III. (1340) we observe the name is written "de la Leye de Stangap." The present hall recently vacated by them is temporarily unoccupied. Crossing the road at four-lane ends (*see* p. 214) a descent is made into Lothersdale, with the village and square-towered church just below, and looking west the precipitous ravine of Surgill and the Town Edge with the moors above, obtrude a commanding and somewhat wild scene upon the landscape. The fact may afford some satisfaction to the lover of genuine rusticity that gas has not yet invaded the quietudes of Lothersdale, and in the church here he may see the cleanly oil-lamps suspended from the roof of its neat interior. The church, which is of Norman aspect, is not old, having been built in 1838, and restored in 1884. It contains a beautiful memorial window to the late vicar, Mr. Holdsworth, and there are also stained memorial windows by Gibb and Howard, of London, to Francis J. Lace, Esq., B.C.L., J.P., of Stone Gappe, who died Dec. 4th, 1882, and of Elizabeth his wife, who died on Christmas Day, 1866, which were put in by their fourteen surviving children, in Aug. 1884. A neat inscribed brass, erected in 1887, by the widow of the late rector, reads as follows : "In loving memory of Wm. Elliott Dutton, for four years priest of this parish. His body lies at Luxor, in Egypt, but his memory lives in the hearts of those who loved him." Lothersdale is also provided with its places of Dissent, and some of these are of old date, the Friends having been established here for over two centuries.

To Raygill and Colne, *see* p. 214.

CONONLEY TO CARLETON.

Leaving the village by an ascending road past a house inscribed A B we continue along the breezy elevation on the south M 1799, side of the valley, and looking northward over Bradley notice how the land has been subdivided and cut up into numberless fields, whose dividing walls run off in all shapes and directions to the very summits of the hills. We have left the corn lands, and here enter upon a tract of the greenest pasture. Below us, in Bradley Ings, we can trace the old course of the river down to the sidewash above Cononley Bridge. A dip in the road goes past a denuded rocky knoll, where the exposed sandstone reveals *in situ* a huge fossil tree lying horizontally in the face of the rock. There is a pleasing view hence of Skipton, with the solid-looking towers of its two churches conspicuous, and the green *ings* of Carleton spreading below. At one time these were subject to wide inundations from the river, so much so that rafts have been used in communicating with the two places. Descending to the three-lane ends we now turn left to Carleton, and at the bottom of the road, near Mr. Eddy's, the steward's office, Carleton Glen may be conveniently visited. It is one of the many beautiful properties of the Duke of Devonshire, and is open every day except Sundays. It is of no great extent, the path going only a few hundred yards through the luxuriant woods above the fish pond, which latter is fed by a small stream and discharged by an artificial waterfall. It is needless to say that the gathering of ferns, primrose roots, &c., is strictly prohibited. Opposite the glen house is a field path to Skipton, but our walk continues along the road about a half-mile to Carleton.

CARLETON.

LIKE Bingley, Keighley, Kildwick, and other places in this Deanery, Carleton (formerly Carlton) has preserved in its name plain proof of a Saxon personality; *carles* (*vulg.* churls) or *ceorls* being the Saxon word for husbandmen. How many Carltons there are in Yorkshire, or in England, we do not know, but this is the fifth* village of this name which we have passed on our journey up from Goole. During the Saxon period, say a thousand years back, the land must have been largely set in corn and a much more fruitful and important place than Skipton, which, then only consisting of a few shepherds' huts, was but an insignificant dependency of the great Earl Edwin, who lived at Bolton on Wharfe. At the Conquest, Carleton (with Lothersden) had ten carucates taxed, whilst Skipton had four. The Scots after Bannockburn made great raids on the district, and in 1318 the accounts of Bolton Abbey show that the grange at Carleton was destroyed by them and the cattle driven off. The churches were pillaged, and in consequence the tax upon that of Carleton, then existing as a chapel to the Priory of Bolton, was reduced by nearly one-half. Up to the reign of Elizabeth the township lay wholly unenclosed, there being one common pasture for cattle, and one town-field for corn. Corn was still grown here until a comparatively recent period, and conveniently disposed of in Skipton, which continued an important corn market up to the present reign.

Of the origin of the first church at Carleton we have no exact knowledge, but at the foundation of Embsay Priory in A.D. 1120, there was a chapel here, and a list of the vicars

---

* The others being near Snaith, Pontefract, Rothwell, near Leeds, and Yeadon.

has been preserved since the first appropriation of the chapel in 1292. The church was rebuilt in the time of Henry VII., and was restored in 1858, when the floor of the nave was relaid and the old gravestones covered in. An exact transcription of the stones was, however, carefully made by the late vicar, Mr. Morris. The present building is an elegant structure in the Early English style, and consists of nave, aisles, chancel, and tower with clock. The latter instrument, with its twelve-foot pendulum, is a mechanical wonder of Craven, and is the production of a self-taught native rustic named " Billy " Cryer. It consists of seven wheels only, and is said to keep excellent time. The interior of the church contains a beautiful east window by Clayton and Bell, and in the chancel there is a remarkable painting on canvas (in size about ten feet by six feet) of the entombment of Christ, executed by the talented daughter of the present vicar, the Rev. T. C. Barker, M.A. The well-preserved registers of the church are amongst the oldest in the country, and date from 1538. The oldest gravestone we have noted in the burial yard bears the date 1667.

In the Churchwardens' Accounts are many entries relating to the old custom of allotting apprentices. Here is a bargain to ' keep, clothe, and maintain ' one who apparently needs no other recommendation but a pair of hands. and the clothes she stands up in !

"2 April, 1777. That Hez. Swire doth agree to take a Female apprentice as soon as one shall be found, and in the same apparel that the said apprentice shall then have and wear: instead of Will Sagar his present apprentice who is afflicted with the Evil.   Signed John Calvert, } Ch. Wardens.
                                   Wm. Driver,
Hez. Swire.   Wm. Burton, Overseer."

Both the Carleton and Skipton registers contain many records of soldiers slain during the Civil Wars, and buried at these churches, but many of them it is evident, were interred where they fell. A few years ago, whilst digging in some fields north-west of Carleton Hall, a quantity of human bones was discovered, doubtless of "soldiers" or " rebels," (as the Royalists and Parliamentarians were respectively styled here), who perished during the siege of Skipton castle.

Not far from the church, and fronting the road, stand the ruins of **Carleton Hall**, and over a five-light mullion on its tottering gable may still be read the brief story of its foundation: "*This made: Will-yam Farrand and Elizabeth his wief, iiii. Aprill; 1584.*" A portion of the building is now used as a farm loft, and the other is without roof. The original oak beams that support the principal apartment are still remarkably sound and perfect, and the floor here is also peculiarly noteworthy, being constructed of huge pavestones, about a foot square, laid diagonally in the earth. The Ferrands, of Norman descent, are still lineally represented by the family at St. Ives (*see* p. 172); and the Carleton estate and hall (not the manor) were acquired by them through the marriage, in 1454, of Roger Ferrand with Isabell, daughter and sole heiress of Willm. de Altaripa, of Carleton, and held by them until 1651, when the estate was sold to a Mr. Thomas Parkinson. The *manor* was held by the Cliffords, who had a house and park at the **Biggin**, probably built and enclosed by Henry first Earl of Cumberland. About twenty years ago, during repairs to this house, a number of silver and bronze coins of the time of Charles I. were found, doubtless concealed during the troublous period of the War, (*see* p. 209). During the lifetime of George, the spendthrift Earl of Cumberland, who died in 1605, and whose portrait painted on oak (dated 1588) is preserved in Skipton Castle, a great many freehold and leasehold tenancies were created, and Whitaker quotes a long petition addressed to this Earl by the tenantry of Carleton, about 1580, on the state of husbandry in the parish. To this we may add, that after the proposed survey, by fine passed 1588-9, George, Earl of Cumberland demised to

"Francis Clifford, esq., Anthony Wright. gent., and Willm. Farrande, gent.. the Manors of Gressyngton, Steton, Idle, *Carleton*, Lothersdaill, Bradley, Conondley, Gysburne, Settyl, Gyglesweeke, Langstroth and Langstrothdaill, Preston, Threaplande, Crakowe, Woodhouse, Appletreeweeke, Lytton, and Lytton Daill, and 1500 messuages, and 20 mills, with lands in the same and in Newhall, Buckden, Heslywood, Storthes. Hawkesweeke, Stodderhale, Coyshe, Overhessilden, Netherhessilden. Foxoppe, Sleight, Glousburne, Cowlynge, and Drawghton; all the mines of lead and other metals in the above manors, &c., being excepted."

Carleton Hall was for sometime the property and residence of the celebrated naturalist and court physician Dr. Martin Lister, who married a daughter of the above Thomas Parkinson, and in 1670 removed from Carleton to York. Here he did admirable service by bringing to light many hitherto unrecorded antiquities of the great Roman city. He afterwards removed to London, and died there in 1712, aged 74. The Carleton Hall estate was sold by his family to the Bensons, Lords Bingley, now represented by Mr. Lane Fox, and the hall was last occupied by a Quaker named Wormer, about sixty years ago.

Trappes Hall is another historic Carleton house, but we know very little about it. It is now occupied as cottages, but was once the seat of the family of Trappes, who forfeited it to the Crown through a treasonable alliance with the last Scottish rebellion.

East of the church, and near the vicarage, is the curious little court-yard, with its massive stone portal, surrounding the Hospital or Alms Houses, founded about 1700 by Ferrand Spence, Esq., of the General Post Office, London, for twelve poor widows belonging to Carleton and Market Bosworth, in Leicestershire. A handsome legacy of about £17,000 bequeathed to this trust in 1871 by the late Miss Ann V. Niven, of Skipton, has considerably increased the allowances and the number of recipients.

Carleton has produced many instances of longevity, and if statistics can be relied on, not a few of persons who have reached the age of 100 and upwards. Dr. Lister mentions two such natives; one Frances Woodworth, who died in 1662, aged 102, being "a lean woman, yet upright as a young girl, and of perfect memory." The other was Thos. Wiggin, who died in 1670 in his 109th year, and who "went about till within a few weeks of his last." We may add that the Carleton registers yield no proof of these instances of unusual longevity. From 1551 to 1562, and again from 1664 to 1674 the registers are deficient.

From Carleton to Skipton (1½ m.) the visitor should take a field path leading from the church, as the highroad makes a considerable circuit.

HIGH STREET, SKIPTON.

SKIPTON.

TO picture Skipton at its most characteristic epoch we must go back a long stretch of time, when after the building of the Castle at the close of the Conqueror's reign, its feudal lords held almost regal power. Before the arrival of Robert de Romillé, its first Norman owner, the place was held by a few Saxon shepherds as its Domesday name *Sciptone* (A.S. *sceap*, a sheep) or *Town of Sheep*, implies. The Barons lived in great state at the Castle; they had a numerous train of attendants, and kept huntsmen, falconers, &c.; they gave costly banquets, entertained royalty, formed royal alliances and otherwise intermarried with the best blood. The grant by King John, in 1204, of a weekly market and a bi-annual fair here promoted Skipton to a town of chief importance, and fit capital of Craven,—the *Craey van*, or land of crags. It has always retained this distinctive title, and is the oldest chartered market town in Airedale, as well as one of the oldest in Yorkshire. About the time mentioned vast tracts of sheep walks began to be appropriated to the range of my lord's deer, and a long and blood-stained era of might against right set in. The hapless serf, with fear and trembling, stole beneath the castle walls, or made a detour believing he should lose his head if, meeting his mighty master, he should incur his displeasure, or mayhap be lynched for a frown! Now, indeed, like the shadow of a cloud upon the rock this old sovereign glory has departed, and we stand in face of a mightier power, before the Castle portal looking up at its significant motto in stone,—
Desormais—*Hereafter!*

Even so it is now as in the days of Homer, when the great poet wrote,

"Like leaves on trees the race of man is found,
Now green in youth, now withering on the ground,
Another race the following spring supplies,
They fall successive, and successive rise.
So generations in their course decay,
So flourish these when those are passed away."

Of the Castle and Church (founded at the same period) we give a more particular account below. Skipton, now a busy extending town of some 12,000 inhabitants, and on the verge of incorporation, has several cotton spinning and weaving mills, the handsomest and largest, that of Messrs. John Dewhurst & Sons, Ld., employing about a thousand workpeople. The famous quarries of limestone at Hawbank employ also a large body of men, and there are besides two corn mills, tanneries, and important lead works. Among other principal buildings are the Town Hall, Temperance Hall, Grammar School, Christ Church, the Catholic Church of St. Stephen, the Convent, Presbytery, Mechanics' Institute (the old Tollbooth), several Nonconformist Chapels, &c. Dissent laid hold of Skipton at an early period. Fox, the Quaker founder, visited it in 1658. It was at Skipton and Carleton, about 1650, that the celebrated Rev. Oliver Heywood first preached in public, and no places suffered more severely than these during the religious persecutions that followed. Many took refuge in little accessible places where preaching houses were established, but where they were often found out and their adherents heavily fined or otherwise punished. A public Pillory stood opposite the Craven Bank in the High Street, until 1770, when it was taken down. All classes of criminals were put in this "wooden collar," which was not abolished by act of Parliament until the year of her present Majesty's accession. Near this Pillory in the High Street, — the principal thoroughfare in the town, leading to the church and castle, — was the old Market Cross, with its stone awning, and by it the Stocks. They were removed about the year 1840. Up to the end of last century sheep-stealers and others convicted of felony were publicly flogged at the Cross. This infliction was carried out almost within living recollection to the very letter of the Act, which ordained that the " bodie be beaten with whips until bloodie by reasone of such whipping." Whether the punishments of ear-cropping and slitting of nostrils existed here is doubtful, but there is evidence of an engine having been kept in the Tollbooth for branding felons. Another old-time punishment here was the Ducking Stool, once common in Airedale villages, for ' cooling ' female scolds. The custom of bull-baiting continued to the present century, and the ring that secured the bull-rope is kept at the *Bay Horse* Inn, opposite which is the flagstone to which the ring was fixed. According to the Court Leet accounts quoted by Mr. W. H. Dawson in his valuable History, the vendors of beef of bulls not previously baited were fined, an enactment that arose, we opine, from the belief that baiting, like game hunted, improved the flesh. Skipton has an old renown for its cattle fairs, and for the general excellent quality of the animals shewn. The celebrated 'Craven Heifer,' which has given name to many an inn, and whose bulky image (the animal weighed over 150 stones) figures on the notes of the Craven Bank, was reared on the rich sward of this parish, near Bolton Abbey.

Turning to the past history of Skipton, from the Romillés the barony, in 1152, came by marriage of Alice de Romillé to William Fitz Duncan, nephew of David, King of Scotland, and then through their daughter to the Earls of Albemarle, the last of whom, again a heiress, married in 1269, Edmund Plantagenet, second son of Henry III., surnamed Crutchback. Leaving no issue, the barony passed to the Crown,* and in 1311 was granted by Edward II. to Robert de Clifford, a descendant of a warlike family that joined the Conqueror, and was ultimately established at Clifford Castle, in Herefordshire. That frail beauty, the 'Fair Rosamond,' paramour of Henry II., and who is supposed to have been poisoned by his Queen at Woodstock, in 1177, was daughter of Walter de Clifford, whose son, Walter, was attainted for enforcing an officer who waited upon him, to "eate the King's Writ, waxe and all," for which offence he narrowly escaped confiscation of his whole patrimony. With the exception of two short intervals the lordship of Skipton has remained continuously with this

---

* That the castle and manor were Crown property early in the reign of Edward I. is evidenced by the following Royal grant made A.D. 1281. " Pro Hospitale Sanctæ Mariæ extra Bishopsgate London. Rex concessit Alienoræ matri suæ pro vita *Castrum et Manerium de Skipton*, Manerium de Pokelington in Com Ebor, Maneria de Middleton et de Dertforde in Com Kanciæ ac alia." *Vide Calendarium Rotul Patent.* (Vol. 4. Record Office.)

family for over five hundred years. It is now vested in Baron Hothfield, and consists of some 13,000 acres.

The Castle. Of the original building erected by Robert de Romillé after the accession of William I. in 1066, nothing is believed to remain but the western doorway of the inner castle, (consisting of a treble semi-circular arch resting upon square piers), and possibly the north tower of the gateway and the dungeon. In the 12th century it appears to have been overthrown by the Scots, and remained in a semi-ruinous state until the installation of the first Lord Clifford in 1311. He set about the building of an impregnable fortress, as now existing, and which consists of seven massive round towers, connected by rectilinear apartments enclosing a spacious irregular quadrangle, and an inner one, known as the Conduit Court, in the centre of which is a large old yew tree. Upon foundations of solid rock, the thick, firmly-built walls on the north side are raised above a lofty natural precipice, whilst on the opposite side the great gateway with portcullis was protected by a deep moat, over which a draw-bridge was thrown. This Lord Clifford fell with many another English noble at the battle of Bannockburn in 1314. During the rule of his successor, Roger Lord Clifford, King Edward II. visited the castle in Oct. 1323, and again in 1324. In 1367 a royal license to enclose 500 acres of land for a park was obtained. John, ninth Lord Clifford, and a conspicuous character in Shakespeare's *Henry VI.*, lost his estates for the part he played on the side of the Lancastrians during the Wars of the Roses. His son Henry, the 'Shepherd Lord,' regained the Skipton lands on the accession of Henry VII. He took a principal command at the battle of Flodden, in 1513, and died at Barden Tower ten years later. Henry, eleventh Lord of Skipton, was created Earl of Cumberland. He made a fortunate alliance with the Lady Margaret Percy, and his son Henry, at the age of twenty, (1537) married the Lady Eleanor Brandon, daughter of the Duke of Suffolk, by Mary, Queen Dowager of France, and granddaughter of Henry VII. The ceremony took place in the Royal presence in the magnificent gallery of Skipton Castle, built specially with the Octagon Tower by the young knight's father for their reception. This august Lady Clifford during her residence at Skipton was made co-heir-presumptive to the Throne of England. Her son George, third Earl of Cumberland, (1558-1605), won the admiration and favour of Queen Elizabeth for his gallantry against the Spanish Armada. He had a strong love of adventure and made many voyages to the West Indies. He was one of the peers who sat in judgment on the ill-starred Mary Queen of Scots, whose Room in Skipton Castle is pointed out as the traditional place of her temporary incarceration. This Earl was father of Lady Anne, the celebrated Countess of Dorset, Pembroke, and Montgomery; who was born in the castle on Jan. 30th, 1590, and died at Brougham at the age of 85. It was she who repaired the castle after the siege in the Civil Wars. She was a noble-minded woman, of great Christian piety, and high accomplishments. She restored Barden Tower, and the tower, &c. of Skipton church, and she has left some interesting literary *Memorials*. The large family painting, now at Appleby Castle, contains her portrait with a biography.* By the hand of her daughter the estate descended to the present noble family of Tufton.

Skipton Castle has sustained two important sieges, first during the insurrection of 1536 known as the Pilgrimage of Grace, when it was the only stronghold in the West Riding that held out for the King; and again a long three years' siege during the Civil War, which terminated in its surrender to the Parliamentary army on Dec. 21st, 1645. The story of the Siege has been often told, but the Terms of Surrender of the Castle to Col. Richard Thorneton, Commander-in-chief of the opposing forces, have only recently come to light.

Appended are the ARTICLES agreed upon :—

1. That Sir John Mallory with all the rest of the Officers, Gentlemen, and Souldiers, shall march out betwixt this and Tuesday next before twelve of the clocke, surrendering the Castle, with all the Armes, Ordnance, and Ammunition, without any prejudice done to them, with all the goods and provisions whatsoever in the said Castle, not to be purloyned or imbezzled, and whosoever shall be found offending after the sealing of these Articles for the misdisposing of goods, shall be given up to Justice and treble satisfaction to be given for the goods so conveyed by the said party, if he be worth it, if not, then to be made good by the Governour.

2. That all prisoners now in the Castle, of what quality or condition soever, shall be set at liberty upon the sealing of these Articles.

3. That after the signing of these Articles two such Officers as Col. Thorneton shall appoint shall be admitted to go into the Castle, and see the evidence houses lockt up and sealed, and have an accompt of all spare Armes and Ammunition, and such a guard at such a time as Col. Thorneton shall appoint to goe in.

4. That the Governour, Officers, and Souldiers of Horse and Foot with their Horses and proper Arms as to horse and foot, that march out accordingley to the Honour of a Souldier, (viz.) with Colours flying, Trumpets sounding, Drums beating, Matches lighted at both ends, and Bullets in their mouthes, every Trooper and every Foot Souldier three charges of powder, and the Officers of Commission to march with their wearing appareli that is properly their owne in their Portmantles, and not have anything taken from them, and that the Common Souldiers shall not march away with any Bag and Baggage.

5. That all Gentlemen not in the condition of a Souldier have their horses and swords, and be allowed to march to the King or his Garrisons, or their own homes, and be protected in either condition as they shall make choyce of.

* For an admirably penned story of her life *see* Hartley Coleridge's *Northern Worthies*.

6. That all Officers and Souldiers of Horse and Foot, Gentlemen, Townesmen, or other persons whatever belonging to this Garrison, shall have liberty, conduct and protection to go to his Majesty, or such of his Garrisons as shall be agreed of.
7. That all Officers, Souldiers, Gentlemen, Townesmen or others desiring to goe and live at home, shall have free leave there to remain under the protection of the Parliament.
8. That all Souldiers or other persons that are sick or hurt, and not able to goe to their homes or other places where they desire, shall have leave to stay here at Skipton, and shall be allowed necessary accomodation untill it please God they shall recover, and then to have Passes upon their desires to goe to their home or to such of his Majestie's next Garrisons they shall make choyce of.
9. That all women and Children within this Garrison be suffered to go with or to such as they shall desire to their own habitations.
10. That all the hangings and other goods given in by Inventory to be the Countess of Pembroke's shall be there secured by themselves and not made sale of untill the Lady of Pembroke bee made acquainted therewith, but to be prized with the rest.
11. That all the evidences and writings whatever belonging to the Countess of Pembroke or to the Countess of Corke in any of the Evidence Houses of this Castle, shall not be looked into by any, untill both the Countesses be acquainted therewith, and for that end that two Moneths time for notice to be given them, and the Kayes to be delivered to Col. Thorneton, who is interested with them in the meantime.
12. That all possible care be taken to preserve the Woods and Parks belonging to both the Ladies.
13. That those that intend to march to his Majesty or any of his Garrisons march but six miles a day, and free Quarter during all their March, and that a sufficient Convoy be allowed them, and may conduct them to Nottingham, and from thence to one of these foure Garrisons as shall be there named by them to the Commander in Chiefe of the Convoy, viz., Banbury, Worcester, Hereford, or Litchfield.
14. That if any persons belonging to this Garrison shall misdemean themselves in the march, it shall not extend further than the parties offending, upon whom Justice shall be done according to the fault committed.
15. That if any Officers or Souldiers shall be necessitated to buy horses, or anything else in their march, shall have liberty for that purpose, and after payment enjoyment thereof during the protection of the Convoy.

These Articles are agreed of us who were appointed to trente for the rendition of Skipton Castle, in the behalf of Sir John Mallory, Govenour of Skipton.

FERDINANDO LEIGH.   FRAN. COBB.
JOHN TEMPEST.   MICAH TOMPSON.

The Castle walls are in some places ten to eleven feet thick. A peculiar feature of its interior arrangements, is that no two rooms in it are on the same level, whilst each is provided with two doors for egress in case of danger. On the left of the court yard is the castle dungeon, a gloomy apartment 16 ft. by 8 ft., and 9 ft. high, in which it may be guessed that many a luckless prisoner has grown pale within its damp and cheerless environment. Many of the lower apartments of the castle were used for storage of provisions and for cattle lairs in times of siege. The Banqueting Hall, facing the court-

SKIPTON CASTLE.

yard, is lighted by three windows, and is a fine apartment about 50 ft. in length. Adjoining it are the Drawing Room, Muniment Room, and Mary Queen of Scots room. On the right of the archway is the Shell House, so called from one of its rooms being decorated with sea shells, trophies of the buccaneering Earl of Cumberland. On the west side a narrow staircase conducts to 'Fair Rosamond's Chamber.' This is in the oldest part of the castle, and her visit or birth here (as is traditionally reported) must have taken place long before the Cliffords came into possession, as already stated, in 1311. In several of the rooms, and notably in the State Chamber, are preserved many specimens of antique furniture and curious old tapestry. Many relics, including paintings, have, however, been transferred to Appleby. Visitors, we may add, are shewn through the Castle after 9 a.m. on application at the Custodian's Office.

The Parish Church. Founded probably towards the end of the Conqueror's reign. From the foundation of their monastery at Embsay to the Dissolution it formed an endowment of the Canons of

Bolton. The present building, of different periods, comprises nave with clerestory, chancel, side aisles, and gallery at west end. The only portion left of the original Norman church is the sedilia of four stone seats, with pointed arches and cylindrical columns, in the south wall of the nave. From appearances in the stonework the whole chancel of three aisles has been added to the original building eastward, probably about 1483, for in that year Richard III., who, when Duke of Gloucester, occasionally resided at the castle, decreed a payment for the repair of this church. The handsome flat oak roof is also referable to this period. In 1655 the church was beautifully restored by the able Countess of Pembroke, whose initials A.P. appear on many of the windows. The elegant oak screen, originally surmounted by a rood-loft, is said to have been the gift of the monks of Bolton. Over the gallery is a curious 'poker painting,' burnt on sycamore wood, representing the "Angel and Shepherds of Bethlehem." It is the work of a native artist named George Smith, who also executed in 1798 the painting of the Royal Arms hung above the sedilia. The church contains many monuments and inscriptions of interest, a splendid reredos, and some admirable illuminated windows by Capronnier, of Brussels. There are three tombs of the Cliffords, Earls of Cumberland, with brasses, restored by the Duke of Devonshire in 1867 at a cost of £1000. The vault was opened in 1803 for inspection by Dr. Whitaker, who describes the appearance of the bodies in his "History of Craven."* In 1854 the floor of the church, beneath which hundreds of interments have been made, was covered with nine inches of concrete. From the tower, 'curfew' bell is tolled nightly at eight o'clock, and the mediæval custom of burial by torchlight was only discontinued early in the present century.

Castle Woods. This beautiful domain that once formed part of the private grounds of the early Cliffords, is now generously open to the public. The woods clothe the sides of a deep and picturesque dell, with a stream in the bottom, and paths in various directions. The trees are more remarkable for their altitude than for their girth, being closely planted on the steep acclivities, amongst them the pine tribe, which have a peculiarly vitalizing influence on the air, and thereby enhance the salubrity of a place, do very well here. A nice round (1½-2 hrs.) through the woods is to follow the Embsay road (¼ m.) to the Bailey Cottage on *l*. A fine old rosemary tree 8 ft. high is a noteworthy object in the garden here. Follow the path along the top about ¾ m., descending over the footbridge, where the stream is seen foaming over low rocks, and ascend *l*. along the opposite side of glen (a way hardly practicable in wet weather), emerging over a step-style into the lane, whence *l*. 20 yds. and over style on *l*. up fields to the top when a splendid **View**, the best of any around Skipton, is had. Below the spectator lies the whole town, with its two

---

* Similarly, in 1813, the vault and body of the unfortunate monarch, Charles I., whose cause the Cliffords ever heroically upheld, were examined by Sir Henry Halford and other gentlemen. The remains were tolerably entire, and in good condition, amidst the gums and resins used for their preservation.

churches at opposite extremites, forming from this point an irregular crescent. Southwards we see Farnhill Crag, Rumbalds Moor, Cononley Moor, &c.; westwards the ascending roads to Colne, over Elslack and Carleton moors, whilst north of these Pendle Hill, with Easington Fell beyond Clitheroe, rear their majestic elevated lines on the horizon. North again is all the range of Flasby Fell, and to the east we see Hawe Bank (Skipton Rock), Embsay Crag, and the road to Barden, with Beamsley Beacon beyond. As this beautiful panorama can be viewed by a walk of 5-7 mins. from Skipton church it is worth seeking on its own account. Opposite the *Royal Oak* ascend the hill to the gas lamp above the Wesleyan Chapel, whence turn *l.* to the field top.

As affording some idea of the natural vegetable productions of this part of Airedale we here furnish, by the help of Messrs. T. W. Edmondson and L. Rotheray, members of the Craven Naturalists' Society, a list of the more interesting species occurring in these woods. The soil is calcareous.

Trees. Oak, ash, elm, sycamore, birch, beech, hornbeam, alder, horse-chestnut, hawthorn, bird-cherry, holly, elder, mt.-ash, goat-willow, crack-willow, black poplar, yew, Scotch fir, and four or five other species of pine.

Shrubs. Blackthorn, guelder-rose, dog-rose, honeysuckle, ivy, wayfaring-tree, hazel, raspberry, dewberry, bramble, broom, woody-nightshade, &c.

Flowers. Wood anemone, crowfoot (*R. auricomus* and *bulbosus*), winter-cress, rock-cress, bitter-cress (*C. amara*), whitlow-grass, stitchwort (*S. Graminea*). St. John's wort (*H. perforatum* and *hirsutum*), wood-sorrel, bitter-vetch (*L. macrorrhizus*), water-avens, alternate and opposite-leaved golden-saxifrage, gt. hairy willow-herb, enchanter's nightshade, wood-sanicle, moschatel, cross-wort, sweet wood-ruff, burdock (*A. minus*), wall-lettuce, hawk-weed (*H. boreale*), hawk's-beard (*C. paludosa*), yellow goat's beard, cowslip, comfrey, giant bell-flower, sweet marjoram, bugle, yellow pimpernel, wood-rush, early purple and spotted orchis, herb-paris or true-love, wild basil, cuckoo-pint or wake robin, yellow flag, tway-blade, greater toothwort, scorpion-grass (*M. Sylvatica* and *cæspitosa*), wood-betony, blue-bell, &c.

Ferns *Lastrea filix-mas*, *Athyrium filix fœmina*, var. *rhæticum*, *Polypodium vulgare* and *rœbertianum*, *Scolopendrium vulgare*, *Polystichium aculeatum*, &c.

Skipton-Rock Quarry. This is one of the 'sights' of Craven, and especially to the geologist, as shewing the extraordinary stratification on the north side of the great Skipton anticlinal. The quarry is reached by entering a stile about ¼ m. on the Harrogate road, and thence by a cottage at its west end. This portion is not now worked, and has recently been planted by the Castle authorities. The quarry, which is leased by the Leeds and Liverpool Canal Co., extends for about 1000 yds., and at its greatest elevation is about 260 ft. high. The limestone is largely used for the repair of roads, and for the smelting of iron, &c. The beds at the west end have a dip W.N.W. of 40° to 50°, increasing almost vertically eastwards. As much as 20,000 tons of rock, we are told, have been dislodged by one blast. The stone is conveyed in waggons from the quarry by an inclined tram, worked by steel-wire ropes from the engine-house at Embsay, down to a branch of the canal behind Skipton Castle to the boats. As much as 40 tons (in 8 waggons) can thus be lowered at once; but before 1836 the stone was carted through the town to the canal.

Craven Baths and Sulphur Wells. There is nothing of much visual interest here now, but the spot was formerly a noted and favourite resort. Pass the Devonshire Hotel and across Draughton beck by the old Grammar School, and then along the Addingham old road about ¼ m. to first house on *l*. The sulphur spring rises at the dip of the hill, where is a pleasantly-wooded dingle through which a stream runs that formerly supplied the baths. These consisted of plunge, shower, and swimming baths, and were organised by the late Dr. Dodgson about fifty years ago. Around the Well House opposite were pleasure grounds maintained by subscription. Two or three years ago the well fell into disuse, and is now flagged over. In dry seasons it was said to have a very disagreeable smell. Its constituent gases are sulphuretted hydrogen and carbonic acid, and solid contents, carbonate of iron, sulphate of magnesia, muriate of soda, and muriate of lime and iodine. A little higher up the road are three reservoirs that supply Skipton with water.

The visitor will find Skipton a capital centre for many delightful walking and driving tours, and there is excellent accommodation at the various hotels in the town.

'BUSES PLY BETWEEN

Skipton and Grassington, (10 m.) **and Buckden,** (18¼ m.) *Daily,* (Mail). Leaves S. (Post Off.) 6-0 a.m., arr. B. 9-20 a.m. On Sunday leaves S., 8-45 a.m., arr. B. 12-5 p.m. On *Mon.. Wed.*, and *Sat.* leaves S. at 3-0 p.m. for Buckden, and 4-50 p.m. for Grassington only. **Return** (Mail) from B., 3-40 p.m., arr. S. 6-40 p.m. On Sunday leaves 2-0 p.m., arr. 5-0 p.m. On *Mon., Wed.*, and *Sat.* leaves B. 6-15 a.m., arr. S. 9-15 a.m. From Grassington, 7-30 a.m. daily. Single fares: Grassington, 1s. 6d.; Buckden, 3s.

Skipton and Broughton (3¼ m.) **East Marton** (5¼ m.) **Horton Lane Ends** (9 m.) **Gisburn** (11 m.) Daily, (Mail). Leaves S. 6-0 a.m., arr. G. 7-45 a.m. On Sunday leaves S. 8-45 a.m., arr. G. 10-30 a.m. **Return** (Mail) from G. 4-15 p.m., arr. S. 6-0 p.m. Sunday leaves 3-10 p.m., arr. 4-50 p.m. Single fares: Broughton, 6d.; East Marton, 9d.; Horton Lane Ends, 1s. 2d.; Gisburn, 1s. 6d.

Skipton and Bolton Abbey P.O. (6 m.) (Mail) week-days only. Leaves S. 6-0 a.m., arr. B. 7-15 a.m. **Return** from B. 5-0 p.m., arr. S. 6-20 p.m. *From Nov. 1st to March 31st, leaves B. at 4-0 p.m.* Single fare, 1s.

In the season (on week-days) Messrs. Cook & Son issue day-tickets from **Leeds and Bradford** by rail to **Skipton**, and thence by conveyance by any of the following routes: (1) **To Barden Tower,** Appletreewick, Burnsall, and return by Grassington and Rylstone. (2) **To Malham** and back by Eshton and Airton. (3) **To Kilnsey Crag** by Threshfield, returning through Grass Woods and Grassington. Return fare for any route 5s.

EXCURSIONS FROM SKIPTON.

Skipton to Broughton, 3½ m., **Elslack**, 5 m. Crossing the Aire bridge two miles out of Skipton, through a rich open country, just after passing the old *Bull* inn (3 m.) a fine view of **Broughton Hall**, occupying a low warm situation is had. The present building dates from 1597, and was anciently called Gilliot's Place. The knightly family of Gilliot were settled at Broughton at an early period, and their name occurs in the oldest charters. In A.D. 1300 we find John Gyliot (*milit*) witness to a deed relating to lands at Glusburn, and again in 1340 Peter Gilliott occurs in a quit-claim dated from the same place. In the reign of Edward II. the Broughton estate was granted to John Tempest, of Bracewell, and since 1406, when Roger Tempest married Katherine, sole heiress of Peter Gilliott, Broughton has been their property and residence. The late Sir Chas. Robt. Tempest, who was High Sheriff in 1839, was created Baronet in 1841, and died unmarried in 1865. He devised his estates at Broughton in Yorkshire and Coleby in Lincolnshire to his great-nephew, Henry A. J. Tempest, who was born in 1863, and died in April, 1891, and whose father, Sir Chas. Hy. Tempest, Bart., is the present occupant. The Hall was some time the residence of the late Chas. Semon, Esq., founder of the Semon Convalescent Home at Ilkley, in 1874. Immediately on passing the Hall, a road on *l.* crosses the bridge before the lodge gates, which may be followed up a shady lane on to the fields direct to **Broughton Church**. This is a Norman foundation, but nothing of the original structure is believed to remain but the doorway and font. Whitaker gives a list of the vicars from A.D. 1247. On the south side of the present building is an old stone with a rude cross enclosing two minor crosses. The tombs of the Moorhouses, of Elslack, Englands of Bingley, and Ayrtons of Rylstone, who were of one family, lie close together on the left of the path before the church porch. Near here are several very old dated gravestones, and one (dateless) bears the device of a sword. The interior of the church contains several lengthy monumental inscriptions, in Latin, to the Tempest family.

The tourist may follow the rural church lane (the old Roman road to Ribchester) past the White House to **Elslack**, or leave the lane by a path through the fields by the railway side to the station. Hereabouts he will see traces of the furrows made when the now green pastures once smiled with corn. The manor of *Eleslac* (as it is written in Domesday) was in Henry III.'s time a possession of the

Norman family of De Altaripa, and afterwards of the Malhams, Royalist officers in the Civil Wars. **Elslack Hall**, their seat (now the property of Mr. Lane Fox), had, in Dodsworth's time, a dungeon, which he describes as having a "hole in the top to let folks down, and no door." There are two stones on different parts of the building inscribed R B 1672, doubtless meant to commemorate the restoration of the hall by its, then proprietor, Robt. Benson, father of the first Lord Bingley, who had acquired it from the Malhams. At the east end are two old mullions of six lights, and on the west side are the perfect remains of a moat. Some years ago a human skeleton was found behind one of the panels in the interior, but how or why it came there is not known. The house is now occupied as a farm by Mr. R. Horner. The **White House**, already mentioned, was the home of the Moorhouse family from about the period of the Rebellion of 1745 until 1876, when old Mr. John Moorhouse, having no issue, retired with his wife to Cowling. They farmed about 100 acres, including the wood, and glebe lands at Broughton. The family came from Skibeden, where they were settled at the time of the Civil Wars, in which they took an active part. For fully six centuries they have resided in the liberty of Skipton; three of this family being enrolled in the Poll Tax of Richard II., A.D. 1379. There are several memorials of them in Skipton Church. Adjoining the beck close by is the **School-house**, for many years tenanted by a worthy veteran, Mr Enoch Hall. He served in the Peninsular wars, and was also one of the guards of Napoleon at St. Helena. Ultimately he came to Elslack, where for many long years he taught the village school, giving plums and delicious gooseberries from his well-kept garden as prizes to his apt scholars. He died in June, 1883, in his 90th year. Often during our many weeks' stay at this place have we chatted with the old man, who was full of racy anecdote and stories of his early soldier life abroad. When newspapers were scarce the late Mr. Ed. Baines (Sir Edward's father) used to come over here occasionally, and bring with him a copy of the *Leeds Mercury* for an old Chartist named Cooper, living up on the moor side, and who was a particularly intelligent man, and the only one who took a paper in these parts. During the French wars people came to him for many miles round to hear the news. On one occasion an anxious wiseacre from Cracoe passed a night at his house, and on the following day, when Mr. Baines arrived with the newspaper, it was reported that Napoleon had reached Cracoe, at which the old man was in a terrible plight. He threw up his arms, exclaiming, "Oh! my dear wife and bairnies, they will all be murdered when I get hame!" But when he did get 'hame,' his delight knew no bounds when, seeing his family all right, it was explained that Cracow in Russia, was meant! But he vowed he would never leave home again. At that time the guards were stationed on Elslack Moor (*see* p. 215). Near the station is a hill (cut through by the railway) called Burwins, on which there was a castle, conjectured by Dodsworth to be Danish, but which Whitaker believes may have been Roman. Not a vestige of the building now remains. But the name is certainly indicative of a Saxon structure, from A. S. *Bur*, a strong house or dwelling, and *win*, a victory, from which it may be inferred that it was a fortified outpost or castle erected by a conquering army as a defence to the surrounding communities; the populous Saxon settlement at Carleton, and likewise Skipton, being at no great distance. *Apropos*, it may be observed that there is a street in Norwich leading up to the ancient Castle, called Ber Street, and in Leeds (with its traditional castle) there is Boar Lane, anciently Bur Lane.

Skipton to Marton, 5¼ m.; **Gisburn**, 11 m. By road past Broughton Hall (3 m.) as last route, and Crickle Ho. (5 m.). In a field below this house is a large sulphur spring, which is mentioned in *Bray's Tour*, 1783. The spot was considered dangerous, and is now covered in. The water upon analysis was found deficient in saline matter, and consequently little benefitting to the human subject, but by bathing it is said to have been very efficacious for the cure of mange in dogs. There is a similar spring at Broughton, near a row of dwellings called after it Sulphur Well Houses. About **East Marton** (inn) the land is nicely wooded and undulating, and the canal intersecting the east end of the village, winds under the picturesque old church. On the village green is a large plane tree, encircled with a good seat. From the rising ground the Weets, above Barnoldswick, and Pendle Hill form an attractive view. On the south side of the church are the remains of a moat that once surrounded the manor house of the Martons, now represented by the family at Capon Wray, near Lancaster. Pedigrees of these mesne lords, and of the Hebers, to whom the estates came by purchase, are given by Whitaker in the *History of Craven*. The church is a venerable edifice of Norman date, built upon a foundation probably destroyed by the Danes.* It has a low embattled tower, with sundial inscribed "Dono Ant. Hartley, 1714." On the north and east walls there is some evident Norman stonework of the 'herring-bone' type. The interior consists of nave, divided by a row of octagonal pillars supporting pointed arches, and chancel, with flat plaster roof. It is fitted entirely with oak, and contains interesting memorials to the families of Roundell, Heber, Stockdale, and Currer, of Gledstone, as well as tablets of arms. In the belfry is a rude stone font (believed to be Saxon) placed upon three short cylindrical supports of later date. The coloured windows are by Taylor (late O'Connor), of London. Proceeding hence to **West Marton** (1 m.), at the turn of the road (11 m. to Settle) a pleasing view is had of the white

---

* On this supposition the church, like many others known to have existed before the Conquest, is not mentioned in *Domesday*. Moreover, no official injunction was laid on the jurors at this Survey to return the churches. Ellis, in his Introduction to Domesday Book, says the mention of them, if made at all, was likely to be irregular. "The whole number returned," he observes, "only amounts to a few more than 1700; one only can be found in Cambridgeshire, and none in Lancashire (between the Ribble and the Mersey), Cornwall, or even Middlesex, the seat of the metropolis. It is acknowledged that the Conqueror destroyed 36 churches to make the New Forest, and therefore churches must have been plentiful."

R

gleaming front of Malham Cove, with Ryeloaf and Kirkby Fell, and N.N.W. the top of Giggleswick Scars and half the height of Ingleborough. There is a neat well-to-do look about this picturesque little place. It possesses a capital village Institute, with a spacious lecture or ball-room. library, &c. By the road side is an admirably arranged fountain, 'for man, horse, and dog,' a Jubilee gift of Mrs. Roundell. Marton was anciently much more populous and important than it is now. In the Poll Tax of A.D. 1379, among the 76 towns and villages comprised in the wapentake of Staincliffe, Marton ranks *second* in the amount (35s. 4d.) contributed. Bolton coming first with 48s. 4d., and Skipton third with 35s. Some of the houses are of old date. One we notice is inscribed B another S and another G— Yew Tree House, AM 1703 so called IM 1711, from a large 1690, old yew in its garden, was the family seat of the Hartleys, and afterwards of the Roundells, before the erection of Gledstone Hall about a century ago. In 1739, by the marriage of Danson Roundell, Esq., D.L., of Marton, with Ellen, heiress of Christopher Hartley, Esq., the Marton estate of the latter was thus transmitted. Marton Hall, the seat of the Hebers for upwards of two centuries, lies pleasantly sheltered amid wood. It had once a fine deer park attached. The building is 'rough cast,' and has a spacious gateway and ponderous oak door that opens into a porch and court-yard, which give the place a very strong and castle-like look. "No house," observes Whitaker in the *History of Craven*, "mentioned within the compass of this work, and in the present generation, has been connected with greater virtues or equal talents." Of this family was the celebrated Bishop Heber, "the Christian, the scholar, and the poet," born at Malpas in 1783, and died in India in 1826. The hall here was bought by Thomas Heber, of Elslack, about 1535.

Passing Yew Tree Ho. the tourist may now proceed by way of Gledstone, a delightful walk, and shortly regain the Gisburn road. In descending the hollow, and overlooking the Mere House,* Malham Cove, and Gt. Whernside are well seen. The rich gardens and glass-houses of **Gledstone Hall** (C. S. Roundell, Esq., J.P.) are now passed, with their choice stock of fruit and flowers. A speciality among the latter is a splendid assortment of chrysanthemums, which have taken many prizes. Last year (1890) a remarkably fine pumpkin weighing 84 lbs. was grown here. Taking the first road on *l*. in view of the hall, a pleasant country walk brings us on to the main road again by Crook Ho. and over Monk Bridge, probably so called from the monks of Kirkstall (who owned Bracewell church, &c.) having been the original builders of it. Here a road diverges to Bracewell (1 m.) and opposite is Horton Bridge (Lane Ends). **Horton** is mentioned in *Domesday*, but the old hall and manor-house are now both tenanted as farms, and possess nothing of special interest. 2 m hence is **Gisburn**, (pop. 530), a pleasant, old-fashioned market

* Marton is supposed to be *Mere town*, from the low grounds having once been covered with water.

town on the old coach-road from York to Liverpool, (and now noted for its sheep and cattle fairs). In monkish days it was the property of the Abbots of Sallay. The manor was purchased, 13th Elizabeth, by the family of Lister, afterwards Lords Ribblesdale, who now own some 5-6000 acres here. Gisburn Park, their seat, was formerly noted for its fine herd of wild cattle, descendants of the indigenous race which once ranged the Lancashire forests. The animals were hornless and of a creamy white, with the exception of the tips of their noses, ears, and feet. The race died out about thirty years ago. The house, situated upon an eminence near the confluence of the Ribble and Stockbeck, contains, amongst other things, some notable paintings, and an ancient drinking-horn (of buffalo) supported by three silver feet, and inscribed in Latin : " He that fights against three shall lose two." The park-lodge is a handsome piece of Gothic architecture, ornamented with figures, &c., designed by the late Lord Ribblesdale. The church here is probably not older than the time of Henry VII., although of Norman origin, and given in the reign of Henry II. to the Nunnery of Stainfield, co. Lincoln. It contains some good stain-glass, &c., and is well worth inspection.

Skipton to Flasby over the Fell, 5½ m. A trip for dry weather only. Take the Rylstone road to the 2-mile stone from Skipton (4 m. to Cracoe). Just above is Crookrise Ho., where permission should be obtained to cross the fell. Make then for the depression between the north hill and Sharper, whence the view in every direction is grand. There is little doubt that when sufficiently clear, the white scar of Malham Cove might be seen between this depression from the hills about Sawood, Wadsworth, and Haworth, as well as from Pendle Hill. Looking N., we have Gt. Whernside, Fountains Fell, Ingleborough, &c.; to the S., Denholme, Haworth, and Boulsworth moors, and S.W., Pendle Hill. To the S E. Cullingworth and Bingley moors, with the Druids' Altar, and a grand sweep of Airedale from Farnhill Crag up towards Hellifield. E. is Embsay Crag, and N.E. Norton Tower, Rylstone Fell, and the little limestone town of Grassington, with the white road over Grassington Moor backed by the great Wham. Follow the wall down through a gateway, and straight away down Black Lane (a narrow miry way) to the beck at Flasby. The beck may be crossed and an ascent made to an old house inscribed RMO 1685. whence a charming walk may be had by way of Hetton to Rylstone (2 m.), or a return can be made to Gargrave by Eshton Bridge, (an ancient structure mentioned in A.D. 1314) 2 m. From Flasby there is also a path over Scarnber Fell by the new reservoir on to the Hetton and Winterburn road for Malham, &c. **Flasby Hall** (Capt. J. N. Preston) lies quietly and charmingly embosomed in deep woods. A chapel oratory and burial-ground appear anciently to have existed here, from the number of human bones that have been dug up. Possibly it was one of the 'Seven Churches' of Gargrave traditionally destroyed by the Scots.

Skipton to Bolton Abbey, 6 m. Follow the Knaresborough (24 m.) road past the Castle, which gradually ascends to High Skibeden (2 m.), where the hard, blackish limestone on the south side of the long anticlinal ridge is well observed in a quarry north of the highway. Here the rocks dip sharply  to the south-east, or in a precisely contrary direction to those described at Haw Bank (see p. 237). The farm here has been in the occupation of Mr. Robt. Birtwhistle for about half a century past. The Birtwhistles are descendants of the old yeomanry class, and have been settled in Craven for ages. In 1478 we find W. Britwysall installed vicar of Kildwick and Skipton. Kildwick being the mother church, Skipton was then, and up to 1843, served by a curate. The tourist now descends to the railway, which here attains, between Skipton and Ilkley, its highest level (513 ft.) On this side the bridge is a 'Holy Well,' a common resort of pilgrims in monkish days, and the brook issuing from it is now called Helliwell beck. At the four lane ends a turn *l.* is made, when soon the Wharfedale hills appear, with Beamsley Beacon occupying the centre of vision. The little village of Draughton is seen away up on *r.*, and a descent is made past Bolton Abbey sta., near which, at the Hambleton Quarry, is a grand exposure of the carboniferous or mountain limestone, traversed by veins of calcite, and contorted, as is often the case along this remarkable anticlinal, in the most curious fashion. On the east side the beds dip north-west at an angle of about 40 degrees, and at this end form one of the finest examples of a trough, or synclinal, that is to be found anywhere. To the west the beds appear vertical, showing the immense lateral pressure they sustained during formation. The well-known walk hence to Bolton Woods needs no description.

Skipton to Draughton, 3¼ m., **(for Bolton Abbey).** From the High Street, on Otley Street, and along the Otley road, 2 m., where Skibeden quarry and farm (above) are seen, and up on *r.* Close House, for more than a century from the time of Queen Elizabeth the home of the Moorhouse family (see p. 239), above which, under Rumbalds Moor, at an altitude of 1000 ft., runs the old Roman road and former coach road from Skipton to Addingham. Between our road and Close House is a line of thorns which marks the old and rather narrow thoroughfare constructed in 1802 from Skipton to Bolton, which crossed the present highway at the 'Half-way Ash' (near the 2 m. to Skipton mile-stone) and continued through the fields to Draughton, and by the school-house under Haw Pike to Bolton Bridge. We emerge at Draughton opposite the wonderful Quarry and small Wesleyan Chapel. Views of this famous Draughton Quarry have frequently been engraved for illustrating the phenomena of contorted strata in geological text-books, &c. The section here worked occupies a basin-like cavity open to the north, and at the east end forms a double anticlinal; the limestone dipping sharp N. and S. at an angle of 80°, resembling the pointed arch of some majestic fane. It is a site of extraordinary geological interest, which as we have remarked, has often been described. Formerly the stone was burned for lime on the spot and used by local farmers for the land. Just above is the *Matchless* Inn, a name that will readily be conjectured to be derived from the natural aspect of the above quarry. This, however, is not the case; it was so-called from a splendid entire horse, which earned in a single season (now about a century ago), sufficient for its owner to purchase the property and build the inn which has since stood here. The old whitewashed Manor House at the low end of the village was built by the

DRAUGHTON QUARRY,—CONTORTED LIMESTONE.

Wainmans of Carr Head. Over the door appear the initials and date R M W 1669. There is a thoroughly rustic charm about this little country place. It is partly wooded, undulating, and tolerably well sheltered; on the mossy walls we have noticed the pretty toad-flax continue in flower until the snows of a November day have extinguished the tiny blossoms.

Skipton to Embsay, 2 m., **Barden,** 7 m. By the Bailey road past the Castle and forward between Flasby Fell and Haw Bank (*see* p. 237). From the *Cavendish Arms* the road ascends through **Embsay,** and at the *Elm Tree* Inn diverges r. up to the church. Opposite the church a field path shortens the road to Eastby (3 m.) Embsay (in Domesday, *Embesie*) formed part of the ancient Saxon Cure of Earl Edwin, whose seat was at Bolton. The Augustinian Priory founded here 21st Henry I. by William de Meschines, lord of Egremond, &c., and Cecily, daughter of Robert de Romillé, his wife, was endowed with the village of Embsay and the churches of Skipton and Carleton. To these original benefactions were added by Cecily de Romillé (only daughter of the above), who adopted her mother's name, the "village of Kildewic, with the mill, and soc, or suit thereof, and the Hagh* (of Crookeris), and all the premises of Aspsiche from the boundaries of Fern-Hill to those of Silesden to Aspsiche, and following Aspsiche to the river Ayre."† The Priory was translated to Bolton about A.D. 1154, according to the well-known tradition of that "endless sorrow" to Cecily de Romillé caused by the loss of her only son, the " Boy of Egremond," in the Strid, a story which is in the main a fiction, as he was a witness to the charter of translation. A charter for the holding of a fair at Embsay was granted by Edward I., A.D. 1305, when the Canons of Bolton had a rent of the mill here with the tolls. In 1318, during a most unsparing raid by the Scots, their grange was destroyed. For some centuries after the removal of the Priory to Bolton, a church was continued at Embsay, but after the Dissolution of the monastery in 1540, it appears to have lapsed into ruins. Interments, however, continued to be made here until a late date. Embsay Kirk (Capt. John Hodgson), which occupies the site, was built about 1780 by Wm. Baynes, a lawyer, and a relative of John Baynes Garforth, of Steeton Hall, and doubtless much of the material of the old priory was utilized in its erection. Possibly some of the under portions and out-buildings may have been restored upon the original structure. The outer wall of the vaulted cellar is about a yard thick, and the arched roofs of several out-houses contain stones, which appear from the masons' marks, to have occupied different positions to what they do at present. No plan of the Abbey has yet been made, nor have the foundations been fully excavated. In 1889, whilst cutting a walk at the east end of the house portions of three walls were discovered, all running east and west ; the two north ones coming to an angle at their eastern extremities, and the south and middle walls forming a passage about two yards wide. Just below this south wall were found several human skeletons, one entire, uncoffined, lay between two long blocks of stone, covered by a slab ornamented with a cross, which from its design cannot be older than Edward II., when the Knights of Malta arose in England. It is well known that none of the Priors of Bolton were buried here after the translation in 1154, excepting perhaps Prior Grene, who retired to Embsay about 1417. The stone is preserved in the arbour, near which are several ancient yew trees. Behind the house is an old disused spring, said to have been enclosed by the monks. It is called St. Cuthbert's Well, after the patron saint of the original priory. The present church was built shortly before Embsay was constituted a separate parish in 1855.

Ascending through Eastby by the ruined mill, built for a cotton-mill about middle of last century by the family of Chamberlain, memorials of whom are to be seen in Skipton church, the tourist

* HAGA : Every lesser estate, indeed even a single field, was called haga, since every particular property with the Anglo-Saxons was enclosed. The strong masculine inflection hegr (gen. heges or heages), signifies a hedge or fence ; and haya, a plot of ground fenced in and surrounded by hedges." Leo's Local Nomenclature of the Anglo-Saxons.

† Burton's Monasticon Ebor.

arrives at a fragrant fir plantation, and continues along the elevation, with an expansive and enjoyable panorama before him. Westward are Pendle Hill and the Lancashire moors with Bolland Fells. On the opposite side of the valley is Draughton Height, with its solitary farm, and below it Chelker reservoir. Beyond the dip of the moor above Seamoor House is the small gap leading to the Double Stones and Gill Grange. At the foot of the hill is Addingham, and S.E. Rumbalds Moor, with Otley Chevin, Yeadon Haw, &c. About 2 m. from Barden a descent is made in view of the far-extending lake-like reservoir; the upper (53¾ acres) having an elevation of 1170 ft., and the lower reservoir (56 acres) being 697 ft. above sea level. Before us are the beautiful woods of Bolton, with the wild heathery moors of upper Wharfedale beyond. There is the rocky knoll of Simon Seat, and away on our left the craggy top of Cracoe Fell, whilst northwards stretch the long boundary line of Grassington Moor, crowned by the Gt. Wham (1900 ft.) The tourist leaves the moor road near Scale House, within a few minutes walk of Barden Tower.

Skipton to Rylstone, 5 m., **Grassington**, 10 m. The road skirts Flasby Fell with Embsay Crag on *r.*, and at 2 m. passes a substantial residence known from remote times as *None-go-by*, which

in the days of the early Cliffords was the lodge or keep of their Foresters. At that period, we may observe, matrimony was subject to a singular toll in the Forest of Skipton, which explains the origin of the name *None-go-by*. "Ev'rie bryde," says this ancient edict, "cumynge this waye shulde eyther gyve her lefte shoo or liis. ivd. to the Forester of Crookrise by way of custome or gaytcloys."

About half-a-mile further on and the old Bar-house is passed. The pedestrian who wishes to escape the heat and dust of the highroad may leave it here and follow the path up to Norton Tower, (whence there is a grand view), descending on to the road again near Rylstone. The direction of the former coach-road (now grass grown) can be traced west of the present highway, which was made in 1853. **Norton Tower** is a conspicuous and impressive object seen from the road, particularly when the old sombre ruin is observed against a clear evening sky. Says the late poet-laureate, Wordsworth,

"High on a point of rugged ground,
  Among the wastes of Rylstone Fell,
Above the loftiest ridge or mound
  Where foresters or shepherds dwell,
An edifice of warlike frame
Stands single,—Norton Tower its name!"

The Protestant Cliffords and the Catholic Nortons, whose estates joined here, long continued in deadly feud, and many bitter quarrels arose as to the right of one or the other to impound the deer and hunt in the other's domain. The fortalice erected on Crookrise by the Cliffords, almost within bow-shot of the watch-tower of their opponents, has long ago disappeared. After the attainture of Richard Norton for his share in the 'Rising in the North' (A.D. 1569) in favour of Mary Stuart and the Catholic succession, the manors of Rylstone, Threshfield, Cracoe, Linton and other lands belonging to the Nortons in Craven were granted to their great territorial foemen, the Cliffords, Earls of Cumberland. The tourist now passes the turretted **Scale House**, one of the stateliest and most compact old mansions in Craven, associated with the troublous times of Craven Quakerism, where the Friends had a meeting-house and a burial-ground as early as 1650. The late Capt. Blake, who died in 1870, and from whom the property was acquired by its present owner, Capt. Henderson, J.P., added two wings to the house, and otherwise improved it. The Blakes are an old Derbyshire family who settled at Rylstone about a century ago. Mr. Blake was for nearly forty years steward to the Earl of Burlington, and his daughter married a Mr. Moorhouse, a gentleman farmer at Gargrave, and a captain in Lord Ribblesdale's yeomanry. His relative, Nancy Moorhouse, sister of Thomas Moorhouse, who died at Elslack in 1863, married a Mr. Ayrton, who for some time resided at Scale House (*see* p. 239). The only representative of the Blakes now at Rylstone is Miss Blake, who formerly lived at the Manor House, and who now occupies a pretty little mansion near the ornamental lake in the village. Descending a rich avenue we come upon this beautiful and sequestered little place; the old walls decked with herb-robert and dainty saxifrage; the whole embowered with flowering thorns, red and white, tall chestnuts, limes, elms, copper-beeches, laburnums, and towering larches, &c., surrounding the bird-haunted little mere, and from whose water-reflected boughs the throstle and blackbird pipe their sweet matin and evening lays! **Rylstone** gave name to the ancient family of Rilleston, who were settled here probably at the time of the Conquest. A chapel of their foundation is known to have existed here as early as A.D. 1160. About 1434 they became matrimonially allied with the Radcliffes, a family that expired in an heiress (*temp.* Henry VIII.) who was married to John Norton, father of Richard, attainted as before stated after the Rebellion of 1569. The Norton woods here are still called by many of the aged inhabitants in the vicinity *John's Wood*, after this old John Norton. The ancient Manor House, with its Elizabethan *Vivery*, or pleasure-grounds, with fish-ponds, &c., disappeared many years since, and all that remains of the latter are a few mounds that once formed the ground-work of the rockeries, &c., adjoining the present building. A very old (undated) sun-dial on the south gable is said to have been preserved from the original building, and there is also a carved stone taken from it now set up in the clerestory of the church. The present Manor Hall (J. Proctor, Esq.) is a large modern mansion, whose front windows frame an exquisite picture of Norton Tower surrounded by an extent of native wood and fell. The church at Rylstone was wholly rebuilt in 1854. It contains some choice stain-glass and several memorial brasses, and outside are some ancient stones recovered from the old church, and bearing sculptured devices. The ancient bells, re-cast by Mears, bore a co-eval inscription, "In God is all." This, engraved in Gothic letters, was misread by antiquaries, and oft quoted, for '*I.N.* (John Norton) *God us ayde*,' and is so alluded to by Wordsworth, in the 7th canto of the *White Doe of Rylstone*. The story of Emily, the last of the Nortons, and of the milk-white doe and its weekly pilgrimage to the grave of the Nortons at Bolton Priory need not be repeated here. The traditional track of the mysterious animal is still pointed out in the depression below the old stone cross on Rylstone Fell and the lower Norton Tower. The reader should consult Wordsworth's beautiful poem on the subject.

Continuing through a pleasant and invigorating country we reach **Cracoe** (6 m.) with its two inns, and **Linton** (8½ m.), when the road ascends to Grassington, which is nearly 200 ft. above the Wharfe. Just before the road diverges to Linton there is a quarry of fossiliferous limestone, of passing interest to the geologist. Linton is picturesquely placed, and it possesses a conspicuous charity hospital, founded in 1751. Its ancient Norman church has been largely rebuilt, and in 1862 was thoroughly restored. The Rev. Benj. Smith, B.D., an eccentric nephew of the celebrated Sir Isaac Newton, was for many years, until his death in 1776, rector of this parish. He regarded the parishioners as "baptised brutes," and they denounced him equally unceremoniously as a "perfect ass." Their admiration was evidently mutual. Stories of the parson's peculiarities and habits have been often recounted.

Cracoe to Thorpe by Elbolton Cave, 2¼ m. Visitors to Cracoe may conveniently explore **Threapland Gill**, a picturesque ravine a little east of the village. To Elbolton, soon after leaving Cracoe a lane on *l.* (2 m. to Thorpe) continues for about a mile to the first farmhouse, opposite which a path leads up through fields about ¾ m., until the crest of the hill is reached, when just over top on *l.* the fossiliferous *debris* of the famous bone cave will be seen. In the fields *en route* abundance of the mountain violet (*V. lutea*) and pretty pink-eyed primrose (*P. farinosa*) may be seen in flower about June, whilst growing on the slopes about the cave are the beautiful rock-rose, sand-wort, and several saxifrages. **Elbolton Cave**, or Knave Knoll Hole (as anciently known) is remarkable for the discovery of pre-historic animal remains made in it in 1888, otherwise there is little to attract the visitor within its gloomy cells. The cave has a narrow pit-like entrance descended by ladders to a (total) vertical depth of about 70 ft. The first chamber is about 20 ft. deep, the second 32 ft., and a third 15 ft., the latter terminating in a pool of water reduced by excavating to a depth of 4 ft. From this point a passage runs to what looks like an old lead-working. The entire length of the cave from the summit mouth to the pool may be taken as 140 ft. At the base of the first chamber were found, mingled with loose angular pieces of limestone and a little brown earth, four entire human skeletons, *in situ*, as buried (in the usual sitting postures) and the remains of at least eight others, together with bone implements, fragments of pot, and remains of wild-boar, horse, dog, wolf, wild-cat, red-deer, and Celtic short-horn, all of Neolithic age (2-4000 years old). Below this upper cave earth was a layer of clay containing more loose stones and much stalagmitic breccia, and in this deposit have been found quantities of well-preserved bones of bears (amongst them the huge grizzly, now extinct in the Old World), and Alpine foxes, hares, and reindeer. The complete absence of iron, bronze, or even flint implements would appear to indicate either a remarkable poverty of these humble cave-dwellers, or the extreme antiquity of the race inhabiting the cave,—before metal was generally wrought or the traffic in flint commenced. Only bone implements have been found. The worn and polished footholds in the upper chamber shew that the present entrance was also that used by the cave-men. The excavations have been conducted by the Rev. E. Jones, F.G.S , late of Embsay, and last year a grant was made by the British Association for the further exploration of the cave. The visitor, after enjoying the ample prospect that is to be obtained from the summit of this knoll may descend to the path by which he came, which soon developes to a cart track and crosses the stream to the hidden little hamlet of Thorpe. There is no inn here. To Grassington or Burnsall it is 1½ m.

Rylstone to Hetton, ½ m.; **Malham**, 6 m. This is a fine but rather rough cross-country trip. A lane by the lake drops to a stone foot-bridge, when a narrow lane and field are ascended to **Hetton**. Much of the land in this township once belonged to the monks of Furness, and after the deposition of the Nortons in 1569, the manor was granted by the Crown to the Earl of Cumberland, and is now held by the Duke of Devonshire. Hetton is a quiet, retired place, upon an elevated plateau commanding a pleasing view of the opposite fells. It has a neat Wesleyan chapel, built in 1839, whilst church folks go to Rylstone. It has a small way-side inn, and if a *name* can presage comfort and fair treatment, the traveller ought to obtain it here. Hetton Rushbearing, as the annual Feast was called, is now hardly remembered, and has been substituted by annual sports, held about the middle of July, when wrestling matches, races, &c., take place, but these, however, have now almost died out. The population is decreasing.

At the low end of the village (opposite a green-gabled house) a broad grassy lane leads over Hetton Common, commanding a picturesque view of the round, green knolls of Elboiton, Skelterton, and Cale, with the high, rocky summit of Cracoe Fell. At the top of the road cross a (temporary) tram-line laid down by the Leeds and Liverpool Canal Company for the conveyance of gritstone from the summit of Boss Moor (1100 ft.) to their new reservoir now being constructed in the Winterburn valley. This reservoir, we may here remark, is a gigantic undertaking on which the Company has been engaged some years. It is calculated to hold, when full, 285.000,000 gallons, the area of the top water being about 40 acres. The approximate cost, when complete, is estimated at £85,000 to £90,000.

Descend the fell-side into the lonely Hetton Beck dale,—one of the most solitary valleys in all Yorkshire, and crossing the handsome little bridge, lately built by the Canal Company of the excellent Boss Moor stone, a gate is opened opposite, and the fell ascended by a well-defined track. Continuing through a number of gateways, with fine retrospective views of Flasby and Cracoe Fells, &c., the head of Whetstone Gill is passed a short distance to *l.* of an old quarry; when, after crossing a small gill, the depression between the Weets on *r.* and Hanlith Moor on *l.* is traversed, whence are seen the Kirkby Fells and Ryeloaf with the village of Malham below. [Coming *from Malham to Hetton*, a good guide for the direction to be taken is the white quarried summit of Boss Moor looking east from the Weets; a little south of the quarry the path runs over Hetton Common from the Beck bridge (as above), or the tourist may pass down the valley to Winterburn. 2 m.] From the Weets (1380 ft.), a plain, peaty, gritstone height, which can be ascended in a few minutes from here, a magnificent view over Lancashire, West Craven, and eastward as far as Gt. Whernside and the Wharfedale hills, is obtainable. Our track now goes down sharp, keeping Hanlith Gill on *l.*, and when in the bottom the stream is crossed by a footbridge near a barn, and the path followed up fields on to the Gordale road, ½ m. above Malham.

SKIPTON TO GARGRAVE.

WE have now reached the very interesting upper region of the Aire, where our river waters some of the richest of pastures in the heart of Craven. Twenty to thirty years ago there were hundreds of acres under the plough, but now there is hardly an acre of corn land to be seen. It is the practice of the present generation of farmers to buy lean stock and fatten it for the local markets, and on some of the best grazing it is possible to turn out two lots of cattle in a season, by giving the land only a fortnight's rest in mid season. But quality rather than quantity is the farmers' chief aim, and in this respect Craven fed beef is admittedly highly nutritious, and is unsurpassed in grain and flavour. It is worth noting that five to six centuries ago, under the feudal system, land in this district was let at about 9d an acre: in 1612 we find it fetched 6s., and latterly £4 to £5!

To Gargrave there are several routes; by the highroad, (4 m.), or along the south side of the canal (4½ m.), or through Stirton and Thorlby (4½ m.), all nice walks. Another route (4½ m.) which we will describe, is from Skipton station to ascend to the far bank of the canal and continue as far as Mr. Dewhurst's boat-house, about half-a-mile. Before the canal was made rather over a century ago, there stood at its junction with the road to Broughton, a stately old residence of the Republican Lamberts, (afterwards of Calton), called Winterwell Hall. It is described as having in Henry VIII.'s time a tower, great parlour, and chamber over it, with study under it. A large and very cold well near the house was swallowed up by the canal. Observing from the bank the beautiful Elizabethan mansion of Aireville (J. B. Dewhurst, Esq., J.P., C.C.), occupying a warm and sheltered situation, though standing, perhaps, somewhat low for effect, we come to the private boat-house, and here enter a gate-way, and turning into the field sharp to the right, keep the bed of the stream on our right all the way up. Some lofty and luxuriant thorn trees are passed on the way, as well as some maples and ash trees, and we observe also one large oak. The oak, however, is ill-suited to the limestone of Craven, but it agrees well with the ash, which in some places where the oak is of stunted growth, spreads her roots over the rich, shallow soil, and attains the stateliest proportions. An old flowery lane is presently entered, which veers left on to the high road, 3 m. from Gargrave. From this point the northern slope of Pendle Hill stands out grandly, but it is seen even to better advantage when opposite Thorlby, a half-mile further on.

Having Bracewell's Cotton Mills,* and the huge glacial mounds referred to elsewhere, about Gargrave before us, we reach the summit of the road (420 ft.), and look down on to the low ground on the far side of the river under Butter Haw. There in the days of Roman sovereignty in Britain some wealthy Roman magister had his stately seat. Of this once splendid villa, however, no traces now remain, but in the middle of last century, when it was first opened, extensive foundations, along with coloured tiles, &c., were discovered. Dr. Whitaker assumes the building to have occupied a parallelogram about 300 feet long and 180 feet wide. The site is now known as Kirk Sink, from a tradition that a great ecclesiastical edifice once stood there and somehow mysteriously disappeared !

We now proceed under the rugged and picturesque Flasby Fell, once wholly clad with native wood, which two

* The chimneys of these mills are seen a long way off (*see* p. 217). But it is a fact worth recording that chimneys are no modern innovation at Gargrave, for at a time when such objects were exceedingly rare in England, there was a chimney at Gargrave as appears by the following entry in the *Compotus* of Bolton Abbey for A.D. 1311. "*Pro camino rect. de Gayrgrave faciendo, et dato eidem, IXs.*" This we should think is the earliest extant reference to a chimney in Yorkshire. Beckman, an authoritative writer on this subject, observes " The oldest certain account of chimneys with which I am acquainted occurs in the year 1347 ; for an inscription, which is still existing, or did exist at Venice, relates that at the above period, a great many chimneys were thrown down by an earthquake." It is, however, tolerably certain that there was a form of flue for the conveyance of smoke in some of our castles and abbeys before this time.

or three centuries ago gave cover to antlered and other kinds of game, but now looking stiff and formal with a recent plantation of fir along its upper slope. Hares are the only game hunted in the locality now. Crossing the canal at the first "lock" upon it from Bingley, we go over Holme Bridge, and pass the kennels of the Craven Harriers, where a subscription pack of hounds is kept. A few foxes, however, are found, and occasionally reynard descends on 'my neighbour's farm' and runs off with a prime-fed duck or goose.

GARGRAVE.

Gargrave, Ghergrave, Gayregraf, or Gerigraph, as it is variously spelled in old charters, is very delightfully situated, and round about it is trim, rich, and park-like, having a semi-private aspect even about the public ways. There is indeed a real look of country pride and unbusied retirement about the place, truly refreshing to the town dweller. Picturesque old lanes, lined with noble ash trees and sycamores, converge upon the village, and hereabouts we see, too, in this warm, wooded vale, well-kept gardens mantled with sweet-smelling roses, clematis, and scarlet-runners, and peaches even ripening their fruit under sheltered walls—pictures of luxuriant beauty! Dr. Whitaker supposes Gargrave to mean the *graf* or trench of *Garri*, a personal name, which, with slight variations, is still retained in the district and elsewhere, not only as a personal but also as a place-name. In the latter respect, for example, there is an old village called Garrigill, near Alston, in Northumberland, which has similarly an ancient chapel.

The parish of Gargrave, which includes Coniston, Eshton, Bank-Newton, and Flasby-with-Winterburn, contains 11,358 acres, and from an unpublished record of half-a-century back, (1841), we find it apportioned as follows: Meadow and Pasture, 10,427 acres; Woodland, 483 acres; Common land, 246 acres, (of which 223 were at Winterburn); and Arable land, 201 acres. Of land in furrow there is now, as before stated, but very little. It is interesting, however, to compare the present absence of tillage with the state of things say five centuries ago, when the monks of Sallay held the lands here. In 1381, according to their *Compotus*, they received tithes of 41½ quarters of wheat, 62 qrs. of barley, 5½ qrs. and 3 bushels of beans, 208 qrs. of oats, and 40 stones of wool. Multiplying these quantities by ten, and assuming, says Dr. Whitaker, that every statute acre yielded three quarters, we get at an approximate idea of the amount of land in tillage at that time, which would not be less than 1000 acres.

Of the Church, the most interesting feature of the village, nothing now remains of the previous structure but the tower, built, according to a date upon an oak board preserved there, in 1521. With this exception the church was wholly rebuilt in 1852, and its present spacious interior is one of the most beautiful and interesting among country churches in Yorkshire. There is no doubt a chapel existed here long before the monks of Sallay, its early owners, founded their abbey in A.D. 1147. A Roger, *clericus de Gerigraf*, was witness to a charter before the foundation of that house. In the vicarage garden we have had shown to us portions of ancient Saxon crosses, the heads of two being pierced with triangular holes, about two inches at their broadest diameter, and the shafts are ornamented with Saxon knotwork and a mutilated *Agnus Dei*. There is also the base of a Norman pillar; and another very perfect oblong stone, about 40 in. in length and 10 in. in thickness, bears the incision of a floriated cross on the top and a sword on one side. Another (broken) stone has the representation of a bow and arrow carved upon it, a memorial stone, doubtless, of some Saxon or early Norman archer. These were all recovered at the restoration in 1852, and point to the existence of a building antecedent to any historic notice we possess of the church. Of the Manor House here at this early period we know nothing, excepting that it occupied a piece of land near the present National School, called yet Garris Close, a name suggestive of what has been said above, and where are indications of a deep moat that once apparently surrounded it. At the end of last century there was found here a singular relic of brass and steel (engraved in

Whitaker), supposed to be the girdle of a purse of Henry II.'s time. The old Tithe barn which formerly stood near this site was taken down about sixty years ago.

There is a tradition that Gargrave had once *seven* churches and that the ravaging Scots destroyed all save that dedicated to their patron Saint Andrew. This belief has probably reference to several chapels-of-ease and chantries anciently existing in the district, of which few or no traces now remain. No visitor to Gargrave should go away without inspecting the very beautiful interior of the present church. The ornamental glass particularly is of a very high order of merit, there being altogether thirty-one stained windows. Those who have recollections of the great Exhibition of 1851, will doubtless not have forgotten the splendid show of illuminated glass by Hardman, of Birmingham, which extended nearly half-a-mile in length. On that occasion he was awarded the first prize for English stain-glass. The whole of the windows (twelve in number) in the nave of the church are by that firm, and these illustrate in a connected manner the story of the Life of Our Saviour. When the church was re-built in 1852, it was resolved that all memorial windows in the nave should be apportioned in rotation of the subject already fixed upon. This design has been carried out, and beneath each of the windows there is now a neat memorial brass. Several of the windows are by Capronnier of Brussels, that on the east side of the north aisle being the first erected by him (in 1854) in England. There is a handsome reredos in Caen stone, and mural tablets to the Wilson and Coulthurst families. One of these is to the memory of Mathew Wilson, and Frances, his wife. (ob. 1798). sister of the first Lord Clive, whose only surviving daughter Margaret, married (1) the Rev. Henry Richardson-Currer. Rector of Thornton, and (2) Mathew Wilson, Esq., J.P., D.L., her first cousin, a Solicitor in London, and father of the late Sir Mathew Wilson, Bart., M.P., D.L., of Eshton Hall, who was born Aug. 29th, 1802, and died Jan. 18th, 1891. The registers of the parish date from 1557. The only piece of ancient church plate preserved is a silver chalice bearing a Latin inscription (undated), the gift of Henry Coulthurst, Esq., of Bank-Newton, who died in 1656, leaving a son Henry, who died in 1706. The living of the church has been in the gift of the Marsdens, (neè Lister), of Wennington and Giggleswick, since 1673, and since 1852 the Rev. Chas. J. Marsden, M.A., has been incumbent. Mr. Marsden, who is in his 74th year, is, we believe, with the exception of the Rev. J. Mann, the venerable Vicar of Kellington, (aged 86), the oldest beneficed clergyman now living in our Dale. The Marsden family, it may be added, were lords of the manor of Bradford, from 1667 to 1795, when John Marsden, of Hornby Castle, conveyed it to Benjn. Rawson, of Bolton-le-Moors, in whose descendants it is now vested.

Most of the buildings at Gargrave are comparatively modern, and amongst them the Methodist Chapel is a conspicuously neat edifice. There are several inns and old houses, and the Aire bridge here is moreover a structure which carries with it a history probably as far back as the foundation of the church. The oldest dated house is one inscribed 1693, besides which, at the north end of the village, is the Old Hall, a large, roomy dwelling, rough built of water-smoothed limestone and sandstone cobbles, evidently taken from the bed of the Aire. It is now occupied as cottages. A wide carriage entrance (now walled-up) once fronted the road on the south side of the garden. One of the windows bears an old incision, 'Cromwell 1709'—an evident anomaly. Yet the troops of Cromwell are said to have actually occupied the building as a barracks during the siege of Skipton Castle. There is good ground for this assumption for we find 'bold Capt. John Hodgson' writing in Aug. 1648, that the enemy "marched towards Kendal; we towards Rippon where Oliver met us with horse and foot. We were then betwixt 8000 and 9000, a fine smart army, and fit for action. We marched up to Skipton * * * *—at which time Captain Currer, a dreaping commander we had in these days, should have delivered up the castle to Langdale, if he had come on, but stout Henry Cromwell commanded the forlorn to Gargrave, but the Langdale's over-run him. The next day we marched to Clithero." From remains that have been found there was no doubt some fatal skirmishing in the vicinity of Gargrave at this time. Several adult skeletons have been unearthed during the process of grave-digging in a piece of ground added to the east side of the church-yard about twenty years since ; and on removing a large ash tree in a field near by, three human skeletons were discovered lying parallel beneath the roots; victims no doubt of the same great Civil fight. The tree had probably been planted over their bodies *in memoriam*.

There are several fields at Gargrave belonging to the poor of the parish. The charities (dating from 1669) now amount to about £98 yearly, derived chiefly from land and the inn at Hellifield.

There are two or three cotton mills in this neighbourhood, the principal of which is run by Mr. Henry Bracewell. On Jan. 31st, 1874, this mill was burnt down, and damage sustained to the extent of £60,000.

Robert Story, the poet, though a native of Northumberland, was long resident at Gargrave, where he built a row of cottages in South Street, in one of which he first lived (about 1822) when master of the School, then conducted in the old Wesleyan Chapel behind. Afterwards he took a larger and better house in the village, where the school was continued until his removal, through Sir Robert Peel, to London in 1843, where he remained until his death in 1860, aged 65. It was at Gargrave, however, that his best work was written.

Gargrave to Eshton, 1¼ m., **Airton,** 5 m. Near the *Swan* Hotel a field path leads over the canal bridge and on to the Eshton road, which passes through richly wooded park-land belonging to Eshton Hall. Here we find but little oak though the ash and sycamore and common thorn attain a large size. Turn *l.* along the Malham road (forward one goes to Flasby and Rylstone) by **Eshton Hall**, (Sir. W. M. Wilson, Bart., J.P.), the ancient and beautiful seat of the Wilson family, which for many years until his death in Jan.. 1891, was occupied by Sir Mathew Wilson, Bart., first elected (1885-6) Member of Parliament for the Skipton Division, and whose statue adorns the principal street in Skipton. The Hall property was bought by an ancestor of the present owner, Mr. Mathew Wilson, a London merchant, in 1642. It is a very ancient manor-house, dating back to Norman times, when the family of De Eston were the mesne lords. The building is of different periods, the latest portion having been added in 1825-6, and it contains amongst its varied collections one of the largest and finest private libraries in England. These include many important historical manuscripts and rare printed works, the collection chiefly of the late accomplished Miss Frances Richardson-Currer. There are also some valuable paintings, including portraits.

&c., by Rubens, Vandyck, Rembrandt, Turner, Sir Peter Lely, &c. A portrait here of Charles the First by Vandyck, is, says Montague, "the best I ever saw of this *murdered* monarch." The pleasure grounds comprise about thirty acres, all laid out and planted during the lifetime of the late owner, and with consummate taste and skill. The timber in the park is now well-grown and presents an aspect of great luxuriance. Visitors are frequently admitted, but previous application should be made. About 1¼ m. further on our way **Eshton Tarn** is passed in the hollow on r., which from the spongy nature of the ground around it must formerly have been three or four times its present size. It is now less than a mile round. Abounding in excellent fish, it was in ancient Catholic times, an important source of revenue to the lords De Eston, to whom it was granted by Edward I., about A. D. 1280. Crossing shortly the Aire bridge the handsome and imposing mansion of New Field (H. Illingworth, Esq.) is seen upon a verdant elevation to the right, whence the road continues direct to Airton for Malham, &c., (*see* p. 269).

Gargrave to Winterburn, 3½ m., **Airton**, 6 m. This is a delightful walk. By the last route to Eshton Hall, and ¼ m. beyond, at Eshton House, (M. A. Wilson, Esq., J.P.), an old flowery lane turns r., and winding, shortly dips into the hollow on l., where is an ancient and copious spring called **St. Helen's Well**, so named from an old endowed chapel-of-ease dedicated to that early Christian saint, and which is mentioned in a commission relating to the manor of Flasby, in 1429. No vestige of the building remains, but the adjoining site is still known as Chapel Field. Probably a cross stood here, and an alms-box to receive the passing charity of those who drank at the well. The water is very pure and cold, and bubbles up with remarkable regularity and force, at the rate of several hundred gallons an hour. At its junction with Eshton Beck, a short distance lower down, the water is said to petrify. The stream side is starred with the beautiful grass of Parnassus, and other marsh-loving plants, not very commonly met with. Crossing here the Nappa Bridge, we are soon in sight of a large and picturesque old mansion called **Friars Head**, which since the death in 1886 of Mr. Dawes, a nephew of the Dean of Hereford, has been occupied by his widow and another family. The house is the property of the Wilsons of Eshton, having been purchased by the late Sir Mathew Wilson's father about 1825, from Mr. Townley Parker of Cuerdon, Lancs. It is a stately looking 16th century building, comprising four front gables of three stories, and there are said to be no fewer than 1470 windows around the house. These had formerly all leaded, diamond panes. The rooms are large and lofty, but the interior fittings are now all altered and modern. One of the upper rooms is stated to be haunted, but by whom or what we have not been able to ascertain. Near the roof is an unlighted apartment called the Dungeon, reported to be the place where the monks consigned their refractory,—possibly the lurking place of the traditional ghost! Originally a grange and hunting-box to Furness Abbey, we find Friars Head valued at the Dissolution at £8 3s. 4d., or about one-sixth of the whole value of the Furness estate in the manor of Winterburn. We are told that after his submission to King Henry VIII. the last Abbot (Pyle) passed a night here on his way to the Consistory at York. Adjoining the house is an orchard which is supposed to have been the monks' burial ground. A few years ago in making a new road to the house a number of

FRIARS HEAD, WINTERBURN.

bones were dug up, which corroborates the belief. Doubtless there would be a private chapel attached. On Scarnber Hill, above the house is the well-preserved outline of an extensive earthwork. probably Danish, forming an elliptic about half-a-mile in circumference. The view from the summit (670 ft.) is very beautiful, comprising Pendle Hill and the ranges westward.

From Friars Head **Winterburn** is reached by a pleasant walk of ½ m. The village lies immured in the lap of gentle hills overshadowed by such dense foliage as to form in reality a perfect bower, —a retreat fit for the Dryades! It is recorded that upwards of 3000 persons die annually in New York from effects of heat, arising mainly from the city lacking trees; at Winterburn they must surely perish from the opposite cause, for it would be difficult to conceive a place more completely protected from the sun's rays. Amid this bowery landscape the songs of many birds mingle their music with that of the on-flowing crystal, pebbly trout-beck beneath, so deliciously cool and clear that you can hardly resist the temptation to stoop over its murmuring waters and drink! The birds haunting this woody wilderness include, as might be expected, many beautiful and uncommon kinds, such as the jay, kingfisher, wagtails, brown and snowy owls, pied-flycatcher, &c. And in the stillness of a fine

Autumn evening we have stood on the little rustic bridge and watched the shy heron winging its way lazily beside the trout-dappled stream within a few yards of our abiding place. It is a curious instinct with this bird to know, as it evidently does quite well, that fish avoid a shadow, for it seldom if ever preys in sunshine. On the bank near stands a large ash tree divided into two main branches, the base of the trunk up to this division having a cavity so large that a tall person may enter and with the aid of a walking-stick not be able to touch the top of it. The tree maintains an appearance of vigour in spite of this extensive decay. Such canker is very often prevented from spreading at the outset by that useful bird, the strong-billed woodpecker eating out the fungoid particles, when new wood heals up the wound, and the tree is saved from further injury. It is erroneous to suppose, as many do, that the woodpecker 'taps' sound wood to the detriment of the tree. The manor of Winterburn, which included the townships of Hetton, Eshton, Flasby, and Airton, belonged as already stated to the monks of Furness. At the Restoration it was claimed by Thomas Wilkinson, Esq., ancestor of the present owner, T. C. Wilkinson, Esq., J.P., of Newall Hall, Otley. The manor hall is now under a separate tenancy. The old **Independent Chapel** at Winterburn is interesting from its association with the family of Major-General Lambert, one of the most conspicuous characters in the Parliamentary wars. The Lamberts lived at Calton Hall, which will be presently mentioned. The chapel was founded by Lady Lambert, wife of the general's son, probably soon after the repurchase of the family estates. She was an ardent Presbyterian, whilst her husband, John Lambert, who was Sheriff of Yorkshire in 1699, was an equally zealous member of the Church of England, and regularly attended Kirkby-Malham church. It is said that Cromwell, whose signature appears in the Kirkby parish registers in 1655, attended service here, but this is not likely as Cromwell died in 1658, and the chapel would not be founded until some years after that. The first ordained minister, however, was the Rev. John Isott, who was appointed in July, 1678. At that time the sittings consisted of rude benches, whilst the floor was strewn with rushes. It is now neatly pewed, with accommodation for about 150 worshippers. Since 1882 the little building has been rented by the Vicar of Gargrave, who holds a service here every Sunday afternoon. There is no burial ground attached, the nearest being at Rylstone and Gargrave, about three miles off.

From the stone bridge, Winterburn, a country lane winds at easy gradients 1¼ m. to Calton Hall. About midway the farmhouse of Cowper Cote, where the Craven Harriers sometimes meet, is passed on r. Cowper Cote, as part of the possessions of Furness Abbey, was valued in the 'First Fruits' at the Dissolution at £8 10s., about £80 of present money. From the summit of the road (Abbey Hill) near here an excellent retrospective view is obtained of Flasby, Rylstone and Cracoe Fells, with the encampment prominent on Scarnber Hill above Friars' Head. The original **Calton Hall**, occupied by the celebrated General Lambert, was burnt down during the lifetime of his son, who erected a plain stone mansion on its site. The building having fallen into decay was replaced in the early part of this century by the present white house. It occupies an elevated, yet retired position, such an one as a military commander might choose with obvious advantage. From the lawn is derived an expansive and very beautiful view extending from Flasby Fell westwards to Pendle Hill. Here is preserved an ancient Sun-dial, inscribed IL. (John Lambert) WF. (Wm. Fairfax) 1688; the only relic of the old family now remaining here. The great Parliamentary commander, John Lambert, sixth heir-descendant of John Lambert, of Preston, Vice-Chancellor of the Duchy of Lancaster, was born here Sept. 7th, 1619. At the age of twenty he married a daughter of Sir William Lister, Kt., of Thornton, another chief militant of the great Civil strife. In the twenty years of his life that followed the event of his marriage, Lambert stands out in bold relief in history as one of the wisest of leaders, yet upholding staunchly the rigorous discipline of that stormy period. A man of iron resolve, of firm and independent character, (after Cromwell's own heart), cool, calculating, and discerning, these lines of Smollett may not inaptly be applied to him,

> "Thy spirit, Independence, let me share,
> Lord of the lion-heart and eagle eye,
> Thy steps I follow with my bosom bare,
> Nor heed the storm that howls along the sky."

The successes of Cromwell in the open field are in large measure due to the skill and determination displayed on all occasions by this brave young chief. In his thirtieth year he was advanced to the Commissary-Generalship of the northern army, and in 1655 appointed one of the twelve Major-Generals installed by the Protector for the military government of England, an office which all authorities allow he deservedly held, and it is certain he acted with great circumspection, wisdom, moderation and justice. At this time Cromwell appears to have visited him, for, as mentioned above, the Lord Protector's autograph as witness to a notable local wedding is found in the Kirkby church registers for that year. Lambert sat in Parliament during the Protectorate, and on the death of Cromwell in 1658, and subsequent retirement of his son Richard, he parried, we might say, single stick with Hazelrig for chief dictatorship. His fortunes, however, were soon reversed, for in 1660, at the Restoration, he was apprehended on a charge of high treason, imprisoned, and ultimately condemned to perpetual banishment in the island of Guernsey, where he died some thirty years after, at the age of 75. His forfeited estates in Craven were afterwards re-purchased by his son, John Lambert,* father of

* The famous General's son does not appear to have been exempt from the roisterous bacchanals of the time, to judge from the following lively bit of gossip extracted from the Diary of the Rev. Oliver Heywood, A.D. 1681:
"1681.—Mr. Lambert, of Caulton, Mr. Heber, Col. Carre, Sr Walter Hawksworth, &c., drunk at Skipton, 10sh. a-piece in wine, were laid aside to sleep, amongst whom was Mr. Sutton, preacher at Skipton and Carleton, he grew very abusive, he played upon Col. Carre, who left them, then upon Mr. Heber, told him his father had been a traytour, but his own father (Mr. Sutton, formerly minister

the last heir male, who died young, March 9th. 1675-6. Frances Lambert, sole heiress, married in 1699, Sir John Middleton, of Belsay Castle, Northumberland.

But, as it was with Lambert, so it is with most people,

"Life is a journey,—on we go
Through many a scene of joy and woe,"

so leaving Calton Hall on *l.* we emerge on the road (9 m. to Grassington) and wind down a picturesque thoroughfare to the substantial Aire bridge at Airton Mills. A path hence by the river leads by Hanlith Mill to Malham (3 m.). It should also be stated that from Winterburn Malham may be reached (6 m.) by the route described on p. 251.

Gargrave to Bell Busk by the Pack-horse road, 2½ m. A pleasant deviation from the ordinary highway through Coniston may be made by leaving Gargrave station and crossing the Aire bridge, and up West Street over Ireland (canal) bridge, whence the road runs through the magnificently wooded park (about 800 acres) of Gargrave House, (J. Coulthurst, Esq., J.P., D.L.), where the stately beeches and sycamores are seen rising from thirty to forty feet in height before a branch is given off from their straight boles. Ascending the lofty avenue the road passes a barn and shortly developes into a grass-covered way between walls, with nice open view north of Malham Cove, Kirkby Fell, Ryeloaf, and part of Fountains Fell. This road was anciently the old pack-horse road from Skipton to Settle, and continued to be the regular highway until the new road was cut through Coniston about 1820. An old dwelling called Granny House is passed on *r.*, which up to that time was a 'public,' and a familiar rendezvous of the packmen in ancient days. It is a stout old edifice which has braved the winters of, we should say, a round three centuries. In a quarter-of-a-mile the Aire bridge, and shortly the Red bridge (so called from the colour of the stone) are crossed, whence *l.* to Bell Busk station, or *r.* to Malham, 5 m. About fifty-five years ago the Aire bridge was almost too narrow for a single cart to pass; it was then widened by the County authorities, but is still narrow. It is one of our oldest pack-horse bridges, and has existed now a good many centuries

at Skipton) was a loyal person, a good man, gone to heaven, and there prayed for him every day, saying God will hear his prayers, &c. He again abused Mr. Heber, who gave him a blow on the head, they squabbled, they turned Sutton out of door as not fit for their company. He is a strange man—he will drink till 3 or 4 o'clock on Sabboth-day morning, yet preach and rant it agt drunk-nnes notably in the pulpit, he sth himself that he hath the knack of preaching; oh. dreadfull, other sad storys I hear of a debauched clergy, yet hector it strangely agt Presbyterians."

GARGRAVE TO BELL BUSK.

Through an umbrageous country from the bridge opposite the *Grouse* and *Swan* Inns the road descends under the railway and crosses the Aire to Coniston Cold, 2 m. Just above the bridge the river makes a curious natural bend locally known as the Coniston S, which is also seen from the railway. A few years ago the proprietor of the Haw Crag quarries, who held the land in which this remarkable curvature is situate, in order to prevent or mitigate flooding, caused a straight channel to be cut through one portion of it and a retaining-wall built, so that this end now makes an island, which would have been washed away but for the stone banking. Below the bridge there is another bend where the river passes over damstones constructed for a water-hold used for driving the wheel at the old corn-mill lower down. The mill, which has not been run these sixty years, is now a ruin, but the old mill-goit is still intact.

Coniston in our earliest charters is spelled *Coniyston* and *Conyngeston Cald*, (Saxon, *conyng*, a King), from having been royal land in Saxon times. The meaning of the distinctive appellation *Cold* is obvious; a name, however, that is hardly deserved at the present day, for the village lies snugly amid well-wooded and picturesque surroundings. These plantings were effected about a century ago when the Garforths came into possession of the manor, whose descendants, now represented by A. A. Tottie, Esq., of Coniston Hall, still hold the same. Its previous history is traced by Whitaker. In the Subsidy Roll of 2 Richard II., Coniston we find paid a poll-tax of 9s. 4d., or about the same as Linton and Addingham, and a third less than its namesake in Kettlewell-dale.

From Coniston to Bell Busk (1 m.) we go along a leafy road by the Hospice Howe Plantation and the handsome modern church, founded by the late J. B. Garforth, Esq., in 1846, and following the course of the river reach Bell Busk station by the large silk mills of Mr. C. A. Rickards.

BELL BUSK.

BELL Busk is not one of those places enshrined in the pages of *Domesday*, nor even in documents of a much later period. It does not appear on Speed's Yorkshire map of 1627, although Otterburn, the next hamlet does. The fact is Bell Busk consisted anciently of a single house situate on the east bank of the Aire near its confluence with the Otterburn and between the ancient bridge and still older ford. The present village is of comparatively new growth, having sprung into existence with the mills erected towards the end of last century. The old house mentioned lay near a track used from the earliest times, in passing between Skipton and Settle and the north, and in pack-horse days we are led to understand a *bell* used to be suspended in a conspicuous *bush*, and rung as an indication of the route to be taken, or as a warning after dark that the waters were out. Then as now this was the central and most thinly populated part of the whole Deanery of Craven, and in such a lonely spot a 'guide' of this kind would be very acceptable. Hence this is how the place is believed to have got its name, and the Good Templars of the village have in consequence called their association the "Bell in the Bush Lodge." Such another 'out-of-the-way' village called Bell-on-the-Hill lies about midway between Whitchurch and Malpas, in Cheshire,—Malpas by the way signifying *Malsus Passus*, or 'bad passage or road.' The custom of bell-ringing, like horn-blowing, as a guide to benighted travellers is very ancient, and was one of the usages prescribed and long practised by the Knights Hospitallers of St. John of Jerusalem, and has doubtless in various combinations given name to both places and persons. But as doubt has often been expressed as to this having been the true origin of the name Bell Busk, we have in vain sought for a possible explanation of it in the sign of an inn. Such signs have frequently originated place-names, and at Oswaldtwistle, near Accrington, is an inn called the 'Bell in the Thorn,' but this it should be stated was named after the man who originally kept it, *Bellthorn*. But there has been no such inn that we can ascertain at Bell Busk.

A more likely theory is that of the Celtic *bal* or *bel*, a dwelling, or place of sacrifice, near a *bush*. We have seen that all along the valley of the Aire (as at Baildon) such places with the root-word *Bel*, lying adjacent to remains of remote antiquity, lend much countenance to this belief. Here about Bell Busk we have traces of pre-historic barrows, cairns, and earthworks; relics undoubtedly in some instances of an age when Baal worship prevailed in this country. Five years ago two broken urns were unearthed on an eminence called Lingber, about a mile south of Otterburn, and which contained cremated ashes, along with a copper dagger or knife, the whole being overlaid by a slab of gritstone. In the pit close by a farmer had previously picked up a thin silver coin, and a beautiful gem of amethystine quartz, incised with a figure, the latter being of good Roman workmanship. In an elevated pasture, about a mile north of Bell Busk, on the way to Airton, another barrow was opened in 1887, and found to contain a rude urn enclosing calcined bones of a human subject, with fragments of charcoal. Again, upon an eminence a mile north of Otterburn, is a large earthwork that probably occupies the site of a temple when the ingle fire burned in commemoration of the Druidical god Baal. The stream that descends to the Pot Ho. at the foot of the hill is still called Ingle beck. But whether these early evidences of Celtic occupation gave rise to an older derivation than that of the 'Bell in the Bush' cannot, we think, with any certainty be ascertained. A perfectly tenable origin may still further be advanced by the fact that the word *bel* is often found in conjunction with other words to signify *a ford*, such as Belfast, (anc-*Bel-feirsde*), meaning the *ford* of the *farset* or sandbank; Belclair, the *ford* or entrance to the plain; Lisbellaw, the fort at the *ford* mouth; &c. We have already referred to the ancient ford here. Bell Busk may, therefore, mean simply the *ford* by the *bush*.

The little rustic village possesses nothing specially noteworthy. The silk-spinning mills belonging to Mr. Rickards are the principal source of employment to the non-farming class, and there is also some quarrying at Hawcrag Rock. In Jan., 1877, an enormous blast was discharged at this quarry, when upwards of 30,000 tons of stone were removed. Bell Busk was an early seat of Yorkshire Quakerism, and under the Toleration Act licence was obtained in 1689 to hold meetings here and at other villages in Craven.

Bell Busk to Otterburn, 1¼ m., **Settle,** 7½ m. This is by the old pack-horse route described on p. 263. From Bell Busk the road *l.* crosses Otterburn beck direct to **Otterburn.** This we may remind the reader is not the Otterburn of the well-known ballad of *Chery Chase*, which is in Northumberland. The name is obviously derived from that amphibious creature the otter, which, whatever may have been the warrant in early times (and *Otreburne* is included in Domesday in the parish of Kirkby-Malham), is now seldom if ever seen here. The district is richly wooded, but a century ago there was hardly a tree to be seen. Now the pleasant trout-beck courses through the village in summer-luxuriant shade, where revels the gaudy dragon-fly, and where the quick-eyed kingfisher darts with painted wing beneath the old stone bridge spanning the stream. The present bridge was built to replace an older one about 1813, when the common land was enclosed. Anciently the greater part of Otterburn belonged to the monks of Fountains, who had probably a small chapel or cell here. In A.D. 1257 we find the following local confirmation of a grant of land to that monastery. "Ric. de Otterburn, Clerk, son of Hugh de Otterburn, confirmed all that Thomas, son of Willm. de Malghum had given, and also gave lieve to enlarge and repair the conduit at Malghum [Malham]." The old Hall here was rebuilt early this century by Robert Nightingale, father of the late Judge Nightingale, the well-known coursing judge. It is now attached to an extensive farm. Many of the better-class old houses in Craven were built in 'stirring times' of inordinate strength, no doubt for defence. Such an one is that occupied by Mr. Wm. Gomersall, at Otterburn. The parlour has cupboard recesses 5 ft. deep, behind which are 3 ft. thick walls. Formerly the house had large open fire-places fit up with mediæval "bee-hive" ovens similar to those found in our old abbeys. Mr. Gomersall, whose fame as a scientific writer and local investigator has been long established, possesses a unique collection of Craven fossils, amongst which we are pleased to note the uncommonly rare *Pleurorhythicus minax*, from the neighbouring Yoredales.

The tourist leaves Otterburn by a rustic shaded lane, (the old pack-horse route to Settle), emerging in a good ¼ m. from between a plantation on an open field, which he must cross up to the gate, and ascend field again to the two gates at the top. Entering *l.* descend the moor to a gate which opens on to a lane—a broad grassy lane, which in ¼ m. passes Bookilber Farm and the extensive rabbit-warren belonging to Mr. Harrison. From the farm (which commands an extended view over Airedale to Pendle, no house is now passed for over three miles,—the road continuing between low hills where the botanist may find diversion among the various kinds of plants. These include the interesting little butterwort, St. John's wort, grass of Parnassus, mt.-willow-herb, scabious (*S. succisa*,) &c.,—all beside the stream bordering the way. After crossing the small beck dividing the parishes of Settle and Long Preston, the terraced heights of Langcliffe Scars come finely into view, when a descent is made upon **Scaleber Bridge** (1010 ft.) at the Waterfall. A path from the stile on *l.* makes a somewhat precipitous descent into the finely-wooded ravine. The scene is extremely grand. The Scaleber beck (which enters the Ribble below Long Preston) here comes over lofty cliffs in two broad cascades of about 20 ft. and 30 ft. respectively, whose wild environment luxuriates in various spray-spangled greenery. A large mossy and many-hued rock in the bottom must be a perfect feast to the eye of the artist. During a hard winter, like the last (1890-1), when King Frost mantles tree and stone with the most exquisite and delicate tracery, and about the half-frozen waterfall huge pendant icicles gleam like silver in the mellow sunlight, a fairy-like scene of wondrous beauty is revealed, worth coming a long way to see.

Proceeding, the junction of the road to Malham is soon reached (*see* p. 293), where is a defaced ancient encampment, which once contained a large water-cistern, doubtless used by the Roman soldiery stationed here. Their road went (as now) by Scaleber and Ebor Gate on High Side, connecting the Roman roads of Settle with upper Airedale. Fragments of deer bones have also been dug up at this camp. The tourist now descends to Settle, 1 m.

BELL BUSK TO MALHAM.

AIRTON, 2 m.   KIRKBY MALHAM 3¼ m.   MALHAM 5 m.

UST above the peculiar Coniston S, previously described, the river takes an abrupt turn from the east, and for the remainder of its six miles' course runs due north. It traverses a landscape half-wild, half-beautiful, consummating in lofty scars and mountain scenery of unrivalled grandeur and scientific interest. Were this valley filled with a large lake, (such as doubtless to some extent once existed), following the sinuosities of the hills, the view revealed would not be inferior to any of the grand lake scenes of similar extent in Cumberland.

If no conveyance has been ordered, the tourist may shorten the road to Airton a little by taking through the gateway at the bottom of the station road, and following the field path into a rustic lane which emerges on the Settle and Hellifield road at Airton. This is a pleasant walk if fine. About midway the stream at Kirk Sike is crossed; Kirk Sike being the traditional site of a Christian place of worship before the building of Kirkby Church, and the adjoining pastures are curiously enough still known as Great and Little Church Door and the Parson's Crook (or Crozier).

AIRTON AND SCOSTHROP.

From the time of *Domesday* these have been separate townships, though only the road (or sike) divides them. Whilst the Wesleyan Chapel and the Post Office are in Scosthrop the houses opposite are in Airton. After the Conquest the manor of Airton was held by Robert de Bulmer, and that of Scosthrop conjointly by the Abbot of Dereham and Thomas de Scostrop. There are several old dated houses in the locality. Garris House on the Hellifield road, is probably like that of the same name at Gargrave, a survival of the residence of the ancient lords of the manor. The present edifice is said to have been built in 1602 by John Topham, founder of the Free Grammar School in 1606. Another old house is inscribed EWA 1696. From the time of Henry VIII. (*ca.* 1540) until its confiscation after the Civil Wars, the manor of Airton, with half that of Scosthrop, was held by the Lamberts, of Calton Hall, whose history we have already traced on pp. 261-3. According to a deed of gift to Fountains Abbey, confirmed 10th Richard I., or A.D. 1198, there was a corn-mill at Airton thus early. The mill most probably stood on the site of the old portion of Messrs. Dewhurst's cotton mill down by the river side. This is known to have been a water corn-mill in former times. Calton it may be remarked, was originally wholly abbey land, belonging to Fountains, Dereham (in Norfolk) and Bolton, and the monks would have part of their corn ground here, as there was at least one Cell in the neighbourhood. At present there is no inn here, but post-horses and conveyances may be obtained at Berry's in Scosthrop. The minimum charge for horse hire from Bell Busk to Malham is 2s. 6d.

The pedestrian may take the river-side route from Airton Mill, crossing the plank-bridge on to Hanlith Mill. **Hanlith Hall**, picturesquely situated on the hill side above, is the ancient seat of the Serjeantson family, who have been local property owners for fully three centuries. The manor in the 16th century was held by the Metcalfes, of the historic family of Nappa, in Wensleydale, by whom it was sold to the Listers, of Midhope, and acquired, about 1615, by Josiah Lambert, of Calton Hall, father, by his third wife, of the celebrated Parliamentary General (*see* p. 262). A stone on a lathe (near where an old tithe-barn stood) bears the date 1694. Seven horse shoes have long been suspended before the hall door, an interesting relic of Craven folk-belief in their efficacy as a charm against ill-luck. Such signs are still not uncommon in Craven. The tourist now crosses the stone bridge between the hall and the mill and wends his way onward about a mile through flowery meads to Malham, passing about midway the two springs of Airehead near two conspicuous ash trees (*see* p. 281).

From Airton by the road to

KIRKBY MALHAM

we pass an old house, with a sun-dial on its west gable, called Skellands, built by the family of King, now about two centuries ago. Thomas King, of Skellands, gent., married a daughter of Wm. Serjeantson, Esq., of Hanlith, in 1714, whose five grandsons were, with one exception, all eminent church dignitaries. This exception was the celebrated James

KIRKBY MALHAM.

King, LL.D., F.R.S., a captain in the Royal Navy, who accompanied Captain Cooke on his last great voyage of discovery round the world, of which he wrote an able and graphic account. Dr. King died in 1784, at the early age of 31. A long epitaph on the family may be seen in Kirkby church.

The parish of Kirkby-Malham comprises the whole valley from Otterburn on the south to Malham Moor on the north, and has an area of 23,727 acres. The population in 1881 was 821, or an average of nearly 29 acres to every soul.* The Domesday name *Chirchebi* premises the existence of a church here in Saxon times, but it was probably ravaged by the Danes, and at the time of the Conqueror's survey practically non-existent. The first legal mention of it occurs in a charter of confirmation by King John, in 1199, to the Abbot and Canons of West Dereham, in Norfolk. In possession of this monastery the rectory and advowson remained until the Dissolution, when it was granted to George, Earl of Shrewsbury. In 1621 we find Sir Thos. Wentworth, afterwards the great Earl of Strafford (who died upon the block), patron of the living, and who about the above date had married a daughter of Francis, 4th Earl of Cumberland, of Skipton Castle ; whose niece, Elizabeth Clifford, married in 1634, Richd. Boyle, Earl of Burlington, from whom is descended the present noble family of Cavendish. To this house the patronage was subsequently transmitted, and is now held by W. Morrison, Esq., M.P., of Tarn House, Malham. The church underwent a thorough restoration some few years ago. It is in the Perpendicular style of the time of Henry VII. The roof is only partially battlemented, and on the tower are some shields and the initials G.N.R., probably those of Geo. Norwych, the vicar in 1485. The interior pillars have on their western faces canopied niches, which in the old Catholic days no doubt held statues of saints. This is a peculiarity found only in the churches of which the Tempests were principal benefactors, namely at Broughton and Bracewell, in Craven. About fifty years ago several interesting old frescoes were partially restored from beneath coats of whitewash which had concealed them. The ancient font here exhibits an admirable example of the dog-tooth ornament, and is probably of Saxon age. The registers, dating from 1597, possess an uncommon interest in that they contain the autograph of England's

* Compare this population and area with the manufacturing districts of mid Airedale (*see* p. 121).

Lord Protector, **Oliver Cromwell**. He has written his name as witness to a 'capitulation' of a very interesting kind, to wit, the marriage between 'Martine Knowles, of Middle House in this parish and Dorothy Hartley, of West Marton,' on 17th Jan., 1655. At this time Cromwell was on a visit to General Lambert, at Calton Hall (*see* p. 261), and may we not imagine the great "uncrowned king" forgetting for an hour the turmoils of state and enjoying the pleasing ceremony,—nay, perhaps, amid flowing bumpers proposing the health and happiness of the newly-married pair! An old house at Kirkby goes by the name of Cromwell House, doubtless so called in honour of his visit. The church, containing memorials of General Lambert's family, was doubtless garrisoned in his service during the Civil Wars.

In the picturesque Kirk Gill, about ten minutes' walk from the village, is a Spa Well, situate at the foot of a small Yoredale-limestone cliff, and which is said to possess virtues similar to the waters at Harrogate. In these woods the botanist will discover many rare species. Here also may be found in Spring, the pink and white varieties of the common blue-bell, besides other attractive kinds of wild flowers.

Ryeloaf (1790 ft.) may be most conveniently ascended from Kirkby, and a descent made to Malham. Time required, 2¼-3 hours. Ascend the Settle road about 1 m. to the 'red gate' at the guide-post (4¼ m. to Settle), whence alongside the plantation of Acraplats, as described on p. 290. The summit is plainly seen, and from it is obtained, perhaps, the finest view in upper Airedale.

From the Hotel *(Victoria)* at Kirkby a pleasant run of 1½ m. brings us to Malham, the *Ultima Thule* of our journey up Airedale.

MALHAM.

" A realm of mountain, forest haunt, and fell,
And fertile valleys beautifully lone,
Where fresh and far romantic waters roam,
Singing a song of peace by many a cottage home."
J. C. PRINCE.

NOT the least charm about Malham is its complete retirement from the distracting influences of town life. Its soothing, wholesome environment seems to breathe of perpetual quietude, especially felt in the long, hot days of summer, when the unobstructed sun-rays flush the white scars with radiant light, the cloud shadows lie motionless, and a drowsy stillness fills the warm air,—a stillness broken only, perhaps, by the bleating of mountain sheep, the lone cry of the curlew, or perchance the familiar voice of some lingering cuckoo heard afar off among the treeless fells ! The place, however, is not always in this happy and tranquil atmospheric mood ; sometimes the storm-clouds lower and vaporous rains and wind rush along the wild hills grandly, but in a manner which most people, we opine, would much rather simply witness than bodily experience.

The straggling little village, through which the first waters of the Aire pour, stands (640 ft. above the sea) at the foot of its guardian hill, Cowden (1000 ft.) (locally *Cawden*), whilst on either side tower the familiar cairns on Gordale Crag and Pike Daw, from all of which there are capital prospects. Perhaps the best convenient view of the place is to be obtained from the Tranlands road behind the Wesleyan Chapel. The village wears a weathered, mountain look, in keeping with its situation and surroundings, and the houses are for the most part substantially built of native grit and limestone. There are two comfortable hostelries, the *Buck* and *Lister's Arms*, besides several very good temperance hotels and private lodging-houses. The terms vary from about 30s. to 50s. per week inclusive.

The chief attractions of the place are, of course, the majestic amphitheatre of the Cove, and Gordale Scar, but there are other scenes and walks, to be hereafter enumerated, in the neighbourhood which well merit the visitor's attention. With respect to the origin and history of Malham, the opinion expressed by Dr. Whitaker that it received its name from *Malgh* its supposed Saxon owner, has been generally quoted and accepted. But in a place so removed, and so predominant

MALHAM.

by its physical aspects, we are disposed to look for an appropriate descriptive nomenclature, as is the case with all the other townships in this extensive parish. The earliest spelling of the name we find occurs variously as Malgham, Malgum, (in *Domesday*) Mawlam, Mawm. The latter carries with it a pronunciation which the place has always borne. Consequently if we allow for the misapplication of sound in the Saxon *sub*. Norman spelling of the word (a circumstance of common occurrence in early charters) we arrive at a very different meaning to that usually accepted, for places compounded of

Maum, *Moym*, and *Mam* are from the Celtic-Irish *madhm*, *a mountain pass or chasm*; thus Maum-Turk, *the boar's pass*, Maumakeogh, *the pass of the mist*, Mam Tor, the hill pass, (above the Windyats, Derbyshire) and Malham, locally Mawm (*the way* to or at) *the pass*, now *the village or hamlet of the pass or gorge*, in allusion either to Gordale or the narrow approaches to the village. The crooked ascent from Malham on to the Gordale road bears the name of Finkle Street, evidently from the Danish *rinckl* (Belgic *winckel*), an angle or corner, a very meet term for this part of the road. Other similar thoroughfares in and about Airedale (as at Selby and Armley) are also known by this singular name, and in Cheshire is a romantically situated little village called Wincle, and below Wincle Grange is the old Dane's Bridge.

Of the Celtic occupation of Malham there is undoubted evidence in local cave deposits of animal remains belonging to a primitive people, and in stone circles and cairns which, however, have never been sufficiently investigated. About forty-five years ago a large barrow containing human bones was opened on the upper east side of the Cove. It had never hitherto been disturbed and was locally known as the Friar's Heap or Monk's Grave, but it is much more likely to have been a British or Danish burial mound.

In Saxon times the great Earl Edwin belonged lands in Malham, and at the Conquest the manor of East Malham was bestowed upon the Norman William de Percy, and soon after the place gave name to its mesne lords the notable family of Mawm or Malham, who died out in Craven at the close of the seventeenth century. The Mauleverers were also lords of thirteen carucates (probably not less than 5000 acres here) in East Malham, of which twelve oxgangs (eight oxgangs constituting a carucate) were early given by them to the Priory of Embsay, afterwards Bolton. Prior Hall, the oldest building now standing in Malham, doubtless retains the original site of the edifice first occupied by the monks of Bolton, where they remained till the Dissolution, and where their courts were held. But the Courts Baron, tradition avers, were held within the sheltering corridors of Gordale, a spot (if this were so) that may readily be imagined would contribute not a little to the impressiveness of the ceremonial.

East Malham, together with a moiety of the manor of West Malham, was after the fall of the monasteries acquired by the Lamberts, and afterwards, about the middle of the 17th century, alienated to the Listers, Lords Ribblesdale. West Malham, originally also held by William de Percy, founder of Sallay Abbey, included the Tarn, and was in possession of the monks of Fountains, whose vast estates, extending from Ripon on the east to Fountains Fell westward, comprised in Craven an area of not less than 60,000 acres. Their lands in this district were appropriated mostly to the grazing of sheep, and on Fountains Fell they had a spacious bercary or lodge, at one time occupied by five shepherds, and in East Malham the monks of Bolton had a similar establishment, to which were attached pens, folds, and wash-pits, besides every other requisite of a great sheep-farm. Frequent reference is made to the repair, &c., of this bercary by the Bolton monks in their Compotus from A.D. 1290 to 1325. Yearly the herdsmen of Fountains drove their flocks over the high moor down to Kilnsey, in Wharfedale, where the animals were clipped, and whence the wool was afterwards conveyed in wains drawn by oxen with a pole, as was the custom then, all the way to Fountains Abbey. Stone crosses, the sockets of which may still be found, served to guide them, or any passing pilgrim, over these wild moors. At the Dissolution West Malham was granted by the King to Sir Richd. Gresham, Kt., and his heirs for ever, who however disposed of it ; and in 1560 it came into the hands of the Assheton family, by whom it was devised to the noble house of Ribblesdale as stated above.

The former possessions of the old monks of Fountains and Malham, are preserved now only in such names as Prior Rakes, (the extensive pasture between the Tarn and Cove), Abbot Hills, Friars' Garth, Cross Field, &c. In the time of the Asshetons there was a deer park, still known as such, adjoining the west side of Prior Hall, where some sixty head of deer were kept, and whence an animal was occasionally liberated for a stalking-hunt over the hillocky scar-rent mountains as far north as Langstrothdale Chace.

Touching the subject of wild animals, besides the fox, rabbit, stoat, and weasel, little is seen here now. But three years ago a badger was observed above Malham, and hunted down to Hanlith, where it was captured, and it is now in the possession of Mr. Rickards, of Bell Busk. Also another of these rare animals was recently (Feb. 1891) taken on the high ground at Stockdale, between Malham and Settle. But the district is more especially noted for its rare birds, plants, mosses, lichens, &c., and in this respect is one of the finest hunting-grounds of the naturalist in Britain. We shall make further mention of this subject later.

Malham has a very old and great reputation for its sheep-fairs, as many as 80,000 head having been exhibited on a single fair-day. There are three fairs annually; the first for lambs on June 30th, the second for lambs on the second Thursday in Aug., and the third for sheep on Oct. 15th. But besides sheep and cattle rearing there is another local industry of some consequence, viz.: lead mining. The veins are worked under Pike Daw, and are upon the whole highly metalliferous; the "Rich Groove" mine here having, we may add, yielded an abundance of very good metal. In April, 1887, a block or "knocking" of lead was brought to the surface weighing upwards of a ton, and containing 85 per cent, of lead, 4 oz. of silver to the ton, with a surface of carbonate of copper. This fine block was afterwards sent to the Newcastle Exhibition. At the beginning of the century occupation was found for a portion of the inhabitants at a small cotton-mill, situated on the stream near the Pan Holes waterfall, a little north of the village, but the mill having been given up some years ago, it fell into ruin and has since altogether disappeared. The old free school at Malham is now also a thing of the past, yet the building still stands beside the road near Prior Hall. It was founded by Rowland Brayshay in 1717, and endowed by him with land valued now at about £110 a year. This endowment, with others, is now applied under the late Act to the maintenance of the Kirkby-Malhamdale United School, conducted since 1877 in a good building situate midway between Kirkby and Malham. For many years during the last and present centuries, Thomas Hurtley, author of a quaint and entertaining volume entitled, "A Concise Account of some Natural Curiosities in the Environs of Malham in Craven," was master of the village school. His book, which is now scarce, was published by the help and patronage of the first Lord Ribblesdale in 1786. It contains some curious and, of course, long exploded notions, not the least remarkable of which are the altitudes quoted of British hills, proving "unquestionably" that the 'mountains of Craven' top the rest of the United Kingdom. This is a statement for which at that era the author himself was not wholly responsible, yet the comparisons at this day possess a peculiar interest, and some may be mentioned; thus Whernside (2414 ft.) is stated to be 5340 ft.; Ingleborough (2373 ft.) as 5280 ft.; Penyghent (2273 ft.) as 5220 ft.; Snowdon (3571 ft.) as 3568 ft.; Skiddaw (3058 ft.) as 3270 ft.; and Benewewish (Ben Nevis, 4406 ft.) as 4350 ft. It is noteworthy that while the Yorkshire hills have their true altitudes more than doubled, the other British 'monarchs' are if anything underrated. But the Yorkshireman is proverbially proud of his county, and if his hills are not 'in the run' among British mountains, they at all events cover plenty of ground, so he may still boast that what they lack in height they make up for in breadth! Hurtley died about 1835 and was buried in Kirkby churchyard. His granddaughther, Miss Hurtley, lives at Malham now. She is an active, chatty old dame, (in her 80th year) and keeps a small lodging and refreshment house on the Gordale road.

Malham Cove, which we must now describe, is about 15 minutes walk from the village. It is one of the grandest inland cliffs in Britain, and has certainly no parallel in Yorkshire, having been likened to the great cliff which rises above the fountain of Castalia at Delphi, in Greece. It is caused, we may remark, by the great Craven Fault which has thrown down the limestone southwards from about 1200 ft. at Malham to at least 3000 ft. at Ingleton. Here the white rock * is exposed for nearly a quarter of a mile in a crescent-shaped battery rising perpendicularly to a height of 286 ft., and the limestone descends still another 200 ft. below the base of the cliff. It is formed of three

---

* This singular *whiteness* is caused by the perpetual action of the water dissolving the carbonate of lime which so thoroughly "whitewashes" the surface as to render it very clean and often distinctly visible at very long distances.

successive narrow ledges, along which small animals have strayed, and helplessly perished in the attempt to return. Such an incident occurred many years ago when a fox and dog in full chase got on to the narrowest point of the middle ledge, and being unable to proceed further or turn round, both were precipitated into the bottom and killed. The cliff is the habitat of innumerable jackdaws, and is also one of the few natural breeding places of the house-martin. The vicinity of the Cove also abounds in many botanical rarities.

MALHAM COVE.

—too rare indeed to be specially localized as some are now unfortunately nearly extinct. In inaccessible crannies of the limestone pavement above, grow the maiden-hair spleenwort, green spleenwort, harts-tongue and other beautiful ferns, which at one time were very abundant on the surrounding moors. But large quantities have been carried off, only to perish beneath the smoky canopies of large towns. This is a great pity, as fern and flower in profusion in their natural haunts give unspeakable charm and interest to a place, of untold value to the beholder in many a dull after-day. Ruskin once visited Malham, and this is what he wrote of the Cove in the Parable of Jotham (Prosperina). "In Malham Cove the stones of the brook were softer with moss than any silken pillow ; the crowded oxalis leaves yielded to the pressure of the hand, and were not felt ; the cloven leaves of the herb-robert and robed clusters of its companion overflowed every rent in the rude crags with living balm ; there was scarcely a place left by the tenderness of the happy things where one might not lay down one's forehead on their warm softness and sleep."

The **Source of the Aire** is popularly accepted to be Malham Cove, but frequent experiments have been made with the result that the bulk of the waters issuing from the base of the Cove are found to be derived from the stream flowing from the Tarn and disappearing at two 'swallow holes' a short distance below. The Tarn again is fed by other streams descending from the neighbourhood of Capon Hall, Fountains Fell and Hard Flask. There are also two springs known as 'Airehead,' about a half-mile below Malham village, and strange to relate, when the waters of the tarn have been held back and suddenly liberated these springs are found to be 'flooded' fully half-an-hour before the Cove water, although the latter is a mile nearer the 'sinks' below the tarn. This can only be explained on the supposition that the passage to Airehead is comparatively straight and rapid, whilst that to the Cove is over a series of lofty waterfalls (the drop from the tarn to the base of the Cove being about 600 feet) into deep or expansive pools or reservoirs, and along a channel, broad, shallow and cavernous ; and from the ordinarily sluggish and tardy exit of the waters at the Cove, it would appear to indicate the presence of some such stupendous wide-spreading cavern behind the face of this cliff in which is one or more lofty cascades. During the great floods of 1775 and 1824 when the tarn overflowed and choked the "sinks," the water poured down the open gorge and over the depression in the middle of the Cove in a broad magnificent cataract, "superior," says White in his *West Riding of Yorkshire*, "in depth and little inferior in grandeur to the falls of Niagara." Such indeed was the volume of water (stated by an eye-witness to have been nine yards in width)  and expanse of spray that spectators were unable to approach within a hundred yards of the fall without being drenched through. But to return ; we may observe that the underground limestone appears to be so fissured and bisected with hidden unknown streams, that to determine accurately the sources and directions of the many springs that go to feed the Aire seems practically impossible. Still many useful experiments may be tried. The stream, it is worth noting, descending near the old Smelt Mills on Malham Moor was long considered to be identical with that appearing at the Cove, but on analysis the upper current was found to be from two to three degrees harder than at its issue, notwithstanding its subterranean passage over a limestone bed of at least $1\frac{1}{2}$ miles ; a degree of hardness we may add approximating nearly to that of an old well situated in front of Prior Hall. This well is 42 ft. deep, and maintains a degree of extreme coldness even in the hottest weather, and is regularly resorted to at such seasons by local farmers for use in butter-making. It is supposed to flow from a spring rising in Cowden Hill, but singularly another well in the same direction close by is often found to be dry when the other has preserved its never-failing supply. A very remarkable phenomenon is also attached to this hill. About every five years we are told a body of water rushes out of the foot of Cowden and down Finkle Street to the *Lister's Arms* Inn, with such violence as to tear away the macadam of the road in parts down to the rock. This torrential discharge continues for seven or eight hours, after which the scene resumes its wonted stillness and the grass reclothes its denuded slopes. The Sabbatic river of Syria, which in the time of Josephus flowed every Sabbath day, but now flows every third day, is an analogous phenomenon. Last Autumn (1890) there was a slight eruption, but it is now about ten years since any serious damage was done by this singular freak of Nature.

Malham Tarn may next claim our attention. It

is situated on Malham Moor at an altitude of 1250 feet ; the beautiful Tarn House (W. Morrison, Esq., M.P., J.P.) above its northern shore, clothed with luxuriant wood, having an elevation above mean sea-level of 1314 feet. It was built and occupied as a summer residence by the first Lord Ribblesdale. The lake (the largest natural expanse in Yorkshire) covers about 150 acres, and occupies a shallow basin of impervious Silurian slate, overlaid by a loose conglomerate, which thus holds the water—nowhere more than 14 feet deep. It abounds in fine trout and perch, "the best fishing," declared Charles Kingsley, "in the whole earth." Trout of 11 lb. and perch of 5 lb., observes our old friend Hurtley, have been taken from its waters, but unless the author's native pride, already alluded to, which doubled the heights of the Craven mountains likewise doubled the weight of the fish, they must have very much deteriorated, for ordinarily the trout (of two kinds) run from 1 lb. to 3 lb., sometimes a little over. The fish were probably introduced by the monks of Fountains, to whom the tarn was a valuable means of income. The shingly margin of the lake is fringed with the creamy flowers of Parnassus, and other rare and damp-loving plants. Over the waters skim or dive numbers of coots, moorhens, teal, and occasionally a few mallard. The wood wren, little grebe, and (on one occasion) the tufted duck, nest in the vicinity of the tarn. In winter-time many rare migratory birds also visit this interesting neighbourhood. Just above the north shore are a couple of small but beautifully-incrusted caverns.

Gordale Scar, about a mile east of Malham, though formed by the same natural convulsion which produced Malham Cove, is as a scene much more impressive than it, inasmuch as it creates a feeling of wonderment almost akin to horror on first beholding "its ponderous and marble jaws." The visitor unaware of the approach to this sublime scene is taken by surprise, for suddenly, as by the power of some giant necromancer, the angle which bounds the desolate valley is turned, and the spectacle of astonishing grandeur stands revealed. As a rock scene it has few if any peers in these islands, and no less an authority than the great traveller Bishop Pocock, declares that during the whole of his wanderings in Syria and the East, he never met with anything

so sublimely impressive. The overhanging cliffs on the left
tower to a height of 300 feet, in gloomy weather touched by

GORDALE SCAR.

floating clouds, whilst the opposing massive stone walls of
scarcely inferior altitude likewise project, thus forming as it

were, a great roofless cavern. Hundreds of sable-plumed jackdaws make the gloomy place their home, whilst from the yew-clad, dizzy, topmost heights, a quick-sighted kestrel may now and then be seen darting down upon its unsuspecting prey. The centre of the ravine is piled up with boulders and loose fragments of stone, the accumulated debris of countless centuries, denuded from the encompassing strata. Coming from the moors above a body of water rolls down about a third of the height in a series of foaming cascades, which in times of flood present an unusually wild scene, blowing their "hoarse trumpets from the steep" with deafening noise. And particularly so after the autumn rains, when the volume and sound of the water, combined with its gloomy environment, renders the scene inexpressibly grand, and far exceeding in impressiveness the famous cataract of Lodore, in Cumberland. Ordinarily it is quite practicable to ascend the chasm and reach the moors above by crossing the stream and climbing the rocks by footholds on the left side of the waterfall. This is frequently done by ladies at the risk, perhaps, of a little wetting by the ascending spray. The present course of the stream was occasioned, about the year 1730, by a terrific thunder storm bursting the rocky barrier through which the current is now diverted. Formerly it descended the centre of the pass above, as is evident from the coating of tufa or thick limy deposit covering the large rock in the middle of the old channel observed on the way up. The water is of a decided buff colour, caused by its holding in solution the lime dissolved and re-deposited on its passage downward; these incrustations in the bed of the stream giving it a very clayey appearance. The action is what is erroneously called 'petrifying;' objects immersed in the water becoming in time incrusted (not permeated) or fossilized with the carbonate of lime. The whole of the cliffs forming this stupendous chasm consist of carboniferous limestone, excepting a bed of older Silurian grit exposed at the foot of the gorge. The original dislocation must, one would think, have involved a dynamic power sufficient to shake the whole earth. That it is due in the first instance to a 'fault' or throw in the strata, and subsequently to the slow operations of Nature, is perfectly evident. Several minor 'faults' are observable in and around the chasm; one such appears at the top of the first fall where the rock is divided by a gap a few inches wide; the throw being slight, and is well seen higher up,—not the result of water separation, but an obvious dislocation caused at the great upheaval. The worn and cavernous character of the base suggests the battery of sea waves at some time. That both sea and ice have filled this valley (as they have covered the rest of Yorkshire) is of course admissible, but the period of such attrition is too remote to have left sufficiently identifiable traces of their intrusion at this spot. The stones of the dry bed are sharp and angular and not water-worn, and every appearance of ice-scratchings must long since have weathered off. The appearance of the gorge must in fact be attributed to the combined chemical and mechanical agency of the atmosphere: to frost and rain, and the erosive power of water, which are grinding it back, so that in ages yet far remote the chasm will become a huge winding defile in the mountains. There is no doubt, however, that it was originally a great cavern, the roof having fallen in when worn down to a mere shell. It was then much higher then at present. The laureate Wordsworth wrote a sonnet on the place, and the poet Gray (whose description of it appears in almost every account of Gordale) said that it made an impression upon him that would "last with life."

As already stated the district is singularly rich in plant-life, and the following list of specialities will be useful to the botanist. It will be noted that among the species named several Arctic and maritime types occur.

Flowering Plants.—*Thalictrum montanum. Armeria maritima. Actæa spicata, Cochlearia alpina, Draba muralis, D. incana. Thlaspi occitanum, Viola lutea, Alsine verna, Hypericum montanum. Geranium sanguineum. G. sylvaticum. Hippocrepis comosa, Rosa tomentosa. R. pimpinellifolia, Poterium sanguisorba. Alchemilla montana. Potentilla alpestris. Rubus saxatilis. Geum intermedium, Pyrus rupicola. Ribes petræum, Saxifraga hypnoides. Sedum villosum, S. telephium. Galium boreale, G. sylvestre, Scabiosa columbaria. Carduus heterophyllus, C. nutans, Taraxacum erythrospermum, T. palustre. Antennaria dioica, Hieracium Gibsoni, Vaccinium oxycoccos, Polemonium cœruleum, Pinguicula vulgaris, Calamintha acinos. Myosotis sylvatica* (a mountain form). *Primula farinosa. Salix phylicifolia, Taxus baccata.*

Potamogeton densus, P. lucens, P. perfoliatus. Orchis incarnata, Gymnadenia albida, Serratula tinctoria, Convallaria majalis.

Mosses.—*Sphagnum deflexum, Gymnostomum curvirostrum, G. tortile, Dicranum calcareum, Seligeria pusilla, Trichostomum tophaceum. T. mutabile, T. crispulum* and *v. elatum. Barbula recurvifolia, B. intermedia, Zygodon viridissimus. Z. Nowellii, Ulota Bruchii, Orthotrichum Lyellii, Splachnum sphæricum, S. ampullaceum, Funaria calcarea, Philonotis calcarea, Breutelia arcuata. Zieria julacea, Bryum roseum, Cinclidium stygium* (at the north-west of the Tarn, one of its three English stations), *Mnium cuspidatum, M. affine, M. serratum, M. subglobosum, Fissidens crassipes, Cinclidotus fontinaloides, Fontinalis gracilis, Antitrichia curtipendula, Anomodon riticulosus, Pseudoleskea catenulata, Cylindrothecium concinnum, Orthothecium rufescens, Brachythecium rivulare, Eurhynchium pumilum, Rhynchostegium murale, Hypnum rugosum. H. virescens. H. giganteum. H. stramineum,* and *H. scorpioides.*

Lichens.—*Leptogium lacerum, Ramalina calicaris. R. fastigiata, Peltigera polydactyla. Parmelia perlata. P. olivacea, Squamaria crassa, S. gelida, S. saxicola, Placodium murorum, Physcia tenella, Solorina saccata. S. limbata. Ramalina farinacea. Evernia prunastri. Lecanora rupestris. L. calcarea, Lecidea cupularis, L. concentrica. L. exanthematica. L. cœruleo-nigricans, Endocarpon miniatum* and *v. complicatum. E. fluviatilis. E. rufescens,* and *Graphis scripta.*

The walks and drives from Malham are many and varied. For the day visitor the following are recommended.

Malham to the Tarn and Water-Sinks and back by the Cove; or by Janet's Cave to Gordale, climbing the Scar (*as described on p.* 285) **and across the Moor to the Tarn, and back by the Cove.** Time required in either case about three hours. To the Tarn ascend the Cove road about 1¼ m. to the gate at the road top, which enter and proceed to the end of the pasture, whence the path diverges *r.* to the Lower Tarn Ho., and the water side is reached in view of the Tarn Ho. on its north slope. After viewing the **Tarn** follow the stream at its outlet about ½ m. down to the **Water-Sinks**, (1250 ft.), where the water may be seen in two places, divided by the wall, disappearing amongst limestone pebbles at the foot of a low hill. The water is clear and drinkable. Hence the wall may be followed straight down 1¾ m. to the Cove, following the old channel of the stream that once ran over its summit, but the limestone is now so much 'denuded' and abounding in 'sinks,' that the chances of a repetition of such a scene as we have mentioned, as witnessed twice within the last century, are becoming day by day more remote. This gorge is very rough and in parts precipitous. The better way from the Aire-Sinks is to round the hill (where the upper water drops) by a distinct track, and follow the wall side east about 100 yds. to the stile. Here a well-defined path continues beneath the scars about ¾ m. until a field is reached on the east side of the **Cove** top, which is descended to a gate that opens on to the summit pavement (1000 ft.) The view hence over Lancashire as far as Pendle Hill (whence the Cove is visible) and the long range of the Pennines, is very fine. The sharp top of Flasby Fell to S.E., and the peculiar glacial knolls about Gargrave stand out very conspicuously. Crossing or skirting the outer edge of the deeply-fissured pavement, the wall may be followed a short distance and the grassy slopes descended (try the echo!) on the west side to the foot of the Cove. The Cove, Tarn. &c., are described on the preceding pages.

Malham through Little Gordale to Janet's Cave and back, 2½ m. About a ¼ m. above the last houses on the Gordale road a step-stile on *r.* (op. a row of thorns) leads down fields towards a barn, near which a foot-bridge crosses the Gordale beck, with the fine woods of Hanlith Gill in front. By keeping this side of the stream, a walk of little more than ½ m. conducts through the wooded ravine of Little Gordale to **Janet's Cave**, a charming sylvan retreat, of which, in the words of Milton, we may justly exclaim,

"In shadier bower
More sacred and sequestered, though but feigned,
Pan or Sylvanus never slept, nor Nymph
Nor Faunus haunted."

A small cascade set within a living framework of moss and foliage,— in Autumn the scarlet berries of the rowan or witch-tree contrasting beautifully with the white foam, renders the scene exceedingly attractive. And what more fit abiding place than this for Queen Janet and her airy little people, whose humble dwelling, guarded by the oft-swollen stream. we see in the rock above! Imagination alone is left to picture the lone witching hour when the moon-silvered waterfall pours forth its music to the dance of the fairies! Emerging from this cool and shady recess the visitor descends a field path to a small gate, whence the return to Malham may be made *l.* by the high-road ; or *r.* to Gordale Scar.

Malham to Tranlands Gill and back by Kirkby, 3½ m. Round by the Wesleyan Chapel and up an old lane *r.* and then *l.* proceeding through the gate-way at the top to Tranlands House. with its witch-scaring horse-shoe conspicuous on the door. Many other houses around Malham may be found with one or more such horse-shoes nailed to their doors, in accordance with a belief. still more or less prevalent in Craven. in their power to act as a charm against the evil doings of witches and wise men ; and associated likewise from an unknown era in the minds of most people at the present day as omens of good luck. Lord Nelson, we are told. had a horse-shoe nailed to the mast of the *Victory*—for luck ! But, alas! it ill-requited him on the day of Trafalgar. From the house the Gill can be descended, and the stream followed to its head, about half-a-mile. The water flows beneath crumbling Yoredale shales, by a larch plantation, and the grassy way is strewn with wild geraniums. stitchwort. milkwort, and other floral treasures, and in the Spring-time primroses, violets, and flowering thorns display their odorous bloom. A rough track hence leads up to Acraplats House and on to the Settle road, whence a descent is made to Kirkby (1 m.) and back by the main road.

Ascent of the Weets (1380 ft.) **by Hanlith Gill and back.** Time 3-4 hours. The rugged woods of Hanlith Gill constitute an attractive walk in themselves. Proceed by the route described to Janet's Cave as far as the foot-bridge near the conspicuous barn. The watercourses forming the acclivitous Gill give it some likeness to a large W, the left lateral branch shaping the ravine of Little Gordale, already mentioned, whilst the tripartite eastern branches, rising before the spectator, form the Gill proper. The woods are very luxuriant, and reveal many pretty glimpses of dell scenery. In Autumn they teem with hazel nuts, blackberries, and groups of scarlet-fruited ash, which, amid the various tinted foliage, conspire to make up a delightful picture. To the top of the Weets from the foot-bridge we must keep on the left side of the middle gill, ascending the open grassy slope with this gill on our *r.*, and so round the top of it, and through the pasture that lies just below the moor-land ridge which forms the summit of the Weets. A few dark weathered gritstones mark the top. The view is very fine, especially southwards over the fells and villages of the Lancashire border country. In this direction we see Pendle, Boulsworth, and various points of the south-western Penines, with the moors about Hebden Bridge, Haworth, and Keighley. Westward, Ryeloaf, Kirkby Fell, and the cairn on Pike Daw are conspicuous, whilst that on Gordale Crag stands a little north of our view-point. Eastwards, the eye takes in a wide range of country bounded by Gt. Whernside and the Wharfedale hills, with the white-quarried summit of Boss Moor intervening. To the south-east the sharp cones of Flasby Fell appear, and the fertile district of middle Craven. The tourist may descend by the way he came, or pursue a track northward about ¼ m. on to the Gordale road 1¼ m. from Malham.

Ascent of Ryeloaf (1790 ft.) **and Kirkby Fell** (1790 ft.) **and back by Kirkby.** Time about 4 hours. This is a capital half-day's outing, the views, especially from Ryeloaf, being unsurpassed in interest and extent by anything in Craven. Opposite Armstrong's Temperance Hotel a stile is entered leading up to a lane, which cross and ascend the lane, forward through fields by a path and stiles all the way until the stone barn in the hollow is reached, with the cairn on Pike Daw up on *r.* Cross the Sell Gill burn (a tributary of the Aire) here, and continue straight up the fields by a path skirting the wall-side, with a small plantation a short distance on *l.* By this route no more complete or characteristic view of Malham Cove can possibly be had ; its entire circumference being exposed almost from base to summit. The whole of the rock on the north side, it will be observed, is composed of the scar limestone, which is cut off by the 'fault' that brings up the grits southwards to the line of scars. When opposite the plantation an early outcrop of the sandstone grit may be seen in the stream by the wall side. Follow the path up to the broken gritstone summit, which the path skirts on *l.*, and make straight for the wall and on to the heather, whence the cairn on **Kirkby Fell** is reached in five minutes. The view is very fine but scarcely equal to that from **Ryeloaf**, which is soon reached by crossing the depression opposite (to the west). Here our stand-point (1790 ft.) is central, and in every direction unobstructed. Northwards the whole of Hard Flask is spread out, looking in any weather magnificently wild. From Kirkby Fell the Tarn House and all the watery expanse before it can be seen, but from here no house or sign of visible life appears to break the impressive solitude of the vast plain. Far away it stretches until the scars of Littondale separate it from the huge bulk of Great Whernside, seen towering to the north-east, and divided by the depression in upper Wharfedale from the conspicuous eminence of Buckden Pike. Eastward the Great Wham caps the summit of Grassington Moor, and S.E. we are able to descry the craggy top of Simon's Seat, with the intervening range of Cracoe and Rylstone Fells as far south as Embsay Crag. South again we have Pendle and the Lancashire moors, whilst the volcanic-like cones of Flasby Fell look extremely picturesque. with the broad vale of Airedale narrowing down to Bingley, and backed by the heights of Baildon and Idle Hill. To the north and west the view is wild and grand, including four principal Craven mountains, viz.: Whernside (2414 ft.), Ingleborough (2373 ft.), Penyghent (2273 ft.), and Fountains Fell (2170 ft.), with a vast tract of upper Ribblesdale reaching almost to the confines of the Lake District. Lunesdale, and when sufficiently clear, the sea off Morecambe are also discernible. After enjoying this extensive and magnificent prospect, a descent may be made towards a plantation S.E., and the wall-side followed down by a streamlet to a gate, whence a good grassy road goes alongside the plantation (Acraplats) and through a number of gateways (*please shut the gates*) until the Settle road is reached at the guide post. A descent of 1 m. will bring the visitor to Kirkby, and thence straight to Malham.

Ascent of Fountains Fell (2170 ft.) The southern slopes of this Fell form the northernmost gathering ground of the waters of the Aire, and the tourist, so inclined, may amuse himself by tracing their several courses with a view to elucidating the long-vexed problem of the source of the Aire. A fine whole day should be selected for this trip, and suitable provision taken, as the only 'restaurants' likely to prove serviceable in this sparsely inhabited region are the open-air ones provided by Nature among the clear springs of the mountain sides. The distance from Malham to the top of the Fell may be reckoned at 6 m., covering a rise of about 1500 ft., chiefly at the beginning and end of the walk. Take the

Cove road and leave the Tarn on *r.* to Capon Hall (farms). Between the Lower Train Ho. and the Higher Train Ho. passed on the way is a run of level ground (about a mile) called the Streets, where in old times horses used to be trained for racing, &c. It is the longest piece of open level ground to be found in this wide, rugged district. A century or more ago, when Boss Moor Fair was one of the great farming events of the year in Craven, whole armies, literally, of Scotch drovers came this way with their herds of black cattle, ponies and sheep. They traversed these wilds from the Highlands every Autumn for the big fair held on the lofty summit of the moor (1080 ft.), some two miles north of Hetton, and many strange tales are related of the cute things said and done at these famous annual gatherings, and of deeds perpetrated too, we opine, not always of the most peaceable character. Indeed, more than one human skeleton has been found with bones rotting beneath some cavernous rock on these wild moors, which ominous discoveries would appear to point to one aspect at least of these lawless times. It is now nearly a century since an old public house called the *Waste* Inn, which stood at the top of the lane near the Druids' Circle at Bordley (*see* next route) was taken down, as was another, appropriately named *Lone Head* Inn, a little to the south, also frequented by the drovers in the old days.

About half-a-mile past Capon Hall a long wall runs due north to the south summit of Fountains Fell, which may be followed and along the top as far as the Tarn. On the north-western declivity is a 'swallow-hole' in the limestone called Jingling Hole, into which a stream from the gritstone fell above is lost, to appear again at Neals Ing, about a mile lower down. Stones thrown into the chasm produce a sound like breaking china, hence the name of it. Just above the Hole is a pretty large cave. The bulk of the mountain is built up of main limestone, with a cap of millstone grit, and intervening is a thick bed (580 ft.) of Yoredale shales, &c. The view is similar to that which we have described as obtainable from Ryeloaf, excepting that the contiguity of Penyghent shews the precipitous mass of that mountain to greater advantage, and also the wild extent of country northward over Langstrothdale to the summit ridge of Wensleydale, is seen better than from the more southern hill named. From Jingling Hole a descent may be made by Thornah Gill to Rough Close and Westside Ho. by a track on to the Capon Hall road for Malham. The east side of Fountains Fell is steep, and consequently the ascent from Higher Train Ho. over Knowe Fell is not recommended.

Malham to Grassington by Skirethorns, 8 m. By the Gordale road direct to Lee Gate House (2½ m.). The road is hilly, the highest part between Malham (640 ft.) and Gordale bridge is 827 ft. Janet's Cave (1 m.) may be visited on the way, and also Gordale Scar by leaving the road at the farmhouse. From Lee Gate (1200 ft.) the rambler may shorten the distance a little to Skirethorns (3¼ m.) by crossing to Bordley (1 m.) and thence by Height Farm; but if he prefer to follow the straighter path he must continue to ascend a short distance past Lee Gate Ho. on *r*. to the guide-post (8 m. to Settle ; 3¼ m. to Kilnsey). A wild prospect is obtained of the limestone fells in front, with Hawkswick Clowder (1350 ft.) and the Parson's Pulpit (1760 ft.) conspicuous ; and hereabouts the lover of wild flowers will be delighted with a great profusion of the pretty yellow mountain pansy. Turn *r*. along the lane which terminates in an open pasture opposite a plantation, with Kilnsey moor on *l*. To **Kilnsey** the *l*. wall should be followed ; whilst our route is by the long wall on *r*., obtaining a good view southwards of the pointed summit of Flasby Fell and the bossy end of Rylstone Fell. Near the second gate-way (through which we have to pass) is the remains of an ancient (supposed) Druids' temple, consisting of a mound 3 ft. high and about 150 ft. in circumference, where was formerly a complete stone circle with a large flat stone at one end called the **Druids' Altar**. The circle appears to have been destroyed in building the adjoining wall, and all that is to be seen now are three upright stones raised above the earthwork. We now enter a long lane and in about ½ m. observe on *r*. a three-arched cave situate in a low limestone cliff above the lonely **Height Farm** (1200 ft.). The occupant of this farm was tempted out of a natural curiosity to open this cavern in the Spring of last year (1890). On digging some ten yards into it numerous remains of foxes and deer, and skulls, bones and teeth of various extinct animals and birds, were found embedded in the stiff clay which blocked the passage into the cavern.* They are at present in possession of the farmer. There seems little doubt but what at some distant period the cave has been inhabited, for in the immediate vicinity an iron spear-head and fragments of rude earthen vessels have also been turned up, relics, evidently. of the aboriginal tribes who once roamed over these wild hills. The cave faces the west, and growing upon the scars about it are various kinds of ferns, as the wall-rue, polypody, and black-stalked spleenwort. In a neighbouring pasture, called Long Close, is another (doubtless ossiferous) cavern, but not yet opened. We now descend upon the picturesque and pleasantly-situated little hamlet of **Skirethorns**, with its magnificent plane-tree, covering probably a circumference of shade from 200 ft. to 250 ft. In the Bell Bank wood opposite, near another large and conspicuous plane-tree, there was found in October, 1880, the skeleton of an adult male person. It was stripped of every article of clothing, and there was absolutely nothing left by which the body might be identified. No one from this neighbourhood had been missing within living memory, and how long the body had lain there it is impossible to tell. It was ultimately buried in Linton churchyard. From Skirethorns the Kettlewell road is reached, whence *r*. to the Primitive Methodist Chapel, and sharp *l*. over the substantial five-arch Wharfe bridge up to Grassington.

Malham to Settle, 6 m. By the main road *via* Kirkby it is 7 m., but to those who are not afraid of a little rough walking the bridle route will be preferred. Ascending the Cove (or Capon Hall)

* The discovery was announced by the author in the *Naturalist* for July, 1890.

road about ¾ m. a sharp turn *l.* is made towards a gate in the corner, and the next gate above it (250 yds.), at foot of which is a line of stones, is the point at which to leave the road. It is directly opposite the face of Malham Cove, and a good view of it and of Airedale southwards to Cross Hills is obtained from here. Open the gate and follow the wall side up ¾ m. to the gate at the top before you, whence a broad grassy track continues under **Kirkby Fell** (1790 ft.), over the middle and most elevated part of the way between Malham and Settle. From the highest point (1550 ft.) the path goes down beside limestone crags with the cairn on **Ryeloaf** (1790 ft.) conspicuous up on *l.* The ascent of this notable mountain (*see* p. 289) can very readily be made from here by dipping into the gully and then following the ridge up to its summit, which is visible most of the way. Continuing beneath the ferny scars we soon arrive opposite the large **Stockdale Farm**, a dwelling whose lonely and romantic situation (1250 ft.) reminds us not a little of Wordsworth's description of the abode of the 'Solitary' in the poem of the *Excursion*,

> "Behold!
> Beneath our feet, a little lowly vale,
> A lowly vale, and yet uplifted high
> Among the mountains; even as if the spot
> Had been, from eldest time, by wish of theirs
> So placed,—to be shut out from all the world!—
> A quiet treeless nook, with (two) green fields,
> And one bare dwelling; one abode, no more!"

When the snows of winter fall heavily on this high land, the solitary mansion is sometimes inaccessible for weeks together. According to an incised stone (S F 1688) the house has been built some two centuries, but it has at various times since been added to and improved. The farm comprises some 5000 acres, and extends two miles up and two miles down the valley. Interesting it is to note at this elevation that of bush fruit (especially the rasp and gooseberry) excellent average crops are produced, whilst the soil too seems well adapted for the growth of rhubarb. Apples on the other hand appear unsuited to this situation and may be regarded as a failure. Now resuming our descent, we obtain an imposing view of the magnificent Langcliffe Scars, rising terrace above terrace, and culminating in huge round white bosses like the domes of some mighty citadel. The valley hereabouts bears evidence of excavations by ice, for in the large heaps of mixed gravel we have plain record of that far-back frigid epoch when enormous glaciers ploughed their way down these rugged heights. Coming to the junction of the roads, (*l.* to Kirkby by Scaleber Waterfall, ¼ m., *see* p. 268) a descent of 1 m. is made past the Roman Catholic Church into Settle.

Many enjoyable walks and drives may be combined with the preceding, or with other routes and places already described, making a stay at Malham of almost any length of time a delightful experience.

CORRECTIONS AND ADDITIONS.

P. xxix. "Boragineæ." In column, "Where found," move up a line, thus: Hound's-tongue, Near Skipton, 7.

P. 22, L. 5. Omit, "of St. John of Jerusalem." For an exhaustive and learned account of the origin and career of this ancient military-religious body, the reader should consult the late Mr. Chas. G. Addison's "History of the Knights Templars, the Temple Church, and the Temple." As the seat of the great Lord Darcie (*see* p. 17) there is also a description of the "Castle of Temple Hurst" in Mr. Froude's "History of England."

P. 26. Add "largely" after last word on page.

P. 153, L. 37. For "a few weeks later" *read* "in September, 1890."

P. 153, L. 43. Further confirmatory discoveries of large quantities of iron scoriæ, charred wood, and portions of broken earthen crucibles have been made by Mr. Preston, in the neighbourhood of Eldwick, in April and May, 1891. Also a good flint arrow-head, leaf-shaped, rather over an inch in length, has been unearthed near the spot where the flint scraper was found (*see* p. 154).

P. 191, L. 35. For Wall *read* Hall.

P. 264. The Hospice Howe or Hospital Plantation, so called from a former owner of land having left a cottage (the ruins of which are still here) to accommodate two old people, with a rent-charge to allow them a small sum yearly. Some forty or fifty years ago, when the building fell into disrepair, the then owner commuted the rent-charge by investing, in the name of trustees, a sum in the Funds, the interest of which provides a comfortable yearly allowance to two aged inhabitants.

P. 276, L. 12. To "Selby and Armley" may be added Pontefract.

INDEX.

The figures in heavy type indicate the page where the place is specially described.

A

Aberdeen, 191
Aberford, xx., xxiv.. 79
Addingham, 200, 204
Adel, Botany *pass.*, **66**, 77, 93, 117
Adwalton, 72
Aire, origin of name. 8
  ,, pollution of, 21. 27, 40
  ,, source of, 270, 281
Airedale, Altitudes, lxiv.
  ,, Angling, lix.
  ,, Botany, xiii.
  ,, Drainage Act, 219
  ,, Folk-Lore, xlix.
  ,, Geology, v.
  ,, Heifer, 178
  ,, Ornithology, xliii.

Airedale, Wolf. last in, 43, 68
Airmyn, lxiv., 1, 6, 9
Airton, Botany *pass.*, lix., lxiv., 258, 266, **269**
Aldersley family, 215
Allerton (Bradford), xx.
  ,, (Leeds), 68
  ,, Bywater, Boty., *pass.*
Altitudes, lxiv.
Alwoodley, 74
Angling, lix.
Apperley, viii., lxiv., Botany *pass.*, 107
Arkwright, Sir R., 180
Armley, ix., lxiv., 8, **63**, 276
Arncliffe Clowder, Boty. *pass.*

B

Baildon, x., Botany *pass.*, lxii., **144**, 160, 266
Baildon Moor, Antiquities, 147
Bank-Newton, 254, 256
Barden, xxxix., 173. 245
Bardsey, 77
Barwick-in-Elmet. xiv., liii, 78
Beaconsfield, Lord, 174
Beal, 24, 154
Beamsley Beacon, 204, 217, 244
Beckwithshaw, 77, 143
Beeston, 68
Bell Busk, 144, 263, 264, **265**
Bingley, viii., Botany *pass.*, xlv., xlvi., lxii., lxiv., 9, 10, 29, 148, 154, 160, 161, **164**, 254

Bingley, Vicinity of, 172
  ,, Walks around, 173
Birkin, xli., 23
Bolton Abbey, vii., 157, 202, 204, 238, 243, 246, 249, 277
Booth Ferry, xxxv., 7, **8**, 10
Boston Spa, 62, **80**.
Bowling, x., 109, 121. 123, 126
Botany, xiii.
Bradford, ix., xlvii., liv., lxiv., 72, **121**, 238
Bradford Parks, 135
  ,, Public Build'gs, 130
  ,, Townships, 135
Bradley, lxii., 215, **217**
Braithwaite, xxxiv., 192

B—continued.

Bramham, xvii., **80**, 167
Bramhope, **72**, 113
Bramley, li., liii., lxiv., **96**
„ Hall Ghost, 99
Brayton, xvi., xxv., xxvi., xli.,17
„ Barf, xviii., xix., xxvi, liv., 20
Brighton, 194
British Village, anct., 150
„ relic, anct., 112
Brontë family, 110, 186
„ Museum, 187

Brontë Waterfall, 187
Brotherton, xi., Botany *pass.*, lxiv., 24, 28, 145
Broughton, xvi., xxvii., 27, 238, **239**, 241, 272
Bubwith, 33
Burley, 73, 155
Burwins (Castle), 240
Busfeild family, 168, 172, 184, 195
Byram, 24

C

Calton, 261, 270, 273
Calverley, Botany *pass.*, li., **101**, 115, 129
Calversike Hill, 194
Camblesforth, xvi., xxi., xli.,16
Camhill Cross, 191
Carlton (Leeds), 224
„ (Pontefract), 19, 27, 224
„ (Skipton), liii., lxiv., 223, **224**, 241
Carlton (Snaith), xv., xxvii., lxiii., 16, 20, 224
Carlton (Yeadon), 155, 224
Carr Head, 214
Castleford, xi., Botany *pass.*, lvii., lxiv., 5, 8, 31, **39**
Chapel Haddlesey, 22
Charlestown, xxix., xxxiii.
Chimney, anct., 253
Cleckheaton, xl., 123
Clifford family, 28, 117, 232
Coates family, 218, 221
Collingham, xl., 78

Colne, 189, 212
Congreve, Wm., 77 [294
Coniston Cold, lxiv., 263, **264**,
Cononley, ix., lx., 218, 220
Cookridge, 95
Corrections & Additions, 294
Cottingley (Bingley), Botany *pass.*, lxii., 161
Cottingley (Leeds), 64
Cowick, 16
Cowlaughton, viii., 193, 212
Cowling, xvii., 192, 212
Cowper Cote, 261
„ Cross, 193
Cracoe, 240, 249
Craven Baths, 238
„ Harriers, 254, 261
„ Heifer, 231
„ Superstitions, lv.
Cromwell, Oliver, 218, 257, 262, 273
Crosshills, 29, 212
Crow Hill Bog, 191

D

Darrington, **19**, 27
Devonshire, Duke of, 182, 221, 236
Dewsbury, 151
Dickens, 159
Dobrudden, 151
Dolgelly, 189
Doncaster, 39, 44
Double-Stones, ix., 202

Drake-Hill, 178
Draughton, vii., xviii., 217, 244
Drax, Botany *pass.*, lxiv., 5, **9**, 63, 156, 165, 167, 172
Drighlington, 71
Druids' Altar, ix. 173, **174**, 186, 204, 243, 292
Druids' Circle, 149, 163
Dyke Nook, 191

E

Eastburn, 206
Eastby, 246
Elbolton Cave, xvi., xxi., 249
Eldwick, Botany *pass.*, 150, 153, **154**, 160, 162, 294
Elslack, vii., 20, 215, **239**

Embsay, 237, **245**, 276
Esholt, Botany *pass.*, 109, **113**, 157
Eshton, 258, 259
  „ Tarn, xxxvi., 259
Exley Head, 189

F

Fairfax family, 19, 49, 53, 72, 125, 172
Farnhill, xix., lxiv., 216
Farnley, 71, 154
Farsley, 105
Faweather, 153, 156
Ferrand family, 161, 172. 226
Ferrybridge, xi., Botany *pass.*, **27**, 129, 165
Flasby Fell, 143, 163, 174, 206, 237, **243**, 290

Flasby Hall, 243
Fleet Farm, 212
Flesher, Rev. J., 202
Folk-Lore, xlix.
Forster, W. E., 128, 133, 155
Fountains Fell.vi..Boty.*pass.*, lxiv., 243, 277, 281, 290
Friars Head, 259
Frizinghall, Botany *pass.*, 122
Fryston, 29, 30
Fungus Foray, 80

G

Gale, Rev. Miles, 184
Gaping Goose, 156
Garforth, xxv., lxiv., 70
  „ family, 198. 264
Gargrave, vii., Botany *pass.*, xlvi., lix., lxiv., 6, 173, 217, 243, 252, **254**, 264
Gargrave House, 263
Gawthorpe Hall (Bingley), 173, 178 (Harewood), 75
Geology, v.
Gill Grange, 194, 202
Gilstead, 160, 173
Gisburn, vi., xxiii.. xxiv., xxv., xxvii., 115, 242

Gledhow, ix.. 68
Gledstone Hall, 242
Glusburn, 212
Goit-Stock Waterfall, 176
Goole, xii., xiv., xxi , xxix., xxxvii., xliv., xlvi., lxiii, lxiv., 4, 6
Goose-Eye, lxi., 192
Gordale, v., vii., Botany *pass.*, lix., 251, 283
Grassington, xxxviii.. 247, 291
Great Whernside, 143, 218, 251, 289, 290
Guiseley, 115, **142**

H

Halifax, 51, 72
Halton, xxxv., 70
Hambleton Haugh, Botany *pass*, 20.
Hambleton (Skipton), 244
Hanlith Gill, 289
  „ Hall, 270

Hardcastle Crags, 191
Harden, xxxix, 10, 162, 172, **175**
Hare Hills, 190
Harewood, xxxiii., xlvi., 5, **74**, 141, 169
Harlow Hill, 77

H—continued.

Harrogate, vii., 74, 76
Hastings, Marquis of, 111
Hatcliffe Chase, 2
Hawcliffe, 197
Hawksworth, Botany *pass.*, 117, **154**, 262
Haworth, lxiv., 123, **185**, 190
Headingley, 82, 93,
Heaton, 139, 160
Hebden Bridge, 191
Heber family, 242, 262
Hellifield, 258
Heminghorough, 5
Hermit Hole, 185

Hetton, 243, **250**
Hirst, Jemmy, 11
Hitchingstone, 192
Holden Wood, ix, Botany *pass.*, 194, 202
Hollingworth Lake, 161
Hooke, Botany *pass.*, 4
Hope Hill, 151
Horsforth, xx., xlvi., 93
Horton (Gisburn), 242
Houghton, Lord, 29, **133**
Howden, xlvii., 10
Hunslet, 65
Hurst Courtney, lxiii., 20

I

Idle, ix., x., Botany *pass.*, 110, 117
Idle Hill, 119, 290
Ilkley, 155, 156, 163, 175. 178, 195, 202, 239

Ingleborough, 156, 163, 174, 191, 193, 204, 242, 243, 290
Ingleton, v., vii.
Ingrow, xxvi., xxxi., xxxv., 185
Isle of Axholme, xii., 3
Ivegate, 130

J

Jackdaw Crag, 81
Janet's Cave, 287, 288

Jennings Hall, 201
Jingling Hole, 291

K

Keighley, ix., Botany *pass.*, xliv., l., lvii., lxi., lxiv., 166, 178, **181**
Keighley, Excursions from, 185
„ Tram and 'Bus Guide, 185
Keighley Tarn, 194
Kellington, xv., xviii., 24
Kiddall Hall, 79
Kildwick, Botany *pass.*, liii., lix., lxii., lxiv., 206, **207**, 244, 245
Kildwick Bridge, 210
„ 'Buses, 211
„ Grange, 205, 210, 218
„ Hall, 209

Kilnsey, 292
Kippax, Botany *pass.*, 44
King family, 271
Kingsley, Chas., 283
Kirkby Fell, 174, 218, 289, 293
Kirkby-Malham, lxiv., 261, **271**
Kirkstall, ix., xx., 126
„ Abbey, xv., **84**, 97, 242
Knaresborough, 35, 172, 243
Knottingley, xi., xxiv., xxix., xxxviii., lxiv., 24, **25**, 40, 189, 220
Knowsthorpe, 69

L

Lambert family, 202, 252, 261, 270
Laycock, liii., 185, 192
Leathley, 76, 143
Ledsham, Botany *pass.*, 44
Ledston, Botany *pass.*, 44
Leeds, x., xlvii., li., liv., lxiv., **47**, 121, 127, 151, 211, 238
Leeds Angling Clubs, lxii.
„ Castle, 8, 35, 39, **52**, 124, 165
„ Celebrities, 55
„ Cemeteries, 57
„ Environs, 63
„ Newspapers, 56, 240
„ Parks, 61
„ Public Buildings, 56

Leeds Tramways and Omnibus Guide, 62
Leeds, Walks and Drives from, 66
Leeds and Liverpool Canal, 160, 173, 237, 250
Leegap, 65
Lightcliffe, 159
Linton, 78, 249
Lister, Dr. M., 227
Littlebeck, 153, 162
Little London, 113
Livingstone, Dr., 161
Lofthouse, 41
Longfellow family, 76, 94
Lothersdale, vii., 162, 214, 222
Lumb Head, 193, 213

M

Malham, viii., Botany *pass.*, xlvii., li., lxiv., 238, 250, 263, 272, **274**
Malham Cove, Botany *pass.*, lix., lxiv., **243**, 263, 279, 290
Malham, Flowers, &c., 286
„ Moor Water-Sinks, 281, 287
Malham Tarn, v., Botany *pass.*, lix., lxiv., 282
Malsis, 212

Manningham, 123, 125, 159
Marley, viii., Botany *pass.*, 167, 169, 172, 178
Marsden family, 105, 257
Marton, **241**, 273
Matlock, 164
Meanwood, 67
Methley, Botany *pass.*, 41
Moorhouse family, 26, 212, 240, 244, 248
Morley, 71
Morton, xxi., 195

N

Nevison's Leap, 31, 79
New Delight, 192
New Field, 250
Newlay, xvi., xxviii., 96
Newsholme Dene, Botany *pass.*, lxi., 192

Nicholson, John, 162, 169, 175, 178
Norton Tower, 247
Nottingham, 127, 220

O

Oakwell Hall, 72
Oakworth, lxi., 185, 190
Oastler, Richard, 50, 128
Oldfield House, 190
'Old Three Laps,' 194
Open-field System, 189
Orange Rock, 177
Ornithology, xliii.

Osmondthorpe, 70
Otley, 66, **73**, 113, 261
Otley Chevin, xxxvii., 117, **143**, 204
Otterburn, lxiv., 265, **267**, 272
Oulton, 43
Oxenhope, xxvi., 123, 185, 191
Oughtershaw, xxxiv.

P

Pannal, 74
Pecket Well, 192
Penyghent, xli., 174, 290
Pickering, 35
Pollington, xiii., 18

R

Rawcliffe, Botany *pass.*, lxiii., 6, **11**
Rawdon, 105, **110**
Rawson family, 115, 125, 129, 139, 257
Raygill, 214
Redcar, 194
Riddlesden Hall, 178, 194
Ripley, 76
Ripon, 18, 51, 77
Robin Hood's Seat, 150, 195, 202
„ Well, 189
Rodley, 101
Roman Camp, 268

S

Salt, Sir T., 65, 128, 157, 159
Saltaire, Botany *pass.*, lxiv., 65, **157**
Scaleber Waterfall, 268, 293
Scarnber Hill, xx., 243, 260, 261
Sconce, 156
Scosthrop, 269
Selby, Botany *pass.*, 14, **17**, 23, 37, 56, 276
Senior, Job, 155
Settle, xvii., 267, 292
Seven Arches (Leeds), Botany *pass.*, 67
Seven Arches (Saltaire), Botany *pass.*, 160, 161
Shakespeare, 104, 176
Sheffield, 127
Shipley, **137**, 161 [163
„ Glen, Botany *pass.*, 147,
Silsden, xxxiii., lxiv., **200**, 205
„ Reservoir, lx., 202
Skibeden, 243
Skipton, vii., Botany *pass.*, xlvi., liii., lvii., lxiv., 9, 28, 215, **229**

Ponden, lxi., 189
Pontefract, Botany *pass.*, 27, 31. **32**, 44, 294
Poole, 72, **76**,
Priesthorpe, 172

Roman Chest, 196
„ Pottery, 154
Roundhay, Botany *pass.*, 61, 68
Royd House, 216, 218
Rumbalds Moor, ix., Botany *pass.*, xlvi., xlvii., lxiv., 149, 163, 175, 178, 244
Ruskin, 281
Ryeloaf, vii., 163, 273, 289, 293
Rylstone, Botany *pass.*, liv., lxiv., 243, 247, **248**
Ryshworth Hall, 172

Skipton, 'Buses, 238
„ Castle, 195, 225, **232**
„ Castle Woods, 236
„ Parish Church, 235
„ Rock, 237
„ Excursions from, 239
Skirethorns, xvi., 291, 292
Slippery Ford, 193
Snagill, 217
Snaith, lxiv., 6, **14**, 37
Stanbury, 186
Steeton, xviii., xxxii., xl., lx., 194, 196, **197**
Stirton, 252
Stockdale (Settle), 293
Stone Gappe, 222
Story, Robert, 258
St. Helen's Well, xxviii., liv., 259
St. Ive's, 172, 174
Sutton, 192, 205
„ Clough, 205
Swarthadale, 202
Swillington, xvii., xxxix., 45
Swinnow, 97

T

Tadcaster, 39, 67
Tanshelf, 33, 39
Tempest family, 239, 272
Temple Hurst, 21, 24, 294
Temple Newsam, 69
Tewit Hall, 190
Thackeray, W. M., 187
Thackley, 106, 119, 122
Thirsk, 56
Thistle Holme, 117
Thoresby, Ralph, 52, 54, 55
Thorlby, lxiv., 252, 253
Thornbury, 135
Thorne Waste (Goole), Botany *pass.*

Thorner, 70
Thornton, R., 161
Thorp, 118, 249
Thorp Arch, xx., 81
Threapland Gill, 249
Threshfield, vi.
Throup Gill, 202
Tong Park, xxiv., xxxvi.
Towton, 79
Tranlands Gill, 288
Trent Fall, 6
Tunnel Hall Hill, 67
Two-Laws, 189, 191
Tyersal, 135

U

Upper House (Horsforth), 94, 95
Upperwood (Apperley), 110

Upwood, 168, 178, 195
Utley, 196

V

Vermuyden, Sir C., 3

Victoria Tower, 199

W

Wadlands Hall, 105
Wainman Pinnacle, 193, **206**
Wakefield, 41, 51
Water Fryston, 27
Waterton Chantry, 42
Weardley, 169
Wedding-Hall Fold, 214
Weets, ix., 289
Weetwood, xxviii., lxiv.
Wesley, Rev. J., 71, 109, 170
West Haddlesey, 23
Westmacott, R., 42
Westminster Abbey, 78
Wetherby, 77, 80
Wharfedale Hermit, 155
Wheelhouse family, 16
Wheldale, 27, 29, 31
Whin Moor, 77, 78, 79
Whitecote (Bramley), 96
Whitehead, L., 80
Whitkirk, 45, 70

Whitley, 19
Wickham family, 161
Willow Bank, 195
Wilsden, Botany *pass.*, xlviii., lxiv., 177
Wilson family, 256, 258
Winchester Cathedral, 18
Windhill, 118, 137, 138
Winewall, 191
Winterburn, xxiv., xxvi., xl., 254, 259, 260
Winterburn Reservoir, viii., lxiv., 250
Winwidfeld, 77
Witenagemott, 49, 177
Womersley, xi., xiv., 19
Woodhouse Moor, 51, 61, 82, 143
Woodhouse Ridge, ix., xix., xx., 61, 67
Woodlesford, 43

W—continued.

Wordsworth, W., 247
Worth Valley, 181, 185
Wortley, 61, 67
Wreck Farm, 212
Wroe, 'Prophet,' 107

Wrose Hill, 118, 142
Wuthering Heights, 187
Wycoller Hall, 191
Wykeham, Bishop, 161

Y

Yeadon, xix.,xxiv..li.,lxiv.,113,143 (Low Hall), 113

York, 18, 37, 65, 97, 143, 163, 227, 260

LIST OF ILLUSTRATIONS.

	Page
Near Goole	2
Hooke Church	4
Beverley Memorial Tow'r, Airmyn	7
Snaith Old Church	15
Temple Hurst Preceptory	21
Fryston Church	30
Pontefract Castle	32
Leeds, Briggate	46
,, Red Hall	50
,, Municipal Bu'ld'gs	54
Beeston Church	64
Adel Church Porch	66
Harewood House	74
Shire Oak, Headingley	83
Kirkstall Abbey	85
,, Nave	87
,, Ground Plan	90
Bramley (Ducking-Stool)	98
Calverley Old Hall	103
Rawdon Old Hall	111
Yeadon Low Hall	114
Bradford Exchange	120
,, Toll Booth	129
,, Town Hall	131
Shipley (Oldest House)	140
Baildon, Cup-and-Ring Stone	149
Baildon, Earthwork	152

	Page
Baildon, Urn and Spear-h'd	153
,, Flint Scraper	154
Saltaire	158
View of Ingleborough	163
Bingley Main Street	170
Goit Stock Waterfall	176
Heweuden Rally Viaduct	177
A bend in the Aire, Marley	179
Haworth Old Church	186
Bronte Waterfall	188
Haworth	190
Hitchingstone, K'ley Moor	193
Silsden Old Hall	200
,, Rev. J. Flesher's House	201
Waterfall in Holden Gill	203
Kildwick Hall	209
,, Grange	210
,, Bridge	211
Crosshills (old house)	213
Farnhill Hall	216
Skipton, High Street	228
,, Castle	235
Draughton Quarry	245
Friar's Head, Winterburn	260
Kirkby Malham	271
Malham	275
,, Cove	280
Gordale Scar	284

And others.

www.ingramcontent.com/pod-product-compliance
Lightning Source LLC
Chambersburg PA
CBHW031423230426
43668CB00007B/412